Imperial Alibis

Imperial Alibis

Rationalizing U.S. Intervention

After the Cold War

Stephen Rosskamm Shalom

South End Press   **Boston, MA**

Cover design by Matt Wuerker
Text design and production by the South End Press collective
Printed in the U.S.A. on acid-free, recycled paper.

Library of Congress Cataloguing-in-Publication Data

Shalom, Stephen Rosskamm, 1948-
    Imperial alibis : rationalizing U.S. intervention after the cold war / Stephen Rosskamm Shalom.
        p.   cm.
    Includes bibliographical references and index.
    ISBN 0-89608-449-3 : $40.00. — ISBN 0-89608-448-5 (pbk.) : $16.00
    1. United States—Foreign relations—1989- 2. Intervention (International law) I. Title.
        E840.S43   1993
        327.73—dc20
                                                                    92-30319
                                                                    CIP

South End Press, 116 Saint Botolph Street, Boston, MA 02115
99 98 97 96 95 94 93   1 2 3 4 5 6 7 8 9

® ⬭GCIU⬭ ⬭

for Ev

Table of Contents

Acknowledgements

Chapters 3 through 7 and the first part of Chapter 8 appeared in earlier incarnations in *Z Magazine*. Chapter 2 is an updated and revised version of an article published in *World Bulletin* (Manila), May-August 1988. The section of Chapter 1 dealing with capitalism and U.S. foreign policy is based on my "The United States and the Philippines: 'Sentimental' Imperialism or Standard Imperialism?" in *Art and Politics in Southeast Asia: Six Perspectives,* edited by Robert Van Niel.

I have incurred many debts in writing this book. Bob Rosen and Stan Karp gave me extensive political and editorial criticism that I'm sure I too frequently ignored. Karin Aguilar-San Juan of South End Press suggested that I begin with a chapter on the actual sources of U.S. foreign policy. Barbara Chasin, Noam Chomsky, Bill Clark, Alison Dorsey, Jack Elbrecht, Judy Feldman, Greg Mantsios, Kimberlyann Mazcko, Bassima Mustafa, Vivian Rosskamm, Charlie Scheiner, Boone Schirmer, Jack Shalom, Carole Sheffield, Bill Vornberger and the librarians at William Paterson College assisted me in obtaining materials. Andy Rabinbach generously translated some articles from German. Maya Chadda, Vivienne Shalom, and Carlos Suarez provided additional valuable comments. Loie Hayes' sharp eye much improved the writing. I alone, and not these good people, am responsible for the interpretations and for any errors that remain.

I thank as well Jessica, Alex, and Evelyn Rosskamm Shalom: Jessie for her skepticism which helped keep me honest, Alex for his sartorial advice (which had no impact), and Evelyn for everything.

Introduction

The Cold War is over.

Only yesterday Washington was warning that the Soviet threat was everywhere. The Soviet Union, declared former President Richard Nixon in 1980, was "the most powerfully armed expansionist nation the world has ever known." There was "no mystery about Soviet intentions," Nixon asserted. "The Kremlin leaders do not want war, but they do want the world. And they are rapidly moving into position to get what they want."[1] Anywhere in the Third World where there was trouble, said Ronald Reagan, it was the Soviet Union that "underlies all the unrest that is going on."[2] Even Moscow's signing of a fishing agreement with the small South Pacific nation of Vanuatu was viewed as part of its inexorable plan for world domination.[3] Soviet designs were seen as well in Central America, despite the absence of a single Soviet soldier. When a new U.S. Assistant Secretary of State for Inter-American Affairs was appointed, his first trip was not to Central or South America but to Moscow, the presumed source of all Third World problems.[4]

But today, the Warsaw Pact military alliance has been abolished. The Soviet Union itself has ceased to exist and the capacity of its successor states to threaten the security of the United States is essentially nil. "The threat to the United States of deliberate attack from that quarter," testified CIA Director Robert Gates, "has all but disappeared for the foreseeable future."[5]

So why, if the Cold War is over, is the U.S. government so eager to retain its monstrous military establishment? Abandoning the rhetoric that just a few years ago saw Moscow as the source of all the world's problems, Defense Secretary Dick Cheney now tells us that the "idea of a security threat was not invented by the communist party. It will remain long after the party is gone."[6] The "underlying causes" of Third World conflicts, Army leaders told Congress in 1990, "exist within the developing nations themselves and will not necessarily diminish even if Soviet international behavior continues to moderate."[7]

A recent Pentagon document foresaw seven threats that might endanger the United States, coincidentally requiring a continuation of the bloated military budget. One of them was that 300 Americans at work on closing down Subic Naval Base might be seized and held hostage by a faction of the Philippine armed forces in 1999. That U.S. officials claim they will be out of Subic by the end of 1992 seems not to have bothered Pentagon planners. Another scenario had "right-wing elements" of the Panamanian national police force allying themselves with "narco-terrorist" elements of the left-wing Revolutionary Armed Forces of Colombia, and threatening to close the Panama Canal unless the Government hands over power.[8]

One might dismiss such ravings as typical Pentagon propaganda when its budget is challenged, but scenarios and justifications for U.S. interventionism are unfortunately not confined to fanatical generals and admirals. Consider liberal *New York Times* columnist Leslie Gelb, who ridiculed the Pentagon planners for their seven scenarios, yet supported their call for preserving NATO, maintaining the United States "as a military power of the first magnitude" in Asia, and standing ready to use force to prevent the spread of weapons of mass destruction. And he criticized the Pentagon document for not saying anything about ensuring Israeli security—that is, about singling out for protection the strongest state in the Middle East which continues to rule over foreign territory and a subject population.[9]

To take another example of the continuing penchant for intervention, one can turn to the *New Republic*, where senior editor Morton Kondracke recently lashed out at candidate Paul Tsongas's foreign policy record. "In virtually every case when America came in conflict with an adversary during his career, Tsongas found that this country was somehow to blame. And in virtually every case when the United States faced the choice of using or threatening military force, Tsongas was opposed to it." Tsongas was hardly a principled anti-interventionist: as Kondracke himself notes, the former Senator supported the presence of U.S. troops in Europe, considered the U.S. invasion of Panama "probably justified," and does not rule out force as a final resort to curtail Iraq's nuclear program.[10] Yet to Kondracke, Tsongas represents dangerous America-bashing wimpiness, having opposed the Contras and Star Wars.

Another *New Republic* senior editor recently argued that it was important to keep U.S. troops deployed abroad. "The case is simple and compelling," he wrote. "The presence of American troops overseas gives the United States considerably more power and influence in the world than it would otherwise have."[11]

"Interfering in the affairs of other states," *New Republic* contributing editor Charles Krauthammer wrote, "is the whole purpose of foreign policy." The call for a peace dividend Krauthammer likened to "unilateral disarmament." The United States has to maintain "a large, technologically advanced, worldwide military force." Even if the Soviet threat is gone,

Krauthammer remarked in March 1990, there's always the Russian threat, and if that doesn't pan out, "we simply have no idea where Germany, China, Japan are headed."[12]

How is it possible that interventionist sentiment remains so strong after the demise of the Soviet Union? The puzzle is resolved by realizing that the Soviet threat was never the real motive for U.S. interventionism. The Soviet Union did indeed behave in an imperial manner and did have armed forces far larger than needed for its legitimate self-defense. But U.S. officials always exaggerated the Bolshevik bogey in order to justify their own inflated military machine, which has primed the U.S. economy and been deployed against the forces of social change in the Third World that challenge U.S. hegemony and economic interests.

Although Moscow was never the real reason for U.S. interventionism, it served an extremely useful purpose as the rationalization for military and covert ventures abroad. With the collapse of the Soviet threat, U.S. officials have had to work overtime to concoct new alibis to disguise U.S. foreign policy. And, indeed, new enemies have been discovered and new missions for the military have been found. Washington tells us that U.S. armed forces will now be deployed to prevent the spread of weapons of mass destruction, to safeguard resources vital to the survival of the Western world, to protect the victims of human rights abuses or American citizens in danger, to combat international terrorism, and to secure the American public from the scourge of drugs. Each one of these justifications is noble-sounding...but false.

Chapters 3 through 8 of this book analyze these new rationales for intervention. I try to show that the record of U.S. foreign policy provides no reason to take any of these rationales seriously. The new rationales are simply taking the place of the previous all-defining rationale supplied by the Soviet Union. Chapter 2 reviews the history of the Soviet threat to demonstrate that it too was always more public relations gimmick than anything else.

To argue that the justifications of the past and of the future have not been and will not be the real reasons for U.S. interventionism, it is necessary first to suggest what the actual motives driving U.S. foreign policy have been. This is the task of Chapter 1 where I will argue that U.S. foreign policy has been rooted in the dynamics of U.S. capitalism and the racist, sexist, and heterosexist ideology that prevails among U.S. policy-makers.

That U.S. interventions will persist does not mean that U.S. foreign policy in coming years will be identical to what it has been for the previous half century. In the Conclusion, I will briefly indicate some of the probable differences between U.S. international behavior of the past and of the future. But notwithstanding these differences, there will be a great deal about U.S. foreign policy that will remain unchanged. And, unfortunately, it is likely to continue that way until the domestic structures and values of American society are fundamentally reformed.

Chapter 1

The Sources of U.S. Foreign Policy

It should not be very controversial to assert that a country's foreign policy reflects the interests of those who control the country's political system. In a country where wealth is distributed in a highly inequitable manner, where it takes enormous amounts of money to wage a political campaign, where the mass media are owned and controlled by the well-to-do, and where crucial investment decisions are in the hands of the rich, the political system will be controlled by either those who own great wealth or those who serve their interests. Formal democracy is not irrelevant: it is in fact a precondition for building the union movements and popular organizations that can challenge the power of entrenched wealth. But in a country where only one out of six workers is a union member, where a political party challenging capitalism has never been able to get more than a handful of votes, the rule of capital is largely uncontested. Given this situation, it should not be surprising that state policy represents the interests of those who control the state: namely, the wealthy. Since the wealthy owe their fortunes to the workings of a capitalist economy at home and abroad, it stands to reason that the state will try to preserve capitalism and expand it where possible, and ensure the position of the wealthy within that capitalist environment. Specifically, the state will seek to promote markets for U.S. investment, to secure a dominating position over resources that are needed by U.S. corporations or their competitors, and to crush those who might try to challenge the smooth functioning of the global capitalist system.

Despite the rather obvious nature of these observations, U.S. ideologues have sought for years to hide this reality. U.S. foreign policy, wrote the prominent diplomat Charles Bohlen some time ago, "is not rooted in any national material interest of the United States, as most foreign policies of other countries in the past have been."[1] A 1981 book on "The American Experience in Asia" refers to U.S. policy-makers as *Sentimental Imperialists*[2] to distinguish them from the standard imperialists who act out of economic self-interest. Indeed, there is a common argument—popularized by Hans Morgenthau and George Kennan among others—that the problem with

U.S. foreign policy is that it has been too concerned with morality and legality. Morgenthau, for example, retells the famous story of how President William McKinley decided to annex the Philippines only after praying for divine guidance.[3] But even if we ignore the question of whether McKinley really believed God told him to take the Philippines in order to "Christian-ize" the people (a majority of whom were already Christian), consider the fact that the purported heavenly advice included the admonition that the United States could not turn the islands over to France or Germany—"our commercial rivals in the Orient"—for "that would be bad business and discreditable."[4] So even if McKinley was following what he regarded as the will of God, his God conveniently was not blind to commercial considera-tions. To say that U.S. policy-makers were guided by the word of a God who just happened to recommend profit-maximization is not much differ-ent from saying that policy-makers worshipped and were motivated by profits.

Moral and legal rhetoric have been constant features of U.S. foreign policy, but morality and legality have been essentially irrelevant to those making policy. As Henry Kissinger explained in closed testimony after betraying the Kurdish minority in Iraq, "covert action should not be con-fused with missionary work."[5] Robert Kennedy, in a famous passage of his memoir of the Cuban missile crisis, explained how he couldn't support the United States engaging in a Pearl Harbor-like sneak attack, but we now know that in private the Attorney General was suggesting that the United States fabricate some incident like the explosion of the Maine in order to have an excuse to invade Cuba.[6] Even if one considers the U.S. official most responsible for attending to legal considerations—the State Department's Legal Adviser—one finds a marked indifference to questions of legality. During the missile crisis, when the United States imposed a blockade around Cuba to prevent the Soviet Union from doing what the U.S. had already done (place nuclear missiles near the borders of its adversary), the State Department Legal Adviser argued that to even ask whether the U.S. action was legal was an inappropriate question. "The object of a first-year law school education is to teach students not to ask such questions."[7]

Under the Reagan administration, the Legal Adviser justified the 1986 U.S. bombing raid on Libya, arguing that while the assassination of foreign leaders was barred by presidential order, a military operation aimed at the barracks where Qaddafi was thought to be located did not count as assassination. The Adviser also argued that the long-standing and accepted interpretation of the U.S.-Soviet Anti-Ballistic Missile treaty was incorrect, thereby allowing the Pentagon to go forward with its Star Wars program. In the words of a Reagan-administration Deputy Assistant Secretary of

Defense, the Legal Adviser "used his creativity and legal skills...in order to advise his client on how to do what he wants to do."[8]

Senator Daniel Moynihan often denounced the Reagan administration for its cavalier attitude toward the law. But he justified U.S. covert operations against Nicaragua, clear violations of international law.[9] More recently, Moynihan introduced a resolution in the Senate—unanimously adopted—declaring an undivided Jerusalem to be the capital of Israel. When Israel annexed East Jerusalem in 1967, the General Assembly had twice declared the action illegal, both times by votes of 99-0 with 18 abstentions. The United States abstained but issued a statement saying it would not recognize the validity of the annexation. Nevertheless, Moynihan wished this conquered territory to be Israel's "eternal capital,"[10] simply ignoring the basic legal principle of "the inadmissibility of the acquisition of territory by war" and the wishes of the local inhabitants.

Is it possible that U.S. policy-makers have been pursuing global democracy rather than capitalism? The view seems currently popular in the media that the two concepts are one and the same. But anyone aware of the minimal definition of democracy as requiring rule by the people knows that this has never been the U.S. goal. As Henry Cabot Lodge acknowledged at the turn of the century, if justice requires the consent of the governed, "then our whole past record of expansion is a crime."[11] Woodrow Wilson proclaimed his devotion to democracy while sponsoring interventions in Haiti, Nicaragua, and Mexico. In 1949, the CIA backed a military coup that deposed the elected government of Syria.[12] In the 1950s, the CIA overthrew the freely-elected, democratic government of Guatemala and blocked free elections in Vietnam; in the '60s, the United States undermined democracy in Brazil and in the Congo (the first scrapping of a legally recognized democratic system in post-colonial Africa[13]); in the '70s, the CIA helped to snuff out democracy in Chile. As Kissinger told a top-secret meeting, "I don't see why we need to stand by and watch a country go Communist due to the irresponsibility of its own people."[14] When the vice-president of the United States told dictator Ferdinand Marcos of the Philippines in 1981 that "We love your adherence to democratic principle,"[15] it was obvious that the U.S. commitment to democracy didn't run very deep.

Capitalism and U.S. Foreign Policy

Those who deny the economic motive in U.S. foreign policy sometimes point to alternative explanations that, when examined carefully, prove to be not so independent of economic concerns. Thus, in *Sentimental*

Imperialists, we read that U.S. power projection abroad provided "social discipline and a restoration of national purpose"; the authors cite the views of Captain Alfred Mahan who felt that unless the masses accepted the great challenge of expansionism they would move toward rebellion and socialism.[16] But this is hardly a non-economic explanation of imperialism; it is in fact precisely one of the points advanced by Lenin in his classic work on imperialism, only he cited the example of British imperialism and the views of Cecil Rhodes.[17]

Often U.S. foreign policy has been motivated by the desire to acquire a strategic position or a military advantage over some rival. But this does not contradict the claim that U.S. foreign policy has economic roots, any more than it would prove that bankers are not motivated by profits because they spend some of their money on vaults instead of lending it out at interest. This confusion is evident in much of the writing on the topic of imperialism. Thus, for example, one writer considers that he has disproved economic explanations of European expansionism because, among the other instances he cites, Upper Burma was seized by Britain not for investment purposes but in order to protect India's frontiers.[18] Given the undeniable British economic stake in India, however, this is no refutation at all.

Of course, the United States never had a large, formal overseas empire as did Britain. Its overseas empire has been mostly an informal one: a neo-colonial rather than a colonial empire. This has meant that while the United States has generally not sought to bring distant territories under its legal control, it has tried to preserve and extend its economic domination over as many countries as it could. Even some of those who deny that the term "imperialism" is appropriate for describing the United States essentially concede this point. Henry Pachter has written, for example: "The national interest is not to protect individual American firms but to preserve a system of business.... The American empire expresses its presence and exercises its influence through the capitalist mode of operation for which it keeps as much of the world 'open' as possible."[19] Benjamin Cohen, another analyst who rejects the view that the United States is imperialist, has stated that what was threatened in Vietnam was not the physical security of the United States, but

> the security of an economic and social system dependent upon the fruits conferred by America's hegemonial position. A world in which others controlled the course of their own development, and America's hegemonial position was broken, would be a world in which the American system itself would be seriously endangered.[20]

Regarding Vietnam, many think they have refuted economic explanations of U.S. policy there by noting that the total cost of the war waged by the United States exceeded by any reasonable measure the value of the Vietnamese economy to U.S. capitalism. But the logic here is faulty. No one would have any difficulty understanding why the cost of capturing a bank robber might sometimes exceed the value of the money stolen: obviously, the rules of the game have to be enforced if the profit system is to be maintained. To allow one bank robber to escape without any serious effort at apprehension would encourage thousands of others to do likewise. In the same way, what was at stake in Vietnam was not one small market for foreign investment, but the stability of global capitalism. If one Third World country could simply opt out of the system, and succeed at some form of independent development, what would keep other countries—perhaps Brazil or Mexico, where the U.S. economic stake was far larger—from doing the same? To make sure that Vietnam would not be such an example to others, Washington spent billions of dollars in a ferocious military assault; and when that effort failed, U.S. policy-makers instituted a fanatic economic embargo of Vietnam, still motivated by the desire to make sure that there would be no model of a successful alternative to capitalist subservience.

One scholar has done a study that shows there to be a rather weak relationship between the amount of U.S. foreign investment in a country and whether the United States has intervened in that country.[21] But this is irrelevant to the imperialism thesis. Would one expect to find a correlation between a bank's assets and whether the police were sent to the bank? Surely the police are not dispatched to banks whose assets are highest but to those whose assets are threatened. Likewise it would be a foolish imperialism indeed that in 1965 sent the U.S. Marines to Mexico rather than to the Dominican Republic merely because the investment stake was greater in Mexico.

To be sure, the United States has a much more substantial economic stake in the developed countries of Western Europe, Canada, and Japan than in the Third World. Thus, no one would dispute the fact that were the United States faced, for example, with the choice between safeguarding its investments in Great Britain or in Guatemala it would choose the former. But this formulation is exactly the opposite of the problem as perceived by U.S. policy-makers. That is to say, from Washington's point of view it has not been a question of *either* the developed countries *or* the less developed countries, but rather of *both* or *neither*. As former ambassador to Japan Edwin O. Reischauer put it, "No clear line exists between our very immediate interests in the security and stability of the advanced nations (such as those of Europe, Japan, and Australia) and conditions in the less developed world."[22] Oil is one aspect of this interconnection, but perhaps the best illustration is the attitude of U.S. officials to the relationship between Japan and Southeast Asia in the 1950s.

In a very literal sense, Japan's economic survival has required foreign trade. Geography and complementarity made China the natural trading partner for Japan; U.S. officials feared, however, that any Japanese dependence upon trade with China might lead to political accommodation between the two nations and Japan would be lost by the "Free World." Accordingly, Washington had to assure Japan access to other markets and Southeast Asia was considered to be the natural choice. This meant that the United States had to prevent Southeast Asia from becoming dominated by China or even from choosing to develop along self-sufficient lines which might deny a major role to trade with Japan.

By the mid-1960s, of course, the situation had changed. Washington found that by assuring the economic viability of Japan it had permitted Japan to escape its subordination to the United States and to become a major economic competitor. But during the 1950s, U.S. policy-makers held the view that it was crucial to secure markets for Japan in Southeast Asia and the evidence showing that this was so is overwhelming. One can find this argument referred to in official public speeches, in the reports of prestigious study groups, and in secret government policy documents.[23] So the claim that the United States has no serious economic interests in the Third World nations of Southeast Asia because Japan is many times more important is simply beside the point. It was precisely in order to preserve Japan within the "Free World" orbit that it was felt necessary to keep Southeast Asia fully integrated into the world capitalist economic system.

In retrospect, of course, many U.S. policy-makers may wish they had acted otherwise and not provided the markets for Japan that helped it become the economic power it is today. But to say that the United States is imperialist or driven by economic concerns does not mean that U.S. officials are all-knowing. The failure of the Japanese economy to remain subordinate to the United States does not mean that this was not the goal of U.S. policy-makers in the 1950s. This same response applies to those who believe that economic motivation was absent from U.S. foreign policy at the turn of the century because the China market that so tempted U.S. political and business leaders never amounted to very much.[24] But, again, the ultimate failure of the China market to develop as anticipated in no way invalidates the claim that it was this anticipation that drove much of U.S. policy in Asia in the early years of the 20th century.

Some have tried to refute the claim that the United States is imperialist by pointing to what they consider to be decisive counter-examples: instances where a foreign government has nationalized some U.S.-owned assets but where Washington did not intervene against, and may even have tolerated, the government in question. This line of argument, however, confuses the contention that the United States is imperialist with the very different view that the United States is both imperialist and omnipotent.[25] If the latter were claimed, then U.S. acceptance of any diminution of its global hegemony would indeed constitute decisive counter-evidence. But, in the real world, there are obvious limits to U.S. power and to the U.S. ability to control events.

In some instances both U.S. government policy-makers and corporate officials have concluded that economic interests would not be best served by Washington's involvement in corporate disputes with indigenous governments. In Peru in the early 1970s, for example, the majority of U.S. business interests opposed calls for imposing sanctions on Peruvian sugar in retaliation for the expropriation of the U.S.-owned International Petroleum Company; the oil company's behavior was viewed as excessive by most U.S. firms and the Peruvian government was still generally supportive of foreign investment.[26] Whether this assessment of the Peruvian government turned out to be correct or not (by 1980 Lima moved sharply rightward), the fact that Washington followed the wishes of most U.S. corporations, rather than those of a single firm, does not disprove the imperialism thesis; rather, this fact is basically consistent with the thesis.

Another critic of the imperialism thesis argues that it "overpredicts" in that it would have predicted U.S. intervention in many other cases, such as Cuba after the Bay of Pigs, Chile in 1970-71, and Iraq in 1958.[27] But the imperialism thesis does not predict that the United States will intervene whenever its interests are threatened—any more than Newtonian mechanics predicts that an object will invariably move in the direction of an applied force. Before predicting in the latter case, one would have to know whether there were countervailing forces and so on. Likewise, one has to know the costs and benefits of intervention in any particular instance; only then can one evaluate the actual imperialism thesis: namely, that Washington will intervene whenever so doing appears to U.S. policy-makers the best course for maximizing key U.S. economic interests.

In the specific cases cited, the United States did not send in troops but its behavior hardly showed a commitment to a policy of non-intervention. U.S. covert operations were conducted against Cuba after the Bay of Pigs[28] and in Chile throughout the Allende years.[29] As for Iraq in 1958, the United States and Britain deployed troops to adjoining Lebanon and Jordan, but judged that there was no one in Iraq who could restore the monarchy, and that, in light of the Iraqi government's assurances of friendliness to the West and to western oil interests, the best that could be done was to attempt to work with the new regime.[30] Significantly, following these assurances—not unrelated to the presence of the U.S. troops in Lebanon and the *New York Times* headline "West to Keep out of Iraq Unless Oil is Threatened"—shares of the oil companies with Iraqi investments rose briskly on the London stock market. And the major foreign oil firm in Iraq soon announced its intention to expand its operations there.[31] A few years later the situation changed: in 1961, the Iraqi leader Abdul Karim Qassim moved against the oil companies. But—as the imperialism thesis would suggest—U.S. policy changed as well. The CIA tried to assassinate Qassim,[32] and there is suggestive evidence that when the Ba'ath party overthrew and executed him in February 1963, the CIA cooperated at least to the extent of providing the names of Qassim's communist backers to be murdered.[33]

To argue that the dynamics of the capitalist system have been a major source of U.S. foreign policy, is not to suggest that economic factors are alone determinative. If foreign policy reflects the interests of those who control the state, it will reflect not just their narrow economic interests, but their racial and sexual outlook as well. There are some who would reduce all of racism, sexism, and heterosexism to their economic origins. U.S. racism, for example, grew out of the mass expropriation of the land of Native Americans and the labor power of Africans. But such reductionism, even if useful for understanding how and why U.S. racism developed in the specific form it did, seems to miss much of the current-day force of racist ideology. This is even more true with respect to sexism and heterosexism which usually operate at a more subconscious level than racism. Whatever their origins, these ideological constructs are worthy of separate consideration in studying the sources of contemporary U.S. foreign policy.

Racism and U.S. Foreign Policy

Racism was one of the key founding principles of the United States. The Puritans exterminated Pequot Indians, hoping, in the Puritans' words, to "cut off the Remembrance of them from the earth." To George Washington, Indians and wolves were both "beasts of prey, tho' they differ in shape." In the Declaration of Independence, one of the indictments against King George was that he had inflicted on the colonists "the merciless Indian savages, whose known rule of warfare, is an undistinguished destruction of all ages, sexes and conditions"—a rather accurate characterization of the rules of warfare employed *against* the Native Americans. Repeatedly, in the Indian wars that raged across the continent, U.S. soldiers would proclaim as they massacred infants, "Kill the nits, and you'll have no lice." "We must act with vindictive earnestness against the Sioux," wrote General Sherman in 1866, "even to their extermination, men, women and children."[34] To Theodore Roosevelt, the "most ultimately righteous of all wars is a war with savages, though it is apt to be also the most terrible and inhuman," but no matter, because it was "idle to apply to savages the rules of international morality which obtain between stable and cultured communities...."[35] Not that Roosevelt went "so far as to think that the only good Indians are dead Indians, but I believe nine out of ten are, and I shouldn't inquire too closely into the case of the tenth."[36] How did this jibe with everyone being created equal? As Harvard President A. Lawrence Lowell explained, Jefferson's doctrine applied "only to our own race, and to those people whom we can assimilate rapidly." Indians "are not men, within the meaning of the theory" that all men are created equal.[37]

Racism against Africans was another fundamental building block of American ideology. Deemed to be sub-human, they were subjected to a barbaric and brutal system of slavery. Lincoln was willing to accept slavery so long as the union could be preserved; and when the Civil War drove him to abolish slavery he did not change his belief in black inferiority. When the South introduced Jim Crow laws to maintain the descendants of slaves as second-class citizens, the northern elite went along. Even after World War II, President Harry Truman was referring to blacks as "niggers."[38] Derogatory references to blacks were standard fare for President Nixon and the senior officials of his administration. "I wonder what your dining room is going to smell like," Kissinger chortled to Senator Fulbright, regarding a dinner for African diplomats.[39]

With racist views deeply embedded in the minds of U.S. policy-makers and rooted in domestic structures of domination and subordination, it is not surprising that these views have influenced the way in which Washington looked at and acted in the world outside.

When Haiti became independent in 1804—the second independent nation in the Western hemisphere—the United States withheld recognition for more than 50 years: Haiti was a black-led state that had abolished slavery, and an obvious challenge to the racial order in the South.[40]

But the racism that was one of the driving forces of U.S. expansionism at the turn of the century was not centered in the South. One of the leading figures in this imperialist upsurge was Senator Albert Beveridge of Indiana. Americans, he declared, were "of the ruling race of the world"; "ours is the blood of government; ours the heart of dominion; ours the brain and genius of administration."[41] Anglo-Saxons, asserted Teddy Roosevelt, were the most advanced race, and the U.S. branch had been strengthened by its frontier experience where inferior races had served as its "natural prey."[42] And it was precisely this U.S. experience dealing with the "lower orders" that was said to justify the conquest of other people of "lower orders" around the world, such as in the Philippines. To grant self-government to the Philippines under Philippine leader Aguinaldo, said Roosevelt, "would be like granting self-government to an Apache reservation under some local chief." "The reasoning which justifies our having made war against Sitting Bull also justifies our having checked the outbreaks of Aguinaldo and his followers."[43] And this seemed to be the way U.S. soldiers in the Philippines viewed the situation: "I am in my glory when I can sight my gun on some dark skin and pull the trigger," wrote one. U.S. troops routinely referred to the Filipinos as "niggers" and one officer explained: "We exterminated the American Indians, and I guess most of us are proud of it, or, at least, believe the end justified the means; and we must have no scruples about exterminating this other race standing in the way of progress and enlightenment, if it is necessary."[44] Almost all the U.S. generals assigned to crushing the Philippine revolution were veterans of Indian wars and most of the regiments were from western states.[45] Atrocities were commonplace and went essentially unpunished. Asked why fifteen Filipinos were reported killed for every one wounded, Gen. Arthur MacArthur told a Congressional committee that inferior races succumbed to wounds more easily than Anglo-Saxons.[46]

The decision to acquire an overseas colonial empire was a controversial one, but aside from a small core of principled anti-imperialists,[47] the debate pitted one group of racists against another. Favoring annexation of the Philippines, Senator Borah of Idaho pronounced that the Filipino would not be suited for self-government for 200 years. Opposing annexation, Senator Vardaman of Mississippi asserted that preparing "the Filipino or any other mongrel race" for the duties of citizenship or self-government could not be done in a hundred thousand years because it was not in their blood to accomplish it; nevertheless, it was their country and they had the right to do what they wanted. Southern Senators generally voted against annexation because, as Senator Benjamin Tillman of South Carolina explained, they had experience with the "colored" race. "It is to the injection into the body politic of the United States of that vitiated blood, that debased and ignorant people, that we object."

The *annexationist* racists won this debate, but they did not fare as well on the subject of Cuba. Arguing for taking over this Caribbean island as well, Senator Newlands of Nevada remarked: "I hear it often said that Cuba would be desirable if for half an hour she could be sunk into the sea and then emerge after all her inhabitants had perished…. The objection that is urged is to the people themselves. And yet today Cuba has been practically dipped into the sea" since so many had been killed in its struggle against Spain. But there were still too many Cubans to convince the *non-annexationist* racists, and Cuba became a neo-colony instead of a colony of the United States. Puerto Rico, with its smaller population, was colonized and brought the blessings of liberty after centuries of Spanish misrule: the United States imposed a literacy and property requirement on voting, disenfranchising 70 percent of the adult males who had been allowed to vote under autocratic Spain.

The United States has often pointed to its historically rather meager overseas colonial empire and its granting of independence to the Philippines in 1946 as proof of American high-mindedness. In fact, however, it was the particular mix of racism and economic interest that accounted for the colonial ambivalence. Tellingly, the legislation providing for Philippine independence specified that Philippine immigration to the United States was to be limited to 50 people a year, compared to more than 25,000 per year from each of the racially favored countries of northern and western Europe.

In the conferences following the first World War, Japan proposed that race equality be adopted as an international principle. Woodrow Wilson stood with the other racialist states of South Africa, Australia, and New Zealand in opposing the Japanese move.[48] Anti-Japanese racism played a particularly significant role during World War II, both in terms of the treatment of Americans of Japanese descent living in the United States and in the attitude toward the Japanese population. Historian John Dower has documented how U.S. hatred was much more intense toward the Japanese than the Germans, both before and after Pearl Harbor. The well-publicized taking of battlefield trophies from Japanese war dead (skulls, ears, and so on) and the torturing and killing of Japanese prisoners were commonplace. Race hatred surely facilitated the decisions to target civilians for conventional and nuclear bombing: prominent U.S. citizens personally favored "the extermination of the Japanese in toto" (Paul V. McNutt) or bombing until half the Japanese population was wiped out (Elliott Roosevelt), while public opinion polls throughout the war showed more than 10 percent of Americans supported annihilating the Japanese as a people; after the war was over, more than one out of five wished the United States had had the opportunity to use many more atom bombs on Japan before it surrendered.[49]

As the war drew to a close, the U.S. attitude toward decolonization was colored by racism. To Franklin Roosevelt, "there are many minor children among the peoples of the world who need trustees," particularly "the brown people of the East."[50] To Assistant Secretary of State Sumner Welles, liberation for Africans was even further off than for Asians since they were "in the lowest rank of human beings."[51] Consistent with this worldview, when the French began massacring thousands on the island of Madagascar in 1947, crushing a movement that U.S. officials considered "wholly indigenous," the U.S. consul on the scene expressed delight that the French offensive was "going very well indeed."[52] Washington opposed UN General Assembly resolutions calling for self-determination for native peoples (1952); the independence of Tanzania, Togo, and Burundi (1957); and the designation of 1962 and then 1972 as the end to the era of colonialism.[53] The State Department did not even have a Division of African Affairs until 1957.[54] After the 1960 Sharpeville massacre in South Africa, President Eisenhower showed his outrage at apartheid by referring to it as "a touchy thing."[55] In 1971, the U.S. Congress passed and President Nixon signed the Byrd amendment calling for the importation of chrome from the white minority regime in Rhodesia, in explicit violation of mandatory economic sanctions imposed by the UN Security Council, with U.S. support. The United States thus became one of only three UN members—the others were Portugal and South Africa—to officially violate the sanctions.[56] One Nixon administration insider recalls that at the rare National Security Council meeting on Africa, Alexander Haig "would begin to beat his hands on the table, as if he was pounding a tom-tom. It was all very manly—a locker-room mentality. Haig would make Tarzan jokes—'Where's your pet ape?' or, talking about blacks, say, 'Henry [Kissinger] can't stand the smell.'"[57]

Asians continued to obsess U.S. policy-makers. The Pacific, said General Douglas MacArthur in 1949, was an "Anglo-Saxon lake."[58] Lyndon Johnson warned that "without superior air power, America is a bound and throttled giant, impotent and easy prey to any yellow dwarf with a pocket knife."[59] Not until the 1960s did the United States revise its immigration laws that treated Asians as inferior.[60] Twice more after World War II, the United States sent large numbers of its troops across the Pacific to fight "gooks" and lay waste an Asian society. A U.S. veteran of the My Lai massacre related that GIs took scalps, "like from Indians. Some people were on an Indian trip over there."[61] A civilian volunteer worker testified that a U.S. adviser compared Vietnam's Montagnard minority to the Native American population and "said we could solve the Montagnard problem like we solved the Indian problem."[62] And it was standard practice among the Americans in Vietnam to refer to dangerous areas as "Indian country."[63]

Other Third World people too were victims of U.S. racism and the stereotypes that such racism generated. When Lyndon Johnson sent U.S.

Marines to the Dominican Republic in 1965, one of his key advisers was Thomas C. Mann, whose view was: "I know my Latinos. They understand only two things—a buck in the pocket and a kick in the ass."[64] Arabs and Muslims have been victims of virulent stereotypes as well: in recent years, a thesaurus listed "tramp," "vagrant," and "huckster" among the synonyms for "Arab." A popular postcard declared: "Fight High Oil Prices! Mug an Arab Today."[65] The *New York Times* printed a letter in 1979 arguing that claims of Israeli torture of Palestinians were actually the result of a failure to appreciate that "the Western notion of telling the 'truth' is, under certain circumstances, seen by Arabs as inappropriate."[66] In 1981, Martin Peretz reprinted in the *New Republic* a 17th-century racist essay on "The Turk" to illustrate how Muslims behave.[67] And almost the only images Americans see of Arabs are of terrorists, oil sheiks, or belly dancers. Such stereotypes no doubt made it easier to rationalize attacks on "Mad Dog" Qaddafi or to go to war in the Gulf.[68]

Of course, at the same time that race hatred helped Americans inflict great suffering on Japanese or North Vietnamese or Iraqis, there were other people of similar races who were viewed as U.S. allies: Chinese, (some) South Vietnamese, Kuwaitis. This inconsistency might suggest that racism was irrelevant, that it was something concocted for the moment with no real impact on policy. But it would be a mistake, I believe, to treat racism as something that could be simply turned on and off at will by U.S. policy-makers. Racist hostility even to allies interfered with the war effort: the "good" Vietnamese were "gooks" too, and racist stereotypes of the enemy overrode rational intelligence gathering in World War II.[69] And the fact that certain types of atrocities were not committed against a white enemy, suggests that the behavior was not motivated only by wartime exigency.

The presence of a few non-whites in policymaking circles is not likely to change the nature of U.S. foreign policy very much; to attain positions of power, these individuals would have to have shown substantial conformity to the prevailing values of the elite. A substantial racial diversity among policy-makers, on the other hand, would likely make racism a less significant factor in the way Washington deals with the world. But such an occurrence is by no means imminent, and will not come to pass as long as racial inequality remains a fundamental characteristic of the U.S. domestic landscape. Until this time, racism will continue to be an important factor in U.S. foreign policy.

Sexism, Heterosexism, and U.S. Foreign Policy

Sexism and heterosexism define appropriate roles for individuals. Women are devalued, as are traits considered typically female, such as nurturance and sensitivity. Men who do not adequately adhere to the approved version of masculinity are considered pariahs. If they are heterosexual but appear insufficiently masculine, they are treated as women, which is to say deprecated and excluded from power. It is even worse if they are gay, for then they are subject to job discrimination, arrest, and assault, as well as ridicule. These attitudes are widespread in American society, but they are particularly concentrated in the centers of power because the political system essentially selects for those with over-developed egos and under-developed compassion. As Henry Kissinger put it, "In contemporary America, power increasingly gravitates to those with an almost obsessive desire to win it."[70]

When these policy-makers have responsibility for foreign policy, their machismo is expressed on the world stage. "Be a man—that is the first and last rule of the greatest success in life," advised that mouthpiece of imperialism, Albert Beveridge.[71] If the United States shunned colonies and was unwarlike, Teddy Roosevelt warned, it would "go down before other nations which have not lost the manly and adventurous qualities."[72] In urging U.S. entry into World War I, Roosevelt admonished Americans to avoid "a flabby cosmopolitanism, especially if it expresses itself through a flabby pacifism," which would be "not only silly, but degrading. It represents national emasculation...."[73]

According to Richard Barnet, who served in the Kennedy administration,

> Some national security managers of the Kennedy-Johnson era...talk about the 'hairy chest syndrome.' The man who was ready to recommend using violence against foreigners, even when he is overruled, does not damage his reputation for prudence, soundness, or imagination, but the man who recommends putting an issue to the UN, seeking negotiations, or, horror of horrors, 'doing nothing' quickly becomes known as 'soft.'[74]

Kennedy himself was described by his sister Eunice: "He hates to lose at anything. *That's the only thing Jack really gets emotional about*—when he loses."[75] For Robert Kennedy, one of the first things he wanted to know about someone being considered for the administration was whether he was tough.[76] Secretary of State Dean Rusk cabled his ambassadors to stop using the word "feel" in their dispatches.[77] And Defense Secretary Robert McNamara answered anti-Vietnam War demonstrators: "I was tougher than you were then [in WWII] and I'm tougher than you now." As Barnet commented, McNamara could not even see that the students doubted his humanity, not his *machismo*.[78]

Machismo was crucial to Lyndon Johnson too, who we are told nicknamed his genitals "Jumbo."[79] Bill Moyers recalled that after Johnson met with McNamara and other ex-Kennedy men, Johnson feared that they would think him "less of a man" than John Kennedy if he did not carry through with Vietnam.[80] According to David Halberstam, Johnson

> had unconsciously divided people around him between men and boys. Men were activists, doers, who conquered business empires, who acted instead of talked, who made it in the world of other men and had the respect of other men.... As Johnson weighed the advice he was getting on Vietnam, it was the boys who were most skeptical, and the men who were most sure and confident and hawkish and who had Johnson's respect. Hearing that one member of the Administration was becoming a dove on Vietnam, Johnson said, 'Hell, he has to squat to piss.'... Doubt itself, he thought, was almost a feminine quality, doubts were for women; once, on another issue, when Lady Bird raised her doubts, Johnson had said of course she was doubtful, it was like a woman to be uncertain.[81]

When Johnson ordered the bombing of North Vietnamese targets, he told a reporter: "I didn't just screw Ho Chi Minh. I cut off his pecker."[82]

Similar dynamics prevailed in the Nixon administration. "No one could prosper around Nixon without affecting an air of toughness," Kissinger has written.[83] What Nixon hated most "was to be shown up in a group as being less tough than his advisers."[84] Nixon was quoted as saying that he chose Spiro Agnew as his running-mate because he was a tough guy and had a "strong-looking chin."[85] When Sen. Charles Goodell switched from a hawk to a dove on the Vietnam War, Agnew likened him to transsexual Christine Jorgensen.[86] "Our objective was to purge our foreign policy of all sentimentality," Kissinger explained.[87] One Nixon aide recalls an illustrative incident:

> As we walked out of his office, Henry turned to one of his secretaries and said, "Where is Eagleburger?" She said, "I'm sorry, but while you were in the meeting Larry collapsed and he's unconscious." The extraordinary thing is that he didn't hesitate but said, "But I need him." Then he said to her, "Get me [Patrick] Buchanan" and went into his office and closed the door.[88]

For Kissinger, "power is the ultimate aphrodisiac" and, in his words, "women are no more than a pastime, a hobby."[89] According to Kissinger,

"In crises boldness is the safest course."[90] To undermine Secretary of State William Rogers whose advice Kissinger considered insufficiently bold, Kissinger spread stories that Rogers was gay and had made it with Nixon.[91] Countless corpses around the world are testament to Kissinger's masculine boldness.

Rank-and-file U.S. soldiers are similarly nourished on machismo. From the Army basic training chant, "This is my rifle, this is my gun; this one's for killing, this one's for fun,"[92] to the songbook of the U.S. pilots of the 77th Tactical Fighter Squadron which includes lyrics like "I fucked a dead whore by the side of the road,"[93] militarism and sexism are enmeshed. In the movie *Top Gun,* one pilot speaks of the enemy to another: "They must be near; I've got a hard-on."[94]

Anthropological data shows that one predictor of whether a society is warlike is whether the males have a tendency to be ambitious and competitive.[95] A recent experiment using male psychology students found that subjects who endorsed the use of nuclear weapons were significantly more likely to report being sexually aroused by "forcing a female to do something she didn't want to."[96] Comparing the treatment of women, gay men, and lesbians from society to society is no easy task, and I am not suggesting that the United States is more interventionist than other nations because it is more sexist or heterosexist. Rather, to fully understand the sources of U.S. foreign policy one must take account, in addition to the workings of capitalism and racism, the pervasive sexism and heterosexism throughout U.S. society, and especially among policy-makers.

As with racism, the presence of a few women or, perhaps in the future, openly gay men or lesbians in top positions will likely have little impact: witness the Reagan administration's foreign policy ideologue, Jeane Kirk-patrick. Indeed, given the dynamics of sexist ideology, sometimes the presence of a woman may provoke a more belligerent policy. For example, George Bush may have felt his manhood challenged when British Prime Minister Margaret Thatcher said to him shortly after the Iraqi invasion of Kuwait, "Remember, George, this is no time to go wobbly."[97] But, in any event, women have been basically absent from U.S. foreign policymaking circles,[98] and there have been no openly gay men or lesbians. Until these realities change in more than token ways, one should expect little moder-ation in the brutality and militarism of U.S. foreign policy.

The various sources of U.S. foreign policy discussed here manifest themselves in different ways. In the chapters that follow one generally won't find foreign policy-makers telling their colleagues "Here's how we can maintain global patriarchy" or "Let's do such and such in order to keep gays and lesbians in their place around the world." Sexism and heterosexism do not influence U.S. foreign policy in terms of conscious, explicit plotting to perpetuate discriminatory structures on an international basis; rather they provide a set of implicit, even subconscious, assumptions about appropriate behavior: policy-makers glorify "masculine" traits like toughness and lack of emotion and deride "feminine" traits like sensitivity and empathy. Thus, they will frequently choose the aggressive or the callous course of action because it is the "manly" thing to do, or take irresponsible risks for fear of appearing effeminate.

Occasionally, policy-makers will discuss options in explicitly racist terms. More often, however, their racism reveals itself in their tacit devaluation of people of other races. To be sure, wealthy policy-makers also devalue the poor of their own race, but racial stereotypes make it easier to dismiss someone's humanity and to be oblivious to the horrific suffering one's policies cause.

Economic self-interest is the motivation most consciously acted upon, but even this will rarely be acknowledged explicitly by policy-makers. They don't sit around and say to each other, "How, in complete disregard for morality and law, can we make ourselves immensely wealthy?" The virtues of capitalism they take as axiomatic, and so the arguments in its behalf seldom make it into the documentary record. The managers of the U.S. state rationalize their actions in terms of the national interest—as if all the American people have the same interest. The view that what's good for General Motors is good for the United States (as Defense Secretary Charles E. Wilson put it)[99] is half obfuscation and half part of the self-evident belief system of policy-makers. Wilson probably never told his staff to choose policies designed to serve the needs of General Motors, but his understanding of the needs of the United States was likely to lead to the same policies.

This chapter has argued that the roots of U.S. foreign policy are the workings of the capitalist system and the racist, sexist, and heterosexist ideology of policy-makers. Because explicit statements of underlying motivation are rare, the real test of this argument lies in an examination of alternative explanations. The next chapter looks at the explanation that has dominated U.S. thinking throughout the Cold War years, the Soviet threat. Subsequent chapters take up the new rationalizations that are likely to be put forward in the post-Cold War era.

Chapter 2

The Soviet Threat

Just a few years ago a precocious sixth-grader by the name of Todd Patterson decided that he wanted to compile an encyclopedia. With typical youthful enthusiasm, he wrote to 170 different countries requesting information. However, since one of the countries he wrote to was the Soviet Union, the FBI paid young Patterson a visit; they opened a secret national security file on him and refused to reveal its contents to him for "national security" reasons. This was not simply the action of some overzealous FBI subordinate. When challenged by the American Civil Liberties Union, senior FBI officials defended their treatment of Patterson as entirely routine, and a judge agreed that the Bureau had not acted improperly.[1]

This story may suggest a certain irrationality in the U.S. attitude toward the Soviet Union. But, in an important respect, the magnification of the Soviet threat has played a useful function for U.S. policy-makers over the years. The managers of the U.S. state have known the reality of Soviet military capabilities and the relative caution of Soviet foreign policy. But in their public statements they have exaggerated Moscow's military strength and distorted its foreign policy record. They have done so for a variety of reasons.

1. Mobilizing the U.S. population against the Soviet threat facilitated the preservation of the domestic status quo: any pressure for social change could be conveniently denounced as part of the internal communist conspiracy, which was allied with the international communist conspiracy.[2]

2. The Soviet threat was used to build support among the American people for greater U.S. military spending (always called "defense" spending). A large Pentagon budget benefits the military, military contractors, and the U.S. economy, which has no other readily available means of Keynesian pump-priming or mobilizing capital for research and development.[3]

3. The Soviet threat pressured the Europeans and Japanese to accept U.S. leadership. "The United States has global interests and responsibilities. Our European allies have regional interests," Kissinger explained in 1973. Zbigniew Brzezinski repeated the same idea in 1987: "We must recognize

that the United States holds the status of a world power, and our allies are simply regional powers."[4] But without the Soviet Union, things would be different. As Sen. David L. Boren put it recently, "the decline of the Soviet Union…could very well lead to the decline of the United States as well…." Will the Europeans and Japan be as willing in the post-Cold War environment to follow the U.S. lead, Boren asked rhetorically. "I don't think so."[5]

4. The Soviet threat provided the rationale for frequent military interventions in the Third World against indigenous social forces. The U.S. population might well have opposed sending in the Marines to crush some local nationalist, but public opinion could often be recruited to the global crusade against Moscow.

Demonstrating the exaggeration of the Soviet threat, of course, does not mean that there were not substantial grounds for criticizing Soviet foreign policy, just as there are solid grounds for condemning the policies of all major states. The Soviet Union played an extremely harmful role in the nuclear arms race, a secondary role to be sure, but a detrimental role nonetheless. It intervened in the internal affairs of other nations, often brutally, as in Hungary and Afghanistan. And it invariably subordinated the struggle for its professed ideal of international socialism to its own national interests. These were all valid grounds for denouncing Soviet foreign policy, but they had very little to do with the Soviet threat as publicly understood. Certainly U.S. policy-makers never issued a condemnation of Moscow for "selling out" revolution in one part of the globe or another. Rather U.S. state managers publicly charged the Soviet Union with having a relentless plan to conquer the world, and the military means to do so; if it weren't for Moscow, we were told, "there wouldn't be any hot spots in the world" (Ronald Reagan).[6] This is what U.S. officials told us, but—not to put too fine an edge on it—they were lying.

The Early Cold War

More than 60 years ago, at a time when Soviet military power was inconsequential, U.S. Secretary of State Frank Kellogg told a Senate committee that the Mexican president was secretly conspiring with Nicaraguan revolutionaries and Soviet agents to impose a "Mexican-fostered Bolshevik hegemony" in Central America.[7] "The Bolshevik leaders," Kellogg declared in 1927, "have had very definite ideas with respect to the role which Mexico and Latin America are to play in their general program of world revolution…. Latin America and Mexico are conceived as a base for activity against the United States."[8] Did U.S. leaders believe this? Of course not. They wanted to intervene against social revolution in Mexico for the same reasons they had been intervening in Latin America for 100 years before the Russian Revolution. The Soviet Union provided a useful pretext for U.S. intervention.

At the end of World War II, the Soviet bogey became the centerpiece of U.S. foreign policy. Moscow, the American people were told, had cynically violated all its wartime agreements, despite Washington's scrupulous compliance with all its obligations. But examination of the documentary record reveals a rather different picture. According to Melvyn Leffler's careful study:

> In fact, the Soviet pattern of adherence was not qualitatively different from the American pattern; both governments complied with some accords and disregarded others. American policy-makers often exaggerated Soviet malfeasance.... Truman Administration officials themselves sometimes violated key provisions of wartime agreements.[9]

One Soviet violation about which U.S. policy-makers made much noise was Moscow's delay in removing its troops from Iran after the war. But the U.S. Joint Chiefs of Staff, with State Department concurrence, secretly wrote in April 1946: "There are military considerations which make inadvisable the withdrawal of U.S. forces from overseas bases on the territory of foreign nations in every instance in strict accordance with the time limitation provision of the existing agreement with the foreign government concerned."[10] For example, Secretary of State Stettinius wrote to Truman on April 19, 1945, that "the question of Philippine independence is conditioned on satisfactory arrangements for [U.S. military] bases."[11]

In 1947, in one of the first major escalations of the Cold War, President Truman asked Congress for funds to help Greece and Turkey resist Soviet aggression. But the genesis of Truman's request shows that policy-makers had a different view of the situation from what they said in public. At an earlier private meeting with Congressional leaders, when the Secretary of State explained the need for U.S. aid, the legislators were unconvinced. Only when Under-Secretary of State Dean Acheson described the situation in terms of vital U.S. interests and the life and death struggle with Soviet communism did Senator Vandenberg, the leader of the opposition, declare that he would support Truman's aid request—on condition that the president's message to Congress employ Acheson's rhetoric and "scare the hell" out of the American people. As one member of the committee that drafted Truman's message put it, "The only way we can sell the public on our new policy is by emphasizing the necessity of holding the line: communism vs. democracy should be the major theme." This theme was false and Washington officials knew it to be false. The "democratic" Greek government they asked the U.S. public to defend was in fact a reactionary, corrupt, and brutal monarchy.[12]

The American people were worried in the early post-war years, having been told by their leaders that the Red Army enjoyed conventional superiority in Europe and that it was poised to attack Western Europe. In fact, the claims of U.S. policy-makers were simply false, as recent scholarship has demonstrated. For example, as late as 1950 half of the transport of the standing Soviet army was horse-drawn—hardly a situation likely to facilitate a *blitzkrieg.*[13]

In the months before the outbreak of the Korean War, a crucial document, NSC-68, was drawn up at the top levels of the U.S. government. The document called for massive U.S. rearmament and signalled another crucial escalation in the Cold War. Again the evidence shows that exaggeration was critical in getting this policy approved:

> Dean Acheson later spoke of the importance of being "clearer than truth" in writing the document, so as to better "bludgeon the mass mind of 'top government'...," while [Paul] Nitze told a later interviewer that bureaucratic infighting demanded a certain sharpening of the language of "the Soviet threat."[14]

In fact, the early fifties presented one of the most significant opportunities to reduce Cold War tensions. On March 10, 1952, the USSR proposed that Germany be unified, with internationally supervised free elections, and that all foreign troops be withdrawn, on condition that this reunified Germany be prohibited from joining any military alliance. This would have been a tremendous step forward for peace, but Washington was determined to incorporate West Germany into NATO, and so it rejected the Soviet proposal.[15] A few years later, Secretary of State John Foster Dulles told a meeting of NATO ministers: "If I had to choose between a neutralized Germany and Germany in the Soviet bloc it might be almost better to have it in the bloc. That clearly is not acceptable but disengagement is absolutely not acceptable either."[16] Despite this record, however, the American people were told—and largely believed—that only further military spending could keep the Russian hordes at bay.

The presence of Soviet troops in Eastern Europe lent some credibility to the exaggerations of the Soviet threat by U.S. policy-makers. But there were no foreign troops in Guatemala when the reformist Arbenz government nationalized the unused lands of the United Fruit Company in the early 1950s. The CIA engineered the overthrow of Arbenz and the military regime that took over promptly un-nationalized United Fruit's lands. Washington pointed to a Soviet bloc arms shipment as justification for deposing Arbenz. We now know, however, that the planning for Arbenz's overthrow began before the arms shipment occurred.[17]

The American people might have been reluctant to support intervention on behalf of United Fruit; they had few qualms in intervening against the Soviet Union, nor against communism in general, which their leaders assured them was identical to the Soviet Union. Thus, the head of the Senate Foreign Relations Committee, Alexander Wiley, who presumably was aware of the independence of Yugoslavia, declared in 1954: "There is no Communism but the Communism which takes its orders from the despots in the Kremlin in Moscow. It is an absolute myth to believe that there is such a thing as homegrown Communism, a so-called native or local Communism."[18]

In 1957, General Douglas MacArthur—whom no one could accuse of excessive sympathy for the Left—gave a speech in which he remarked:

> Our government has kept us in a perpetual state of fear—kept us in a continuous stampede of patriotic fervor—with the cry of grave national emergency. Always there has been some terrible evil at home or some monstrous foreign power that was going to gobble us up if we did not blindly rally behind it by furnishing the exorbitant funds demanded. Yet, in retrospect, these disasters seem never to have happened, seem never to have been quite real.[19]

In March 1960, at a White House meeting, there was "a general discussion of what would be the effect on the Cuban scene if Fidel and Raul Castro and Che Guevera should disappear simultaneously." One of the officials present, Admiral Burke, warned that the communists were the best organized group in Cuba and might take control if the three leaders were eliminated. To which CIA director Allen Dulles replied that "this might not be so disadvantageous" because it would facilitate action against Cuba.[20] In short, communism was not a real threat to U.S. policy-makers, but a rationale for U.S. intervention. It is often noted that U.S. policy with respect to Cuba seemed irrational; Washington appeared to be forcing Havana into close alignment with Moscow. But this is not irrational if one's goal is to establish an excuse for invasion and destabilization.

John Kennedy was elected president of the United States in 1960 in part because he warned of the dangers of the "missile gap," a frightening Soviet lead in intercontinental ballistic missiles. It turned out, however, that the only missile gap that existed was a dramatic imbalance...in favor of the United States. What accounted for the "error"? Robert McNamara, who served as Secretary of Defense from 1961-68, acknowledged in 1982 that the "missile gap of 1960 was a function of forces within the Defense Department that, perhaps unconsciously, were trying to support their particular program—in that case, an expansion of U.S. missile production—by overstating the Soviet force."[21]

Exaggeration was not just confined to missiles. Two civilian specialists assigned to the Systems Analysis office of the Pentagon have related their experiences at trying to measure the conventional balance in Europe. "In 1961, the usual comparison was 175 well-equipped, well-trained, fully ready Soviet divisions facing about 25 ill-equipped, ill-trained, unready NATO divisions in the center region." But when they bothered to count the number of soldiers on each side, they found that "…the Soviet forces alone were substantially outnumbered by the NATO forces, even after mobilization." This didn't look good for those wanting to point to the Soviet threat. So,

> despite the increasing independence of the East European countries from the Soviet Union, intelligence reports and Service staff estimates began to count the satellite divisions as nearly equivalent to Soviet divisions…. Indeed, it appeared that whatever headway the Systems Analysis office made in reducing the number of Soviet divisions was offset by an equivalent number of newly found satellite divisions. One way or another, the number of well-equipped, well-trained, combat-ready Pact divisions stayed at 175 in military threat estimates.[22]

This same sort of exaggeration continued in the 1970s. In the words of Deputy Under-Secretary of Defense Charles Duncan, Jr.:

> Why, you may ask, do some have the view that the Soviet Union has become the world's number one military power? The answer is that, to a large extent, we have created that image ourselves…in the understandable desire to reverse the anti-defense mood and propensity for reduced defense budgets of the early 1970s….[23]

To many U.S. policy-makers the "Vietnam syndrome"—the reluctance of the American people after the Vietnam War to support foreign military interventions—was a serious ailment, leading to "the understandable desire to reverse the anti-defense mood" by exaggerating the Soviet threat.

The Continuing Cold War

In the 1970s, Soviet military spending, while high, was consistently overstated by U.S. government sources. CIA accounting techniques, in fact, led to an automatic upward revision in estimated Soviet military expenditures whenever the United States increased the base-pay of its own soldiers.[24] The capabilities of the Soviet military machine were also consistently exaggerated. Few Americans were told, for example, that the Soviet logistics system almost proved unable to support the *unopposed* Soviet invasion of Czechoslovakia in 1968.[25]

The large number of Soviet emigrants to the United States in the 1970s, many of whom had served in the armed forces, provided first-hand evidence on actual Soviet capabilities. Consider the testimony of a former Soviet radar specialist:

> In the unit where I served, for example, I had a radar. According to regulations I should have had two of them. But only one of them actually worked, and then only half the time. Why? Because the officers in my unit liked to drink, and to get extra money, and how are they going to get it? They would immediately think of selling spare parts. What kind of parts? Cables, various generators for the radar, various kinds of radio equipment which is in short supply in civilian stores but which is available in the army. As a result the station would work only for a short time and then die out…my equipment was on its last legs. The second radar would not work because there was no generator—the officers sold it, and drank away the money.[26]

A former lieutenant in the Soviet strategic rocket forces stated that "the time for the Americans to attack would be New Year's Eve, because everybody was drunk and there was no one on duty." But then he paused and added, "New Year's Eve wasn't that much different from any other time."[27]

In 1967, at Moscow's 50th Anniversary war games, an impressive 10,000-man division was on display. Unannounced, however, was the fact that the division consisted exclusively of officers. The highlight of these 1967 war games was a demonstration of tanks crossing the Dnieper River under fire. In reality, however, the tanks actually used concrete tracks constructed on the river bed over the preceding four months, hardly a realistic simulation of wartime conditions.[28]

In the 1980s, U.S. magnification of the Soviet threat went into high gear. Ronald Reagan, taking a page from John F. Kennedy's campaign two decades earlier, charged there would soon be a "window of vulnerability," a time when the Soviet Union would be able to launch a nuclear first strike at the United States and get away with it. This was a preposterous claim: even if the Kremlin had been able to destroy every land-based U.S. missile there was no way to eliminate the U.S. ballistic missile submarine fleet; if even a single one of these vessels survived, it would be able to incinerate over a hundred Soviet cities—a rather robust deterrent. But in any event, Reagan's handpicked "Scowcroft Commission" admitted in 1983 that there was no window of vulnerability (while of course still recommending production of the MX missile, based in the same silos used by older missiles and hence no less vulnerable to Soviet attack).

Reagan accused the previous Carter administration of allowing a precipitous decline in U.S. military strength. The actual facts were that under Carter, military outlays went up every year, and the rate of growth in military spending probably exceeded that of the USSR.[29] This didn't stop the Reaganauts from declaring that Moscow had achieved strategic superiority, and they were joined in this by Democrats such as David Boren, head of the Senate Intelligence Committee. But when a Boeing official T.K. Jones (later appointed to the Reagan Pentagon) could publicly warn that the United States was so weak that "if we are threatened we ought to give them what they ask for," it was obvious that the threat was being concocted to justify more military spending.[30]

Under Reagan, the Pentagon began publishing a glossy annual booklet entitled "Soviet Military Power." The publication regularly included inapt comparisons, tendentious statistics, and paranoid warnings. Numerous pictures of menacing Soviet weapons systems were presented. Only on close examination did it become clear that these pictures were often not photographs, but artists' renderings, some of them artists' renderings of weapons systems that did not yet exist.[31] "Soviet Military Power" claimed ominous Kremlin advances in its land, air, and sea forces that could only be adequately addressed by supporting the Reagan administration's military build-up.

Eager to deploy a 600-ship navy, the Pentagon laid particular stress on Soviet naval developments. The Soviet Navy did grow substantially in the years since World War II, but official U.S. sources rarely pointed out its continued inferiority to the U.S. Navy. Great significance was attributed to Moscow's acquisition of two aircraft carriers in the Pacific, without noting either the decisive U.S. quantitative lead in this regard or the fact that the Soviet vessels were not true carriers. They carried only helicopters and vertical take-off fighters, the latter using so much fuel on take-off and landing that they could not stay in the air very long; none had been observed aloft for more than sixteen minutes.[32]

Despite U.S. Navy claims that the Soviet Navy was preparing to challenge the United States for control of the seas, the facts were rather different. A leading authority on "gunboat diplomacy" noted that Washington was the leading practitioner of the art in the 1980s and the "strongest and most interventionist of the naval powers."[33] Aside from engaging in military actions against Grenada, Lebanon, Libya, and Iran, the United States sent its warships into Soviet territorial waters in the Black Sea,[34] dispatched a carrier task force into the Bering Sea, and had its naval aircraft make mock bombing runs at Soviet territory.[35] In the meantime, Moscow had most of its Navy "swinging uselessly at anchor,"[36] "remaining snugly alongside in their home fleet areas."[37]

U.S. exaggeration of the Soviet threat was particularly mendacious with respect to Central America. To justify U.S. interference in El Salvador, it was necessary to portray the revolution there as Soviet directed. On February 23, 1981, the State Department issued a White Paper on "Communist Interference in El Salvador." According to U.S. officials, the eighteen pounds of documents proved that the Salvadoran insurgency was a "textbook case of indirect armed aggression by Communist powers through Cuba." But when one looked carefully at the evidence, one saw instead (in Ray Bonner's apt phrase) "a textbook case of distortion, embellishments, and exaggeration."

> The documents, it turned out, didn't weigh eighteen pounds; that was the total weight of [White Paper author Jon] Glassman's suitcase, which also contained his personal belongings. Moreover, many of the documents weren't even written by the guerrilla leaders that the administration claimed had written them....
>
> [A] close reading of all the documents revealed that contrary to the white paper's assertions, [Salvadoran Communist Party leader Shafik] Handal had not been very warmly received in Moscow. He met with a middle-ranking official in the Latin American section in the Soviet Communist party and received no firm assurances of any arms shipments.

Two U.S. journalists "reported that some of the documents were provided to the United States by [death squad organizer Roberto] D'Aubuisson...." Even the author of the White Paper later conceded that parts of it were "misleading" and "over-embellished."[38]

In November 1984, the Reagan administration leaked word that a Soviet freighter was on its way to Nicaragua with 21 MiG fighters aboard. The information turned out to have been concocted, but it served the purpose of deflecting attention from the positive reports by international observers of the Nicaraguan election and got the compliant Democrats to agree that the Sandinista government had no right to defend itself from U.S. attack. This was not the first fabrication regarding Soviet arms to Nicaragua. A study sponsored by the State Department found that:

> All-too-many U.S. claims [about Soviet bloc military aid to Nicaragua] proved open to question. In May 1983 the White House announced that

reconnaissance photos proved the Soviet ships Novovolynsk and Polotosk carried heavy military equipment; American reporters present at the unloading saw only field kitchens from East Germany, and 12,000 tons of fertilizer.... President Reagan later declared that the ship Ulyanov was "loaded with weaponry"; yet a respected Conservative British observer saw "no signs of offensive weaponry or armoured vehicles," only 200 transport vehicles, 80 jeeps, 5 ambulances, and assorted civilian equipment.[39]

Much attention was given every trip Nicaraguan officials made to Moscow, as if this proved Soviet control of the Sandinista government. On the other hand, little was heard of the Honduran delegation sent to Moscow in September 1987 to discuss trade expansion with Eastern Europe.[40] This differential coverage was part and parcel of the effort to discredit Nicaragua as a Soviet pawn.

In May 1987, Ronald Reagan told newspaper publishers that Lenin had once said that "the road to America leads through Mexico." A few days later a Soviet official appeared at a press briefing with the collected works of Lenin, challenging anyone to find such a remark. Naturally, no one could.[41]

In 1988 it was revealed that three days before President Reagan declared that there was "no way" a Soviet pilot could have shot down a Korean Air Lines jet in 1983 by mistake, U.S. intelligence had concluded that a mistake was in fact the likely explanation.[42] One might note also that the fact that it took four hours to shoot down a foreign aircraft, thought by Moscow to be a spy-plane, flying over one of the most militarily-sensitive regions of the Soviet Union, rather effectively undermined the Pentagon's claims of the efficiency of the Soviet air-defense system. But neither in 1983 nor in 1987 (when a West German amateur pilot flew into Red Square) did the U.S. government acknowledge that the Soviet air-defense network was rather unimpressive. In Pentagon reports, the most porous Soviet defenses appeared invulnerable.

In 1986, the White House claimed that the Soviet Union could deploy an X-ray laser without the need for any further nuclear tests. But, as the *New York Times* reported,

> In a sharp contradiction to Congressional testimony by the Reagan Administration, a Central Intelligence Agency report released yesterday says the Soviet Union would have to conduct further underground nuclear tests before it could deploy an X-ray laser, an advanced antimissile weapon.

This was "a classic case of threat inflation," pointed out Rep. Edward Markey of Massachusetts. "The Department of Energy has exaggerated Soviet X-ray laser capabilities to justify its budget request for the U.S. X-ray laser program."[43]

Moscow's Troubling Absence

In 1984, Assistant Secretary of Defense Richard Armitage was testifying before the U.S. Congress on the New People's Army, the insurgent guerrilla movement in the Philippines. Rep. Benjamin A. Gilman, Republican of New York, asked him: "Is there some external support for the terrorists and the insurgency? Where are they getting their help from?" Armitage replied: "This is one of the most troublesome aspects of the insurgency. There is no apparent external source of support, Congressman."[44] Note that Armitage did not say "Thank goodness there is no outside support." He did not reply "Fortunately, there is no Soviet involvement." Instead, he found the lack of external support to be troubling, indeed one of the most troubling aspects of the insurgency. Why? Because it would be hard to mobilize the U.S. public to support massive intervention in the Philippines if the enemy was only other Filipinos. Fifteen years earlier, Senator Symington had complained about U.S. aid to the Philippine government designed only to protect U.S. bases "from the Philippine people who do not agree with the policies of the Government or do not like Americans."[45] How much better for U.S. officials if they could portray the enemy as the Soviet Union.

The absence of any evidence showing Soviet involvement in the Philippines was troublesome, but not insurmountable to resourceful commentators. One U.S. military intelligence analyst claimed that the Soviet-NPA link was proven by, among other things, the fact that the Communist Party of the Philippines opposed U.S. intervention in Nicaragua.[46] But even more sober U.S. observers tried to raise the specter of Soviet involvement. In 1987, Richard J. Kessler, then with the Carnegie Endowment for International Peace, wrote an article in the *Washington Post* ominously titled "Are the Soviets Sneaking Up on the Philippines?"[47] Kessler began by observing that:

> analysts have been so preoccupied with finding concrete evidence of Soviet arms—which has not yet emerged—that they have missed what has been happening: The rebel forces have grown strong; reports of Soviet military aid have increased; and leadership of the Philippines

Communist party has changed its once wary attitude toward accepting foreign support.

Kessler thus stated that there was no concrete evidence of Soviet arms, but yet there were increased reports of Soviet military aid. But why tell us about reports for which there was no evidence?

Kessler went on: "Moreover, the Soviets have been courting the Aquino government with offers of investment and expanded commercial ties." Now this was certainly subversive, to be courting the legitimate, recognized government, with such devious tactics as trade and investment—while at the same time supporting the opposition. But Moscow's diabolic activities went further:

> As part of an effort to improve their image, the Soviets replaced their ambassador, the only diplomat to congratulate Ferdinand Marcos for winning the 1986 presidential election. Construction has also begun on a new Manila office building and home for the Soviet trade representative in fashionable Forbes Park, also home of the American ambassador.

Presumably, the U.S. ambassador was distressed that his neighborhood would no longer be so exclusive. Who knows who they would allow in next? In addition, "Now the Soviets want to open consulates in the southern cities of Cebu and Davao, where the United States also maintains diplomatic presence."

"The Soviets," Kessler continued, "have long been interested in gaining a foothold in the Philippines.... Now the Soviets have a base in Vietnam and are eying the South Pacific. Their persistence is impressive." The Soviet base in Vietnam will be discussed below. But what evidence was there of Soviet "persistence"? "The Soviets began translating Philippine books and training linguists in the dominant dialect, Tagalog, in the early 1960s even though diplomatic relations were not established with the Philippines until 1976." Was there no end to Soviet cunning?

> The Soviets are testing the waters, but so far there is little evidence that they have done more, according to American intelligence sources. Nor is there any concrete evidence of CPP cadres being trained abroad in such countries as Vietnam. Foreign journalists traveling with the NPA rarely report seeing AK-47s, and Philippine military have not yet recovered any M-16s that are not traceable. Lt. Gen. Salvador Mison, vice-chief of staff, stated in a Washington meeting in May [1987] that reports of Soviet arms are the "products of very fertile minds."

These remarks of Kessler's were quite sensible. But then he added:

> Reports of Soviet submarines and subsequent denials make good copy but are not the story. The NPA do not need Soviet trainers or even Soviet arms. They have done quite well with U.S. Army field manuals and can buy or capture arms locally. What they need is money and credibility. These the Soviets can provide.

Ah ha! So now Kessler was going to give us evidence of what really mattered, Soviet funding. "If the Soviets wanted to, they could ensure a steady supply of weapons. That they haven't indicates the war has not yet reached a critical point." So the real story was that there was no Soviet money, but they could have provided it if they wanted to. But that wasn't all.

"More importantly, the Soviets do not have to provide direct aid to have influence." So what are the cagey Russians up to?

> A more lucrative Soviet approach to low-intensity conflict in the Philippines is their current strategy of obtaining intelligence and securing a political foothold. In November 1984 the World Peace Council held a meeting in Manila at which time Soviet agents reportedly met with the CPP. More importantly, two Tass correspondents visited Davao City, a center of NPA activity, in early December 1984, presaging a growing Soviet interest in Davao. Over the past year the Soviets have returned to Davao several times.

In this Soviet low-intensity conflict, the intensity is so low as to be virtually non-existent.

"Whether or not the Soviets have a long-term plan for turning the Philippines into a satellite state is beside the point." On the contrary, one would think this was a rather significant question. "What they do have is a strategy for positioning themselves to influence events in the Philippines." And what underhanded means are they using to "position" themselves? "The Soviets, for example, distribute their press releases in Tagalog while the USIA publishes its in English." It would have been admirable if the USSR actually had distributed its press releases in Tagalog, but in fact it did not.[48]

Kessler summarized his outlook with these ominous words: "The conflict is escalating, with the Soviets poised to play on what was once exclusively American turf." And this, one suspects, was what really worried Kessler: that the Philippines was supposed to be U.S. turf and those uppity Russians didn't seem to appreciate the fact. That the Philippines might be Filipino turf presumably didn't occur to Kessler.

To take another example of this descent into the world of make-believe, consider the late Robert Shaplen, long deemed the dean of U.S. Asia correspondents. In a lengthy two-part article on the Philippines that appeared in the *New Yorker*, amid some rather insightful analysis, appeared the following:

> ...what is significant is the increasing amount of attention the Soviet Union has been paying to the Philippines.... In addition to their embassy in Manila, the Russians are seeking to establish consulates in Cebu and Davao, and are building a new home and office for the Soviet trade representative in fashionable Forbes Park, where the American Ambassador's official residence is also located. Correspondents of Tass, the Russian news service, regularly visit the Philippines, and their press releases are written and distributed in Tagalog, though the United States Information Agency uses only English.[49]

Presumably Shaplen spoke to the same sources as Kessler did, repeating the same mix of paranoia and error.

Shaplen, Kessler, and others wrote ominously of the Soviet presence at Cam Ranh Bay in Vietnam. In 1987, the commander of the U.S. Pacific fleet called Soviet access to Cam Ranh Bay "the second most dramatic change to the strategic equation in Asia," second only to the invasion of Afghanistan,[50] and many other analysts claimed that the Soviet presence in Vietnam required that the United States maintain its military bases in the Philippines as a counterweight.[51] But in fact, according to the *Far Eastern Economic Review*, U.S. analysts were at a loss to explain the rather modest scale of Soviet deployments at Cam Ranh.[52] And when Gorbachev suggested trading off the Soviet facilities in Vietnam for those of the United States in the Philippines, Washington greeted the proposal with disdain.[53]

This is a standard pattern: to characterize Soviet forces or facilities as possessing crucial military significance, only to dismiss these same forces or facilities as militarily trivial when an offer is made to give them up. To take another example of this, the "Soviet Military Power" booklet noted that a "major portion" of Soviet naval strength lies in its submarine force, "the world's largest."[54] Yet when Moscow proposed cutting its underwater fleet in return for U.S. reductions, a U.S. Navy officer scoffed: "They've got a bunch of subs copied from World War II German U-boats that haven't left pier-side for 10 years, and they want to trade these for our new carriers?"[55]

Under Gorbachev, the Soviet Union started unilaterally paring back its military forces. It agreed to remove its SS-20 missiles from Asia without any corresponding reduction in the U.S. Pacific nuclear arsenal; it accepted asymmetrical cuts in its conventional forces in Europe; it reduced its overseas naval deployments.[56] But the U.S. Chief of Naval Operations, petrified of budget cuts, warned that Soviet policy was "if anything, even more aggressive under Gorbachev." He went so far as to suggest that by operating at a lower tempo, the Soviet Navy might be even more prepared for "rapid force generation."[57] And another commentator warned that the "absences" of the Soviet Navy from the high seas "must now be a cause for panic," possibly indicating an impending Soviet attack.[58]

But even the heroic efforts of Pentagon propagandists cannot resuscitate the Soviet threat any longer. Other threats need to be invented if the American people are going to be duped into continued funding of the U.S. war machine and support for foreign interventions. The chapters that follow examine these new threats.

Chapter 3

Stopping The Spread of Weapons of Mass Destruction

The Bush administration put forward a multitude of rationalizations for going to war against Iraq in January 1991: to preserve the American way of life, to counter aggression, to restore the Emir of Kuwait, to protect oil supplies, to save jobs for U.S. workers. Polls showed that the American public was convinced by none of these excuses except one: the need to prevent Saddam Hussein from acquiring nuclear weapons.[1] As estimates of when Iraq would get the bomb were conveniently reduced—from five years to less than one year—people were understandably concerned about the spread of weapons of mass destruction. Iraq's nuclear potential *was* frightening, as was its chemical weapons arsenal, and as indeed was its massive conventional military capability.

But these horrendous armaments did not appear overnight, and they certainly did not burst into existence on August 2, 1990, when Iraq invaded Kuwait. The proliferation of conventional, chemical, and perhaps nuclear weapons to the Gulf region was deeply rooted in the policies of many outside countries, not the least of them the United States. An examination of this historical record is useful for explaining the spread of each of these types of weapons to the Gulf and elsewhere, as well as for revealing the remarkable level of hypocrisy issuing from pundits and policy-makers in Washington.

Grooming the 'Policeman of the Gulf'

The impetus behind the growth of the Iraqi military was established in the early 1970s. Great Britain had at that time reached the end of its imperial pretensions and was preparing to withdraw its forces from the Gulf and grant independence to Oman and the small sheikdoms that would become Bahrain, Qatar, and the United Arab Emirates. The Nixon administration—chastened by the debacle in Vietnam—had concluded that U.S. interests could be better protected by local surrogates than by the direct use of U.S. troops. The logical candidate for this role as "policeman of the Gulf" was Iran, whose leader, Shah Mohammed Pahlevi, owed his throne to the CIA (which had helped to overthrow nationalist Prime Minister Mossadeq in 1953) and whose internal security force, SAVAK, had been established and trained with CIA assistance.

As Britain retired from the region, it arranged (possibly with U.S. connivance) for Iran to seize three small islands at the mouth of the Gulf that were claimed by Arab sheiks.[2]

In May 1972, just 24 hours after agreeing in Moscow to a set of basic principles on U.S.-Soviet relations that committed both nations to minimizing international tensions, Nixon and his National Security Adviser Henry Kissinger were in Teheran offering to sell the Shah any U.S. weapons he wanted—other than nuclear weapons. Over the next seven years, the United States sold $21 billion worth of arms to Iran, compared to $1.2 billion in the previous 22 years. Iran became the largest U.S. arms recipient in the world, buying the latest U.S. aircraft, as well as destroyers more advanced than those being produced for the U.S. Navy. According to a study for the mainstream Council on Foreign Relations, by the mid-1980s Iran would have been a regional superpower, with ground forces roughly equivalent to those of West Germany, a better air force, and a navy that would have given it control of the Gulf and a presence in the Indian Ocean. This arms build-up "might well have amounted to the most rapid expansion of military power under peacetime conditions of any nation in the history of the world."[3]

By arming the Shah, Washington hoped to have a means of suppressing any radical movements that might arise in the Gulf, as when Iranian troops were dispatched to Oman in 1975 to crush a rebel group there. Weapons sales to Iran were also a windfall to U.S. arms manufacturers, though to pay for his new arsenal the Shah became a leading figure in pushing up the price of oil.[4]

In the same May 1972 meeting at which the Shah was given the blank check for arms purchases, Nixon and Kissinger worked out with the Iranian leader that both their countries would give military aid to the rebellious Kurdish minority in neighboring Iraq.[5] It is important to note that concern for the welfare of the unfortunate Kurds was the furthest thing from the minds of Nixon and Kissinger. According to a classified report by the House Select Committee on Intelligence leaked to the press:

> documents in the Committee's possession clearly show that the President, Dr. Kissinger and the [Shah] hoped that our clients [the Kurds] would not prevail. They preferred instead that the insurgents simply continue a level of hostilities sufficient to sap [Iraqi] resources.... This policy was not

imparted to our clients, who were encouraged to continue fighting. Even in the context of covert action, ours was a cynical enterprise.

The Select Committee concluded that had the United States not reinforced Iran's prodding, the Kurds might have "reached an accommodation" with Baghdad, "thus gaining at least a measure of autonomy while avoiding further bloodshed. Instead, our clients fought on, sustaining thousands of casualties and 200,000 refugees."

In 1975, the Shah and Saddam Hussein of Iraq signed an agreement giving Iran territorial concessions in return for Iran's closing its border to Kurdish guerrillas. Teheran and Washington promptly cut off their aid to the Kurds and, while Iraq massacred the rebels, the United States refused them asylum. As noted in Chapter 1 above, Kissinger justified this U.S. policy in closed testimony: "covert action should not be confused with missionary work."[6]

(One might turn to Kissinger's memoirs to get his public justification. In his first volume, he discussed the situation only in a footnote, saying that a full discussion would have to await volume 2. Volume 2 has 1255 pages, but not a single word on the Kurds.[7])

Iran's shopping spree for arms, its grabbing of Gulf islands claimed by Arabs, its fueling of the Kurdish insurgency—all of these served to feed Iraqi militarism. Between 1973 and 1980, Iraq's armed forces doubled in size and the number of armored and mechanized divisions grew four-fold.[8] The situation has been summarized this way by a mainstream analyst, Ephraim Karsh:

> By and large the course of the Iran-Iraq strategic relationship in the [1970s] was dominated by [the Shah's] persistent thrust for regional hegemony. Iraq played a reactive and defensive role.[9]

One cannot know, of course, what Baghdad would have done in the absence of the Iranian build-up. But certainly if the Gulf arms race was a concern, here was an opportunity for the United States to approach the other arms suppliers to the region—the Soviet Union and France—to agree on multilateral restraint.

Arms Are For Hugging

The Nixon and Ford administrations, however, had no interest in such mutual undertakings. They refused to begin multilateral discussions on arms transfers and an internal study to reconsider the U.S. refusal was never completed.[10] President Jimmy Carter, on the other hand, pressured by congressional criticisms of the U.S. arms bazaar,[11] announced a new unilateral U.S. policy on weapons sales and agreed to talks with Moscow on mutual restraint.

His unilateral commitment, declared in May 1977, was that U.S. arms sales in 1978 would be less than in 1977 and that the United States would not be the first supplier to introduce advanced weapons with new or significantly higher combat capability into a region. The presidential directive, however, explicitly excluded sales to NATO countries, Japan, Australia, and New Zealand from the ceiling on arms transfers. The directive then declared that "We will remain faithful to our treaty obligations, and will honor our historic responsibilities to assure the security of the State of Israel,"[12] which, according to Secretary of State Cyrus Vance, excluded Israel too from the ceiling.[13] Moreover, commercial arms sales were not covered by the ceiling either. In short, almost half of all U.S. arms sales were counted outside the ceiling, so while the new policy gave the illusion of reductions, in fact total U.S. arms sales actually increased: from $12.8 billion in 1977 to more than $15 billion in 1978, and over $17 billion by 1980.[14]

Unilateral U.S. restraint, of course, would not have kept arms out of the Third World. From 1977 to 1980, U.S. arms sales to developing nations increased 14 percent, compared to a 55 percent increase for the Soviet Union, and a 78 percent increase for Britain, France, West Germany, and Italy. Arms transfer data are extremely controversial, but it seems that in 1980 Moscow was the Third World's largest individual arms source, while sales from the United States and its allies together exceeded those from the USSR and its allies.[15]

It was thus clear that any reduction in the spread of conventional weapons would require multilateral agreement. In March 1977, in response to an earlier suggestion from Soviet leader Leonid Brezhnev, the United States and the Soviet Union agreed to set up a bilateral working group to consider arms transfers, and talks got under way at the end of the year. The U.S. side insisted—and Moscow went along—that they consider region by region concerns. The United States proposed for discussion Latin America and sub-Saharan Africa; the Soviet Union accepted these and made its own suggestions of west Asia and east Asia (presumably Iran and China). At this point, the U.S. delegation was instructed by Washington to refuse to listen to the Soviet proposals and to walk out if the Soviets persisted in bringing them up. "Such a refusal may have been unprecedented in the annals of American diplomacy," commented one prominent scholar.[16] Others noted that "Never before…had one side refused to listen to the other's presentation at a U.S.-Soviet arms control negotiation" and this after the United States had explicitly pledged to discuss any legitimate geographic region suggested by the USSR.[17]

Then in 1979 the Iranian revolution occurred. U.S. arms deliveries to Teheran were cut off, and the revolutionary turmoil left the Iranian military in disarray. Iraqi President Saddam Hussein, seeing an opportunity to finally even the score with his regional foe, invaded Iran in September 1980.

The Reagan administration took office in January 1981 proclaiming its opposition to even the limited global arms restraint of Carter. For example, there had been a tacit arrangement between the United States and the Soviet Union not to provide the latest model combat aircraft to their respective allies on the Korean peninsula; in 1981, the United States broke the arrangement and sold F-16s to South Korea.[18]

In the Iran-Iraq war, the United States officially declared its neutrality and announced that it would not provide military aid to either side. In fact, however, Washington provided assistance to both sides. This shameful record will be discussed in detail in Chapter 4; suffice it to note here that the result of U.S. policy was the prolongation of the war. The Reagan administration may have thought that dragging out the war served its interests, but Iraq emerged from the fighting with a vastly larger and more threatening military machine than when the war began. In 1980 Iraq had 200,000 troops;[19] in 1988 it had more than three times as many first line soldiers, and perhaps a million all told. As Saddam Hussein bragged to the Iraqi people in November 1989: "you entered the war with 12 divisions...now we have about 70."[20] And the numbers of tanks and aircraft grew comparably.

At the close of the Iran-Iraq war, Iraq's desperate economic situation made it difficult to continue financing its military machine. Washington, however, came to the rescue. In October 1989, President Bush signed top-secret National Security Directive NSD-26 calling for closer ties with Baghdad and permitting $1 billion in new aid. As late as the spring of 1990, the Bush administration allowed Saddam Hussein to buy U.S. "dual-use" technology—advanced equipment with both civilian and military applications.[21]

One would have hoped that after the Iraqi invasion of Kuwait Washington would have learned its lesson about reckless arms sales. Unfortunately that seems not to be the case. In September 1990, the Bush administration announced $20 billion in arms sales to Saudi Arabia, the largest arms deal in history, though Congress cut this to $7.5 billion. In March 1991, Secretary of Defense Dick Cheney declared that the United States would sell *more* not *fewer* weapons to the Middle East in the wake of the war. And sure enough the United States has become the world's leading weapons supplier to the Third World and to the Middle East. Characteristically, on May 29, 1991 President Bush pledged to curb the Middle East arms race, and in the next week the United States announced two major weapons deals in the region; in October, at a conference in London, Washington committed itself to restraining its arms sales to the Middle East, and within two weeks began negotiations with Saudi Arabia for a $5 billion sale of F-15 fighters.[22]

It was not simply conventional military forces that grew during the course of the Iran-Iraq war. As the *Washington Post* reported,

> U.S. and Israeli intelligence analysts blame the Iran-Iraq war for most of the developments destabilizing the Middle East military equation—the extensive use of missiles against civilian populations in cities, local engineering to extend vastly the range of missiles and acquisition of chemical warheads.[23]

Chemical weapons in particular were used on a large scale in the Iran-Iraq war, first by Baghdad and then, in retaliation and on a smaller scale, by Teheran. Neither country had ever used poison gas before, and it was in the context of their drawn-out conflict that the warring parties resorted to chemical arms. But to make sense of the spread of chemical weapons to the Gulf, it is necessary to look at the historical antecedents.

Better Dying Through Chemistry

The use of chemical and biological weapons in warfare has a long and gory past. In the fifth century B.C., the Spartans tried to overwhelm opposing cities with sulphur fumes.[24] In 1346, the Tartars catapulted the bodies of plague victims into the walled city of Caffa to defeat its defenses. Four centuries later, the British used blankets infected with smallpox against rebellious North American Indian tribes.[25]

In 1907, all the major powers—except the United States—signed the Hague Convention outlawing the use of chemical projectiles in combat.[26] Nevertheless, chemical warfare was widespread in World War I, causing more than a million casualties, almost 10 percent of them fatal.[27] In the aftermath of the war, the British used gas warfare against rebellious Iraqis, though not on the scale urged by Winston Churchill, who explained,

> I am strongly in favour of using poisoned gas against uncivilized tribes. The moral effect should be good...and it would spread a lively terror.... We cannot in any circumstances acquiesce in the non-use of any weapons

which are available to procure a speedy termination of the disorder that prevails....[28]

In 1925, many nations came together and signed the Geneva Protocol, prohibiting the use in war of "asphyxiating, poisonous, or other gases, and of all analogous liquids, materials, and devices" as well as "bacteriological methods of warfare." Most countries ratifying the Protocol reserved the right to employ such weapons if used by others first. Among the major powers, most ratified within the first few years, and all but two had ratified by the early 1950s. Japan did not do so until 1970, and the United States refused to ratify until 1974.[29]

Chemical weapons were not considered especially useful against an enemy well-prepared with gas-masks, but against Third World people the results could often be devastating. Italy, though it ratified the Protocol in 1928, used mustard gas during its invasion of Abyssinia in 1935-36.[30] Japan used chemical weapons on a small scale in its war against China;[31] in addition, the Japanese military secretly developed bacteriological warfare agents (such as infected fleas) and used them in a few instances against Chinese targets.[32] When the United States entered the Pacific War, Japan became more circumspect—fearing U.S. retaliation—and none of the other World War II participants is known to have used chemical or biological weapons in combat. The Germans, who had developed new deadly nerve gases, mistakenly assumed that their enemies also had such weapons and refrained from employing them. In 1944, Churchill urged the use of gas ("what is to their detriment is to our advantage," he reasoned), but his advisers rejected the idea and Churchill reluctantly gave in.[33] Roosevelt pledged that the United States would not be the first to use chemical weapons, but after his death some key advisers, such as chief of staff Gen. George Marshall, recommended their use against Japanese outlying islands. The war ended before a final decision was made.[34]

The secret Japanese unit in charge of bacteriological warfare had conducted experiments on prisoners of war, killing 3,000 human "subjects" including Americans, and compiling voluminous data on the effects of various biological agents. The United States captured the officers in charge of this unit and shielded them from war crimes prosecution in return for their cooperation with U.S. biological warfare efforts.[35] In 1946, members of Congress boasted of U.S. germ warfare weapons, and in 1947 President Truman withdrew the Geneva Protocol from consideration by the Senate (where it had been languishing since 1925).[36] When the Soviet Union in 1949 placed some Japanese officers on trial for war crimes involving biological warfare, U.S. officials dismissed the whole thing as a propaganda ploy.[37]

During the Korean War, the North Koreans and the Chinese accused the United States of engaging in biological warfare. The charge has not been proven, and large-scale use almost certainly did not occur, but whether some experimental attacks were conducted cannot yet be ruled out.[38]

In any event, the United States did develop an extensive chemical and biological warfare capability. In 1956, the U.S. Army revised its *Field Manual on the Law of Land Warfare* to point out that Washington was not party to any treaty banning chemical, toxic, or bacteriological warfare, and thus such prohibitions were not binding on the United States.[39] In 1959, a resolution was proposed in the House of Representatives reaffirming the position, originally enunciated by Franklin Roosevelt in World War II, that the United States would not be the first to use chemical or biological warfare; the resolution was strongly opposed by the Departments of Defense and State and was defeated.[40]

The United States pursued a particularly vigorous program of research on germ warfare. This was sometimes described as "defensive" research, but as the official Pentagon history acknowledged, "Research and development in the offensive aspects of BW proceeded hand in hand with defensive developments for, in truth, the two are almost inseparable."[41]

To test the dispersion of biological agents, starting in 1949 the Army conducted open-air tests of "simulated" organisms over populated areas of the United States. The Army said these tests were totally harmless, but the medical literature showed the simulants to be potentially fatal to sick and sometimes even to healthy individuals. No medical follow-up was ever done to determine the health effects of the tests. In 1950, after San Francisco was secretly sprayed with the bacteria *Serratia marcescens* in a germ warfare test, a city hospital recorded its first ever outbreak of *Serratia marcescens* infection, with one man dying. The Army claimed this was just a coincidence. In 1951, another test was conducted in Virginia, with the Army intentionally exposing a disproportionate number of African Americans to a potentially fatal simulant in order, it alleged in a classified document, to be prepared for an enemy attack using a fungus that affects blacks in particular.[42] In 1966, a secret germ warfare test was carried out in the New York City subway system. The Army claimed that the test enabled them to devise counter-measures to prevent an enemy from engaging in such an attack. The Army concluded, for example, that "enforcement of an ordinance against litter would make clandestine deposit of agents in the system more difficult"—a counter-measure so valuable that it was never shared with police or transit authorities.[43]

The U.S. biological warfare program was not simply a research effort. Rep. Richard D. McCarthy revealed in 1970 that contingency plans were drawn up for the first use of biological weapons against Cuba. McCarthy reported that he was told by officials that the United States came close to actually using such weapons during the Cuban missile crisis, intending to infect the Cuban sugar crop and to incapacitate human beings. One informant told him that germ warfare agents were actually placed aboard planes.[44] The United States also used biological agents in attempting to assassinate foreign leaders, though in no case were the attacks known to be successful. Castro and Lumumba were intended targets, as was Iraqi leader Abdul Karim Qassim.[45]

But it was chemical, not biological, weapons that the United States employed on a wide scale. During the Vietnam War, U.S. military forces used massive amounts of tear gas and herbicides. The United States claimed that these chemicals were not outlawed by the Geneva Protocol, but the UN General Assembly passed a resolution in 1969 declaring that riot control agents and herbicides violated international law—law, the Assembly said, that was binding even on nations that were not party to the Protocol. The vote was 80 in favor, 36 abstentions, and only three opposed—the three being the United States, Australia (then using herbicides in support of the U.S. invasion of Vietnam),[46] and Portugal (also using herbicides at the time in its colonial wars in Africa).[47]

While tear gas is not generally lethal, one of the types used in Indochina carried warnings that it was not to be used when "deaths are not acceptable."[48] And all types were potentially fatal to children, the elderly, and the infirm and to those in enclosed spaces. So-called "non-toxic" gas and smoke even killed an Australian soldier wearing a gas-mask who was caught in a tunnel.[49]

When the United States began using tear gas in Vietnam, Secretary of State Dean Rusk announced that it would only be employed in situations comparable to domestic crowd control, and not in the course of ordinary military operations. Then the United States argued that tear gas could save lives—when civilians and enemy soldiers were commingled in a tunnel, for example, tear gas could ferret them all out, allowing the civilians to be separated from the military personnel. But tear gas was in fact routinely used to enhance killing—as when it was dropped by helicopter on underground bunkers and then followed by B-52 attacks with conventional ordnance, a tactic that did not distinguish between soldiers and noncombatants.[50]

In 1969, the State Department sent one of its officials, Thomas R. Pickering, to face congressional critics. Pickering explained that tear gas was not prohibited by international law because it *could* be used to reduce casualties. Rep. Donald Fraser was perplexed: "In other words, if theoretically, it could be used to reduce casualties, the fact that it is used to increase casualties is of no account as long as it could be used to reduce them?" Pickering indicated that this was indeed a correct understanding of his view.[51]

Pickering also tried to justify the use of herbicides. He read from the Army's *Field Manual on the Laws of Land Warfare* that food may be destroyed by chemical means if "intended solely for consumption by the [enemy's] Armed Forces (if that fact can be determined)."[52] Pickering was apparently unconcerned that a study for the American Association for the Advancement of Science found that the United States had sprayed herbicides over 6 percent of South Vietnam's entire cropland, destroying enough food to feed 600,000 people for a year, nearly all of which would have been consumed by civilians.[53]

Chemical weapons became increasingly controversial with the U.S. public in the late 1960s. In addition to photos of napalmed Vietnamese children, public opinion was aroused by an accidental spread of nerve gas during open air tests in Utah (killing more than 6,000 sheep) and by an Army plan to transport tons of obsolete chemical weapons across the country for disposal in the ocean off New Jersey. In response to growing popular pressure, Congress prohibited open-air testing and banned the further production of lethal chemical weapons. President Nixon announced on November 25, 1969, that he would resubmit the 1925 Geneva Protocol to the Senate for its ratification, with reservations regarding the right to use chemical weapons in retaliation and excluding from its coverage herbicides, riot control agents, smoke, and napalm. Nixon further declared that the United States would unilaterally destroy its biological weapons stocks, that it would never use such weapons, even in retaliation, and that it would only do defensive research on biological warfare.[54] In April 1970, the Pentagon ordered the suspension of Agent Orange use in Vietnam as a result of studies showing the compound's devastating human effects. (The Army admitted continuing use of it, however, for at least another four months.) In December 1970, the White House announced that all herbicide use in Vietnam would be phased out and in May 1971 U.S. military use ended, though low-level use was evidently continued by the South Vietnamese government.[55]

The U.S. renunciation of biological warfare was not a major concession, given the prevailing military thinking which considered biological agents impractical weapons because of their unpredictable effects. Nevertheless, the unilateral U.S. move was helpful in getting multilateral agree-

ment to the 1972 Biological and Toxin Weapons Convention which outlawed the use, production, and stockpiling of such weapons. Not helpful,
however, was the apparent U.S. use of biological agents against Cuba in
1971: according to intelligence sources interviewed by *Newsday*, a U.S.
agent passed a vial of African swine fever virus to anti-Castro terrorists; six
weeks later an outbreak of the disease forced the slaughter of half a million
pigs to stem a national epidemic.[56] Also unhelpful was the fact that as late
as 1975 the CIA was still holding on to offensive biological warfare stocks.[57]

Bee Shit and Bull Shit

In 1981, the Reagan administration charged the Soviet Union with
violating both the 1925 Geneva Protocol and the 1972 Biological and Toxin
Weapons Convention.[58] The United States claimed that Moscow and its
Vietnamese and Laotian allies were using mycotoxins—fungal poisons—in
Afghanistan, Laos, and Cambodia. This "yellow rain," as the lethal agent
was dubbed, was said to be employed "almost on the scale of genocide" in
Laos.[59] The United States asserted that refugee testimony as well as physical
evidence supported the charges. The administration asked the *Wall Street
Journal* to play up the story,[60] and the paper ran some 50 articles in the 18
months following the initial U.S. accusation.[61] By December 1982, the U.S.
media generally accepted the charges,[62] and in February 1984 the *Journal*
editorialized that "Among men of affairs the 'yellow rain' debate is closed."[63]
This may have been an accurate characterization of the views of "men of
affairs," but serious analysts found gaping holes in the evidence. The
refugee testimony was shown to be extremely unreliable[64] and no laboratory—not even a U.S. Army lab—was able to replicate the identification of
mycotoxins on leaf samples. It finally turned out that the "yellow rain" on
the samples was nothing but bee feces.[65]

As Elisa Harris, a chemical and biological warfare specialist with the
Brookings Institution, concluded:

> although it is impossible to prove that lethal chemical warfare has not
> occurred in Southeast Asia and Afghanistan, the failure of any govern-
> ment, including the United States, to positively identify any specific
> agent—such as mustard or nerve gas—raises doubts about the Reagan
> Administration's more general chemical warfare charges against the
> Soviet Union and its allies.[66]

The Soviet Union or the Vietnamese may well have used *tear* gas in
Afghanistan or Southeast Asia, but given U.S. policy in Indochina it is

obvious why Washington had no interest in exploring or publicizing this particular crime.

There was nothing wrong with urging careful investigation of the "yellow rain" claims of refugees—as the editors of the left-wing *Southeast Asia Chronicle* did,[67] for example. But we now know that U.S. experts had serious doubts about their own evidence. A special U.S. government investigating team found major problems with the previously conducted refugee interviews; medical tests showed no clear cases of chemical attack. Yet, publicly, U.S. officials insisted on calling their evidence "incontrovertible."[68]

Thus, the "yellow rain" episode was not simply a case of honest error, caused by the inherent difficulties of getting conclusive proof in such situations. Rather, there was clear intent to deceive. Washington hoped that charging Soviet use of mycotoxins would help to discredit Moscow generally, slow down arms control efforts, and smooth passage in the U.S. Congress of appropriations for a new generation of chemical weapons. Back during a congressional hearing in February 1980, Rep. Robert I. Lagomarsino questioned U.S. intelligence officials: "Do we have any information on the use of chemical warfare in Afghanistan other than just rumors?" "There is no confirmation at all," was the reply. Lagomarsino then commented that "the common perception is that the Russians are using it there because there have been a lot of rumors in the papers." To which a high CIA official responded: "I don't see anything wrong with letting that rumor run."[69] Some years later, James Leonard, a former ambassador who helped negotiate the 1972 Biological and Toxin Weapons Convention, called U.S. management of its side of the Convention "shameful." "It is our responsibility *not* to make charges we can't substantiate."[70]

Kenneth Adelman, a director of the Arms Control and Disarmament Agency under Reagan, has written: "Whether Iraq would have been emboldened to introduce nerve agents on the battlefields of the Middle East in the absence of the recent Soviet and Vietnamese precedents remains an open question."[71] There is a more telling open question, however: whether inundating the media with charges of mycotoxin warfare, charges that were known to be unsubstantiated, might not weaken world reaction to instances of actual chemical weapon use.

Iraq and Chemical Warfare

Starting in 1984, UN investigations confirmed that Iraq was using chemical weapons against Iranian troops. The *Wall Street Journal,* characteristically, charged that mycotoxins were being used and that Moscow was the only plausible source. UN experts, however, never found toxins (poisons produced from living organisms), only mustard gas and perhaps the nerve gas tabun. According to the U.S. government, Iraq made its own chemical agents after purchasing precursor chemicals and equipment legitimately from western chemical companies.[72]

In 1986, Kenneth Adelman wrote regarding Iraq and chemical weapons, "Meaningful sanctions have yet to be imposed. Regrettably the United Nations General Assembly too often appears content with passing hollow resolutions condemning chemical warfare in general terms, while permitting violators to escape without the punishment they deserve."[73] Adelman's words were actually a precise description of the U.S. reaction. In March 1984, the State Department issued a mild condemnation of Iraq's use of chemical weapons[74] and then, in November, Washington and Baghdad restored diplomatic relations (ruptured since 1967).

For two years of Iraqi chemical warfare use, the UN Security Council did not criticize Iraq by name; later the United States made clear that it would oppose any Council action against Iraq.[75]

By the end of the Iran-Iraq war, chemical weapons had become fully integrated into Saddam Hussein's armed forces,[76] with apparently no effect on the U.S. tilt toward Iraq. Then Baghdad turned its military might on its own Kurdish minority and used chemical weapons against them.[77] Members of Congress called for sanctions on Iraq, but the administration opposed the move.[78] In the meantime, Iraq continued to receive U.S. dual-use exports and agricultural credits, despite evidence that the latter may have been financing military purchases.[79]

While ignoring Iraqi chemical weapon use, the U.S. government proclaimed throughout the 1980s that the Soviet Union had a decisive lead in chemical and biological warfare, including in the area of genetic engineering, thus requiring the development of a new generation of U.S. chemical weapons. In fact, a study by the General Accounting Office of the U.S. Congress, based on classified as well as unclassified sources, found little hard evidence to support the dire warnings.[80] As for gene warfare, evidence of a Soviet effort in this area was scanty,[81] and the U.S. Army was advertising for specialists on recombinant DNA and toxins three years before the Pentagon even claimed Moscow was using genetic engineering for military purposes.[82] Nevertheless, in 1986 the United States resumed open-air testing of biological agents,[83] and in 1987, with the help of three tie-breaking votes cast by Vice-President George Bush in the Senate, Washington ended its eighteen-year moratorium on the production of chemical weapons.[84] It was obviously hard to convince Third World nations that such weapons were reprehensible and unnecessary when the United States continued producing them. (Mikhail Gorbachev announced in 1987 that the Soviet Union had stopped producing chemical agents.)

In January 1989, 149 nations meeting in Paris unanimously agreed to condemn the use of chemical weapons. Their declaration expressed concern that such weapons "remain and are spread," thus censuring both those nations with chemical arsenals and those seeking to acquire them. The declaration further urged the swift completion of a treaty to ban the possession or production of chemical weapons, then being negotiated by 40 nations (including the United States) in Geneva.[85] There was a long-standing consensus among the 40 nations—based on a draft proposal submitted by Vice-President Bush in 1984—that all new production of chemical weapons would cease when the treaty took effect. In October 1989, however, it was revealed that the Bush administration intended to keep producing poison gas even after a global pact was in effect.[86]

Public pressure, however, forced Bush to reverse himself, though he still insisted that the United States would retain 2 percent of its chemical stockpile until all nations had signed on,[87] thus continuing to reserve for Washington a privileged status. Finally, in May 1991 Bush agreed to destroy all U.S. chemical weapons within ten years of a global ban. He also announced that once the treaty was in force, the United States would forswear any use of chemical weapons, even in retaliation.[88] The way was at last open to a chemical weapons treaty—though negotiations slowed again when Bush reversed himself once more, this time withdrawing his previous call for fully open and immediate inspections, stating instead that challenge inspections should be limited near certain installations for national security reasons.[89]

The U.S. renunciation of chemical weapons was no doubt motivated by the realization that U.S. hypocrisy would make it impossible to convince other nations to give up their chemical weapons, weapons that the United States can do without given its nuclear capability. It will still be difficult, however, to get universal adherence to a chemical ban, given the continued existence of nuclear arsenals. Chemicals are the inexpensive weapons of mass destruction, and, as Arab nations have argued on numerous occasions, states cannot be expected to renounce such weapons so long as their enemies maintain atomic arms.[90] The nuclear powers have taught by example over the last four decades that real international status comes from being able to threaten the incineration of large numbers of people. Accordingly, aspiring global players in the Third World have sought to obtain nuclear weapons or, where that has not been possible, the cheaper alternative. Thus, the spread of chemical weapons and nuclear proliferation are inextricably linked.

Nuclear Arms

The spread of nuclear arms, beyond the United States, the Soviet Union, and Britain, had its roots in the 1950s. Washington contributed to the proliferation in three ways. First, U.S. policy stated that in the event of hostilities nuclear weapons were to be "as available for use as other munitions," in the words of a secret 1953 National Security Council directive.[91] Believing that the American public had to get over its squeamishness regarding these weapons, Eisenhower administration officials publicly declared in 1955 that they considered atomic arms interchangeable with conventional ones.[92] This was hardly a message designed to discourage other nations from seeking nuclear weapons of their own.

Second, the United States, which had used the bomb in World War II against a non-nuclear foe, made clear that it was prepared to do so again. In 1955, the United States threatened and intended to use nuclear weapons against China if Beijing persisted in its efforts to take over Quemoy and Matsu, two minor groups of islands just off the Chinese coast of no importance to the defense of Taiwan, but from which Chiang Kai-shek's forces had been launching attacks—quietly appreciated in Washington—against the mainland.[93] China ultimately backed down, but, not surprisingly, decided in the midst of the crisis to begin its own nuclear program.[94]

The third way in which U.S. policy promoted nuclear proliferation was in placing more emphasis on nuclear weapons cooperation with its European allies—even at the cost of encouraging and stimulating independent atomic weapons programs—than it did on working toward international agreements to prevent the spread of nuclear weapons.[95] So eager was the United States, that it gave West Germany atomic bombs under "dual control," meaning that (until the Kennedy administration installed safety locks) the Germans would have had only to overpower a single U.S. sentry in order to drop a nuclear bomb on Moscow.[96]

When China detonated its first atomic weapon in 1964, U.S. officials began to worry about proliferation. The solution they considered was unilateral action, possibly with tacit Soviet cooperation, to destroy Chinese nuclear weapons facilities.[97]

But even at this point, key top policy-makers were privately unenthusiastic about non-proliferation, despite a public U.S. posture favoring it.[98] Not until 1966 did Washington decide that it favored non-proliferation over the possibility of establishing a NATO or European nuclear force.[99] Accordingly, in 1968 the United States joined with Britain and the Soviet Union in putting forward the Treaty on the Non-Proliferation of Nuclear Weapons (NPT), which they invited all other countries to sign. The treaty obliged signatories who possessed nuclear weapons to refrain from transferring nuclear weapons or the technology for such weapons to any non-nuclear state; non-nuclear states undertook not to accept nuclear weapons or nuclear-weapons technology and to accept international safeguards on all their peaceful nuclear energy facilities. Many non-nuclear states considered that they should not be the only ones to give up something by signing the treaty; accordingly, Article VI of the treaty was designed as a crucial concession to them: it obligated all nations to pursue good faith negotiations leading to the cessation of the nuclear arms race, nuclear disarmament, and complete disarmament.[100]

Progress on stopping nuclear proliferation would thus require taking steps to reverse the superpower arms race and getting as many nations as possible to ratify the NPT. On the first of these requirements, the U.S. record was unimpressive.

In 1968, when the NPT was signed, the United States had 4,500 strategic nuclear warheads and the USSR 850. A decade later, thanks to the introduction of new technology, the numbers stood at 9,800 for the United States and 5,200 for the Soviet Union.[101] And the warheads were far more lethal in 1978 than in 1968.

In 1973, Washington and Moscow signed an agreement on the Prevention of Nuclear War. Henry Kissinger called it at the time "a significant step" in reducing the likelihood of a nuclear holocaust. In his memoirs, however, Kissinger admitted that he had negotiated "a bland set of principles that had been systematically stripped of all implications harmful to our interests."[102] During the negotiations Kissinger had insisted that the agreement include a paragraph guaranteeing non-intervention in other countries. With considerable reluctance, Soviet leader Brezhnev and Foreign Minister Gromyko assented, whereupon Kissinger withdrew the paragraph[103]—not much of an indication of a good faith effort to end the arms race.

For many non-nuclear states, the issue of nuclear testing was the litmus test by which they judged the devotion of the nuclear powers to non-proliferation. New kinds of weapons require testing, and thus a prohibition on testing would at least halt the race to develop new, more deadly nuclear arms. In 1963, the United States, the Soviet Union, Britain, and many other nations had agreed to ban atmospheric tests and committed themselves to seek the discontinuance of *all* nuclear tests for all time. In fact, however, in the seven years following 1963 the United States conducted more underground tests per year than total tests—atmospheric and underground—it had conducted in all but two pre-1963 years.[104]

Annually, beginning in 1962, a large majority of the UN General Assembly passed resolutions condemning all nuclear testing. The 1968 NPT in its preamble specifically recalled and renewed the commitment to ban all testing.[105] And in 1973 the Swedish government declared a day of mourning over the failure to make progress in this regard.[106] Then, in 1974, the United States and the Soviet Union showed the extent of their good faith by negotiating the Threshold Test Ban Treaty. As William Epstein, a Canadian special consultant on disarmament to the UN Secretary General, noted, the treaty

> allows the parties to continue unrestricted underground tests of whatever size they wish until March 31, 1976; thereafter they will limit weapon tests to 150 kilotons each, which is about 10 times larger than the yield of the bomb that was dropped on Hiroshima and which exceeds in size all but a few of the tests conducted in recent years.... This is not just a cosmetic agreement; it is a mockery of a test-ban treaty.[107]

Even this treaty, however, was not ratified by the United States until September 1990.[108]

In 1975, a conference was held to review the NPT. As the Swedish delegate reported, the "nuclear-weapons powers had nothing substantive to offer to stem the trend toward proliferation. Their cynicism was made obvious by a categorical nonacceptance of all proposals, symbolized by a giant United States test explosion in the middle of the Conference."[109] By the time of the 1985 review conference, the Soviet Union had come to accept a comprehensive test ban, while the United States continued to reject the notion. But Moscow apparently decided that it would not be helpful for the superpowers to embarrass each other and thus did not press the issue.[110]

In September 1990, another NPT review conference was held. Once again Third World countries urged a comprehensive test ban, warning that the future of the NPT was endangered. And once again the United States refused.[111] And at a UN conference in January 1991, Washington opposed yet another effort to achieve a total test ban.[112]

In September 1991, after the failed Soviet coup, President Bush announced that the U.S. would unilaterally eliminate short-range ground- and sea-launched nuclear weapons. His announcement was motivated by two major concerns: one, given the centrifugal forces in the USSR it was important to make sure that Soviet short-range weapons didn't fall into dangerous hands;[113] and, two, according to public opinion polls, there were renewed pressures in the United States for deep defense cuts, so the Bush administration hoped to give up weapons that were not especially useful militarily as a way to forestall deeper cuts.[114] Accordingly, Bush's announcement included ominous warnings against cutting the military budget, particularly Star Wars and the B-2 stealth bomber,[115] and reserved the right of the United States to be the first to use nuclear weapons.[116] With the leading global superpower still unwilling to accept a comprehensive test ban or an agreement barring first use of nuclear weapons, it is no wonder that leaders of some non-nuclear states continue to pursue nuclear arsenals of their own.

In addition to working to halt the superpower arms race, the other requirement for promoting non-proliferation was encouraging as many states as possible to adhere to the NPT. Here too the U.S. effort was feeble. In fact, in a secret 1969 National Security memorandum the Nixon administration indicated its attitude to the just-concluded treaty: "The government, in its public posture, should reflect a tone of optimism that other countries will sign or ratify, while clearly disassociating itself from any plan to bring pressure on these countries to sign or ratify." [117]

Many nations did adhere to the treaty, among them Iraq, Iran, Libya, Syria, and, in 1981, Egypt. However, some crucial countries failed to do so: among them France, China, India, Pakistan, Israel, Brazil, Argentina, and South Africa.[118] Instead of pressing these nations to sign on, the United States often facilitated their nuclear efforts. Washington was covertly aiding the French nuclear weapons program since 1974,[119] despite the fact that France was a particularly irresponsible nuclear power, insisting until 1975 on atmospheric nuclear testing, conducting underground tests in the South Pacific in violation of the nuclear-free zone established by the countries of the region, and engaging in blatant state terrorism to prevent interference with its testing program (the blowing up of the environmental vessel, Rainbow Warrior).

In 1978, the U.S. Congress passed legislation mandating a cutoff of economic and military aid to countries trying to produce nuclear weapons. Because of strong evidence showing that Pakistan was heavily involved in developing nuclear arms, U.S. aid was halted in 1979. But following the Soviet invasion of Afghanistan, the Carter administration claimed emergency exemption from the congressional aid ban and offered Pakistani President Zia a two-year, $400 million package of economic and military aid. U.S. officials made clear to Zia that aid would continue flowing despite the Pakistani nuclear program so long as a nuclear weapon was not actually tested.[120] Shortly after taking office in 1981, Ronald Reagan (who had declared during the election campaign that non-proliferation was none of America's business[121]) agreed to provide Pakistan with $3.2 billion in aid over six years. When Congress asked whether the administration felt confident that Pakistan was not developing a nuclear weapons capability, Under-Secretary of State James Buckley replied reassuringly: "There is...a distinction between developing a capability and utilizing a capability."[122] And the pattern has continued: in the fall of 1990 the Bush administration tried to get a waiver to provide aid to Pakistan despite its ongoing nuclear program.[123]

Another potential nuclear power was South Africa. In both 1977 and 1979 the United States tried to cover up South African nuclear tests.[124] In 1981, U.S. brokers—with the knowledge of the State Department—arranged the transfer of nuclear fuel from France to Pretoria. The next year Reagan allowed the export to South Africa of "dual-use" items, but he was blocked in this by the Congress.[125] The Reagan administration also circumvented U.S. legislation in aiding the nuclear programs of Brazil, India, and Argentina.[126] And even after the Iraqi invasion of Kuwait, the White House approved the export of parts for a new three-stage missile that Brazil was developing, despite compelling evidence that Brazil had shared missile and nuclear technology with Iraq.[127] Not to be outdone, Congress voted two weeks later to allow the export of supercomputers to Brazil.[128] During the period of the U.S. honeymoon with Saddam Hussein—that is, from the early 1980s until August 2, 1990—the United States allowed the export to Iraq of "dual use" nuclear technology; in August 1989, the Pentagon and the Department of Energy invited three Iraqi scientists to a "detonation conference" in Portland, Oregon, that included lectures on igniting A-bombs and was, in the words of an internal Department of Energy memo, "the place to be...if you were a potential nuclear-weapons proliferant."[129]

The Israeli Bomb

But the real test of U.S. concern with nuclear proliferation is the case of Israel. As early as 1968 the CIA had concluded that Israel had manufactured atomic weapons.[130] Israel did so with a combination of early U.S. assistance to its "peaceful" atomic energy program, secret French support, winking on the part of Washington, theft, and deception. Israeli officials refer to the French as "whores" for selling Saddam Hussein nuclear technology,[131] but a quarter of a century before Paris started "whoring" with Iraq, it was doing so with Israel.[132] Iraq, we now know, set up front companies all around the world to try to buy or acquire nuclear technology.

Israel has done the same thing for years.[133] The CIA believes that Israel stole 200 pounds of enriched uranium from a plant in Pennsylvania (with the connivance of the company president) and that Israeli agents diverted 200 tons of processed uranium ore at sea.[134] In 1960, France illegally transferred to Israel heavy water from Norway, used in making nuclear weapons.[135] In 1990 Iraq was "stung" trying to buy U.S. krytrons (used as triggers for nuclear weapons), but in 1971, the Pentagon approved the sale of krytrons to Israel, and in 1985 Israel was caught trying to obtain additional U.S. krytrons illegally.[136] The sneaky Iraqis allowed international inspectors to examine one of their nuclear reactors while they actually worked on atom bombs at other facilities. They weren't nearly as tricky, however, as the Israelis who built a false control room at their Dimona reactor to fool U.S. inspectors, who paid visits between 1962 and 1969, seemingly eager to be fooled.[137] In fact, when Prime Minister Menachim Begin described a non-existent underground weapons facility at the Iraqi reactor that Israel bombed in 1981, he was actually describing what Israel had built underneath Dimona.[138]

Despite the deception, the CIA knew about the Israeli nuclear program. But whenever Washington found out some more about what Israel was doing, there was no negative U.S. reaction. In fact, the U.S. government—whether under Eisenhower, Johnson, Carter, or Reagan—helped provide cover to the Israelis and U.S. aid to Tel Aviv was increased.[139] U.S. laws calling for the cutoff of aid to states producing nuclear weapons were carefully written in such a way so as not to include Israel.[140] Indeed the author of the legislation, Sen. Stuart Symington, had told Israeli Deputy Defense Minister Shimon Peres back in 1963: "Don't stop making atomic bombs."[141] Israel didn't stop, and we now know that Israel not only has the atom bomb, but it has some 200 thermonuclear warheads, including advanced low-yield neutron bombs.[142] Among the countries targeted by Israeli nuclear weapons has been the Soviet Union,[143] raising the specter that a local conflict could turn into a global Armageddon.

When asked directly about the Israeli nuclear program, the Carter administration noted only that Israel had declared it would "not be the first to introduce nuclear weapons into the area."[144] But U.S. officials knew well what Israel meant by this pledge: only that it would not be the first to test a nuclear weapon in the region or to publicly announce its possession of such a weapon.[145]

In 1974, Egypt and Iran co-sponsored a resolution in the General Assembly calling for the establishment of a nuclear weapons-free zone in the Middle East. The vote was 128 in favor, none opposed, and only Israel and Burma abstaining. In 1975, seven Middle Eastern governments told the

Secretary General that they were prepared to refrain from developing nuclear weapons if Israel would do so as well, with adequate control measures.[146] Israel informed the Secretary General that it favored a nuclear weapons-free zone based on direct negotiations between all the states in the region,[147] implying mutual recognition and hence prior solution of all outstanding political problems in the Middle East. Between 1975 and 1979, the General Assembly reaffirmed the Egyptian-Iranian resolution by the same lopsided margin, with only Israel abstaining in the last four of these years.[148] Then in 1980 Israel voted for the resolution. It is hard to avoid cynical interpretations of the Israeli switch: it may have been motivated by a desire to look good given that Egypt, but not Israel, was about to accede to the NPT. Or it may have been camouflage for the decision made by Israeli officials at the time to attack Iraq's Osirak nuclear power plant.[149]

Though far behind Israel technologically, there is no doubt that Iraq has sought a nuclear capability and was able to hide its effort from international inspectors. Israeli complaints about the limitations of international inspections, however, were rather hollow given Tel Aviv's refusal to accede to the NPT and given its own nuclear arsenal. It would have been a real service if Israel had offered its expertise in evading inspections in order to strengthen the inspection machinery of the International Atomic Energy Administration. But instead of proposing some sort of mutual renunciation of nuclear weapons under the most stringent of international controls, Israel launched a military strike against Osirak in June 1981.

The United States supported a Security Council resolution condemning the raid, though making sure that no sanctions were imposed on Israel. Despite the condemnation, there are reasons to believe that Washington was not opposed to the attack. In October 1980, Israel had consulted with the U.S. Nuclear Regulatory Commission regarding the effect of hypothetically hitting a nuclear power plant with 2,000-pound bombs, the kind used in the Osirak strike.[150] According to National Security Adviser Richard Allen, Reagan's reaction to the raid was, "Well. Boys will be boys."[151] The United States began a study of whether Israel's use of U.S.-supplied aircraft in the raid violated U.S. law, which would require an arms cutoff. The study was never completed.[152]

Even analysts sympathetic to Israel's view that Iraq was up to no good concluded that the Israeli attack may have stimulated, rather than thwarted, the Arab quest for nuclear weapons.[153] The Israeli position, on the other hand, seemed to be that it would maintain its nuclear monopoly by continuing to destroy any Arab nuclear facilities. Prime Minister Begin in fact declared that Israel would not tolerate any enemy, Arab or not, acquiring a nuclear capability, thus including Pakistan, and there were reports of an Israeli overture to India, proposing a joint strike on Pakistan's nuclear facilities.[154]

Shortly after the raid on Iraq, a State Department spokesperson was asked whether the U.S. concern over non-proliferation applied to Israel. The reply consisted of the usual evasions:

> the U.S. has no nuclear cooperation with Israel. Our own policy is clear: The prevention of the spread of nuclear weapons is an important worldwide objective of the United States. We have noted that the Government of Israel has consistently affirmed that it would not be the first to introduce nuclear weapons into the region. Beyond that I cannot go.[155]

A week later, Reagan was asked the same question:

> Well, I haven't given very much thought to that particular question there.... It is difficult for me to envision Israel as being a threat to its neighbors. It is a nation that from the very beginning has lived under the threat from neighbors that they did not recognize its right to exist as a nation. I'll have to think about that question you asked.[156]

Despite Reagan's unique quickness of wit, his argument is actually quite commonly heard: Israel's nuclear weapons program is different from Iraq's because the former is a peace-loving, humane state while the latter is aggressive and ruthless.

There *are* important differences between Israel and Iraq: only Iraq has used large-scale chemical warfare; Iraq has killed a far larger fraction of its own population than has Israel, though most of Saddam Hussein's atrocities occurred during periods when he enjoyed U.S. support. In early 1990, for example, when Middle East Watch denounced Iraq as "one of the most brutal and repressive regimes in power today," twelve western powers tried to get the UN Human Rights Commission to investigate Iraq's abuses, but Washington opposed the effort.[157] Nevertheless, Israeli brutality should not be minimized. The treatment of Palestinians in the occupied territories has been horrific. During the first year alone of the *Intifada,* 66 Palestinians died from exposure to tear gas fired by Israeli troops.[158] Killings, bone-breaking, torture, blowing up of houses, atrocities against children, collective punishment—all these have been commonplace.[159] Additionally, both Israel and Iraq have been expansionist powers, invading weaker neighbors. The Israeli invasion of Lebanon in 1982 (which like the Iraqi invasion of Iran in 1980 received a wink and a nod from Washington) caused thousands of civilian casualties.[160]

If Israel, the strongest conventional power in the region, claims to need nuclear weapons for deterrence, then lesser powers can make a similar claim. Iraq, after all, could point to the Israeli attack on its Osirak nuclear reactor in 1981, and to subsequent Israeli threats. For example, in 1988 Tel Aviv launched a new military satellite which, the *Washington Post* noted, was widely regarded as a symbol of the Israeli commitment to an offensive, possibly even preemptive strategy. Martin Indyk, the Executive Director of the Washington Institute for Near East Policy, reported publicly after extensive talks with top Israeli military officers that the Israeli Air Force wanted to preempt missiles in Syria, Iraq, and Saudi Arabia and that the Air Force view had been accepted.[161]

What makes missiles so dangerous in the region is that they are potential means of delivering nuclear or chemical warheads. Israel, however, has always had the regional lead in this regard. First Israel got the Lance missile from the United States and then developed the Jericho missile. Both are too expensive and inaccurate for other than nuclear missions, so it is probable that they have been nuclear-armed.[162] Subsequently Israel developed—without protest from either the Carter or Reagan administrations—the Jericho II, capable of carrying fusion weapons 400 miles.[163] Israel has shared missile technology with the Shah's Iran, South Africa, Taiwan, and China.[164] According to a report by the Inspector General of the State Department, Israel has engaged in a "systematic and growing pattern" of selling sensitive U.S. military technology to third countries—among them South Africa—which, though in violation of U.S. law, elicited no response from the U.S. government.[165]

Another means of delivering nuclear warheads is via wide-gauge cannon. Iraq was known to have been actively seeking to develop such a "supergun" with the help of Gerald Bull, a weapons expert recently assassinated, probably by the Israeli spy agency, Mossad.[166] In 1975, South Africa obtained the technology for an earlier nuclear-capable cannon from Bull's Canadian/U.S. firm with the help of CIA and Israeli agents eager to facilitate Pretoria's intervention in Angola.[167]

No Nukes and No Gas

Baghdad's nuclear capability was exaggerated by U.S. officials eager to justify the military option against Iraq.[168] But U.S. threat-inflation does not mean that nuclear proliferation in the Middle East is not a serious problem. The question, however, is how this problem should be dealt with?

Shortly before the U.S. attack on Iraq, Ann Lewis, the former political director of the Democratic National Committee, wrote that "no settlement of the gulf crisis can include international negotiations on nuclear proliferation in the region" for this would allow Saddam Hussein to claim a victory.[169] Instead of negotiations, Bush has taken the Osirak approach to arms control, only on a more massive scale. There are serious dangers to this approach.

First, it is highly ineffective. As a Pentagon official acknowledged, "We can bomb all we want, but we'll never get all his material and equipment by bombing."[170] Second, it is likely to be counter-productive. While the Iraqi nuclear program has certainly been set back, can anyone doubt that the Arab people will only be incited to further efforts to produce chemical and nuclear weapons, if not in Iraq then in Syria or Libya or somewhere else, if not next year then five or ten years from now? Being the victim of a military attack by a more powerful country only reinforces the view that a nuclear capability could help even the contest. And, third, if the Osirak approach should be adopted by other countries, the world would be a perilous place indeed. Imagine if India decided to enforce its vision of non-proliferation on Pakistan, or China on India, or South Korea on North Korea.[171]

During a May 1991 commencement address at the Air Force Academy, President Bush put forward an arms control plan for the Middle East. In two paragraph's of this speech, Bush called for an eventual nuclear-free zone in the Middle East and the elimination of chemical weapons and ballistic missiles. But the plan was basically all smoke and mirrors because the missile ban covered only new missiles, thus leaving Israel with a decisive edge, and the nuclear ban required no action from the one nuclear power in the region. In the rest of the speech, Bush cautioned Congress that he would veto any military budget that cut Star Wars or the B-2 bomber.[172]

As U.S. propagandists self-righteously denounce Iraqi instruments of mass destruction, U.S. hypocrisy continues. Despite a law stating that "no military equipment or technology shall be sold or transferred" to Pakistan because of its nuclear weapons program, Washington issued licenses for over $100 million in commercial sales of military supplies to the South Asian nation in 1990 and 1991.[173] And while warning that military know-how from the former Soviet Union might fall into dangerous hands, the Bush administration is trying to buy up Soviet technology to enhance its own Star Wars project,[174] while rejecting limitations on the U.S. nuclear testing program.[175]

Weapons proliferation is an extremely significant global problem. But the last agency in the world one would want to entrust with the job of solving this problem is the Pentagon.

Chapter 4

Protecting Resources

The long lines at the gas pumps in 1973 and 1979 made many Americans concerned about the supply of oil and other resources. This concern might have led to an effort to develop alternative energy sources, but instead Washington chose to increase U.S. dependence on foreign petroleum while preparing the military to intervene abroad to protect essential resources. In 1988, near the end of the war between Iran and Iraq, the U.S. Navy was deployed to the Persian Gulf for the announced purpose of assuring the flow of oil. But, in fact, neither the naval deployment nor U.S. policy throughout the eight-year-long conflict was motivated by the fear of a resource shortage. Rather, the U.S. goal was to control the region's vast oil resources, a rather different matter. Indeed, this determination to control the petroleum supplies of the Middle East has been one of the constants of U.S. foreign policy for decades.

Some Crude History

Much of the world's proven oil reserves are located in the limited area of the Persian Gulf (called by Arab nations the "Arabian Gulf," and by those who try to keep their gazetteers politically neutral, simply "the Gulf").

Less than 4 percent of U.S. oil consumption comes from the Gulf, but, according to the official argument, Western Europe and Japan are extremely dependent on Gulf oil and hence if the region fell into the hands of a hostile power, U.S. allies could be brought to their knees, and U.S. security would be fundamentally and irreparably compromised. If one examines the history of U.S. policy in the Gulf, however, protecting the oil interests of Western Europe and Japan never seemed to be one of Washington's foremost goals.

As far back as the 1920s, the State Department sought to force Great Britain to give U.S. companies a share of the lucrative Middle Eastern oil concessions. The U.S. Ambassador in London—who happened to be Andrew Mellon, the head of the Gulf Oil Corporation (named for the

Mexican, not the Persian/Arabian, Gulf)—was instructed to press the British to give Gulf Oil a stake in the Middle East.[1] At the end of World War II, when the immense petroleum deposits in Saudi Arabia became known, Secretary of the Navy James Forrestal told Secretary of State Byrnes, "I don't care which American company or companies develop the Arabian reserves, but I think most emphatically that it should be *American*."[2] And it wasn't the Russians that Forrestal was worried about. The main competition was between the United States and Britain for control of the area's oil.[3]

In 1928, Standard Oil of New Jersey and Mobil had joined British and French oil interests in signing the "Red Line Agreement," under which each pledged not to develop Middle Eastern oil without the participation of the others. Nevertheless, after World War II these two U.S. firms (together with Texaco and Standard Oil of California) grabbed the Saudi concessions for themselves, freezing out the British and French. When the latter sued on the grounds that the Red Line Agreement had been violated, Mobil and Jersey told the court that the agreement was null and void because it was monopolistic.[4]

In the early 1950s, oil was used as a political weapon for the first time—*by* the United States and Britain and *against* Iran. Iran had nationalized its British-owned oil company which had refused to share its astronomical profits with the host government. In response, Washington and London organized a boycott of Iranian oil which brought Iran's economy to the brink of collapse. The CIA then instigated a coup, entrenching the Shah in power and effectively un-nationalizing the oil company, with U.S. firms getting 40 percent of the formerly 100 percent British-owned company. This was, in the view of the *New York Times,* an "object lesson in the heavy cost that must be paid" when an oil-rich Third World nation "goes berserk with fanatical nationalism."[5]

In 1956 the oil weapon was used again, this time by the United States against Britain and France. After the latter two nations along with Israel invaded Egypt, Washington made clear that U.S. oil would not be sent to Western Europe until Britain and France agreed to a rapid withdrawal schedule.[6] The United States was not adverse to overthrowing Nasser—"Had they done it quickly, we would have accepted it," Eisenhower said later[7]—but the clumsy Anglo-French military operation threatened U.S. interests in the region.

In October 1969 the Shah of Iran asked the United States to purchase more Iranian oil as a way to boost his revenues. But the Shah's request was rejected because, as an assistant to then President Nixon explained, "a substantial portion of the profits from these purchases would go to non-

American companies" if Iranian oil were bought, while if Saudi oil were purchased, the U.S. share would be larger.[8]

By the end of the 1960s the international oil market was far different from what it had been two decades earlier. Oil supplies were tight, the number of oil firms had grown, and the producing countries, joined together in the Organization of Petroleum Exporting Countries, were seeking to improve their financial position.

Crucial talks on oil prices began in 1970 between U.S. companies and the government of Libya. Significantly, Washington did not weigh in on the side of the companies, and in fact, the companies themselves did not put up much resistance to the price increases. For the oil companies, higher prices would be beneficial, making profitable their growing investments in the developed nations (for example, in Alaska and the North Sea).[9] Any higher prices could be passed on to consumers—and, indeed, in 1972-73 the companies raised their prices to a greater extent than crude costs alone warranted.[10]

In 1972, the Nixon administration was advocating higher oil prices.[11] According to a study by V.H. Oppenheim, based on interviews with U.S. officials:

> The weight of the evidence suggests that the principal consideration behind the indulgent U.S. government attitude toward higher oil prices was the belief that higher prices would produce economic benefits for the United States vis-à-vis its industrial competitors, Western Europe and Japan, and the key Middle Eastern states, Saudi Arabia and Iran.[12]

And Henry Kissinger has confirmed that this was U.S. government thinking: "The rise in the price of energy would affect primarily Europe and Japan and probably improve America's competitive position."[13]

Amid growing warnings about a possible oil embargo, the industrialized western countries held meetings to decide their response. Showing its concern for its allies, the United States proposed that any reductions be shared, but on the basis of each country's sea-borne imports, rather than on the basis of total energy requirements. Since the United States was much less dependent on imports than other countries, this formula meant that in the event of an embargo U.S. energy supplies would be cut far less than those of its "allies."[14]

After the October 1973 Middle East war broke out, but before the Arab embargo, U.S. oil company officials wrote to Nixon, warning that the "whole position of the United States in the Middle East is on the way to being seriously impaired, with Japanese, European, and perhaps Russian interests largely supplanting United States presence in the area, to the detriment of both our economy and our security."[15] Note that the Russian threat was considered only a possibility, the allied threat a certainty.

In late 1973 and on into 1974, the Arab oil producers cut their production and imposed an embargo against the United States and the Netherlands for their pro-Israeli position. The public has memories of long lines at the gas pump, rationing, and a crisis atmosphere. In fact, however, in Kissinger's words, "the Arab embargo was a symbolic gesture of limited practical impact."[16] The international oil companies, which totally monopolized petroleum distribution and marketing, pooled their oil, so the shortfall of Saudi supplies to the United States was made up from other sources. Overall, the oil companies spread out the production cutbacks so as to minimize suffering, and the country most supportive of Israel—the United States—suffered among the least. From January 1974 to March, oil consumption in the United States was only off by 5 percent, compared to 15 percent in France and West Germany.[17]

Even these figures, however, overstate the hardship, because in fact,

> *there was at no time a real shortage of petroleum on the European market.* Consumption simply responded to the increase in prices.... Between October, 1973, and April, 1974, the reserves of oil products in the countries of the European Community never descended below the 80-day equivalent of consumption; and in Italy the reserves in fact increased by 23 per cent.[18]

In Japan, there were about two million barrels of oil more than the government admitted, as the bureaucracy, the oil industry, and industrial oil users sought to exploit the crisis for their own advantage.[19]

In the aftermath of the embargo, U.S. allies tried to negotiate their own bilateral petroleum purchase deals with the producing nations without going through the major international oil companies. Washington opposed these efforts.[20] In short, the well-being of U.S. allies has never been the key consideration for U.S. policy-makers.

Nor for that matter has the crucial concern been the well-being of the average American. One former Defense Department official has estimated that it cost U.S. taxpayers about $47 billion in 1985 alone for military expenditures related to the Gulf;[21] former Secretary of the Navy John Lehman put the annual figure at $40 billion.[22] What could be worth these staggering sums?

These expenditures have *not* been necessary for the survival of the West. In the extreme, according to former CIA analyst Maj. Gen. Edward B. Atkeson, if all Gulf oil were cut off, the elimination of recreational driving (which in the United States accounts for 10 percent of total oil consumption) would reduce western petroleum needs to a level easily replaceable from non-Gulf sources. Even in wartime, Atkeson concluded, Gulf oil is not essential to western needs.[23] And in a protracted global conflict, one can be sure that oil fields would not last very long in the face of missile attacks.

The billions of dollars, however, are a good investment for the oil companies, given that they are not the ones who pay the tab. To be sure, the multinationals no longer directly own the vast majority of Gulf crude production. But they have special buy-back deals with the producers, whereby they purchase at bargain prices oil from the fields they formerly owned. For example, according to former Senator Frank Church, U.S. firms "have a 'sweetheart' arrangement with Saudi Arabia, notwithstanding the nominal nationalization of their properties...."[24] Radical regimes want to sell oil as much as conservative ones do, but a change of government in any Gulf state might eliminate the privileged position of the oil companies.

The internal security of regimes like Saudi Arabia depends heavily on outside, particularly U.S., support. Many Saudis believe that in return their country has set its oil production levels to please the United States, to the detriment of their nation's long-term interests. At times, this has meant selling oil beyond the point at which the proceeds could be productively invested, an economically irrational strategy particularly given the fact that oil in the ground appreciates in value.[25] More democratic or nationalistic governments in the Gulf may not be so willing to sacrifice their own interests. And such governments will also be less willing to accommodate a U.S. military presence or to serve as U.S. proxies for maintaining the regional status quo.

And thus for more than 40 years, through many changed circumstances, there has been one constant of U.S. policy in the Gulf: support for the most conservative local forces available, in order to keep radical and popular movements from coming to power, no matter what the human cost, no matter how great the necessary manipulation or intervention. The United States has not been invariably successful in achieving its objective: in 1979, it lost one of its major props with the overthrow of the Shah of Iran, who had policed the Gulf on Washington's behalf. But the basic pattern of U.S. policy has not changed, as is well illustrated by its policy with regard to the war between Iran and Iraq.

The Iran-Iraq War

The war between Iran and Iraq was one of the great human tragedies of recent Middle Eastern history. Perhaps as many as a million people died, many more were wounded, and millions were made refugees. The resources wasted on the war exceeded what the entire Third World spent on public health in a decade.[26]

The war began on September 22, 1980, when Iraqi troops launched a full-scale invasion of Iran. Prior to this date there had been subversion by each country inside the other and also major border clashes. Iraq hoped for a lightning victory against an internationally isolated neighbor in the throes of revolutionary upheaval. But despite Iraq's initial successes, the Iranians rallied and, using their much larger population, were able by mid-1982 to push the invaders out. In June 1982, the Iranians went over to the offensive, but Iraq, with a significant advantage in heavy weaponry, was able to prevent a decisive Iranian breakthrough. The guns finally fell silent on August 20, 1988.

Primary responsibility for the eight long years of bloodletting must rest with the governments of the two countries—the ruthless military regime of Saddam Hussein in Iraq and the ruthless clerical regime of the Ayatollah Khomeini in Iran. Khomeini was said by some to have a "martyr complex," though, as U.S. Secretary of State Cyrus Vance wryly observed, people with martyr complexes rarely live to be as old as Khomeini. Whatever his complexes, Khomeini had no qualms about sending his followers, including young boys, off to their deaths for his greater glory. This callous disregard for human life was no less characteristic of Saddam Hussein. And, for that matter, it was also no less characteristic of much of the world community, which not only couldn't be bothered by a few hundred thousand Third World corpses, but which tried to profit from the conflict.

France became the major source of Iraq's high-tech weaponry, in no small part to protect its financial stake in that country.[27] The Soviet Union was Iraq's largest weapon's supplier, while jockeying for influence in both capitals. Israel provided arms to Iran, hoping to bleed the combatants by prolonging the war. According to a CIA report, 92 countries sold vital military equipment and technology to Iraq from 1983-89.[28] And at least ten nations sold arms to both of the warring sides.[29] The list of countries engaging in despicable behavior, however, would be incomplete without the United States.

The United States did not have diplomatic relations with either belligerent in 1980 and announced its neutrality in the conflict. One typically humanitarian State Department official explained in 1983: "We don't give a damn as long as the Iran-Iraq carnage does not affect our allies in the region or alter the balance of power."[30] In fact, however, the United

States was not indifferent to the war, but saw a number of positive opportunities opened up by its prolongation.

The need for arms and money would make Baghdad more dependent on the conservative Gulf states and Egypt, thereby moderating Iraq's policies and helping to repair ties between Cairo and the other Arab states. The war would make Iran—whose weapons had all been U.S.-supplied in the past—desperate to obtain U.S. equipment and spare parts. The exigencies of war might make both nations more willing to restore their relations with Washington. Alternatively, the dislocations of war might give the United States greater ability to carry out covert operations in Iran or Iraq. And turmoil in the Gulf might make other states in the area more susceptible to U.S. pressure for military cooperation.

When the war first broke out, the Soviet Union turned back its arms shipments en route to Iraq, and for the next year and a half, while Iraq was on the offensive, Moscow did not provide weapons to Baghdad.[31] In March 1981, the Iraqi Communist Party, repressed by Saddam Hussein, beamed broadcasts from the Soviet Union calling for an end to the war and the withdrawal of Iraqi troops.[32] That same month U.S. Secretary of State Alexander Haig told the Senate Foreign Relations Committee that he saw the possibility of improved ties with Baghdad and approvingly noted that Iraq was concerned by "the behavior of Soviet imperialism in the Middle Eastern area." The United States then approved the sale to Iraq of five Boeing jetliners, and sent a Deputy Assistant Secretary of State to Baghdad for talks.[33] In early 1982, CIA director William Casey traveled to Baghdad to meet secretly with Saddam Hussein. On his return, Reagan signed a National Security directive authorizing support for Iraq.[34] On February 26, 1982, Iraq was removed from the State Department's notoriously selective list of countries supporting international terrorism, despite the fact that U.S. officials knew that Saddam's support for terrorism had not weakened.[35]

With Baghdad off the terrorism list, the United States began extending agricultural credits as well.[36] The United States also started secretly passing Iraq highly classified intelligence: satellite imagery, communications intercepts, and CIA assessments that could pinpoint Iranian weaknesses.[37] Washington's professed neutrality prohibited selling arms to either side, but, as the National Security Council's Middle East director explained, "There was a conscious effort to encourage third countries to ship U.S. arms or acquiesce in shipments after the fact.... It was a policy of winks and nods."[38] Significant quantities of U.S. arms were transferred to Iraq as a result of this U.S. policy over the next seven years, particularly from Egypt, Jordan, and Kuwait. And starting in 1983, the CIA looked the other way when private U.S. arms dealers sold Iraq sophisticated Soviet arms bought in

Eastern Europe, again in violation of U.S. obligations as a declared neutral.[39] In November 1984, Washington and Baghdad restored diplomatic relations, which had been ruptured since 1967.[40]

The U.S. Commerce Department approved the sale to Iraq of hundreds of millions of dollars worth of dual-use equipment.[41] For example, helicopters were sold to Iraq as crop dusters, but were probably used for spraying poison gas on the Kurdish population.[42] In January 1988, to take another example, Washington approved the sale of a laser-guided welding system which could be used to repair jet engines and rocket casings.[43] The U.S. Export-Import Bank (that is, the U.S. taxpayer) also provided Iraq with billions of dollars in loan guarantees, thanks to the persistent lobbying of Vice-President Bush who overcame Ex-Im staff objections that the loans would never be repaid.[44] In 1988, U.S. military advisers secretly drew up battle plans for Iraqi officers.[45]

The Soviet Threat and the Rapid Deployment Force

Before turning to U.S. relations with Iran, it is necessary to consider how the Iran-Iraq war was furthering U.S. military relations with the other Arab Gulf states.

Washington typically justified its desire for military ties in the Gulf and the development of forces for use there by warning of the Soviet threat. In January 1980, President Carter proclaimed the "Carter Doctrine," declaring that the United States was willing to use military force if necessary to prevent "an outside power" from conquering the Gulf. As Michael Klare has noted, however, the real U.S. concern was revealed five days later when Secretary of Defense Harold Brown released his military posture statement. Brown indicated that the greatest threat was not Soviet expansionism but uncontrolled turbulence in the Third World. "In a world of disputes and violence we cannot afford to go abroad unarmed," he warned. "The particular manner in which our economy has expanded means that we have come to depend to no small degree on imports, exports and the earnings from overseas investments for our material well-being." Specifically, Brown identified the "protection of the oil flow from the Middle East" as "clearly part of our vital interest," in defense of which "we'll take any action that's appropriate, including the use of military force."[46]

Brown did not explicitly state that the United States would intervene militarily in response to internal threats, like revolution, but after he left office he explained what could be said openly and what could not: "One sensitive issue is whether the United States should plan to protect the oil fields against internal or regional threats. Any explicit commitment of this sort is more likely to upset and anger the oil suppliers than to reassure them."[47]

Gulf sensitivity on explicit U.S. commitments to "defend" the oil fields had two sources. First, the sheikdoms do not like to be seen as dependent on U.S. force against their own populations. And, second, the Gulf states were made nervous by the frequent talk in the United States about taking over the oil fields in the event of another embargo.[48] There was even a congressional study of the feasibility of seizing the oil fields; and though the study concluded that such an operation would be unlikely to succeed militarily, the mere fact that this was considered a fit subject for analysis did not instill confidence in Gulf capitals.[49]

Given this sensitivity, Brown advised that the United States should prepare plans and capabilities for intervention—against coups and other threats—but should avoid an explicitly declared policy to this effect.[50]

The Carter administration began the formation of a Rapid Deployment Force (RDF) to project U.S. military power into the Gulf region. Originally proposed in 1977, the planning did not make much progress until after the Soviet invasion of Afghanistan. The fundamental purpose of the RDF was always, in the words of Carter's National Security Adviser, "helping a friendly government under a subversive attack";[51] nevertheless, to justify the RDF the Soviet threat had to be magnified. Accordingly, Carter spoke in apocalyptic terms about the strategic significance of the invasion of Afghanistan, even though U.S. military experts were aware that a "thrust through Afghanistan would be of marginal advantage to any Soviet movement through Iran or the Gulf."[52]

In 1980, the Army conducted a gaming exercise called "Gallant Knight" which assumed an all-out Soviet invasion of Iran. The Army concluded that they would need 325,000 troops to hold back the Soviet colossus. According to a former military affairs aide to Senator Sam Nunn, the Army deliberately chose this scenario to guarantee that immense forces would be required.[53] And though an RDF of this size might seem unnecessarily large for combating Third World troublemakers, the Pentagon noted that in the mid-1980s Third World armies were no longer "barbarians with knives." The United States could no longer expect to "stabilize an area just by showing the flag."[54]

When Reagan became president, he added what became known as the "Reagan Codicil" to the "Carter Doctrine," declaring at a press conference that "we will not permit" Saudi Arabia "to be an Iran."[55] The codicil did not represent new policy, but merely made explicit what the policy had always been.

Under Reagan, the CIA secretly concluded that the possibility of a Soviet invasion of Iran was "remote"[56]—not surprisingly, given that the Red Army was hardly having an easy time with the Afghanis, who had half the population and were much less well equipped.[57] The remoteness of the Soviet threat, however, did not slow down the build-up of the RDF.

In 1982 the Pentagon's secret *Defense Guidance* document stated that the Soviet Union might extend its forces into the Gulf area "by means other than outright invasion." It continued: "Whatever the circumstances, we should be prepared to introduce American forces directly into the region should it appear that the security of access to Persian Gulf oil is threatened...."[58] In the Senate, many argued that there was too much emphasis on countering the USSR, whereas the focus should be on "deterring and, if necessary, fighting regional wars or leftist or nationalist insurgencies that threatened U.S. and allied access to the region's oil supplies."[59]

The official line was that the RDF would be deployed when a government invited it in to repel a Soviet attack. But, as a Library of Congress study noted, this view was belied by "guidance documents which say that the forces must be capable of coercive entry without waiting for an invitation."[60] Senators Tower and Cohen stated that they favored greater emphasis on Marines who could shoot their way ashore against military opposition. The administration pointed out that RDF plans all along had included a "forcible entry" option, relying on Marines. "We must be able to open our own doors," the Marine Commandant testified in March 1982.[61]

To support the RDF, the Pentagon needed a network of bases, not just in the Middle East, but worldwide. "To all intents and purposes," a former senior Defense Department official observed, "'Gulf waters' now extend from the Straits of Malacca to the South Atlantic."[62] Nevertheless, bases nearer the Gulf had a special importance, and Pentagon planners urged "as substantial a land presence in the [Middle East] as can be managed."[63] The Gulf states were reluctant to have too overt a relationship with the United States, but the Iran-Iraq war served to overcome some of this reluctance. In 1985, as Iranian advances seemed ominous, the *New York Times* reported that Oman "has become a base for Western intelligence operations, military maneuvers and logistical preparations for any defense of the oil-producing Persian Gulf."[64] A few months later, a secret U.S. report was leaked indicating that Saudi Arabia had agreed to allow the United States to use bases in its territory in a crisis.[65] The doors to U.S. influence were opening wider.

Two Tracks to Teheran

U.S. policy with respect to Iran was more complicated than that towards Iraq, because it followed two tracks at once. On the one hand, U.S. officials saw "a great potential" for a covert program to undermine the government in Teheran;[66] on the other hand, Washington tried to build ties to that same government.

U.S. actions in pursuit of the first track showed quite clearly that Washington's opposition to the Khomeini regime had nothing to do with its lack of democracy, for the groups that the United States backed against Khomeini were often supporters of the previous dictator, the Shah.

Starting in 1982 the CIA provided $100,000 a month to a group in Paris called the Front for the Liberation of Iran, headed by Ali Amini, who had presided over the reversion of Iranian oil to foreign control after the CIA-backed coup in 1953.[67] The United States also provided support to two Iranian paramilitary groups based in Turkey, one of them headed by General Bahram Aryana, the Shah's army chief, who had close ties to Shahpur Bakhtiar, the Shah's last prime minister.[68]

In 1980, under the Carter administration, the United States began clandestine radio broadcasts into Iran from Egypt, at a cost of some $20-30,000 per month. The broadcasts called for Khomeini's overthrow and urged support for Bakhtiar.[69] Other broadcasts contained anti-Soviet material.[70] In 1986, the CIA pirated Iran's national television network frequency to transmit an eleven minute address by the Shah's son over Iranian TV. "I will return," Reza Pahlevi vowed.[71]

Simultaneous with these activities, the United States pursued its second track: trying to establish ties with the Iranian mullahs based on the interest they shared with Washington in combating the Left. The U.S. purpose, Reagan announced in November 1986, after the Iran-Contra scandal blew open, was "to find an avenue to get Iran back where it once was and that is in the family of democratic nations"—a good trick, as Mansour Farhang has commented, since pre-1979 Iran was hardly democratic.[72]

Shortly after coming to office in January 1981, the Reagan administration decided to allow Israel to ship several billion dollars worth of U.S. arms and spare parts to Iran. Washington specifically authorized Israeli arms sales to Iran for somewhere between six and eighteen months and after that continued to replenish Israel's stockpile knowing that its U.S.-made weapons were going to Teheran.[73] In addition, U.S.-made arms from Belgium and Holland were sent to Iran which, according to the testimony of arms dealers, the United States also replenished.[74] Gary Sick, who served on the National Security Council under Presidents Ford, Carter, and, briefly, Reagan, believes that these weapons shipments represented payment by the Reagan administration to Iran for its service in delaying the release of the U.S. embassy hostages until after the 1980 election.[75] The evidence on this matter in either direction remains inconclusive, but if we assume Sick is incorrect, then we still have to determine why the United States permitted weapons to be transferred to Iran. There were no hostages at the time, either in Iran or Lebanon. So we are left with the explanation that Washington decided to use the arms trade, in violation of its proclaimed neutrality, to try to win influence with the clerics ruling Iran.

In 1983, according to the Tower Commission:

> the United States helped bring to the attention of Teheran the threat inherent in the extensive infiltration of the government by the communist Tudeh Party and Soviet or pro-Soviet cadres in the country. Using this information, the Khomeini government took measures, including mass executions, that virtually eliminated the pro-Soviet infrastructure in Iran.[76]

These massacres elicited the expected level of concern from U.S. officials. "The leftists there seem to be getting their heads cut off," remarked an Under-Secretary of State from the Carter administration.[77] The United States also passed to the Iranians "real and deceptive intelligence" about the Soviet threat on Iran's borders.[78]

Reagan administration officials claimed that their efforts in Iran were designed to build ties to moderates. In fact, however, they were aware that they were dealing with the clerical fanatics. Oliver North told Robert McFarlane and John Poindexter in December 1985 that the anti-tank weapons secretly being provided to Iran would probably go to the Revolutionary Guards, the shock troops of the mullahs.[79] In August 1986, the special assistant to the Israeli prime minister briefed George "Out-of-the-Loop" Bush, telling him, "We are dealing with the most radical elements.... This is good because we've learned that they can deliver and the moderates can't."[80]

The idea of building a strategic connection to Iran had wide support in the U.S. government, though the policy of using arms transfers to achieve it did not. The Tower Commission, for example, stated that while it disagreed with the arms transfers, "a strategic opening to Iran may have been in the national interest."[81] And it should be made clear that a strategic opening did not simply mean beginning a dialogue with or acting civilly toward a former adversary; rather, it was part of a policy to prevent any comparable access for the Soviet Union. Thus, a CIA position paper in 1985 noted that whichever superpower got to Iran first would be "in a strong position to work towards the exclusion of the other."[82] Another CIA official wanted to achieve "a securing of Iran" so that it would again "have a relationship with the U.S." and be "denied to the Soviets."[83] And McFarlane cabled to Poindexter after a secret meeting in Teheran in May 1986: "We are on the way to something that can become a truly strategic gain for us at the expense of the Soviets."[84]

The main tool by which U.S. policy-makers sought to secure their position in Iran in 1985 and 1986 was secretly providing arms and intelligence information. In the early '80s, U.S. aid to Iran had been funneled through Israel and other allies.[85] In 1984, because of Iranian battlefield victories and the growing U.S.-Iraqi ties, Washington launched "Operation Staunch," an effort to dry up Iran's sources of arms by pressuring U.S. allies to stop supplying Teheran.[86] U.S. secret arms sales to Iran in 1985 and 1986 thus not only violated U.S. neutrality, but undercut as well what the United States was trying to get everyone else to do. The cynical would note that Operation Staunch made the U.S. arms transfers to Iran that much more valuable.

When this arms dealing became known, the Reagan administration was faced with a major scandal on several counts. Proceeds from the arms sales had been diverted to the Nicaraguan Contras in violation of U.S. law. And though the administration's professed uncompromising stand on terrorism was always hypocritical, given its sponsorship of terrorism in Nicaragua and elsewhere (see Chapter 7), being caught trading "arms-for-hostages" was particularly embarrassing.

In any event, political influence, not hostages, was the Reagan administration's objective. Regardless of what was in the President's mind (as it were), the National Security Council was clear that the political agenda was key.[87]

Whatever the arguments for purchasing the freedom of hostages, trading weapons to obtain their release is another matter entirely, since one is exchanging for the lives of some hostages the lives of those who will be fired on by the weapons. And trading weapons for "a strategic opening" is more reprehensible still, particularly so when the weapons are going to the country whose army is on the offensive. Reagan claimed that the weapons were all defensive in nature,[88] but this is nonsense. Anti-tank missiles in the hands of an advancing army are offensive. And U.S. officials knew exactly what Iran wanted the weapons for. As the Tower Commission noted, North and CIA officials discussed with their Iranian contacts "Iran's urgent need" for "both intelligence and weapons to be used in offensive operations against Iraq."[89]

The intelligence that the United States passed to the Iranians was a mixture of factual and bogus information. The CIA claimed that the false information was meant to discourage Iran's final offensive by, for example, exaggerating Soviet troop movements on the northern border.[90] But if the United States simply wanted to discourage an Iranian attack, it could have done this more easily by telling Iran of Washington's contingency plans to use U.S. air power in the event of an Iranian breakthrough against Iraq.[91] The misinformation about the Soviet Union, however, had the added advantage of inciting Iranian hostility to Moscow and to the local communists.

U.S. intelligence did not deal only with the Soviet Union, but covered the Iraqi front as well. CIA deputy director John McMahon claimed that he warned Poindexter that such intelligence would give the Iranians "a definite edge," with potentially "cataclysmic results," and that he was able to persuade North to provide Iran with only a segment of the intelligence.[92] North, however, apparently gave critical data to Iran just before its crucial victory in the Fao Peninsula in February 1986.[93] It is unclear to what extent North was acting on his own here, but it is significant that despite McMahon's warnings, neither Poindexter nor CIA Director Casey reversed the plans to provide the Iranians with the full intelligence information.[94]

At the same time that the United States was giving Teheran weapons that one CIA analyst believed could affect the military balance[95] and passing on intelligence that the Tower Commission deemed of "potentially major significance,"[96] it was also providing Iraq with intelligence information, some misleading or incomplete.[97] In 1986, the CIA established a direct Washington-to-Baghdad link to provide the Iraqis with faster intelligence from U.S. satellites.[98] Simultaneously, Casey was urging Iraqi officials to carry out more attacks on Iran, especially on economic targets. (The CIA provided the intelligence data allowing Iraq to assess its bombing raids on Iranian oil terminals and power plants.)[99] Asked what the logic was of aiding both sides in a bloody war, a former official replied, "You had to have been there."[100]

Washington's effort to enhance its position with both sides came apart at the end of 1986 when one faction in the Iranian government leaked the story of the U.S. arms-dealing. Now the Reagan administration was in the unenviable position of having alienated the Iranians and panicked all the Arabs who concluded that the United States valued Iran's friendship over theirs. To salvage the U.S. position with at least one side, Washington now had to tilt—and tilt heavily—toward Iraq.

The American Armada

The opportunity to demonstrate the tilt came soon. Kuwait had watched with growing concern Iran's battlefield successes, perhaps made possible by U.S. arms sales and intelligence information. Iran was now also attacking ships calling at Kuwaiti ports, and to protect itself Kuwait decided to try to draw in the United States. In September 1986 (before the scandal broke), it approached both Washington and Moscow and asked if they would be interested in reflagging some Kuwaiti vessels, that is, flying their own flags on Kuwaiti ships and then protecting these new additions to their merchant marine. The initial U.S. reaction was lackadaisical. But when the United States learned in March 1987 that the Soviet Union offered to reflag eleven tankers, it promptly offered to reflag the same eleven ships—which would both keep Soviet influence out of the Gulf and give the United States the opportunity to demonstrate its support for Iraq.[101]

The Kuwaitis accepted the U.S. offer, declining Moscow's, though chartering three Soviet vessels as a way to provide some balance between the U.S. and the USSR,[102] the Kuwaitis being less afraid of Soviet contamination than their American saviors were. Under-Secretary of Political Affairs Michael H. Armacost explained in June 1987 that if the USSR were permitted a larger role in protecting Gulf oil, the Gulf states would be under great pressure to make additional facilities available to Moscow.[103] The U.S. view was that only one superpower was allowed to have facilities in the region, and that was the United States. Thus, when in December 1980 the Soviet Union proposed the neutralization of the Gulf, with no alliances, no bases, no intervention in the region, and no obstacles to free trade and the sea lanes,[104] Washington showed no interest.

In May 1987, a U.S. vessel, the USS Stark, was attacked, not by Iran, but by an Iraqi warplane. Thirty-seven Americans died. Reagan used the incident to issue what one scholar has called "an informal U.S. declaration of war" against *Iran*.[105] Cynics have suggested that the Iraqi attack was intentional, with the purpose of drawing the United States into an active role against Iran.[106] More likely is the conclusion of BBC correspondent John Simpson that the Iraqi Exocet missile accidentally homed in on the radio beam from the Stark which was directing the pilot to his target.[107]

Some cautioned that the attack on the Stark showed the dangers of the U.S. headlong involvement in the Gulf. But more influential voices asserted that the high stakes demanded a U.S. role. Senator Daniel Patrick Moynihan declared that the "great geo-political prize of the twentieth century" was now in the Soviets' grasp, and that we could not accept their "intrusion" in that strategic area.[108] And Carter's National Security Adviser

Zbigniew Brzezinski warned that the "major beneficiary of a U.S. retreat would be the Soviet Union."[109] And so, by August 1987, the United States had an aircraft carrier, a battleship, six cruisers, three destroyers, seven frigates, and numerous supporting naval vessels in or near the Gulf,[110] in what a congressional study termed "the largest single naval armada deployed since the height of the Vietnam war."[111]

The Reagan administration claimed that the reflagging was merely intended to protect the flow of oil. It warned that "any significant disruption in gulf oil supply would cause world oil prices for all to skyrocket," grimly recalling how events in 1973-74 and 1978-79 demonstrated that "a small disruption—of less than 5%—can trigger a sharp escalation in oil prices."[112]

In fact, however, oil—and oil prices for that matter—were never threatened. There had been a worldwide oil glut since the early 1980s, with much underused production capacity in non-Gulf nations. Despite the horrendous human costs of the Iran-Iraq war, oil prices had actually fallen by 50 percent during the course of the conflict.[113] By the end of 1987, two-thirds of all the oil produced in the Gulf was carried by pipeline. The congressional study noted that even in the unlikely event of an actual shutdown of the Gulf, the impact on oil supplies and prices would have been minimal.[114] In no sense then could the Strait of Hormuz be viewed as the "jugular" of the western economies.[115]

Fewer than 2 percent of the ships that did transit the Strait came under attack, and even this figure is misleading because many of the attacks inflicted relatively minor damage.[116] Only one Iranian attack in ten caused serious damage.[117]

Significantly, Iran became more aggressive in attacking shipping *because* of the U.S. naval presence.[118] Between 1981 and April 1987, when the U.S. reflagging was announced, Iran struck 90 ships; in the little over a year thereafter, Iran struck 126 ships.[119] As the congressional study noted, "shipping in the Gulf now appears less safe than before the U.S. naval build-up began."[120]

If the United States were concerned with free navigation, it might have given some consideration to a Soviet proposal that the U.S. Navy and all national navies withdraw from the Gulf, to be replaced by a United Nations force.[121] But Washington wasn't interested. Indeed, some, like the *New York Times,* noted that it was the United States that could close the Gulf—to Iranian exports—though the *Times* added that "such action would of course be unthinkable unless requested by the Arab states of the region."[122] So much for freedom of navigation.

It was Iraq that started the tanker war in the Gulf proper in 1981, and Iraq that continued these attacks into 1984 without a parallel Iranian response at sea. Two months after Iraq stepped up the pace and scope of its attacks in March 1984, Iran finally began responding.[123] Iraqi attacks, however, outnumbered those by Iran until after the United States announced its reflagging.[124] The U.S. Navy protected the reflagged vessels, and in April 1988 extended its protection to any neutral vessels coming under Iranian attack.[125] In practice, this meant that Iraq could strike at Iranian vessels with impunity, with the U.S. Navy preventing retaliation by Teheran.

Washington justified its policy by noting that Iraq only attacked Iranian ships, while Iran targeted the ships of neutrals: Kuwait, in particular. This was a dubious legal argument on two counts. First, Kuwait was a neutral engaged in rather unneutral behavior. Among other things, it opened its ports to deliveries of war material that were then transported over land to Iraq.[126] Second, Iraq too hit neutral ships, even Saudi Arabian ships, when they called on Iran.[127] Iraq declared certain Iranian waters a "war exclusion zone," but as an international law expert has noted, Iraq's method of enforcement "closely resembled German methods" in World War II, and "under any analysis the Iraqi exclusion zone cannot be justified." The "attacks on neutral merchant vessels by both sides must be condemned as violations of international law."[128] There was thus no legal justification for the United States to take Iraq's side in the tanker war.

Still less was there any sense in which the U.S. Navy could be referred to as a "peacekeeping" force. Gary Sick asserted that U.S. naval units "have been deployed aggressively and provocatively in the hottest parts of the Persian Gulf." "Our aggressive patrolling strategy," he observed, "tends to start fights, not to end them. We behave at times as if our objective was to goad Iran into a war with us."[129] According to the congressional report, officials in every Gulf country were critical of "the highly provocative way in which U.S. forces are being deployed."[130] When in April 1988 the United States turned a mining attack on a U.S. ship into the biggest U.S. Navy sea battle since World War II,[131] *Al Ittihad,* a newspaper often reflective of government thinking in the United Arab Emirates, criticized the U.S. attacks, noting that they added "fuel to the gulf tension."[132] Washington, however, did not believe that its Navy was being aggressive enough, so plans were developed to fake radio transmissions to simulate a tanker as a way to lure Iranian gunboats into international waters where they could be attacked.[133]

The aggressive U.S. posture was in marked contrast to the posture of the Soviet Union. The Soviet Union too was escorting ships in the Gulf, particularly vessels carrying weapons to Kuwait for Iraq. On May 6, 1987, Iranian gunboats attacked a Soviet merchant vessel,[134] and two weeks later one of the Soviet ships chartered by Kuwait was the first victim of a mine attack since 1984.[135] These facts are not widely known, because the Soviet response was extremely mild.

Soviet policy in the Gulf was the subject of a study commissioned by the U.S. Army and written by reputed intellectual heavyweight Francis Fukuyama of the Rand Corporation. Fukuyama concluded that Gorbachev's "new thinking" in foreign policy was only rhetoric as far as the Persian Gulf was concerned because Moscow continued to pursue "zero-sum" (that is, totally competitive) policies vis-à-vis the United States. But the facts presented in the study suggested a rather different conclusion. Fukuyama noted that the "Soviets, it is true, were facing a U.S. administration that was itself playing very much a zero-sum game in the Gulf.... What the Soviets would have done if faced with a more collaborative United States is untestable and consequently unknowable." Nevertheless, for Fukuyama the USSR was to blame since Gorbachev had been accommodative in other areas of policy in the face of U.S. intransigence and thus might have been so in the Gulf as well.[136]

Fukuyama acknowledged that the Soviet Union refrained from following other, more aggressive policies in the Gulf, such as trying to outbid Washington for influence with Kuwait. He observed that Soviet naval units in the Gulf were not offensively deployed, in contradistinction to those of the United States. (Indeed, Fukuyama pointed out that since the early 1970s Moscow had slowed the development of its power projection capability, unlike the United States.) The USSR sought to use economic and political instruments of policy in the Gulf, rather than predominantly military ones as the U.S. did. And when Moscow did seek its own advantage in relations with Iran, it did so in response to the secret dealings in Teheran by the White House.[137] In short, if Soviet policy in the Gulf could be criticized for insufficient "new thinking," by comparison U.S. policy reflected a Stone Age approach.

The provocative U.S. naval deployments in the Gulf took a heavy toll on innocent civilians. In November 1987, a U.S. ship fired its machine guns at night at a boat believed to be an Iranian speedboat with hostile intent; it was in fact a fishing boat from the United Arab Emirates. One person was killed and three were wounded.[138] Far more serious was the shooting down by the U.S. cruiser Vicennes of an Iranian civil airliner, killing all 290 people aboard. The commander of another U.S. ship in the Gulf noted that while "the conduct of Iranian military forces in the month preceding the incident was pointedly non-threatening," the actions of the Vicennes "appeared to be consistently aggressive," leading some Navy hands to refer to the ship as "Robo Cruiser."[139] It is now known that the U.S. ship was in Iranian territorial waters when it shot down the plane and that no merchant vessel was in distress when it commenced firing at Iranian gunboats.[140]

Washington expressed its regrets for what it said was a tragic accident, but its remorse was qualified. "One thing is clear," Vice-President Bush told the United Nations, "the USS Vicennes acted in self-defense."[141] To fly over a warship "was irresponsible and a tragic error," said Bush, and "Iran must bear a substantial measure of responsibility for what has happened." (The plane was in its normal flight lane.) "After seven unanswered warnings," the ship's captain "did what he had to do to protect his ship and the lives of his crew." (Seven of ten messages from the Vicennes were sent on a frequency no civilian airliner could pick up; the other three would have required the crew to be able to identify their position relative to the Vicennes to know they were the intended recipients.)[142] Even if the Iranian airliner had been an F-14, as the Vicennes erroneously concluded, that warplane had no significant anti-ship capability.[143] "The United States will never put its military in a dangerous situation and deny them the right to defend themselves"—which was, of course, the best argument against sending warships into the Gulf in the first place.

These tensions in the Gulf continued to promote one important U.S. goal: they encouraged the Gulf states to enhance their military cooperation with the United States. As noted above, the United States had used the Iran-Iraq war as a lever for obtaining additional basing rights in the Gulf region. The reflagging operation further enhanced the U.S. position. According to an Associated Press report, the U.S. general in charge of the RDF claimed that the "United States gained unprecedented credibility with Arab leaders as a result of its large-scale naval commitment in the Persian Gulf." This commitment, he said, enabled the United States to establish better diplomatic and military ties with Gulf states.[144]

Indifference and Diplomacy

Aggressive U.S. naval deployments in the Gulf elicited no dissent from the *New York Times*. The editors acknowledged that Washington's "profession of neutrality is the thinnest of diplomatic fig leaves," that in reality "America tilts toward Iraq." But the tilt was "for good reason," for it was a strategy designed to achieve peace.[145] The administration had been confused, the *Times* admitted, but now Washington had developed "a coherent policy to contain Iran. It has thereby earned the right to take risks in the gulf."[146] And when the risks resulted in the destruction of the Iranian airliner, the editors declared that the blame might lie with the Iranian pilot, but if not, then it was certainly Teheran's fault for refusing to end the war.[147]

This is the common view of the war, widely promoted by Washington—that Iran was the sole obstacle to peace. A review of the diplomacy of the war, however, shows that while Khomeini certainly bears tremendous blame for the bloodshed, the blame does not stop with him.

When Iraq attacked Iran on September 22, 1980, the United Nations Security Council waited four days before holding a meeting. On September 28, it passed Resolution 479 calling for an end to the fighting. Significantly, however, the resolution did not condemn (nor even mention) the Iraqi aggression and did not call for a return to internationally recognized boundaries. As Ralph King, who has studied the UN response in detail, concluded, "The Council more or less deliberately ignored Iraq's actions in September 1980." It did so because the Council as a whole had a negative view of Iran and was not concerned enough about Iran's predicament to come to its aid. The U.S. delegate noted that Iran, which had itself violated Security Council resolutions on the U.S. embassy hostages, could hardly complain about the Council's lackluster response.[148]

Iran rejected Resolution 479 as one-sided—which it was. When Norway called for an internationally supervised withdrawal of forces, Iraq replied—accurately—that this violated 479. Iran refused to engage in any discussions as long as Iraqi forces remained on its soil.[149] In the meantime, State Department officials proposed "a joint U.S.-Soviet effort to promote a settlement," but National Security Adviser Zbigniew Brzezinski argued that this "would legitimate the Soviet position in the Gulf and thus objectively undercut our vital interests."[150] No U.S. initiative was forthcoming. A few more unfruitful Security Council meetings were held into October, and then there were no further formal meetings on the subject of the war, despite the immense carnage, until July 1982.[151]

There were a number of third party mediation efforts. The first was undertaken by Olaf Palme, representing the UN Secretary General. Palme proposed that as an initial step the two sides agree to have the disputed Shatt al-Arab waterway cleared. Iraq, however, would only agree if it could pay the full costs (thus legitimating its claim to the entire river), and no agreement could be reached.[152] Then, the Nonaligned Ministerial Committee proposed a cease-fire simultaneous with withdrawal, with demilitarized zones on both sides. Iran accepted and, for a while, Iraq did as well. But Baghdad soon changed its mind, hoping to win on the battlefield. In neither of these instances was any significant outside pressure put on Iraq to settle.[153]

In early 1982 another mediation effort was begun by the government of Algeria, which had helped Iran and Iraq reach a border agreement in 1975 and had also served as a go-between for the release of the U.S. embassy hostages. On May 3, 1982, however, an aircraft carrying the Algerian foreign minister and his team of experts was shot down in Iranian airspace by an *Iraqi* fighter plane. Five years later a captured Iraqi pilot was said to have admitted that the attack was intentional, with the objective of having Iran be blamed for the action.[154] Whether this is true or not, the shootdown eliminated from the scene the most experienced mediators.

By the end of May 1982, Iran had recaptured nearly all its territory and Iraq was looking for a way out of the war. The Islamic Conference Organization and the Gulf Cooperation Council tried to mediate a settlement. On June 3, three men led by an Iraqi intelligence officer attempted to assassinate the Israeli Ambassador to Britain, probably with the hope of provoking an Israeli invasion of Lebanon that would create the conditions for the Gulf combatants to end their fighting so they might face their common enemy, Israel.[155] Israel needed no encouragement to march into Lebanon; it knew the provocation had nothing to do with the Palestine Liberation Organization (PLO) or Lebanon, but invaded anyway. But the Lebanon war did not dissuade Iran from continuing the Gulf war, and may even have derailed the mediation efforts.[156]

Iraq offered to withdraw its remaining forces from Iran and to cease fire. In Teheran a vigorous debate ensued as to whether to accept the offer or to continue on. The militant mullahs had seen their power grow during the war; though the Shah had originally been ousted by a wide range of political forces, the crusade against Iraq had enabled the right-wing clerics to mobilize the population and to prevail over their domestic opponents. In addition, just as Iraq had erroneously assumed that Iran was on the verge of collapse in September 1980, so now Iran assumed Saddam Hussein was about to fall. Khomeini decided to go on with the war, declaring that Iran would not stop fighting until Saddam Hussein was overthrown, Iraqi war-guilt assigned, and reparations paid.

The government of Iran thus bears major responsibility for the death and destruction that followed. But, significantly, no industrial country gave strong support to a peace settlement at this time.[157] Within the United States government, Secretary of State Alexander Haig proposed some sort of international peace conference (though without U.S. participation, and of course with no Soviet participation). The proposal, Haig recalls, "failed to win the attention of the White House." Haig notes that the "war was then at a critical stage, an Iranian offensive having recovered nearly all of Iran's lost territory, and it is possible that a properly designed initiative could have succeeded in ending the hostilities."[158]

On July 12, 1982, the Security Council met on the issue of the war for the first time since 1980 and called for a withdrawal to the pre-war boundaries. Iran considered this further proof of the bias of the United Nations, since the call for withdrawal came at the first moment in the war when Iranian forces held any Iraqi territory.[159]

Iraq responded to Iranian victories on the ground by making use of its advantage in technology: it escalated the tanker war, employed chemical weapons, and launched attacks on civilian targets. Iran retaliated by striking Gulf shipping starting in 1984 and launching its own attacks on civilians, though on a lesser scale than Iraq. Iran charged that the Security Council's handling of each of these issues reflected animus against Iran.

In 1984 the Security Council passed a resolution on the tanker war that was directed primarily against Iran's actions and made no reference to Iraqi conduct except to call for all states to respect the right of free navigation.[160]

On chemical weapons, the Security Council passed no resolution. The United States condemned the use of chemical weapons, but declined to support any Council action against Iraq.[161] The Council did issue a much less significant "statement" in 1985 condemning the use of chemical weapons, but without mentioning Iraq by name; then, in March 1986, for the first time a Council statement explicitly denounced Iraq. This, however, was two years after Iraq's use of chemical warfare had been confirmed by UN investigators.[162]

In 1983 a UN team found that both sides had attacked civilian areas, but that Iran had suffered more extensive damage than Iraq. Teheran wanted the Security Council to pass a resolution that indicated Iraq's greater responsibility, but the Council refused to do so, and no statement was issued.[163] In June 1984 the Secretary General was able to get the two sides to agree to cease their attacks on civilians. Both sides soon charged violations, but UN inspection teams found that while Iraq was indeed in violation, Iran was not. By March 1985, the moratorium was over.[164]

At this time, jockeying for position with Moscow was still a crucial consideration for the United States. In a section of a draft National Security document that elicited no dissent, U.S. long-term goals were said to include "an early end to the Iran-Iraq war without Soviet mediation...."[165]

Iran remained committed to its maximum war aims, a commitment not lessened by the fact that Oliver North, apparently without authorization, told Iranian officials that Reagan wanted the war ended on terms favorable to Iran, and that Saddam Hussein had to go.[166] But it was not just North's *unauthorized* conversation that encouraged Iranian intransigence; the *authorized* clandestine dealings between Washington and Teheran no doubt had the same effect.

In late 1986 the Iran-Contra scandal broke, forcing the United States to go all-out in its support for Iraq in order to preserve some influence among the Arab states jolted by the evidence of Washington's double-dealing. In May 1987, U.S. Assistant Secretary of State Richard Murphy met with Saddam Hussein and promised him that the United States would lead an effort at the UN for a mandatory arms embargo of Iran; a resolution would be drawn up calling on both sides to cease fire and withdraw, and imposing an embargo on whoever didn't comply, presumably Iran. The United States drafted such a resolution, but the non-permanent members of the Security Council altered it to include the formation of an impartial commission to investigate the origins of the war, as Iran had been insisting, and to eliminate the mandatory sanctions. On July 20, 1987 the revised document was passed unanimously as Security Council Resolution 598.[167]

Iraq promptly accepted 598, while Iran said it would accept the cease-fire and withdrawal of forces if the impartial commission were set up first. The United States and Iraq both rejected Iran's position, asserting that Iran had no right to select one provision out of many in the resolution and impose that as a first step.[168]

The Secretary General then travelled to Teheran and Baghdad to try to work out a compromise and he made some progress. According to the leaked text of his private report to the Security Council, Iran agreed to accept an "undeclared cessation of hostilities" while an independent commission was investigating the responsibility for the conflict; the cessation would become a formal cease-fire on the date that the commission issued its findings. This was not an acceptance of 598, but an informal cease-fire might have meant an end to the killing as surely as a formal one. Iraq, however, insisted that "under no circumstances" would it accept an undeclared cease-fire.[169] Instead of seizing the Iranian position as a first step toward a compromise, the United States, in the words of Gary Sick, "pressed single-mindedly for an embargo on Iran, while resisting efforts by Secretary General Javier Perez de Cuellar to fashion a compromise cease-fire."[170]

"Could the war have been ended by a compromise in early 1988?" Sick has asked.

> The answer will never be known, primarily because the United States was unwilling to explore Iran's offer. The U.S. position—and sensitivities about even the perception of any sympathy toward Iran—were a direct legacy of the Iran-contra fiasco. They may have contributed to prolonging the war for six unnecessary months.[171]

Finally, in July 1988, with anti-war sentiment in Iran growing widespread, Ayatollah Khomeini decided to end the fighting. On July 18, Iran declared its full acceptance of Resolution 598. But by this time Iraq had turned the tide of the land battle, having regained virtually all of its own territory, and Saddam Hussein refused to accept the cease-fire. Baghdad continued offensive operations, using chemical weapons both against Iran and its own Kurdish population. It was not until August 6 that international pressure got Iraq to agree to a cease-fire, which went into effect two weeks later.[172] Both regimes continued to kill their own citizens—Kurds in Iraq and dissidents, especially leftists, in Iran—but the Iran-Iraq war was over.

The Iran-Iraq war was not a conflict between good and evil. But though both regimes were repugnant, it was the people of the two countries who served as the cannon fodder, and thus ending the war as soon as possible was a humane imperative. Instead of lending its good offices to mediation efforts and diplomacy, however, Washington maneuvered for advantage, trying to gain vis-à-vis the Soviet Union and to undercut the Left. The United States provided intelligence information, bogus and real, to both sides, provided arms to one side and dual-use equipment to the other, encouraged its allies to supply weapons to both sides, funded paramilitary exile groups, sought military bases, and sent in the U.S. Navy—and all the while Iranians and Iraqis died.

"It wasn't that we wanted Iraq to win the war," explained Geoffrey Kemp, head of the National Security Council's Middle East section. "We did not want Iraq to lose. We really weren't naive. We knew [Saddam Hussein] was an SOB, but he was our SOB."[173] But even after the war was over, the United States continued building ties to the "SOB." As the fighting ended, the State Department secretly recommended that there "be no radical policy changes now regarding Iraq." Then in October 1989, Bush issued a secret National Security Decision directive, NSD-26, ordering closer ties with Iraq. The directive paved the way for $1 billion in new U.S. aid to Baghdad at a time when banks had cut off loans and officials in three agencies were objecting that the U.S. funds were being misused. In the Spring of 1990, the Bush administration continued to allow the sale of dual-use items and to share intelligence information with Saddam Hussein.[174]

Less than a year later, the United States went to war in the Gulf directly, this time against Iraq. Again, the issue was not the free flow of oil, but who would have the decisive say over how this resource was used. Bush did not wage war in order to keep the price of oil low. When Saddam Hussein told U.S. Ambassador April Glaspie just before his troops marched into Kuwait, "Twenty-five dollars a barrel is not a high price," she replied, "We have many Americans who would like to see the price go above $25 because they come from oil-producing states."[175] Glaspie didn't have to mention that George Bush was one of those Americans. The issue was not the price of oil, but who would determine the price. "By virtue of its military victory," *New York Times* business correspondent Louis Uchitelle wrote in March 1991, "the United States is likely to have more influence in the Organization of Petroleum Exporting Countries than any industrial nation has ever exercised." Most capitalist nations want to keep petroleum prices down, but for the United States the right price must be low enough to promote economic growth but high enough to generate profits for the oil companies and give the United States a comparative advantage over its economic competitors. "When representatives of the 13 OPEC nations gather in Geneva next week, Administration officials will not attend, even as observers. But they will be sitting figuratively at the elbow of Saudi Arabia and the other oil-producing states of the Arabian peninsula." In 1986 Vice-President Bush travelled to Saudi Arabia to ask the Saudis to raise oil prices: "In those days, the United States did not have the influence over the Saudis that it presumably has today...." "'It would be disastrous for the American economy if the price [of oil] were to fall into the low teens,' said Sidney Jones, an Assistant Secretary of the Treasury for economic policy."[176]

The struggle for oil is not a struggle to ensure that American cars and factories have adequate supplies of oil so that they won't be forced to grind to a halt. It is a struggle to see who is going to be able to use this crucial resource for its own economic advantage.

Chapter 5

Protecting Americans Abroad

The president of the American Society of International Law noted some years ago that "the claimed right to intervene to protect one's own citizens was the most cited rationalization for the episodic acts of interventionary imperialism all the way to the Boxer Rebellion and on down the line."[1] Now it might seem that the issue of protecting foreign nationals abroad could not be a very significant matter in U.S. foreign policy. After all, as international law expert Thomas Franck once quipped,

> The actual number of Americans killed abroad by events in foreign countries that are intentionally directed at Americans would come somewhere in the list between Category 17 of deaths, which would be a surfeit of claret, and Category 19, which would be a paucity of green vegetables.[2]

In addition, in 1936 the United States signed a convention in Buenos Aires under which it gave up the right to intervene in Latin America "for whatever reason."[3] Nevertheless, the protecting-Americans-abroad justification for intervention has been used quite a number of times by Washington since World War II. Three of the major such instances are worth looking at here for they tell us a great deal about the how this rationale might be used in the future.

The Dominican Republic

In 1962, Juan Bosch was elected president of the Domincian Republic in that country's first experience with democracy after three decades of the U.S.-backed dictatorship of Rafael Trujillo. Just seven months after taking office, Bosch was overthrown in a military coup. On April 24, 1965, Bosch supporters in the armed forces led an effort to restore the constitutionally elected president to office. Key Dominican military officers vacillated and it briefly seemed as if the victory of the constitutionalist rebels would be almost bloodless. Had it been so, of course, the danger to American citizens would have been precisely nil.

But it was not to be. According to Jerome Slater, whose account is not unsympathetic to the U.S. government, U.S. military attachés "urged the military to resist and told them they had U.S. 'support' if they did." Concludes Slater: "Undoubtedly, this U.S. intervention proved decisive with those commanders who were still wavering."[4] The ranking official in the U.S. Embassy endorsed an attack by the military on the rebels, "even though it could mean more bloodshed."[5]

The Dominican Air Force proceeded to strafe the palace and other sites held by the rebels. The latter urgently asked the U.S. Embassy to try to prevent these air strikes, but the Embassy rejected the plea.[6]

The military onslaught was stopped, however, by civilians who had been armed by the rebels, and starting on April 26, military leaders called on the United States to support them with troops.[7] Still confident that the military would prevail, Washington turned down the request for the time being. With their abiding commitment to non-intervention, U.S. policymakers took the position that "We don't want to intervene unless the outcome is in doubt."[8]

As civil war spread, the U.S. Embassy informed those American citizens who wanted to leave to gather at the Embajador Hotel in Santo Domingo. A right-wing radio announcer had tried to hide himself among the evacuees and armed rebels came to the hotel looking for him.[9] Some shots were fired in the air, frightening the assembled Americans. No one was hurt and there was no attempt to terrorize the Americans; shortly thereafter rebel officers agreed to cooperate fully in the evacuation of the U.S. citizens.[10] Washington expected the military to soon be in firm control, and no U.S. official thought U.S. troops were needed to protect the Americans.[11]

The military offensive, however, ran aground the next day, and at 3:00 p.m. the head of the military junta, Colonel Benoit, telephoned the U.S. Embassy to ask for U.S. troops. The request was passed on to the State Department, but neither the U.S. ambassador nor officials in Washington believed troops should be sent.[12] At 4:00 p.m., Benoit submitted a formal written request for U.S. troops. The request warned of the dangers of "another Cuba," claiming that the rebels were controlled by communists, and committing widespread atrocities. No mention was made of any danger to Americans.[13] Washington was still not persuaded that troops were needed.

An hour later, the U.S. ambassador became convinced that the military could not prevail on its own and he cabled Washington urging the dispatch of U.S. Marines. He asserted that U.S. citizens were now at risk, but emphasized the reverses suffered by the military (their officers were dejected, several of them were weeping). "If Washington wished," the ambassador suggested, the Marines could be landed for the mission of protecting the evacuation of Americans.[14]

Lyndon Johnson approved the landing of the Marines, and the ambassador was instructed to get a written request from Benoit asking for U.S. troops specifically to protect American lives. The Marines landed several hours before the revised request arrived.[15] Johnson's speech announcing the intervention justified it exclusively in terms of protecting U.S. citizens.[16]

Secretary of State Dean Rusk and Lyndon Johnson later spoke of the Embajador Hotel episode as though it had been the incident precipitating the decision to land the Marines. As noted, however, it had occurred the day before.[17] The actual danger to American citizens is indicated by the fact that (to quote Slater) "not a single American" was attacked. Moreover, there were "remarkably few [rebel] atrocities of any sort. What few attacks did occur were highly selective, aimed almost exclusively at a few extreme rightists, and then mainly at their property." To be sure, there were many civilian casualties in the civil war, but "many more innocent civilians died as a result of the Air Force bombing and strafing" than at the hands of the rebels.[18]

U.S. officials repeated stories of hundreds of people being lined up against the wall and shot, of hacked off heads being carried around as trophies, of embassies being torn up. In fact, there had been no mass killings, nor disembodied heads, nor torn up embassies, nor even widespread looting in rebel zones.[19] The real bloodbath was yet to come.

Initially, 500 U.S. Marines were landed, but the number was quickly increased to more than 20,000. Within 48 hours, the U.S. troops were deployed so as to block a rebel victory.[20] "Your announced mission," the commander of the U.S. forces was told on April 30, "is to save American lives. Your unstated mission is to prevent the Dominican Republic from going Communist."[21] (The claim that the rebels were controlled by communists was nonsensical.[22] Administration officials rationalized that although they could only identify a few communists amid the rebel forces, Castro had begun with just twelve men and Hitler at one time had had only seven supporters.[23])

U.S. troops interposed themselves between rebel and military units. After the military had regrouped and been resupplied with U.S. assistance, they were then allowed, if not encouraged, to move through the U.S. lines to attack rebel forces who had been cut off from their rural base by U.S. troops. Hundreds of rebel fighters and innocent civilians were butchered.[24] To quote Jerome Slater again:

Although the Johnson Administration had proclaimed as one of the main purposes of the intervention the need to save Dominican lives in a bloody civil war, in fact most of the estimated three thousand Dominican deaths occurred after the intervention, some of them in clashes between the constitutionalists and U.S. troops, and the rest at the hands of a Dominican military that the United States had rescued from probable annihilation in April and thereafter had helped protect and rebuild.[25]

In closed hearings, Secretary of State Rusk had declared that the decision to send troops was "ninety-nine percent the problem of protecting American and other foreign nationals."[26] Yet the U.S. troops remained in the Dominican Republic for seventeen months. Before they left, they organized elections in which an associate of former dictator Trujillo defeated Bosch for the presidency. The elections were stage-managed in a variety of ways by the United States and its local allies, though this did not stop commentators like Slater from praising the workings of Dominican democracy.[27] Slater does acknowledge, however, that the United States probably would not have let Bosch undertake such radical measures as placing supporters of the constitution in military command positions.[28] In subsequent years, death squads appeared in the Dominican Republic, corruption grew rampant, living standards for the majority of the population declined, and the labor movement was repressed to ensure high profits for foreign companies.[29] As a reporter for the *Wall Street Journal* put it in 1971, "The terrorism, corruption and misery that marked Rafael Trujillo's 31-year dictatorship...are even more widespread today...."[30]

Such are the fruits of "humanitarian" intervention.

The Mayaguez

Ten years after the Marines landed in Santo Domingo, innocent American lives were once again said to be in danger, requiring military action. A U.S. merchant ship, the Mayaguez, and its crew of 40[31] had been seized by the new revolutionary government of Cambodia.

Cambodia had been the victim of years of U.S. subversion, bombardment, and direct invasion. This U.S. intervention and the parallel interventions in Vietnam and Laos resulted in a devastating defeat for the aspirations of the people of Indochina: millions of people lay dead, economic life was shattered, and the massive devastation would take decades to overcome. But the wars on Vietnam, Laos, and Cambodia were also viewed in Washington as defeats for the United States; despite the application of unprecedented violence, the United States had been unable to subdue the peasant armies that ultimately took power in April 1975.

On May 10, Secretary of State Henry Kissinger urged his boss, President Gerald Ford, to respond to the defeat in Vietnam with "a tough, even abrasive foreign policy."[32] *Time* magazine reported that Ford "had been searching" for a means to show that the United States was now conducting this "abrasive" foreign policy when the Mayaguez was seized. Even before the seizure, one U.S. official had told *Time,* "There's quite a bit of agreement around here that it wouldn't be a bad thing if the other side goes a step or two too far in trying to kick us while we're down. It would give us a chance to kick them back—hard."[33]

And perhaps the Ford administration decided to help things along. That the Cambodians claimed a 12-mile limit to their territorial waters was known[34]; that they were battling with Vietnam over claims to islands off the coast was also known.[35] And that they had in the previous few days fired on at least one ship and detained another for sailing within 12 miles of islands they claimed was known as well.[36] Nevertheless, the State Department issued no warning to vessels in the area. Kissinger later asserted that though no advisory to ships was issued, maritime insurance companies were informed of the danger. The president of the American Institute of Marine Underwriters, however, denied that any such warning had been received.[37]

In his memoirs, presidential press secretary Ron Nessen wrote:

> News accounts told of a Panamanian freighter and a South Korean vessel being harassed by Cambodian patrol boats a few days before the Mayaguez was seized. Actually there were a number of similar incidents, beginning much earlier, which were never revealed. In addition, the United States had picked up intelligence that Cambodia intended to extend its territorial claims around the offshore islands, including Poulo Wai, and to enforce its claim by seizing ships that strayed too close.

Nessen went on to ask the obvious question: If the United States knew this, why wasn't a warning to merchant shipping issued? "It could have been simply a bureaucratic screw-up, one agency not knowing what another agency knew." And he then added: "I never saw a shred of evidence that the Mayaguez was deliberately allowed to sail into a Cambodian trap in order to provoke an international incident."[38]

On May 12, the Mayaguez sailed, according to its captain, within seven miles of Poulo Wai.[39] Given Cambodia's response to other ships in its waters and given the well-documented xenophobia and paranoia of Khmer Rouge officials—traits not discouraged by two decades of U.S.

interventionism—it is not surprising that the Cambodians reacted by seizing the ship. The captain of the Mayaguez later guessed that the Cambodians "thought I was making a survey of the island to find out just how much military force they had there."[40]

In Washington, a National Security Council meeting was promptly convened and Kissinger argued that what was at stake was far more than the capture of a U.S. cargo ship.[41] As Nessen recalls, Kissinger "said the capture of the Mayaguez gave Ford the chance to assert strongly that there was a point beyond which the United States would not be pushed."[42] The immediate use of force was impossible: as Kissinger's assistant Brent Scowcroft put it, U.S. naval vessels were "heartbreakingly" far away, at least two days steaming time.[43] Ford ordered military forces to be moved into place. He knew that the Thai government wouldn't be happy about the United States using its bases in Thailand for this purpose, "but until Mayaguez and her crew were safe, I didn't give a damn about offending their sensibilities."[44] Bangkok in fact sent Washington a note explicitly telling the United States not to use bases in Thailand for any military operations relating to the Mayaguez, but Ford simply ignored the note.[45]

White House press secretary Ron Nessen announced that the president "considers the seizure an act of piracy."[46] But even by the U.S. account, the ship was within Cambodia's territorial waters. The co-chair designate of the American Bar Association's committee on international law thought that Cambodia at least had a viable claim that it was arresting violators of traditional international law.[47] Ship seizures were not at all unusual in international practice (for example, the United States had seized and detained a Polish fishing vessel off the San Francisco coast that same week).[48] And though there are legal differences between fishing vessels and other ships, and though one can argue the legal merits of the case, there was no justification for characterizing the Cambodian action as an "act of piracy"—and State Department lawyers admitted as much.[49]

Nessen further announced that the President had "instructed the State Department to demand the immediate release of the ship. Failure to do so would have the most serious consequences."[50] Kissinger later asserted that the United States rejected the idea of sending an ultimatum to Cambodia because it was feared that this might harden Cambodia's attitude even more.[51] A number of sources have claimed that in fact in a private message sent to Phnom Penh the United States gave the Cambodians 24 hours to surrender the ship and crew;[52] when the General Accounting Office (GAO) of the Congress later tried to confirm or deny this story, they were blocked by the State Department's refusal to declassify the message.[53] Even if there were no deadline set, however, the threat of force was evident in Nessen's statement and subsequent U.S. statements. As Kissinger put it, "We felt we had, in effect given an ultimatum without giving a specific time."[54]

The Cambodians docked the Mayaguez at Koh Tang island and transferred the crew to a fishing boat, which along with some gunboats set out for Kompong Som (formerly Sihanoukville) on the mainland. The U.S. Air Force tried to get the boats to turn back by dropping bombs in front of them and when this failed U.S. aircraft sank three of the gunboats and immobilized four others.[55] The Deputy Assistant Secretary of Defense testified that he "can't be sure" that there were no Americans aboard the vessels that were sunk.[56] The fishing boat was bombed and strafed 100 times, the captain of the Mayaguez later recalled,[57] and three of the Mayaguez crew were wounded by shrapnel.[58] When U.S. pilots confirmed that Caucasians were aboard the boat, the bombing gave way to gas attacks. In the Mayaguez captain's words, "Everybody on the ship vomited. Their skin was burning."[59] The fishing boat finally made it to Kompong Som.

Blowing the Hell Out of 'Em

The National Security Council met again that afternoon. Kissinger and Ford "felt that we had to do more" than rescue the ship and crew; as Ford acknowledged, they were "eager to use Mayaguez as an example for Asia and the world."[60] Diplomacy was never seriously considered: early that morning a report had been received indicating that a foreign government was using its influence to seek the ship's early release and that it expected the release to come soon; according to the GAO, the report was basically ignored.[61] The United States made its first approach to the United Nations at about 1 p.m. that day,[62] more than 48 hours after the beginning of the crisis. The Secretary General appealed to the United States and Cambodia to refrain from further acts of force to facilitate a peaceful settlement of the dispute,[63] whereupon President Ford gave the order for a military operation.

Ford's battle plan called for Marines to attack Koh Tang island and recover the Mayaguez, while bombing raids were conducted on an airport, a naval base, and a oil refinery on the mainland. Kissinger, Vice-President Nelson Rockefeller, and Scowcroft favored using B-52s for the air strikes; Ford, however, opposed using these incredibly inaccurate planes when he was advised that a U.S. aircraft carrier with tactical bombers was then in the area. "Even so," noted *Time* magazine's correspondent, "the B-52s were kept gassed-up, their bomb bays loaded, and their crews on the line ready for take-off."[64] Reporters were excluded from the air base on Guam so they wouldn't be able to see the planes being loaded with 1000-pound bombs.[65]

Once the military operation was set in motion, Ford called in congressional leaders for a briefing which characteristically began with a standing ovation for the President. Ford explained: "We gave the Cambodians clear orders. They disregarded them. They were not to try to take the ships from the island to the mainland."[66] For this act of disobedience to the ruler of the universe, Cambodian ships had been blown out of the water. Ford then described the military action that had been ordered and the congressional leaders asked a few bland questions. The President Pro Tempore of the Senate, James Eastland, sat slumped down in his chair throughout the session, mumbling several times, "Blow the hell out of 'em."[67]

Just minutes before the Marines arrived at Koh Tang[68] and several hours before the first bombs were dropped on the mainland, Radio Phnom Penh began a 19-minute broadcast by Hu Nim, Cambodia's Minister for Information and Propaganda. After criticizing U.S. interference in Cambodia, Hu Nim declared: "Regarding the Mayaguez we have no intention of detaining it permanently and we have no desire to stage provocations. We only wanted to know why it came and to warn it against violating our waters again." This was the same warning, said Hu Nim, as given to "the ship flying the Panamanian flag which we released on 9 May 1975." The broadcast continued:

> Wishing to provoke no one or to make trouble, adhering to the stand of peace and neutrality, we will release this ship but we will not allow the U.S. imperialists to violate out territorial waters, conduct espionage in our territorial waters, provoke accidents in our territorial waters, or force us to release their ships whenever they want by applying threats.[69]

It took just under an hour for the U.S. government monitoring agency in Bangkok to translate the broadcast and transmit it to Washington. Kissinger and Ford were determined to go ahead with their military plans, ignoring the conciliatory nature of the broadcast. Ford told one journalist, "I said to the secretary, 'They don't mention the crew,' and apparently the information Henry had, he had not been told or the announcement didn't include the crew. So I said to him, 'Proceed as we had agreed, with the air strikes and the full operation.'" It is true that the announcement did not specifically mention the crew; but Ford did not know this for sure ("*apparently* the information Henry had") and even Henry had received only a preliminary translation of the broadcast.[70] Any reasonable reading of the Cambodian message would assume that the release of the crew was intended. Would someone who says he doesn't want to be provocative or make trouble think the United States wouldn't feel provoked if it were given back the ship but not the crew? Hadn't the message spoken of the release of the Panamanian "ship" as a way to refer to the release of that vessel and its crew? And in fact wasn't this very same shorthand of using the word "ship" to refer to vessel and crew employed by the United States in its initial public statement on the crisis (the President "instructed the State Department to demand the immediate release of the ship.")[71]

No pause was ordered in the Marine assault. The air-strikes on the mainland[72] were put on hold, but then ordered resumed just twenty minutes later when no further word was received from Cambodia.[73] It is not surprising that no further word was received in these twenty minutes given that the United States did not issue its message saying it wanted to hear specific word on the crew until an hour later.[74] The operative principle for U.S. policy-makers seems clear here: when in doubt, use force.

In fact, at the very same time as the Phnom Penh radio broadcast, the Cambodians had put the Mayaguez crew on a fishing boat and sent them, unaccompanied, back towards the Mayaguez and Koh Tang island. About three hours later they were spotted by a U.S. plane. Nevertheless, air strikes were then carried out against the mainland air and naval base. Aircraft, hangars, fuel storage facilities, runways, and anti-aircraft sites were hit at the airfield and barracks and fuel storage facilities at the naval base.[75] Within half an hour, the entire Mayaguez crew was reported picked up, all hands safe, by a U.S. destroyer. Ford announced that offensive operations would now cease, but 30 minutes later air strikes were ordered and carried out against an oil refinery, warehouses, and a railroad yard building at Kompong Som.[76] The United States defended these last raids as necessary to protect the Marines trying to extricate themselves from Koh Tang[77]—a rather preposterous claim, given that these targets were hardly going to enable the Cambodians to project military power 35 miles across waters controlled by the U.S. Navy and Air Force—particularly not an oil refinery that Washington knew to have been inoperative.[78] According to the GAO, the Defense Department was unable to cite any indications that Cambodia—which had few boats or planes remaining after the previous air strikes—was preparing to attack the U.S. forces still on Koh Tang.[79]

Kissinger is said to have put the matter a little differently in private: asked by Scowcroft whether there was any reason for the Pentagon not to disengage, Kissinger told him: "No, but tell them to bomb the mainland. Let's look ferocious! Otherwise they will attack us as the ship leaves."[80] Ford makes no mention in his memoirs of the post-release air strike, though he does complain that still another wave of air attacks that he authorized somehow never got carried out.[81]

There was more ferocity. The United States dropped the BLU-82 bomb, the largest non-nuclear weapon in its arsenal, on Cambodian positions on Koh Tang. Again the claim was made that this measure was necessary to extract the Marines from the island, but there are reasons for doubt. The head of the Marine Task Group had originally asked that the bomb be used only when requested by the officer in charge of the Koh Tang assault. But, according to the GAO, the "assault commander had not requested the use of the BLU-82 and stated that he was not informed that a decision had been made to drop the weapon." The GAO was "told that the decision to use the weapon was probably made in Washington."[82]

To "save" 40 crew members who were being released anyway, the Mayaguez "rescue" mission led to the deaths of 41 Americans and the wounding of 50 more: 15 Marines died in the assault on Koh Tang and 23 Air Force personnel were lost in a helicopter crash as troops were being moved into position in Thailand. (The Pentagon tried to exclude the latter 23 from the death toll on the grounds that these Air Force units ultimately were not assigned to combat, but clearly the 23 died as a result of the Mayaguez operation.)[83] Despite these losses, Secretary of Defense James Schlesinger was correct when he remarked that "the outcome was fortunate."[84] It was only good fortune that prevented the Mayaguez crew members from being killed either by U.S. bombs or by Cambodians enraged at U.S. duplicity. Had the Cambodians possessed the evil intent that, according to U.S. policy-makers, justified the whole operation, it is hard to see how any of the crew would have survived the rescue mission.

The captain later asserted that he and the entire crew were grateful for the rescue operation. But one wonders. Some of the crew suffered permanent damage from the gas attacks.[85] The Cambodians were rather more solicitous of the crew's well-being; one member commented later that the Cambodians "were so nice, really kind. They fed us first and everything. I hope everybody gets hijacked by them."[86] More typical was the reaction of chief engineer Cliff Harrington who commented as he boarded the U.S. destroyer: "That's a damn shame they're bombing Kompong Som. Those people didn't do us any harm."[87]

The costs of the "rescue" mission to the Cambodians were far heavier, though the final toll will probably never be known.[88] And, as William Shawcross has noted, one can do no more than "speculate on the effects the attacks must have had on Khmer Rouge paranoia about their enemies."[89]

The reaction in the United States to the Mayaguez affair was general enthusiasm. Said Sen. Barry Goldwater: "It shows we still got some balls in this country."[90] "Let no one mistake the unity and strength of an America under attack," declared Democratic Sen. Adlai Stevenson III.[91] "The

President's firm and successful action," effused Sen. Ted Kennedy, "gave an undeniable and needed lift to the nation's spirit, and he·deserves our genuine support."[92] There were a few voices of dissent, among them Rep. Pat Schroeder: "We have won no 'victory.' We have proved nothing to the world, except that this President is willing—as were his predecessors—to make hasty and ill-considered use of American military force against tiny countries regardless of the law."[93]

Grenada

Cambodia was actually huge, compared to the *really* tiny country of Grenada. In October 1983, U.S. troops invaded this Caribbean island, claiming that they were protecting more than a thousand American citizens, the majority of them students at St. George's University Medical School.

A country of just 100,000 people, Grenada had been ruled since 1979 by a left-wing government headed by Maurice Bishop. In early October 1983, the ruling New Jewel Movement was torn by internal discord, and on the fifteenth Bishop was ordered arrested by the party's central committee. On the nineteenth, a huge crowd of Bishop's supporters freed him; a clash with army units ensued and in the aftermath Bishop and some of his key associates were executed.

There was widespread international condemnation of the killings. Cuba declared that "No doctrine, no principle or proclaimed revolutionary position and no internal division can justify atrocious acts such as the physical elimination of Bishop and the prominent group of honest and worthy leaders who died yesterday."[94] Michael Manley, the leftish former Jamaican prime minister, called the killings a "squalid betrayal of the hopes of the ordinary people of our region."[95] Neighboring Caribbean states imposed harsh economic sanctions. The United States, too, expressed its concern over developments in Grenada, but it obviously wasn't very concerned about Bishop. From the time he first came to power in 1979—overthrowing Eric Gairy, a corrupt and repressive leader with a rather bizarre belief in UFOs[96]—the United States had been hostile to Bishop. Bishop was no democrat, but he was genuinely popular and committed to improving the social welfare of the population.[97] According to the *Washington Post,* the National Security Council considered a proposal to blockade Grenada just after Bishop took over.[98]

Relations worsened when Ronald Reagan became president in 1981. Under the new administration, any government in Central America or the Caribbean not wholly subservient to Washington was a target for destabilization. The CIA developed a plan to undermine Bishop by causing economic difficulty in the country; the plan was said to be aborted because of Senate opposition.[99] But the United States did offer the Caribbean Development Bank a loan on condition that Grenada be excluded,[100] and in general Grenada was barred from receiving U.S. aid.[101]

In October 1981, the United States conducted a military exercise in the Caribbean called "Amber and the Amberines" (a none too subtle reference to Grenada and the Grenadines) which involved the hypothetical freeing of Americans held hostage on "Amber" and installing a government "favorable to the way of life we espouse."[102] Reagan refused to accept the credentials of Grenada's ambassador to Washington and he ordered the U.S. ambassador in Barbados not to follow the usual practice of presenting his letters of credence in Grenada.[103]

In early 1983, a U.S. official warned that Grenada might provide missile bases for the Soviet Union.[104] Other officials claimed Grenada was preparing a submarine base for Moscow, until a *Washington Post* reporter bothered to look at the alleged site and found that it was too shallow for any such facility.[105] The biggest U.S. government propaganda campaign, however, was to suggest that the new airport that was being built at Point Salinas was to be a Cuban or Soviet military base.

It is "difficult, if not impossible to identify any economic justification" for building an airport, a Deputy Assistant Secretary of State testified in June 1982.[106] But, as the World Bank had noted in 1980, the lack of a decent-sized airport was a major obstacle to developing Grenada's tourism industry.[107] The length of the runway was said by U.S. officials to prove its military character, but eight other Caribbean countries had even longer runways.[108] "Grenada does not even have an Air Force," blustered Ronald Reagan. "Who is it intended for?" he asked,[109] neglecting to point out that commercial airlines use airports too. A base at Point Salinas, Deputy Secretary Kenneth Dam charged, would allow Cuban aircraft to strike Puerto Rico, among other targets.[110] But Puerto Rico is closer to Cuba than to Grenada.[111]

The Cubans, of course, were playing a prominent role in the construction of the airport, but so was the British firm Plessey, and even a U.S. dredging company was taking part.[112] Presumably there would have been greater western participation in the project if Washington had not gone to such great lengths to dissuade other nations from becoming involved.[113]

So, unlike most Grenadians, the United States shed few tears over Bishop's death. In fact, the crisis within the New Jewel Movement provided the Reagan administration with a great opportunity.

Right after Bishop was killed, General Hudson Austin, head of the armed forces, announced the formation of a Revolutionary Military Command (RMC) and declared a round-the-clock, shoot-on-sight 96-hour cur-few. U.S. officials subsequently claimed that the draconian curfew endan-gered U.S. citizens, and that Americans could not leave the island. Neither of these claims was true.

In later congressional testimony, Deputy Secretary Dam acknowl-edged that he was unaware of anyone—American or Grenadian—shot pursuant to the curfew.[114] There is no evidence of any action taken or threatened against any foreign citizen during this period.[115] Reagan admin-istration officials announced on October 27 that they had found evidence that the Grenadian government, together with Cuban advisers, was plan-ning to take American hostages,[116] but this claim was retracted a short while later.[117] (Of course, this didn't stop noted legal scholars like John Norton Moore—writing after the retraction—from citing the false claim.[118]) Not only was there no such plan, but both Grenadian authorities and Cuban officials in Havana gave explicit assurances that U.S. citizens were safe. Washington did not bother to disclose these assurances publicly. When they later came to light, the White House explained that the pledges were not trusted.[119]

The Grenadian government was particularly solicitous of the welfare of the American medical students, whose presence on the island was crucial to the country's economy.[120] Austin himself visited the vice-chancellor of the medical school to assure him that there was no danger to the students and to offer any assistance to help the school cope with the curfew; water was specially provided and school officials were given passes to go out despite the curfew.[121] Students who went outside during the curfew re-ported that they were not stopped or threatened.[122]

For the country as a whole, the curfew was temporarily lifted on the third day to give people chance to buy food.[123] The government provided the medical students with vehicles and escorts to get from one campus to the other.[124]

The medical school took a poll of its students and only 10 percent wanted to leave Grenada.[125] On the evening of Sunday, October 23, 500 parents of the medical students met in New York City to discuss the situation. Many had been in touch with their children. They sent a telegram to President Reagan urging him not to "take any precipitous actions at this time."[126]

In the meantime, the Reagan administration was hard at work to make the situation of the students look precarious. Just before the Sunday night meeting, the chancellor of the medical school was called by various U.S. officials trying to get him to say that the students were in danger. He did not believe this to be the case and refused to make such a statement.[127] Medical school trustees were also contacted in an effort to elicit similar statements.[128] Over that weekend, U.S. diplomats flew into Grenada (with the permission of the Austin government) to talk with U.S. citizens. Instead of trying to ascertain the students' views, however, the diplomats tried to convince them of their danger.[129]

Late Sunday night a radio broadcast from outside Grenada announced that an invasion of the island was imminent. This caused many of the students to get worried—as well it might, for, more than anything else, it was an invasion that would put them at risk—and now perhaps half of them wanted to leave.[130] Fear of invasion, however, is hardly a rationale for an invasion, particularly because there was no obstacle to orderly evacuation if it were desired.

British and Canadian diplomats present on the island did not believe an invasion was necessary to protect their nationals.[131] Administrators of the medical school supported this assessment,[132] though one of them, vice-chancellor Geoffrey Bourne, later changed his view on the basis of some rather peculiar reasoning, and who knows what pressure. According to Bourne, Austin had mistakenly thought that all the U.S. students were being taken out of the country and came to him very upset; Bourne explained to him that this was not the intention, but concluded from this that there were grave doubts whether they could have gotten out.[133] The Grenadian government sent a diplomatic note to the United States that Sunday night and broadcast the text over Radio Free Grenada. It condemned any planned invasion and offered to hold talks to ensure good relations. "We reiterate that the lives, well-being and property of every American and other foreign citizens residing in Grenada are fully protected and guaranteed by our government." However, the note went on,

> any American or foreign citizen in our country who desires to leave Grenada for whatever reasons can fully do so using the normal procedures through our airports on commercial aircraft. As far as we are concerned, these aircraft can be regular flights or chartered flights and we will facilitate them in every way we can.[134]

Of course, these were just promises, and Deputy Secretary of State Dam asserted that, "Although the RMC gave assurances that the airport would be opened on October 24 and foreigners allowed to depart, they then failed to fulfill that assurance."[135] This assertion is simply false. The curfew was lifted at 6:00 Monday morning and the airport was opened. Four small planes flew in, picked up passengers—among them, the former director of Reagan's national commission on social security—and flew out.[136] Caught in their lie, U.S. officials later argued that, though a few planes got in and out, "the airport was not open for normal traffic."[137] This too was a lie. There was no normal traffic, but that was not because the airport was closed, but rather because neighboring Caribbean states had prohibited the regional airline from traveling to Grenada as part of the sanctions they had imposed against the Austin government.[138]

The attention that U.S. officials devoted to the question of an orderly evacuation was revealed when Rep. Stephen Solarz asked Deputy Secretary Dam whether, after the four small planes had landed, the United States tried to arrange for other, larger planes to land to pick up Americans. Dam replied: "I cannot answer that question. First of all, I am not clear as to what extent we were aware. We were certainly aware planes were not getting in. To what extent we were aware the small planes had been able to get out, I do not know."[139] Even without the regular regional carrier, alternative evacuation plans could be made: on the evening of October 24, the Foreign Minister of Trinidad and Tobago announced that arrangements had been made to evacuate Trinidadian and Canadian nationals by air the next day.[140] But the next day the United States invaded.

"I think," commented Robert Pastor, a member of Jimmy Carter's National Security Council,

> there is reason to believe that the marines may have got there just in time before the new Grenadian Government could prove publicly the private assurances that it had given to the medical school and the U.S. Govern-ment...that they were going to assure the safety of U.S. citizens....[141]

Perhaps it was this sense of urgency that led the Pentagon to name the invasion Operation Urgent Fury.

Operation Urgent Fury

If there was any scheme to hold Americans hostage, the invasion provided the ideal opportunity. The Grenadians knew of the impending invasion many hours before it began. Then it took U.S. troops more than a day and a half from their first landing to reach the Grand Anse campus of the medical school[142]—more than enough time for the Grenadians to carry out any nefarious deeds were they so inclined. (The time lag was attribut-able to the fact that the students' "liberators" had never been told there was a second campus.[143]) According to Bourne, the Grenadian army did not use school property for offensive or defensive purposes though it would have been a perfect site from which to shoot down U.S. helicopters.[144] (One might compare this Grenadian concern to avoid "collateral damage" to civilian sites with the United States's accidental bombing of a mental hospital, killing dozens.[145])

There is no doubt that the students were finally in danger—they told "of bullets crashing through their dormitory rooms during the invasion, and of wading through surf to board rescue helicopters amid raging gunfire and booming explosions"[146]—but it was the invasion that endangered them.

But even if one believed that U.S. citizens had been in danger, this was a rather weak justification for the invasion, given that U.S. troops did far more than evacuate Americans; they overthrew the Austin government.[147] So the Reagan administration needed some other rationalizations.

One claim advanced was that the intervention had been requested and authorized by the Organization of Eastern Caribbean States as a measure of collective security. This claim, however, was a transparent fig-leaf. While most OECS members did support the invasion, they in fact had no legal authority to authorize force. The OECS treaty clearly requires unanimity for its decisions, but, even aside from the abstentions, the Grenadian government—a member nation—obviously did not concur. The treaty further specifies that collective security measures are permitted only in cases of outside aggression, which was not relevant to the Grenada situation.[148] U.S. officials were privately discussing intervention with OECS nations prior to the latter organization's meeting at which the secret decision to support an invasion was reached.[149] The formal request for U.S. intervention from the OECS was drafted in Washington.[150] The 300 Caribbean "troops" that participated in the invasion were in fact police forces who saw no combat.[151] The largest of these contingents came from Barbados and Jamaica, neither of which is a member of OECS. They were both part of another, larger regional grouping, CARICOM, which did not endorse the use of force.[152] In any event, one might consider for example whether the Soviet invasion of Czechoslovakia in 1968 would have been justified even if the other Warsaw Pact members had begged Moscow to intervene?

Another U.S. claim was that the invasion had in fact been invited by the government of Grenada in the person of Paul Scoon, the Governor-General. Scoon, according to Washington, secretly transmitted a request for intervention that the United States could not reveal until after the invasion out of concern for his well-being. But Scoon's position was entirely a ceremonial one: according to People's Law Number 3 of March 1979, the Governor-General "shall perform such functions as the People's Revolutionary Government may from time to time advise."[153] A report from the British House of Commons (recall that the Governor-General is supposed to be the representative of the British Queen) stated that "the timing and nature" of Scoon's request "remain shrouded in some mystery, and it is evidently the intention of the parties directly involved that the mystery should not be dispelled."[154] The British magazine *The Economist* (which supported the invasion) was more direct: the "Scoon request was almost certainly a fabrication concocted between the OECS and Washington to calm the post-invasion diplomatic storm."[155] Later, Scoon told the BBC that what he had asked for "was not an invasion but help from outside."[156] And he also informed reporters that he had not been aware of the possible involvement of U.S. forces until they landed in his front garden.[157]

With the pre-invasion danger to the students not credible and the legal arguments unconvincing, the White House resorted to its old standby: U.S. troops got to Grenada "just in time," Reagan declared, to prevent a Cuban take-over.[158] This claim was preposterous on its face—Cuba had been outraged at the killing of Bishop.[159] But when U.S. forces captured some 25,000 documents in Grenada detailing such things as weapons deals with the Soviet Union and North Korea, the administration proclaimed that its case had been proven. But the documents,[160] in the words of one right-wing study,

> provide no conclusive evidence that Grenada had become a depot of Soviet arms for future use in the region, nor were there any Soviet or Cuban military bases or facilities at the time of the U.S./OECS intervention aside from the controversial airport, which also had clear-cut civilian purposes.[161]

Moreover, as another scholar notes, the documents "do not provide evidence" that the New Jewel Movement "intended to allow Grenada to be used as a military or political base for the Cubans or Soviets to expand their influence in the region."[162]

The arms deals revealed in the documents do not suggest plans for aggression in the Caribbean. The militia that was to receive these weapons seems to have been intended as a means of building political cadre and for internal security and self-defense.[163] U.S. officials charged that the Grenadian armed forces were larger than any legitimate defense need, but, given the successful U.S. invasion, they evidently weren't large enough. Of course, nothing the Grenadians could have done could have prevented a U.S. military victory, but a large militia might have faced the White House with the prospect of a messy conquest, something that doesn't play as well with the U.S. public as a quick and costless intervention. As it was, the Austin government had disarmed many in the militia before the invasion for being pro-Bishop.[164]

World opinion regarding the U.S. invasion was almost uniformly hostile. In the United Nations, only El Salvador, Israel, and a few of the east

Caribbean states voted with Washington against a resolution of condemnation. (The UN, said Jeane Kirkpatrick afterwards, was "an outdated institution."[165]) In Britain, Reagan's close ally Margaret Thatcher was politely critical of the invasion; a Labour MP was somewhat less restrained, noting that U.S. policy was "conducted by a bunch of ignorant businessmen led by a president who is a dangerous cretin."[166]

Several analysts (though not the U.S. government[167]) have argued that despite the worldwide censure, the Grenadian invasion should be viewed as a humanitarian intervention, not because it saved the medical students, but because it saved all Grenadians from a repressive dictatorship; in this view the intervention promoted self-determination.[168] Given the widespread support among the Grenadian population for the U.S. intervention, this argument has to be seriously addressed. One can dispute particular poll results documenting this support (asking, for example, whether responses weren't colored by the hope of U.S. dollars flowing into the country), but every observer came back from Grenada reporting strong popular support for the invasion.

Grenadian opinion alone, however, is not sufficient to justify one country's invading another. You might be glad that the local tough beat up a malicious neighbor, but vigilantism ultimately makes us all worse off, since once vigilantes are unleashed they are hard to control and the likelihood that their "interventions" will only be for just cause is small. When the vigilante has a record of supporting all sorts of atrocities, and committing many of them him- or herself, then the dangers of vigilantism are even more pronounced.

In any event, the argument that foreign intervention is justified when it is the only way to promote democracy doesn't apply in the Grenada case. The evidence is clear that the Austin government almost immediately realized it had gone too far. As Michael Manley put it,

> The military group that had taken over knew very well they were isolated from the Grenadian population, isolated from the Caribbean, isolated from Cuba.... From the very start, they sent out feelers. They called in the private sector, they issued a statement saying they wanted good relations with the United States, they sent out word into the Eastern Caribbean, they sent word down to a Caricom meeting in Trinidad to say, "We're willing to talk, we're in a hopeless situation."[169]

On October 22, Austin had asked Scoon to help set up a broad-based civilian government.[170] The economic sanctions imposed by the Caribbean nations had been in effect only four days when the United States invaded. There was, noted the leader of Trinidad's House of Assembly (no radical), "a great deal of room for diplomacy."[171] But it was never tried. The use of outside force was embarked upon, as the government of Trinidad and Tobago put it, "as a first resort."[172]

Was Austin bluffing? Was a peaceful solution possible? Did the Marines arrive, as Robert Pastor has suggested, "just in time before negotiations between CARICOM and the Austin regime might have produced a peaceful, negotiated outcome?"[173] One doesn't know. But, the matter was never tested.[174] And, as British correspondent Hugh O'Shaughnessy has commented, had Austin and his supporters "not given up their narrowly dictatorial aspirations it is difficult to see what force they could have relied on to maintain them against the popular anger at the massacre they were responsible for." Specifically, "the militia was demoralized and virtually disarmed," the army's morale "was unreliable and any blockade of supplies to the island would…have caused chaos in Grenada." O'Shaughnessy concluded that "It would have been only a matter of time before the Leninist aspirations" of the Austin group "were swept away by Grenadians themselves. By mounting the invasion the U.S. robbed them of that opportunity."[175]

Why was this opportunity important for Grenadians themselves? The first reason follows from a basic notion of not only radical, but even liberal thought. As John Stuart Mill argued more than a century ago, the internal freedom of a political community can be achieved only by members of that community, for only in the "arduous struggle for freedom" do people develop the capacities and qualities they need to live in freedom.[176] Polls in Grenada after the U.S. invasion revealed that the prospects for self-determination were not auspicious. Many did not want elections held for years, most could not think of any local leader they supported, and 75 percent wanted Grenada to officially become part of the United States.[177] In place of popular enthusiasm for improving their country and their collective lives, there was a growing dependency on U.S. aid.[178]

The second reason U.S. intervention was so injurious to the Grenadian people is that if they had achieved democracy on their own it would have been a model of democracy drawing heavily on the populist and egalitarian aspects of the Bishop legacy. As it was, elections were held, with Washington bankrolling its favored candidate,[179] and the political system that emerged was a democracy in name, but lacking in democratic content.

Supporters of the New Jewel Movement have been purged from the civil service and replaced with supporters of the new government. A British Labour movement delegation found evidence of mistreatment of NJM members during and after the U.S. invasion. The militia under Bishop had been accused of being abusive, but the Council on Hemispheric Affairs reported in November 1985 that the 800-member U.S.-trained police force that replaced it "has acquired a reputation for brutality, arbitrary arrests, and abuse of authority." In 1986, the government obtained parliamentary approval for emergency powers, and it confiscated literature and censored the press and even calypso lyrics. The next year, a leaked document from the ruling party recommended the setting up of a secret intelligence unit to spy on political opponents.[180]

The social and economic program of the new government—urged by U.S. advisers and even made a condition of U.S. aid[181]—has been to cut back the social welfare programs introduced by the New Jewel Movement, cut state spending, and replace the progressive income tax with a regressive value added tax.[182] Unemployment has gone up sharply, health care and education have deteriorated, and the number of Grenadians leaving the country each year is 25 percent higher than under Bishop.[183] The U.S.-sponsored development strategy based on foreign investment has been a failure, and in 1987 the government kept itself afloat only by borrowing from the National Insurance fund.[184] Ironically, what prosperity there is in the country (in the words of a study sponsored by the U.S. government) can be largely "attributed to the completion of the international airport at Point Salinas."[185]

That the interests of the Grenadian people were not foremost in the minds of U.S. policy-makers was obvious. Anonymously, they acknowledged as much. The "overriding" reason for the invasion, they admitted to the *New York Times,* was so that the United States wouldn't be seen as a paper tiger. "What good are maneuvers and shows of force, if you never use it?"[186]

The Dominican Republic, the Mayaguez, and Grenada: in each case Americans were said to be in danger; but the dangers were concocted. In each case, American soldiers and a larger number of Dominicans, Cambodians, Grenadians, and Cubans died, not to save U.S. nationals who would have been far safer without U.S. intervention, but so that Washington might make clear that it ruled much of the world and that it was prepared to engage in a paroxysm of violence to enforce its will.

There have been some cases where American citizens were truly in danger: for example, the four churchwomen who were killed by government-sponsored death squads in El Salvador in 1980. But there was no U.S. intervention there, no Marine landings, no protective bombing raids. Instead Washington backed the death squad regime with military and economic aid, military training, intelligence sharing, and diplomatic support.

Is it possible that there would be a situation in the future where unilateral U.S. military intervention would be justified to protect the lives of Americans? Anything is possible. But the record of how this justification has been used in the past, and the utter cynicism shown by the U.S. government when friendly regimes such as the one in San Salvador have brutalized Americans, ought to make us extremely skeptical.

Chapter 6

The U.S. Response to Humanitarian Crises

One rationale for U.S. interventionism that we are likely to hear with increasing frequency in coming years is that of "humanitarian intervention." Its persuasiveness lies in the fact that even for those who hold the principle of non-intervention to be extremely important, there is a competing principle that is also important: namely, that when possible one ought to try to prevent massive human suffering. Sometimes, these two principles may be in conflict. For example, imagine if a government were to start massacring its population. Should foreign nations intervene to put a halt to the killing? To make the example specific, what if the government of South Africa were to methodically set up gas chambers and proceed to exterminate the black population of the country? Would foreign intervention be justified?

The risk in granting blanket endorsement to humanitarian intervention is that governments are not typically motivated by humanitarian concerns; if they intervene somewhere they will be doing it for their own reasons and in such a way that humanitarianism will probably be ill-served. Indeed, there is the danger that if the doctrine of humanitarian intervention became widely adopted there would be no end to wars and their attendant human misery.

When one looks at the actual occasions upon which claims of humanitarian intervention have been put forward, the record is not very reassuring. Hitler justified his occupation of Bohemia and Moravia in 1939 as humanitarian intervention to protect minorities.[1] To this day some scholars cite the Spanish-American War as another example of humanitarian intervention because the United States freed Cuba from the Spanish yoke. Not surprisingly, such accounts make no mention of the Platt Amendment (which forced Cuba to include in its constitution a provision allowing the United States to intervene) nor the U.S. domination of the island for the next half century.[2]

One leading authority asserts that there was at most a single genuine case of humanitarian intervention in the century and a half before World

War II: the French occupation of Lebanon/Syria in 1860-61 to prevent the massacre of the Maronite Christians at the hands of the Druses.[3] But a British government report on these events leaves doubts even in this instance:

> ...it is an admitted fact that the original provocation proceeded from the Christians, who had been for months beforehand preparing an onslaught on the Druses, which their leaders confidently expected would terminate, if not in the extermination, in all events in the expulsion, of that race.

Moreover, the Christian clergy attempted "to animate the courage of their flocks, by telling them that their endeavor to attain undisputed possession of the Lebanon would be warmly countenanced by the Powers of Christendom."[4] The British, of course, were not themselves neutral observers, but there is certainly the possibility that Maronite hopes of foreign intervention on their behalf helped to precipitate the violence.

One reason we must be extremely cautious before endorsing a right of humanitarian intervention is that this right is, as Richard Falk has noted, an *asymmetrical claim* in international law.[5] That is, it is a claim advanced only by the strong against the weak. No one bothers debating whether Cuba has the right to land marines in Los Angeles to protect the population there from undoubted police brutality. Likewise, people haven't stayed up nights arguing about whether the Philippines had the right to deploy troops in Tiananman Square to protect the democracy movement from cruel repression.

Because humanitarian intervention is this sort of privileged claim of the powerful, we would want to impose the strictest constraints upon its use to prevent abuse—if we were going to endorse it at all. Surely one would want minimally to insist that any humanitarian intervention meet a number of standards: (1) That the intervenor be able to credibly prove genuine concern about the humanitarian issue. (For example, China was outraged at Vietnam's treatment of its Chinese minority in the late '70s. But given Beijing's utter silence while its Cambodian ally butchered 200,000 ethnic Chinese in the same period,[6] a Chinese claim of humanitarian intervention against Vietnam would be highly suspect.) (2) That the intervention use force only as a last resort. (And one ought to be particularly wary of cases where the intervenor itself has blocked the possibility of more peaceful solutions.) (3) That the intervention employ only the least amount of force necessary to achieve the humanitarian end. And (4) that the intervention be reasonably expected to reduce the total level of suffering.

There have in fact been many instances in the last half century of massive violations of human rights in foreign countries which should genuinely have raised humanitarian concern.[7] One way to help in evaluating future U.S. claims of humanitarian intervention is to look at how the

United States has responded to these real cases of widespread atrocities. In some cases, the opportunities for the United States to do much about the situation were limited; in other cases, the possibilities for affecting the outcome were substantial. We will particularly want to consider the U.S. response in the latter cases.

All the cases that will be examined will involve large-scale killings or forced starvation. These are not, however, the only causes of great numbers of deaths. Poverty, for example, leads to lower life expectancy and higher infant mortality. Governments may be limited by the economic where-withal of their societies, but we certainly ought to hold them responsible for "avoidable" deaths, deaths that could have been prevented had there been a more equitable or humane distribution of resources. By this standard, there are many regimes whose human toll is far larger than generally realized. To take a single example, the United States surely has the economic and technical ability to provide its citizens with an infant mortality rate equal to that of Sweden's. Using this measure, in 1970 alone there were some 34,000 avoidable infant deaths in the United States (the excess of the U.S. infant mortality rate over that of Sweden's); in 1986 there were about 17,000. From 1945 to the present, more than a million American infants died needlessly.[8] They were not shot or thrown in gas chambers, but they were nevertheless victims of the U.S. government. This sort of human rights atrocity, however, will not be considered here. The analysis will be confined to situations involving direct killings or forced starvation.

The Holocaust

The greatest outburst of mass killing in the last 50 years took place under the Nazis. There were many victims of Nazi terror—gypsies, gay men and lesbians, Soviet prisoners of war, Slavs generally—but the extermination campaign against the Jews was the most systematic and far-reaching.

Since most of those slaughtered by the Nazis were non-Germans, and since most of the killing took place after the United States was already at war with Germany (Germany had declared war on Washington the day after Pearl Harbor), the holocaust did not pose the usual difficult question regarding humanitarian intervention: namely, whether it is justified to intervene in the internal affairs of another nation in order to promote some humanitarian end. The war rendered the principle of non-intervention inoperative here, so the U.S. concern for the victims of mass murder can be viewed without complication. And, because the United States had a significant Jewish minority (though not nearly as powerful as it would later become), we would expect the U.S. response to Nazi crimes to be stronger than to crimes where the victims were, say, Bangladeshis or Biafrans.

Oppression of Jews by other European countries earlier in the century occasionally elicited mild expressions of concern from the United States government, though the humanitarian motive here was not always self-evident. In 1902, for example, Secretary of State John Hay sent a note protesting the treatment of East European Jews which, he said, was driving to U.S. shores a horde of immigrants which constituted the "mere transplantation of an artificially produced diseased growth to a new place."[9] As might be guessed, such protests had little effect on oppressive policies in Eastern Europe and refugees continued to pour into the United States. Sponsors of restrictive immigration legislation quoted the testimony of State Department consuls warning that the country faced an inundation of "abnormally twisted" and inassimilable Jews, "filthy, un-American, and often dangerous in their habits."[10] In 1924, the Congress passed a law setting immigration quotas for each foreign country based on the U.S. population in 1890, that is, before the large-scale immigration from eastern and southern Europe.

With Hitler's rise to power in 1933, and particularly after November 1938 when Jews in Germany were terrorized and tens of thousands were sent to concentration camps, Jews were desperate to emigrate. Nazi policy at the time encouraged emigration—extermination didn't become policy until after the invasion of the Soviet Union in June 1941—but the world's doors remained closed. In the United States, Congress and even explicit anti-Semites supported the idea of a haven for Jews, as long as it wasn't in the United States.[11] President Franklin Roosevelt, responding to public pressure, convened an international conference at Evian, France, in 1938 to deal with the refugee crisis, but made clear that the United States had no intention of loosening its quotas. Only one country attending the conference offered any substantial encouragement to Jewish immigration—the Dominican Republic, because dictator Rafael Trujillo wanted to increase the white population of his country relative to the black.[12]

The United States didn't even admit Jews up to its low quota limits. The State Department established all sorts of bureaucratic obstacles to immigration that fell within the quota, claiming to fear spies, saboteurs, and those who would end up on the public welfare rolls. In late 1941, after talking with Lawrence A. Steinhardt, the Jewish U.S. ambassador to the Soviet Union, the Department's official in charge of issuing visas recorded in his diary his approval of Steinhardt's opposition to

> immigration in large numbers from Russia and Poland of the Eastern Europeans whom he characterizes as entirely unfit to become citizens of

this country. He says they are lawless, scheming, defiant—and in many ways inassimilable. He said the general type of immigrant was just the same as the criminal Jews who crowd our police dockets in New York and with whom he is acquainted.... I think he is right—not as regards the Russian and Polish Jew alone but the lower level of all that Slav population of Eastern Europe and Western Asia.[13]

The United States entered the war in December 1941, and by the end of the next year U.S. officials knew for certain that Jews were being systematically murdered.[14] Yet U.S. immigration policy remained unchanged: the quotas were maintained and State Department administrative policies assured that only 10 percent of the quota slots were filled, not for any lack of potential refugees.[15] In addition, Washington persuaded Latin American governments to halt all their immigration from Europe.[16]

During the course of the war, numerous opportunities presented themselves for rescuing substantial numbers of Jews. But, as David Wyman's well-documented study *The Abandonment of the Jews* concluded, the State Department and the British Foreign Office "had no intention of rescuing large numbers of European Jews. On the contrary, they continually feared that Germany or other Axis nations might release tens of thousands of Jews into Allied hands."[17] This would have put intense pressure on the United States to admit more Jewish refugees. It also would have put pressure on the British to open Palestine to Jewish immigration, which they were loathe to do, not out of any concern for Palestinians (Churchill called Arabs "a backward people who eat nothing but camel dung"[18]), but to maintain Britain's imperial position in the Middle East. The State Department hoped that the Nazis would not offer to deliver a large number of refugees, because, the Department warned in October 1943, the Allied unwillingness to accept them would transfer the odium from Germany to the Allies.[19]

Some rescue schemes raised tough moral issues: Should trucks be traded for Jews? Should the Allies threaten to bomb German cities in retaliation for killing Jews? (This latter proposal was essentially moot since the Allies were bombing German cities and civilians in any event.)[20] But other opportunities involved no threat to the war effort. Among the possibilities were setting up "free ports" for refugees, establishing a war refugee board, and bombing the death camp at Auschwitz and the railroads leading to it.

U.S. public opinion strongly opposed increasing the immigration quotas,[21] but there was substantial support for the idea of free ports: just as certain goods were allowed to enter free ports as long as they were later going to be transhipped, so refugees might be admitted if they were placed in camps until the end of the war and then sent elsewhere. In addition, such an example might have helped in persuading Spain, Turkey, and Switzerland to accept more refugees. Roosevelt finally agreed to set up such a free port, a camp at Fort Ontario, New York, accommodating a grand total of 1,000 people (this while 55,000 immigration slots remained unfilled). Obviously, this miserly effort was hardly sufficient to set much of an example to other countries. And to reassure the public that the refugees weren't being treated too well, government medical policy provided that the refugees were to be maintained in the same general condition under which they arrived; not even vitamins could be given to children out of government funds.[22]

A government agency assigned the job of helping Jews could have made a big difference: pressuring neutral nations, funding escape efforts, broadcasting warnings to Jews in occupied Europe, and so on. FDR set up such an agency—the War Refugee Board—but only in 1944, after Congress was about to do so, and fourteen months after U.S. policy-makers knew of the death camps. The Board received little power, no cooperation from the administration, and woefully inadequate government funding. Even so, its dedicated staff was able to save some 200,000 people.[23]

In 1944, the U.S. War Department was urged by Jewish organizations and others to bomb Auschwitz. Assistant Secretary John J. McCloy replied that "such an operation could be executed only by the diversion of considerable air support essential to the success of our forces" and would be of "doubtful efficacy." Moreover, said McCloy, "such an effort, even if practicable, might provoke even more vindictive action by the Germans."[24] McCloy never explained what could be more vindictive than mass extermination, but his other excuses were bogus as well. U.S. bombers regularly flew near Auschwitz on their way to other targets, and even did heavy bombing in the area of the death camp, including at the industrial facilities associated with the camp. The camp had taken eight months to build and under the conditions prevailing in 1944 could not have been rebuilt if it were destroyed by bombing. The single-minded focus on the war effort that McCloy said precluded saving Jewish lives did not prevent McCloy from blocking the planned bombing of a German town known for its medieval architecture, or stop Washington from dropping supplies in what it knew was a futile effort to assist the Polish Home Army in its uprising in Warsaw, or prevent a U.S. army tank unit from going out of its way in what the U.S. Senate called a "heroic effort" to save some valuable horses.[25]

The shameful record of the United States and the rest of the world during the holocaust is used by Zionists to justify the establishment of a Jewish state in Palestine. This is not the place to deal at any length with this argument, but it should be noted that the Zionist movement did not distinguish itself either in rescue efforts during the war. Rescue was always subordinated to the goal of establishing Israel. Mainstream U.S. Zionists, for example, refused to back a congressional resolution calling for more immigration to Palestine unless it included a demand for a state. The Zionists also did not support the legislation calling for the establishment of the War Refugee Board. The Zionist movement was not without influence in the United States during the war, but it devoted its major efforts to the drive for a Jewish state and relegated rescue to a secondary position.[26]

Defeating Nazi Germany ended the holocaust. But the United States did not enter the war to save Jews. And when it could have saved many by opening up the immigration quotas or bombing the gas chambers, it did not do so. World War II may have been a "just war," but it certainly wasn't driven by humanitarian concerns on the part of the U.S. government.

Biafra

In May 1967, the eastern region of Nigeria seceded and declared itself the independent state of Biafra. Secession is a basic democratic right that follows logically from the right of self-determination. Sometimes secession will raise thorny political issues, for example when the secessionists themselves oppress a minority living within their territory (as in the case of the South in the American Civil War), or when secession would remove resources vital to the survival of the larger country (as in the case of Katanga and the Congo), or when the secessionists are too small a community to constitute a viable state. None of these considerations applied in the case of Biafra. The Ibo people constituted the majority of Biafra and their leaders expressed their willingness to let any non-Ibos determine their own future through an internationally supervised plebiscite.[27] Though Biafra contained oil resources, the rest of Nigeria retained enough oil reserves to make it a major producer with or without Biafra.[28] And far from being non-viable, an independent Biafra would have been the fourth most populous country in Africa.[29] In addition, the eastern region of Nigeria had long had a separate identity, and the right of secession had rather deep roots in Nigerian political thought.[30]

That secession is a basic human right does not mean that all people ought to secede from larger political units. People will enjoy many advantages from living in larger-scale societies, so they are likely to demand independence only if their grievances are substantial. In September 1966, some 10,000 Ibos were massacred in pogroms in northern Nigeria, which caused more than a million of them to flee to the eastern part of the country.[31] The exact role of the central government in Lagos in these massacres is unclear, but soldiers were prominent among the killers and little effort was made by the authorities to put a halt to the slaughter; nor did the government ever condemn the carnage.[32] Whether these events warranted the decision to secede was obviously a determination that only the Ibos could make for themselves. This their leaders did in April 1967 and a few months later the Nigerian government went to war to crush the secession.

Britain, the former colonial ruler which had transferred power in 1960 to a Nigeria firmly under the control of the traditional, pro-British leaders in the north, immediately declared its support for Lagos in the ensuing civil war. As an official in London explained, it might be right for other nations to adhere to a policy of non-involvement, "but we are the former colonial power."[33] Propelled by this British sense of duty, not diminished by its substantial investments in Nigerian oil, the government of Labour Party Prime Minister Harold Wilson became Nigeria's decisive backer, providing arms, diplomatic support, technical assistance, and advice.[34] The Soviet Union, eager to ingratiate itself with the most populous nation in Africa, joined Britain in sustaining Lagos, becoming its principle supplier of aircraft. France—except for a brief moment when it thought it might be able to get an oil deal from Nigeria[35]—served as Biafra's main weapons source, hoping to weaken the British position on the continent; the French, however, kept their arms shipments below what Biafra needed to win, probably intentionally.[36]

The United States announced that it would supply weapons to neither side in the civil war, but it made clear where its sympathies lay. As the U.S. ambassador to Nigeria explained in July 1967:

> My Government recognizes the Federal Military Government of Nigeria. We have repeatedly made known our complete support of the political integrity of Nigeria. Many times we have expressed our hopes that Nigeria would continue to remain a united country. This is not only an official view, but one that is also felt by American businessmen engaged in the rapidly growing trade between our two countries.[37]

Washington, eager for London's backing in Vietnam, determined to follow the British lead; as Secretary of State Dean Rusk put it, "We regard Nigeria as part of Britain's sphere of influence."[38] The United States suspended aid projects in the east, but continued them in the rest of Nigeria.[39] And some Nigerian military personnel continued to receive training in the United States in 1968.[40] U.S. officials rationalized the British arming of

Nigeria ("I do not really see how they could have made any other choice," explained Under-Secretary of State Nicholas Katzenbach),[41] while criticizing the French for aiding Biafra, and pressuring them to stop doing so.[42]

Lagos's strategy in the civil war consisted of blockading Biafra and trying to starve it into submission. Such a strategy, of course, made civilians the primary victims of the war. Nigerian officials acknowledged as much: "I want to prevent even one Ibo having one piece to eat before their capitulation," proclaimed the Nigerian military commander on the southern front.[43] And Lagos's highest ranking civilian declared, "All is fair in war and starvation is one of the weapons of war."[44]

It must be noted that this brutal approach to warfare was not uniquely African. During World War I, the British instituted a naval blockade of Germany, contrary to international law.[45] It was, said the British Foreign Secretary, "a blockade such as the world has never known, but it was possible only because the United States was not criticizing but cooperating."[46] The caloric intake of the German civilian population fell to about a third of its normal level, with large numbers of deaths—perhaps three quarters of a million—attributable to the resultant malnutrition.[47] When the war ended, moreover, the blockade was left in place, and Germany was denied food for another five months. British officials took the view that they didn't want to relax the blockade "until the Germans learn a few things,"[48] and French Premier Georges Clemenceau is said to have believed that "there are twenty million Germans too many."[49] Food shortages were worse after the armistice than before.[50] Washington, fearing the spread of Bolshevism in Germany[51] and eager to promote its agricultural exports,[52] wanted to send in food, but would not do so until the French agreed that the Germans could pay for the deliveries with gold that Paris hoped to claim as reparations for itself.[53]

So the Nigerians were hardly the first to regard starvation of civilians as a legitimate weapon of war. But this made its use against the Biafran population no more justified. The British Prime Minister told a U.S. official that he would accept a half million dead Biafrans if that is what it took to preserve the unity of Nigeria.[54] Though most governments in the world backed Nigeria, international popular opinion was strongly sympathetic to the suffering Biafrans. Accordingly, British policy—in the words of a Foreign Office official—was to "show conspicuous zeal in relief while in fact letting the little buggers starve out."[55] The United States followed suit. While providing a great deal of the humanitarian aid that was flown into Biafra by private relief organizations, Washington officials did their best to publicly downplay the extent of the starvation.[56] The U.S. Embassy in Lagos even told visitors that Biafran children with rust-colored hair—characteristic of those dying of protein deficiency—were actually members of an obscure red-haired tribe whom the clever Biafrans had starved and put on display as a way to generate international sympathy.[57]

During the 1968 presidential election campaign, candidate Richard Nixon expressed his concern over the starvation in Biafra—he even used the word "genocide"[58]—and when he won the election there was some hope that he might change U.S. policy.

Nixon was repelled by images of children starving. After watching one television report on the famine in Biafra, he telephoned the State Department and told them to send relief and "get those nigger babies off my TV set."[59] Basically, Nixon did not consider Africa to be of any great strategic importance, and he told his National Security Adviser Henry Kissinger, "Let's leave the niggers to [Secretary of State] Bill [Rogers] and we'll take care of the rest of the world."[60]

Kissinger brought his own biases to bear. At one point during a briefing, he asked how one could tell the Ibos apart from northern Nigerians. When told that the northerners

> tended to be more Semitic in appearance and the eastern, coastal Ibos more Negroid, he became confused. "But you have always told me the Ibos were more gifted and accomplished than the others. What do you mean 'more Negroid'?"[61]

Upon taking office, Nixon ordered a review of U.S. policy toward the Nigerian civil war. The review concluded that U.S. policy should be continued and that a Nigerian victory would be "in the long-term interests of the United States"[62] As a sop to growing public concern over the starvation, however, Nixon announced the appointment of a special ambassador in charge of relief efforts, carefully explaining that Washington would still not recognize Biafra.[63] (The special ambassador, C. Clyde Ferguson, Jr., was a black law professor from Rutgers. "Do you think he'll understand the cables?" Kissinger asked.[64])

According to a member of the National Security Council staff, occasionally Nixon would make vague comments suggesting that he wanted to recognize Biafra; Kissinger would give the president a sympathetic hearing, then return to his office and proceed "as if the conversation had never taken place, ordering his staff to do the same." These intermittent pro-Biafran tendencies, the NSC staffer recalls, "seem to have passed as quickly from Nixon's memory as from Kissinger's consideration."[65]

By the Spring of 1969, relief officials were estimating that at least a million Biafrans had already died of starvation.[66] A U.S. relief organization asked Washington if it would be willing to provide helicopters to get food into Biafra. The Defense Department turned down the proposal on the grounds that military needs in Southeast Asia (that is, killing Vietnamese peasants) was a higher priority than feeding Biafrans.[67]

Finally, in January 1970, Biafran resistance collapsed. Following the surrender, there was no generalized massacre of the Ibo population, but Nigerian policies caused hundreds of thousands of Ibos to starve to death after the fighting had ended. One reporter on the scene wrote that he saw no signs of massive atrocities, yet "considering the conditions of the relief operation, the result may very well be the same."[68] Part of the problem was the lack of discipline among Nigerian troops, who often requisitioned Red Cross vehicles in order to carry away their loot,[69] but part was a matter of policy from Lagos.

The Nigerian government announced that it would allow no humanitarian aid to be delivered by any of the organizations that had provided relief supplies to Biafra during the civil war. The problem was not a lack of food—food was available in sufficient quantities just outside the collapsed Biafran enclave, brought there by relief agencies—but rather its transportation into and within the enclave. The area around Biafra's main airfield was particularly needy and the airfield might have served as a crucial means of distribution, but it was not used, and indeed Lagos ordered it plowed up.[70] In the meantime, a Nigerian military governor just 60 miles from the worst starvation held a wedding ceremony with champagne and suckling pigs served by waiters flown in from Lagos for his 500 guests.[71]

Assistant Secretary of State David Newsom testified that observers had reported favorably on Nigerian relief efforts,[72] but Nixon knew better. After hearing an upbeat State Department briefing on the situation, the President called Kissinger. "They're going to let them starve, aren't they Henry?" "Yes," replied Kissinger and the two men went on to discuss other matters.[73]

The most extensive and careful study of Biafra's food requirements was carried out by U.S. health experts who concluded that some 9,500 tons a week were urgently needed; the State Department stalled on presenting this information to the Nigerian government and the White House didn't push the matter.[74] The Nigerian Red Cross set a goal of delivering 4,200 tons per week. In fact, only 3,500 tons a week were delivered.[75]

There are no reliable figures on how many starved after the fighting, just as the death toll for the whole civil war is unknown. One pro-Lagos journalist who puts the total number of deaths from 1967 to 1970 at a million (a low estimate) says that the number of those who died at the end of the war because aid was too slow in reaching them "ran into thousands, possibly even hundreds of thousands."[76]

The U.S. government was not oblivious to humanitarian concerns during the civil war. Largely in response to public pressure, Washington provided about half of all the international relief going to Biafra.[77] But it is hard to believe that the United States could not have done more, such as using its tremendous influence to get a cease-fire (favored by Biafra, but rejected by Lagos), or pressing for an international arms embargo on both sides. Washington claimed it was neutral in the conflict, but, as Senator Eugene McCarthy pointed out, the United States "has been neutral only in refraining from shipping arms," while it has "officially accepted the Nigerian explanation of the situation" and used its "influence to gain acceptance for this viewpoint among other African nations."[78] To support a unified Nigeria when some Nigerians did not want to be unified was not to pursue a policy of neutrality, but to take sides. And when the side taken was starving hundreds of thousands of people to death, it was clear that humanitarian considerations didn't count for very much in U.S. foreign policy.

Bangladesh

In 1971 another country became engulfed in civil war. The nation of Pakistan consisted of two regions separated by more than 1,000 miles, with India in between. The two regions shared a Muslim majority, but differed in language, ethnicity, and culture. West Pakistan politically dominated the more numerous, largely Bengali population of the East and exploited them economically. The callous indifference shown by the authorities in Islamabad in the West to a devastating cyclone that struck the East in November 1970 further inflamed separatist sentiment. When the military government of Yahya Khan permitted the country's first free elections in December, the Awami League, a middle-class Bengali nationalist party headed by Sheik Mujibur Rahman (Mujib), swept 167 of the 169 East Pakistan seats, giving it an absolute majority in the National Assembly. But Yahya then announced that he was postponing the convening of the Assembly. Calls for independence and communal violence erupted in the East and on the evening of March 25-26 the Pakistani army—that is to say, West Pakistani troops—arrested Mujib and launched a brutal crackdown on the Awami League and on Bengalis more generally.

In the center of Dacca, the main city of East Pakistan, the army set fire to 25 square blocks and then mowed down those trying to escape.[79] Thousands were massacred in Dacca in the first few days[80] and the killings spread throughout the countryside. Bengali guerrilla resistance led to further bloody reprisals. U.S. consular officials in Dacca reported privately to Washington that "selective genocide" was going on.[81] A World Bank mission reported in July that in every city it visited there were areas razed and in every district there were "villages which have simply ceased to exist."[82] Sober estimates by the summer put the death toll between two and three hundred thousand.[83] ("When one fights, one does not throw flowers," Yahya told the press.[84]) Literally millions of Bengalis fled across the border into India in what was probably history's largest one-way movement of refugees in so short a time.[85]

World opinion was horrified at the carnage. But from the Nixon administration, there was not a word of condemnation. An official U.S. statement on April 6 referred to the people killed in East Pakistan as "victims," but no other announcements expressed any criticism of the massacres.[86] Officers at the U.S. consulate in Dacca sent a cable to Washington dissenting from the official policy: "Our government has failed to denounce the suppression of democracy. Our government has failed to denounce atrocities. ...we have chosen not to intervene, even morally"[87]— whereupon Nixon ordered the Consul-General transferred.[88]

The U.S. moral failure, in fact, began earlier. At the beginning of March, in a meeting of top policy-makers called the Senior Review Group, a State Department official suggested that the United States try to discourage Yahya from using force. According to one insider, the official did not press the point "after Kissinger cautioned SRG members to keep in mind President Nixon's 'special relationship' with Yahya.... SRG members concluded that 'massive inaction' was the best policy for the United States."[89] Kissinger's memory of the meeting has him telling the group that the president was reluctant to confront Yahya, but that the White House would not object if other countries wanted to dissuade him from using force. "All agencies agreed that the United States should not get involved."[90]

Nixon's "special relationship" with the Pakistani dictator had a variety of sources. One was a general fondness for right-wing generals. (When Yahya had visited Washington in October 1970, Nixon assured him that "nobody has occupied the White House who is friendlier to Pakistan.") The fact that Yahya's adversary—Prime Minister Indira Gandhi of India—was a woman, further cemented the bond between Nixon and the Pakistani leader.[91] Another source of the special relationship was the fact that Yahya had agreed to let Pakistan serve as the jumping off point for Kissinger's secret trip to China in July 1971. Kissinger has written that while Washington could not condone brutal military repression, "Pakistan was our sole channel to China; once it was closed off it would take months to make alternative arrangements."[92] This excuse is nonsense. Romania had already been established as an alternate channel to Beijing,[93] and in fact there was no reason that the trip to China needed a secret channel at all. As Kissinger has acknowledged, the Chinese opposed the secrecy of the trip, which was insisted upon by the U.S. government[94]—or, more accurately, by Nixon and Kissinger, since most others in the U.S. government were kept as much in the dark as was the U.S. public.

By mid-March, ten days before the bloodbath started, the CIA, the Pentagon, and electronic intelligence sources all detected the Pakistani military preparations, yet Washington chose not to warn the Bengalis.[95] On March 26, the day after the violence erupted, Kissinger told a high level meeting that the president "doesn't want to do anything.... He does not favor a very active policy."[96]

If Nixon and Kissinger genuinely believed that they could save more lives by forceful private appeals to Yahya, while forgoing public denunciations, then one would have to view their public silence with some sympathy. But private communications between the United States and Pakistan were extremely restrained, with Nixon warmly praising Yahya for his statesmanship and expressing understanding of his difficult circumstances.[97] (A May 28 letter to Yahya, for example, was, in Kissinger's words, "not exactly strong."[98]) Moreover, according to a State Department official with access to the minutes of the relevant meetings, at no time during March or April was "Kissinger on record as voicing outrage or humanitarian concern as the Pakistani armed forces obeyed Yahya's crackdown orders with a vengeance."[99]

In their rampage, Pakistani troops used U.S. weapons, among others, and public criticism of U.S. policy forced the administration to announce in April a ban on further arms deliveries to Islamabad. Two months later it was discovered that the ban only applied to *new* licenses; any arms covered by licenses issued before March 25 could still be delivered. When the loophole was revealed, the administration explicitly declared that such deliveries could continue. To do otherwise, the State Department explained, would "be interpreted as sanctions" and thus "seen as an unwarranted intrusion into an essentially internal problem."[100]

The pre-March 25 licenses were supposed to cover only "non-lethal" military equipment, but reporters found that the term "non-lethal" included ammunition and spare parts for military aircraft. Asked when ammunition might be considered lethal, a State Department spokesperson replied that this was "a theological question."[101] Thus, after March 25, ten ships sailed from the United States with military cargo bound for Pakistan[102] worth some $5 million.[103] Congress further discovered that the Department of Defense continued to approve weapons requests from the Pakistani military after March 25. The State Department testified that these approvals, worth some

$10 million, could not override the ban on issuing new arms export licenses, but certainly they did not give Yahya a very strong message that the United States disapproved of his actions.[104] By July 1971, the United States was the only western nation still delivering military goods to Pakistan.[105] It was not until early November that Washington finally announced that the pipeline of military equipment had finally dried up.[106]

The pattern was a little different with economic aid. There was substantial international humanitarian assistance sent to East Pakistan (where famine threatened) and to India (where all the refugees were massed), but the World Bank recommended in June that no new development aid go to West Pakistan until a political accommodation was reached in the East. Britain, Sweden, the Netherlands, and West Germany among others suspended their aid, but the United States did not. As the U.S. representative at a meeting of aid donors declared, "The United States was not [using] and did not plan to use aid as a lever to secure a political solution."[107]

Despite administration objections, however, the House of Representatives voted to suspend aid. This provoked Nixon's first public statement on U.S. policy toward the Pakistan crisis: "We are not going to engage in public pressure on the Government of West Pakistan. That would be totally counterproductive."[108] U.S. development aid in the pipeline continued to flow to Pakistan, and, as Malcolm W. Browne of the *New York Times* reported, "Official American comments on the subject have been couched in language ambiguous enough to enable Pakistani newspapers to carry such headlines as: 'U.S. Aid Not Suspended.'"[109]

Whether strong U.S. pressure on Yahya could have prevented further killing cannot be known, though certainly the knowledge that Nixon was publicly allowing military and economic aid to continue and declaring that the crisis was an internal Pakistani matter[110] must have strengthened the dictator's resolve. "Don't squeeze Yahya at this time," Nixon instructed U.S. officials on May 2.[111]

The United States was a major contributor to the international relief operations in the East. A State Department official believes that this aid was intended to "defuse pressures upon the White House to exert influence on Yahya to make meaningful political concessions."[112] At a meeting on July 31, when the Deputy AID administrator suggested that Washington recommend to Yahya that the army be removed from civilian-type administration in East Pakistan so that relief efforts could go forward, Kissinger barked: "Why is it our business how they govern themselves?"[113]

In the meantime, guerrilla war raged in East Pakistan, and India increasingly provided training, arms, and bases for the Bengali guerrillas.

Pakistani and Indian troops exchanged artillery fire across the border and made some cross-border incursions.[114] In late November, Indian troops took up positions within East Pakistan.[115] Then on December 3, the Pakistani air force launched attacks on Indian airfields and a full-scale war was on.[116] Two weeks later, Pakistan's armed forces in the East surrendered to the Indians and a cease-fire was agreed to in the West. Bangladesh became an independent nation.

The Indian intervention in East Pakistan which put an end to the brutal repression of the Bengali population by Pakistani troops is considered by many commentators to be a leading case of humanitarian intervention.[117] In the United Nations on December 4, the Indian ambassador declared: "We are glad that we have on this particular occasion absolutely nothing but the purest of motives and the purest of intentions: to rescue the people of East Bengal from what they are suffering."[118] But when the final version of the Security Council debates was published, India deleted from the record all of its statements which sought to justify its use of force on the grounds of humanitarian intervention.[119] Presumably, New Delhi was wary of establishing a precedent for one country intervening in the internal affairs of another and felt it had other adequate grounds on which to defend its intervention.

The millions of refugees that had poured into India between March and December 1971 had caused incredible hardship for the government in New Delhi. The refugees were concentrated in the Indian province of West Bengal, where they constituted more than 20 percent of a chronically impoverished population. When Nixon boasted that the United States was providing as much aid to these refugees as the rest of the world combined, he obscured the fact that all the international aid together compensated India only a quarter of the cost of supporting the refugee camps, a cost equivalent to all the external development assistance flowing into India. Recurrent outbreaks of disease, including cholera, threatened to spread beyond the camps. And hundreds of thousands of additional refugees were living among the general Indian population, competing for scarce jobs.[120] Indian officials thus considered it essential that the refugees return to their homes, but this was obviously never going to happen as long as the West Pakistani army was running amok in the East. As a motive for intervention, this was not a pure case of humanitarianism, yet one can certainly sympathize with India's concern.

Another aspect of India's concern was more problematic. Indian officials believed that as time went on, the Bengali independence forces would become increasingly radicalized. Eventually the guerrillas would defeat the Pakistani army, which was essentially fighting a colonial war a thousand miles from home; but the longer it took to achieve victory the more likely the leadership of the movement—and of post-independence Bangladesh—would fall to the Left. The Indian government already had enough difficulties with its own volatile Bengali population: New Delhi routinely took over the West Bengal state government for being too radical. Indian leaders were unwilling to accept an independent leftist Bengali nation just over the border.[121] One cannot know, of course, what the consequences of a more radical Bangladesh would have been for the people of that country, but in 1974 alone 50,000 died of starvation,[122] the major causes of which were the inequitable distribution of food and conscious political choice by the government.[123] During periods of starvation, food aid was smuggled out of the country and into India on Bangladeshi navy vessels under the supervision of the President's relatives.[124]

So though the Indian intervention ended Pakistani atrocities in the East, it is not obvious that the people of Bangladesh ultimately benefitted from the intervention, and it is thus difficult to justify India's action as humanitarian intervention. But the U.S. course of supporting Pakistan was based even less on humanitarian considerations.

In November and December the Pakistani dictator virtually cut himself off from all outside influences except his almost daily visits with the U.S. ambassador.[125] Despite this unusual opportunity for leverage, the United States did not press Yahya to accept either the independence of Bangladesh (which, Kissinger claims, U.S. officials knew to be inevitable[126]) or the release of Mujib. When full-scale war broke out in early December, Kissinger told top policy-makers, "I am getting hell every half-hour from the President that we are not being tough enough on India.... He wants to tilt in favor of Pakistan."[127] This tilt was not the result of India's move into Pakistan, for in fact Kissinger had told his Senior Review Group as early as July 30, 1971—more than four months before the war—that "the President has said repeatedly that we should lean toward Pakistan...."[128]

On December 4, the U.S. ambassador to the United Nations, George Bush, began his remarks with what one commentator has called "unconscious irony." "In the months since last March we have all been witness to the unfolding of a major tragedy," Bush said.

> Civil strife in East Pakistan has caused untold suffering to millions of people, has created a new and tragic refugee community in India of unparalleled dimensions and has brought India and Pakistan to open hostilities. It is time for the United Nations to act to bring the great moral authority of this body effectively and quickly to bear to preserve the peace between two of its largest members.[129]

But, of course, the time for the United Nations to have acted was back in March, not nine months and hundreds of thousands of corpses later. Secretary General U Thant had in fact tried to get the Security Council to deal with the crisis in July, but neither the United States nor anyone else was interested in hearing the issue.[130]

Bush declared in the Security Council in December that Pakistan's "tragic mistake" did not entitle India to use force.[131] The United States introduced a resolution in the Security Council and then, after a Soviet veto, in the General Assembly calling for an immediate cease-fire and withdrawal of forces. Kissinger told U.S. officials that he would be willing to have the resolution include a general reference to political accommodation in East Pakistan but "we will certainly not imply or suggest any specifics, such as the release of Mujib."[132] The General Assembly endorsed the resolution by a wide margin.

There was a serious danger that the war between India and Pakistan might spread. For some months, officials in Islamabad had warned that in the event of war, China would not be neutral, and Indian leaders—who signed a friendship treaty with the Soviet Union in October—replied that they would not be alone either.[133] Kissinger is reported to have suggested in Islamabad in July that it would be helpful if India were to receive a signal from China that it was strongly committed to maintaining the unity of Pakistan and that in case of war, China would not remain a "silent spectator."[134] This, of course, may have been intended as a bluff to reduce the likelihood of war. But in December, Kissinger thought there was a real possibility that Beijing might go to war. He instructed his assistant that if the Chinese informed the United States that they were going to move, Washington should reply that it would not ignore Soviet intervention.[135] Apparently no word of discouragement was to be offered, though the entire region might be consumed in warfare, and the U.S. guarantee would if anything make a Chinese decision for war more likely. As things turned out, however, the Chinese—absorbed with their own internal crises—proved more restrained than Kissinger and did not get involved.

Kissinger asked his advisers whether the United States could authorize the transfer to Pakistan of military equipment from allies such as Jordan, even though the United States itself had announced an arms embargo. Told that it would be illegal, Kissinger satisfied himself with having letters sent to Jordan, Saudi Arabia, and Iran keeping open the possibility of weapons transfers and letting the Indians know that such transfers were being contemplated. When Jordan's King Hussein requested permission to send eight U.S. jets to Pakistan, Nixon authorized sending ten and promised Hussein that they would be replaced.[136]

Nixon and Kissinger claimed to be worried that India would not content itself with defeating Pakistani forces in the East, but was determined to destroy West Pakistan as well, even though Indian military moves in the West were basically defensive holding actions. (Virtually no other U.S. policy-maker with access to the same intelligence interpreted India's intentions as did the President and his National Security Adviser.[137]) Washington dispatched a naval task force headed by the nuclear-armed aircraft carrier Enterprise to the Bay of Bengal. On December 10, the commander of Pakistani troops in the East tried to arrange a cease-fire and transfer of power to Bangladeshi officials. Encouraged by the prospects of U.S. and Chinese intervention on his side, Yahya ordered his troops to fight on.[138] (Civilians were the main victims of this prolongation of the war: as it retreated, the Pakistani army killed Bengali non-combatants, and Bengalis killed non-Bengali Pakistanis.[139]) On December 16, Pakistani forces in the East surrendered unconditionally, but Yahya declared that he would continue fighting. India announced that it had ordered a unilateral cease-fire on the western front to begin the next day. On the afternoon of the 17th, Pakistan accepted the cease-fire.[140]

Despite the end of the war, conditions for the people of Bangladesh were still grim. A State Department official had told Kissinger on December 6 that Bangladesh would be "an international basket case," to which Kissinger replied, it would "not necessarily be our basket case."[141] Washington *did* provide food aid, but in September 1974 it threatened to cut off the aid unless Bangladesh stopped exporting jute (its principle crop) to Cuba.[142] In 1975, the Mujib government in Dacca was overthrown in a military coup, perhaps with U.S. involvement,[143] and the new regime became heavily dependent on the United States, China, and Saudi Arabia, while cutting its ties to Moscow and New Delhi.[144]

Burundi

In 1972, killings on a massive scale broke out in the small African country of Burundi, where the Tutsi ethnic group who made up only 14 percent of the population dominated the Hutu majority. On April 29, 1972, a violent uprising was launched by some Hutus. The rebellion was promptly put down, whereupon the army and government-organized youth groups proceeded to massacre Hutus, particularly those with any education. By the time the carnage ended in August, conservative estimates put the death toll at 80,000-100,000 in a nation of 3.5 million.[145]

Despite the fact that the U.S. ambassador and the State Department privately characterized what was going on in Burundi as "selective genocide,"[146] the U.S. government made no public criticism of events in that country. Even in private, however, the U.S. abdicated its moral responsibility. The U.S. ambassador, Thomas P. Melady, spoke with Burundi's president Micombero on May 5 at a time when it appeared that the government was still suppressing a rebellion and not yet engaged in mass murder. Melady claims he urged Micombero to re-establish political control with a minimum of violence and avoid bloodshed, and that the President assured him there would be no unnecessary killing.[147] But five days later, when Melady concluded that selective genocide was going on, he made no further approach to Micombero. In fact, he prepared to leave the country to return to Washington before taking up a new diplomatic post. He requested no further meeting with the Burundian president. On the eve of his departure, Melady was summoned to Micombero's headquarters to receive a decoration. The subject of the ongoing massacres did not come up.[148]

Just before he left, Melady met with some other foreign ambassadors and they agreed that the senior diplomat, representing the Vatican, ought to deliver a letter to Micombero urging an end to the repression. The U.S. Embassy played a role in drafting the letter to Micombero which was presented on May 29,[149] while Hutu school teachers, church leaders, nurses, students, and others were being beaten to death. The letter is quoted here in its entirety:

> I wish to express to Your Excellency, in the name of several of my colleagues, how satisfied we are by recent indications of the beginning of pacification and the re-establishment of law and order.
>
> As true friends of Burundi we have followed closely with anxiety and uneasiness the events of these last weeks. Thus we are comforted by your having constituted groups of wise men (elders) to pacify the country, and by the commands which you have given, to repress the arbitrary actions of individuals and groups, the private vengeances and excess of authority.
>
> We sincerely hope with all our heart that your laudable initiatives will meet the collaboration of everyone, thus fulfilling the aspirations of the population, so tested and contributing to uplift before public world opinion the good name and reputation of the Republic of Burundi.
>
> Finally we have welcomed with the greatest sympathy, your recent appeal in which we discern your desire to assist all victims of the events, and we assure Your Excellency that the governments and the organizations that we have the honor to represent will put everything to work to assist all those who have suffered and who suffer still, at the same time

as they will work to support your efforts to promote the peace, unity, and progress of Burundi and all its inhabitants.[150]

Not surprisingly, this letter did not slow down the killings.

Would a strong protest from Washington have helped? One can't tell. Melady and other U.S. officials later criticized the United Nations, the Organization of African Unity, and individual African states for their inaction,[151] though Secretary General Waldheim at least did what the United States did not—he publicly referred to the massacre[152]—and the OAU said privately to Micombero what the United States did not—that the killings must stop.[153] Melady acknowledges that the "spotlight of an aroused international public opinion might have brought an end to the killings sooner. Some lives might have been saved."[154] Yet he himself tried to keep news of the massacres out of the U.S. press.[155] And Melady concludes that the U.S. government "responded in an appropriate fashion." "Direct unilateral intervention was out of the question," Melady writes, because "it would have been contrary to our policy of nonintervention in the affairs of African states."[156]

It is hard to believe that the U.S. government, which, as Jonathan Kwitny has noted, instigated "the very first coup in postcolonial African history, the very first political assassination, and the very first junking of a legally constituted democratic system,"[157] was so committed to non-intervention that it couldn't issue a strong statement of protest about mass murder. Indeed, even when it was confirmed that U.S. aid was being used by the government of Burundi to lure Hutus to their deaths, there was no U.S. protest.[158]

As a matter of fact, the United States potentially had more influence in Burundi than most other countries because U.S. firms bought 80 percent of Burundi's coffee, accounting for some 65 percent of its foreign exchange.[159] Supporters of U.S. policy have argued that a boycott of Burundian coffee would only have hurt the poor Hutu farmers and that other buyers would have taken up the slack.[160] But the profits from the coffee industry went overwhelmingly to Tutsis, not Hutu farmers,[161] and previous efforts to diversify purchasers had failed.[162] Here too, one can't be sure whether the threat of a boycott would have helped stop the massacres, but U.S. policy-makers did not even consider the idea.

At the end of September 1972, after the killings had come to an end, the new U.S. ambassador (Melady's replacement) was temporarily recalled from Burundi, but no public announcement was made. In Washington, Burundi's ambassador was secretly called in and told that normal relations were impossible.[163] In January 1974, however, the U.S. ambassador cabled

Washington to recommend the resumption of normal relations in order, among other reasons, to "promote viable U.S. investment." "This has assumed particular importance," the ambassador noted, "with the appearance of a UN survey report indicating the possible presence in Burundi of one of the world's major nickel deposits." The State Department's Thomas Pickering then sent a memorandum to the White House supporting normalization because it would provide "opportunities for American corporations that are interested in exploiting the major new mineral discovery." On January 29, Nixon authorized the normalization to proceed.[164]

Cambodia

In Cambodia in the late 1970s, the Khmer Rouge led by Pol Pot carried out massive atrocities against its own population. Before 1975, the United States had destabilized Cambodian society and subjected its peasantry to one of the most intense bombardments in history, thereby creating the conditions for the Khmer Rouge's brutal rule. Once Pol Pot took power, the United States had almost zero direct influence on the Cambodian government. Assistant Secretary of State Richard Holbrooke testified in 1977 that only one country carried any weight in Phnom Penh, and that was China, which, unfortunately, had no desire to prod the Khmer Rouge to stop the killings.[165] But Washington had growing ties with Beijing which it could have used as indirect leverage on the Cambodians. The Carter administration, however, was more eager to solidify its relationship with China and to punish Vietnam for resisting U.S. domination for two decades than to concern itself with Cambodian deaths. In May 1978, National Security Adviser Zbigniew Brzezinski discussed with the Chinese the need for "assistance to Southeast Asian efforts to check Soviet support of Vietnamese expansionism,"[166] the only efforts in this regard at the time being those of the Khmer Rouge.

At the end of the year, Vietnam invaded Cambodia. To many Cambodians, this was a humanitarian intervention, saving them from the brutality of the Khmer Rouge.[167] Hanoi did not officially endorse the humanitarian justification for its intervention, appealing instead to its right of self-defense against continual Cambodian border incursions.[168] There would be reasons to question a humanitarian intervention rationale from Vietnam, even if it had been put forward. Apart from the historic Vietnamese domination of Indochina, there is the fact that Hanoi had publicly supported the Khmer Rouge regime in 1977[169] and even returned refugees to the Khmer Rouge to maintain ties.[170] But however we judge the Vietnamese intervention, the U.S. reaction was clearly devoid of humanitarian considerations.

Though the Vietnamese quickly took Phnom Penh, the Khmer Rouge were able to regroup over the Thai border and with support from China and Thailand wage a guerrilla war against the new Vietnam-backed regime of Heng Samrin. Brzezinski boasted in 1981: "I encouraged the Chinese to support Pol Pot." Pol Pot, he said, "was an abomination. We could never support him. But China could." And while Chinese arms flowed to the Khmer Rouge, the United States, according to Brzezinski, "winked semi-publicly."[171]

As part of its policy of punishing Hanoi, Washington had banned all aid to Vietnam, and even obstructed private U.S. aid agencies from shipping privately donated humanitarian assistance to meet basic needs of the people of Vietnam. Following the Vietnamese invasion of Cambodia, the new Vietnam-backed regime in Phnom Penh was subjected to the same restrictions.[172] The only U.S. humanitarian aid was that sent to the refugee camps near the Thai border from which the Khmer Rouge and other anti-Phnom Penh guerrillas recruited fighters. At the same time, the United States gave diplomatic support to Pol Pot, voting to award the Cambodia seat in the General Assembly to the Khmer Rouge rather than giving it to Heng Samrin, or even leaving it vacant.

Despite Washington's claim that it was following the lead of the Association of Southeast Asian Nations (ASEAN) in dealing with the Cambodia question, in fact, as one conservative scholar has noted, "Over and over again, the U.S. has acquiesced in attempts by Beijing to block a more compromise oriented policy" put forward by some Southeast Asian nations.[173] In July 1981, for example, at a UN conference on Cambodia in New York, ASEAN wanted the final resolution to call for the disarming of the Khmer Rouge in the context of a political settlement; the Chinese instead wanted language that favored the Khmer Rouge. Washington sided with Beijing.[174]

In May 1982, the Khmer Rouge formed a coalition with Prince Sihanouk and Son Sann, two conservative leaders of what the United States dubbed the NCR—Noncommunist Cambodian Resistance. The NCR was of little consequence militarily, but they gave the Khmer Rouge international respectability, with Sihanouk becoming the nominal head of a coalition in which the Khmer Rouge was the dominant force. ASEAN and the United States had pressed Sihanouk and Son Sann to adhere to the coalition, making their joining a precondition for receiving western aid.[175]

ASEAN provided weapons (some of them manufactured under U.S. license) to the NCR, while Washington provided them with financial support, "non-lethal" supplies, intelligence information, military advice, and coordination of all the aid.[176] The United States claimed this support in no way aided the Khmer Rouge, but, as Sihanouk admitted, "We assist one another in every circumstance and cooperate with one another on the battlefield."[177] The U.S. General Accounting Office reported that from 1986 to 1988 there was no U.S. accountability to assure that U.S. aid went to the Sihanouk and Son Sann forces and not to the Khmer Rouge; "serious abuses and diversions of assistance" were found to have occurred, though "the details of these abuses remain classified by the State Department." After 1988, when tighter controls were imposed, the GAO could verify that the NCR received the aid, but had no way of determining how it was used within Cambodia, and whether, for example, it was diverted to the Khmer Rouge.[178]

In 1989, Vietnam withdrew its troops from Cambodia, but U.S. policy remained unchanged. Only under congressional pressure and the defection of the West European allies,[179] did the Bush administration announce in July 1990 that it would no longer vote to give the Cambodian seat in the United Nations to the Khmer Rouge-dominated coalition.[180] But this new policy did not end U.S. aid to the Khmer Rouge's coalition partners nor U.S. endorsement of Sihanouk's insistence that any settlement must be acceptable to the Khmer Rouge.[181] After further evidence of battlefield coordination between the Khmer Rouge and the U.S.-supported guerrillas, Washington suspended aid to the latter in early 1991; but a month later, the aid was resumed.[182] A UN peace-keeping force is now being sent to Cambodia to supervise country-wide elections. Whether the Khmer Rouge will be able to intimidate its way to victory—using military force that it accumulated over the years of its tacit alliance with the United States—remains to be seen.

More Massacres

Unfortunately, the five instances of mass inhumanity examined above do not exhaust the list. Even leaving aside international wars (Vietnam, Afghanistan, Iran-Iraq, etc.), there have been depressingly many occasions in which massive numbers of people have been killed by oppressive regimes.

For example, in 1954, the United States overthrew the elected government of Guatemala and organized a brutal security apparatus to maintain the status quo. Over the next three and half decades, this U.S.-backed security force—"today arguably the most repressive force in Latin America," in the words of a *Wall Street Journal* reporter—was responsible for as many as 200,000 killings, with the help of intelligence files set up by the CIA.[183]

Between 1965 and 1969, at least half a million people were massacred in Indonesia by the army and its right-wing supporters. U.S. diplomatic backing for the Jakarta butchers, and U.S. enthusiasm for the defeat suffered by the Left in the bloodbath have long been noted.[184] Recently, however, Kathy Kaldane of State News Service documented that Washington did more than just serve as a cheering section: the CIA provided the killers with lists of names of leftists to murder.[185] A decade later, when Indonesia invaded East Timor, killing upwards of 100,000, the United States continued to arm Indonesia and blocked United Nations actions to halt the slaughter.[186]

In Uganda, Idi Amin presided over the killing of some 250,000 people between 1971 and 1979.[187] Amin took power in a military coup backed by Britain and Israel;[188] he had been a member of the British colonial armed forces and was known to be a murderous thug, but ferocity in carrying out orders had always been considered a virtue by his British commanders.[189] Amin soon broke with Israel and established ties with Libya, Saudi Arabia, the PLO, and the eastern bloc. Washington called home its ambassador from Kampala in 1973, but publicly attributed the recall not to the mass slaughter then under way, but to Amin's "entirely unacceptable" criticism of the U.S. role in Vietnam.[190] At the same time, the United States became Uganda's main trading partner,[191] and continued to provide the regime with military equipment and training for members of its internal security force.[192] By the end, Amin was an international embarrassment. The U.S. Congress voted (over objections from the Carter administration) to cut off trade with the country. When Ugandan troops conducted a raid into neighboring Tanzania, the Tanzanians responded with an all-out invasion of Uganda and deposed Amin in 1979, in what is often referred to as a humanitarian intervention. The aftermath, however, was not very promising: after an initial euphoria, the country slid into civil war, repression, and mass murder. As many may have died in the half decade following Amin as during his rule, and not a few talked of the "good old days under Amin."[193] Amin obtained refuge first in Libya and then in Saudi Arabia, where he is today.

There have been other murderous regimes where U.S. leverage has been negligible. For example, the governments of China in the 1950s and 1960s and Ethiopia in the 1980s have been responsible for massive death. Washington was hostile to both of these regimes, but there are good grounds for doubting that humanitarianism was the reason for the hostility: the Ethiopian government in power before 1974 was also responsible for mass starvation and a brutal war against secessionist movements, and yet was strongly supported by the United States;[194] and Mao's predecessor massacred immense numbers,[195] while enjoying U.S. backing.

There has been no instance since World War II in which the United States has formally justified a resort to force on the grounds of humanitarian intervention on behalf of non-Americans. More significantly, however, although there have been many opportunities for Washington to have stopped massacres and saved lives by measures short of direct military intervention, it has not done so. Sometimes it has acquiesced in the murders; sometimes it has facilitated them.

The U.S. government has often been generous with food aid, and even though there is an element of self-interest in distributing surplus food supplies, this generosity should still be welcomed. But often—as in Biafra and Bangladesh—the U.S. participation in relief efforts was used to deflect attention from the larger U.S. complicity in mass atrocities.

There have been three recent cases of inhuman regimes deposed by outside intervention—in Bangladesh, Cambodia, and Uganda. I have indicated some reasons for being skeptical regarding the humanitarian intervention justification in each of these cases, though I admit these are not easy situations. But there is no doubt—given the U.S. record with respect to government murder—that U.S. intervention is unlikely to promote humane results.

There will be situations, like the travail of the Kurds in Iraq, where intervention may be considered. In the aftermath of the Iran-Iraq war, Saddam Hussein turned his military machine, including chemical weapons, against his country's Kurdish population. At least half a million Kurds were forcibly relocated, many were killed, and 4,000 villages were wiped off the map, but there was no word of public protest from the Bush administration.[196] In February and March 1991, the United States urged the Iraqi people to overthrow Saddam Hussein; the Voice of Free Iraq—almost certainly a CIA-funded operation—recruited Kurdish exiles to broadcast calls to their compatriots to rise up against the Iraqi leader.[197] When the U.S. calls were heeded, President Bush proceeded to turn his back on the Kurds, just as Kissinger had done in 1975 (while Bush was head of the CIA).[198]

Bush decided to let Saddam Hussein put down the rebellions without U.S. intervention rather than risk the splintering of Iraq. Washington had warned Hussein not to use combat helicopters against the insurgents, but when he ignored the U.S. warning, the United States chose not to act. In fact, a White House spokesperson explicitly rescinded the warning.[199] "We never made any promises to these people," said a senior official. "We don't want Iraq dismembered, since that would go counter to the reason we fought the war," commented another official.

White House press secretary Marlin Fitzwater declared that reports of atrocities against the Kurds would not change U.S. policy. Just a short while before Bush had likened Saddam Hussein to Adolf Hitler; now Fitzwater equated the Iraqi leader with those trying to overthrow him:

> I think it's safe to assume that in the kind of warfare being conducted by the rebel forces and the Kurds, as well as by the Government of Iraq, as well as by other groups, that there are all sorts of atrocities and war repercussions taking place—yes. But it is our belief that the best policy is not to involve ourselves in those internal conflicts.[200]

Only after U.S. and international opinion were aroused by Bush's perfidy did the president move to protect the Kurds.[201] And his continuing hypocrisy was evident from his complete silence while Kurds are being massacred by Turkey—a loyal ally and member of the anti-Iraq coalition.[202] In addition to killing Kurds within Turkey, Ankara has launched major raids by its U.S.-supplied air force against Kurdish villages in Iraq—located within the allied security zone.[203] (In 1983, while NATO maneuvers were going on in Turkey, Turkish troops attacked Kurdish positions in Iraq with Iraqi approval, eliciting no criticism in the West.[204]) Kurds in Turkey have been subjected for years to draconian legislation that, among other things, outlaws the use of their language in books, newspapers, schools, and public meetings.[205] Even a Turkish law banning spoken Kurdish in any circumstance was only lifted recently. (Objections to spoken Kurdish, the *New York Times's* Clyde Haberman sympathetically noted, "were rooted less in racism than in a sincere foot-in-door fear that yielding on language rights today would lead inexorably to separatist demands tomorrow."[206]) Protecting the Kurdish people from the Turkish government would not require sending in foreign troops. Given Ankara's dependence on trade and aid from the West, the United States has ready leverage to save many lives—leverage it has no interest in exercising.[207]

From the point of view of the Left, it is right to safeguard the Kurds from the consequences of U.S. policies that have subjected them to indiscriminate massacre.[208] UN intervention is certainly to be preferred to U.S. intervention, not because other countries have a measurably better commitment to humanitarianism than the United States (many do not), but because the self-interest of the various nations may well conflict, thus eliminating the more obscene instances of self-aggrandizement for which humanitarian intervention is often a cover. But the UN Security Council today is too subject to the whims and financial leverage of Washington to make it a dependable protector of global human rights. A United Nations responsive to U.S. strategic interests (in Iraq and Turkey) rather than to genuine humanitarian considerations is not likely to end Kurdish suffering.

In domestic politics, we oppose forced confessions or arbitrary searches by the police, even though in a particular case such actions might prevent a crime or help bring a criminal to justice. Because giving the police unlimited power is so subject to abuse, we accept a greater incidence of crime in order to reduce even greater threats to our freedom. Similar logic applies in international relations. Landing foreign troops every time a government was alleged to violate human rights would be a prescription for global chaos. Such interventions, even if taken in response to genuine human rights violations, would likely lead to more death and destruction than would have occurred otherwise. And to allow each country, or each powerful country, to judge for itself when human rights have been violated in other countries would be dangerous in the extreme. But there are some cases where the level of human rights violation is so massive, where hundreds of thousands or even millions of lives are at stake, that one might want to permit some exception to the general prohibition against humanitarian intervention.

But when a country has a record of not protesting mass murder (as in Biafra, Bangladesh, and Burundi), of not taking simple steps that might have saved millions (such as opening immigration quotas during the holocaust or threatening to cut off coffee purchases from Burundi), of actually cooperating with mass murderers (as in Cambodia), and of supporting mass murderers (as in Indonesia, East Timor, and Guatemala) then one has to be very wary when that country tries to justify an intervention on humanitarian grounds.

Chapter 7

Terrorism—The Case of Libya

Combatting terrorism, according to U.S. policy-makers, will be a major function of the U.S. military in the post-Cold War era. Terrorism is an extremely convenient alibi for interventionism. Whenever an excuse is needed, Washington can arbitrarily declare certain nations to be engaged in international terrorism, though their behavior may not significantly differ from the behavior of many other nations, including close allies or even the United States itself. If a foreign crisis is needed to generate votes for the party in power or to distract attention from domestic policies that depress the real wages of most Americans, there is nothing like terrorism to provide the justification. If the profits of military contractors need to be increased or if the independence of Third World leaders needs to be squelched, the fight against terrorism can serve as the rationalization.

To be a good target for the U.S. war on terrorism, a nation needs to be relatively weak militarily. The Pentagon could not just go and bomb the Soviet Union whenever it got the urge; nor could it even bomb Syria which was closely tied to Moscow. It helps if the people of the terrorist state are of swarthy complexion, for then the crusade against terrorism will be reinforced by the ubiquitous racism of American society. And the ideal terrorist state must indeed resort to terrorism at least occasionally. It is far easier to construct a lie out of a half-truth than out of the truth. The real level of terrorism, however, is unlikely to be adequate to the needs of U.S. policy-makers, and therefore the target must be one that can be readily provoked into committing some outrage when needed. Provocation and exaggeration can transform the small-scale terrorist into a world-class enemy.

In recent years, Libya has been branded by U.S. officials as one of the world's chief sponsors of international terrorism, and its leader, Muammar Qaddafi, has been portrayed as one of terrorism's leading practitioners. Thus demonized, Libya has been the target of direct U.S. military action on four separate occasions (more than any other country since World War II). Three times—August 1981, March 1986, and January 1989—U.S. air or naval units clashed with Libyan forces in the Gulf of Sidra, off the Libyan coast.

On another occasion, in April 1986, Washington launched air-strikes against Tripoli and Benghazi. And today, U.S. officials ominously warn that they do not rule out the possibility of military action to get Libya to turn over suspects in two plane bombings.

To appreciate what the anti-terror campaign holds in store for the post-Cold War era, it will be useful to look at the history of Washington's relationship with Qaddafi and Libya.

Qaddafi came to power in 1969. For almost a quarter of a century before this, the U.S. government pursued its strategic and economic interests in Libya without regard for the sentiments of the Libyan people.[1] When the aging King Idris seemed no longer able to preserve the U.S. position, U.S. officials hoped that Qaddafi would do the job and, indeed, they were initially encouraged by the new Libyan leader's anti-communist foreign policy.

The euphoria, however, did not last. Qaddafi was determined to take control of the Libyan petroleum industry and in this he came into conflict with the United States. Washington did not oppose the oil price increases of the early 1970s,[2] but it did try to resist the partial nationalizations. Britain and the United States attempted to organize a boycott of Libya's nationalized oil, but the international oil market was not what it had been in the early '50s, when a buyer boycott had helped to bring Iran to its knees. Qaddafi was able to find alternative buyers for his oil in Eastern Europe and thus resist the pressure. The U.S. oil companies eventually settled their dispute with Libya, but the hostility between the two governments remained.

Qaddafi and Washington were also on a collision course because they both endorsed "rejectionist" positions on the Israeli-Palestinian dispute; that is to say, they both rejected the national rights and legitimacy of one of the two contending national groups in that conflict.[3] As the United States and Israel became virtually the only rejectionists on one side, and Libya one of the few on the other, antagonism naturally grew.

Moreover, Qaddafi soon abandoned his reflexive aversion to Marxism, and though Libya was far from "a Soviet satellite" (as Alexander Haig called it in 1981[4]) and farther still from a "Communist, Marxist-Leninist controlled state" (as some inanely charged[5]), he increasingly found himself supporting governments and movements that were anathema to Washington.

However, according to U.S. officials, the fundamental reason for U.S. government hostility to Libya was that Qaddafi engaged in terrorism, subversion, and foreign military adventurism. Qaddafi has done all these things. But any examination of the record shows that Libya's behavior, while often reprehensible, has been much exaggerated and hardly comparable to that of a number of other states, including the United States. Moreover, the evidence demonstrates that Libya's actions have often been responses to deliberate U.S. provocations.

The Terror Connection

Qaddafi has sponsored and supported terrorism. He has executed numerous domestic political opponents within Libya and Libyan agents have assassinated some two dozen Libyans abroad. He has ordered terrorist assaults in foreign countries and has also provided support to the terrorist activities of certain Palestinian factions and others. The covert nature of most terrorist operations has allowed Qaddafi to deny his involvement in incidents in which he may have played a role, but has also permitted commentators to charge Qaddafi with involvement despite the absence of any substantiation.

Claire Sterling and Yonah Alexander, for example, two prominent terrorism "experts,"[6] have asserted without any evidence that the murder of Israeli athletes at the 1972 Munich Olympic games was funded and promoted by Qaddafi.[7] But even the Reagan administration's report on Libya in 1983 mentioned the Olympic murders without charging Libyan responsibility,[8] and two British journalists have written,

> Israeli intelligence officials, in long discussions with the authors on Libyan terror, have denied that Qaddafi had any role in the Munich massacre. "This was purely a Black September operation," said an Israeli official. "We have no information that he took part in the planning or the logistics."[9]

On April 15, 1986, U.S. warplanes bombed Libya. Washington cited Libya's alleged role in two terrorist incidents as major justifications for the air-strikes: the bloody attacks on the El Al airline counters in Rome and Vienna in December 1985 and the bombing of the La Belle discotheque in West Berlin in early April 1986.

For each of these incidents we need to consider two logically distinct questions. First, on the basis of the evidence available to the United States at the time of its air-strikes, was there proof of Libyan involvement in the incidents? And, second, what does later evidence show regarding Libyan involvement? Clearly, it is the first question that is crucial for judging the morality of the U.S. air raids (leaving aside the matter of how one is supposed to respond to terrorist acts under international law). For the government to punish someone because he or she *might* have committed a crime is wrong, regardless of whether it later turns out that the person was guilty. It is improper to act before there is compelling proof of guilt. Where the first question is essential for judging U.S. actions, the second is relevant for judging Libyan behavior.

For both the Rome and Vienna attacks and the La Belle bombing, there is some recent evidence that will be discussed below which suggests Libyan culpability. But when we consider the evidence available to the United States at the time of its air-strike, it is clear that there was a U.S. eagerness to act before the evidence was in.

The Rome and Vienna airport attacks were carried out by the Abu Nidal organization, a Palestinian group that has violently opposed Yasir Arafat and the PLO. In the Security Council, before Congress, and in State Department reports, U.S. officials insisted that in these attacks the Abu Nidal operatives were acting as "Libyan henchmen" and under Libyan sponsorship.[10] Under questioning, however (and not very pointed questioning at that), the evidence at the time for Libyan sponsorship was revealed to be rather thin. Under-Secretary of Defense Fred C. Iklé testified that:

> The evidence for most attacks is very good…. The evidence linking Libya to…the Rome and Vienna attacks is far less concrete….
>
> In the Rome and Vienna shooting, we have only the assertion by Tunisian officials that two of the passports used by terrorists in the Vienna attack were seized from Tunisian nationals by Libya when Tripoli expelled some 30,000 Tunisian workers from Libya last August [four months before the airport attack]. The third passport used in that [Vienna] attack, Tunisian officials said, was lost in Libya by its Tunisian owner.[11]

Assuming the Tunisian assertion to be true, this evidence in fact showed no more than that Libya at some point in the previous four months gave some support to Abu Nidal (or to someone else who in turn passed the travel documents on to Abu Nidal); it hardly proved that Libya was the mastermind or the sponsor or even aware in advance of the airport attacks.

U.S. officials documented all sorts of Syrian links to Abu Nidal and to the airport attacks, yet they insisted that the attacks had Libyan (not even "Libyan and Syrian") sponsorship. In minimizing Syrian responsibility, the director of the Office of Counterterrorism even dismissed the importance of training for terrorists—a point conveniently forgotten when "terrorist training camps" in Libya were later bombed:

> Some of the terrorists involved in the Rome and Vienna attacks may have been "trained" in the Bekka Valley of Lebanon controlled by Syria. But it doesn't take much training to fire sub-machine guns and throw hand grenades against civilian passengers in a crowded airliner terminal.[12]

Also relevant to judging how much Washington knew in 1986 was the fact that U.S. officials claimed to know that "Abu Nidal and his top lieutenants" were "living in Libya."[13] More than a year later, however, in June 1987, the U.S. government trumpeted the fact that Syria had been induced to expel the Abu Nidal organization from Damascus,[14] though no U.S. official bothered to point out what this implied for U.S. claims that the group had already been headquartered in Libya.

Might there have been some *secret* evidence of Libyan links to Abu Nidal in the second half of 1985? If so, it was very secret indeed. Senator Mitch McConnell, a Republican from Kentucky and a member of the Select Committee on Intelligence, wrote to the head of the committee on January 24, 1986:

> I am particularly interested in what information the Intelligence Community has which links Libya with Abu Nidal and this attack and when were they aware of this shift in associations. As recently as November, I had thought Syria was considered Abu Nidal's primary patron.[15]

Iklé's testimony, cited above, was the full response to McConnell's inquiry, and did not suggest that there was any additional secret information.

Officials in Italy and Austria agreed that it was Syria, not Libya, that was responsible for the airport attacks.[16] And the *New York Times* referred to a State Department official "who was openly skeptical about the evidence used to link Libya to last December's Rome and Vienna airport attacks"—though not so openly that the *Times* had bothered to quote him in December, rather than the following April when he had some other charge to make against Libya.[17]

Patrick Seale, a respected British specialist on the Middle East, has recently reported on his interviews with defectors from the Abu Nidal organization who state that Libya was involved in the planning of the airport attacks and in providing the weapons.[18] These stories may well be true. But it is doubtful that this information was available to Washington in 1986. The large-scale defections from Abu Nidal did not occur until some years later,[19] and if the CIA had penetrated the organization at a high level in 1986 it has been singularly inept at thwarting its operations.

The other terrorist attack that Washington claimed justified its air-strike on Libya in April 1986 was the bombing of the La Belle discotheque in West Berlin. For four years all the evidence that was gathered on the case by West German police, including evidence revealed in a related trial in London, implicated Syria, not Libya.[20] The United States claims to have intercepted messages between Tripoli and the Libyan embassy in East Berlin confirming Qaddafi's responsibility for the bombing, but the messages were far from conclusive, and did not alter Bonn's skepticism regarding Libya's role. Nearly a month after the discotheque attack, the Berlin police chief in charge of the investigation denied there was any evidence linking Libya to the incident.[21] Significantly, Seymour Hersh discovered in February 1987, some ten months after the fact, that the intercepts had still not been shown to the National Security Agency's North Africa specialists[22]—those who might have been able to understand the context of the messages or even detect willful manipulation.

In 1990, the German press reported that files and defectors from the former East German secret police, Stasi, showed that individuals working out of the Libyan People's Bureau in East Berlin planned and carried out the discotheque bombing. Moreover, the reports claimed that Stasi not only had foreknowledge of the attack but may even have had an agent under its control involved in the operation from the start. Some accounts stated that this agent was killed by the Libyans a month later, while subsequent versions claim that the agent was arrested by West German authorities in the Summer of 1990.[23] A number of points are puzzling, however.

First of all, it is not clear what motive the East Germans would have had for supporting the discotheque bombing. The U.S. raid on Libya purportedly carried out in retaliation for the bombing proved highly embarrassing to the Soviet Union and its allies. In order to avoid a confrontation with the attacking U.S. forces, Moscow moved 3,500 Eastern bloc personnel in Libya away from the coast, pulled its vessels out of Libyan waters, and retreated its reconnaissance planes from Benghazi to Eastern Europe—hardly an impressive action for the heroic defender of the Third World.[24]

Second, if the Stasi-controlled agent was arrested in the Summer of 1990, why has there been no trial?

And third, there is the curious matter that the German press reports also claim that the CIA infiltrated at least one agent into the terrorist group that carried out the La Belle attack, apparently the same agent who was working for Stasi.[25] Did the CIA know about the bombing in advance but choose not to thwart it, so as to provide a pretext for bombing Libya, or did the CIA try but fail to prevent the bombing? Or perhaps the reports of CIA foreknowledge are themselves erroneous?

Again, it is certainly possible that Libya was responsible for the La Belle bombing. But any justification for the U.S. bombing raid on Libya can only be based on the evidence available at the time of the raid. And well after that raid the evidence was unconvincing enough that the West Berlin police and West German government publicly disputed the U.S. allegation that Libya was responsible. Even today, Washington has not released any evidence that it had at the time that would challenge this view.[26] Shortly after the La Belle bombing, Leslie Gelb wrote in the *New York Times:*

> officials said that even though hard evidence was lacking, the Administration intended to press ahead with its public campaign of identifying Colonel Qaddafi with the attacks. As one official put it, "This is our best way of sensitizing Americans and Europeans about the problems and preparing the groundwork for follow-on responses."[27]

If the evidence in many cases for Libyan terrorism is ambiguous, this does not mean that Qaddafi's hands are clean. There is rather convincing evidence for his involvement in many terrorist actions over the years. What this means, however, is that the Libyan government engages in the sort of actions that many other governments engage in. Noam Chomsky, Edward Herman, and others have extensively documented that the death toll attributable to terrorist forces armed and trained by Washington or some of its close allies exceeds by a considerable margin the toll attributed to terrorists even remotely connected to Qaddafi.[28]

The U.S. government maintains a statistical database on international terrorist incidents. The data excludes—by ideological definition—terrorism carried out by U.S. allies.[29] According to the database, there were 2,264 people killed in international terrorist incidents occurring in or spilling over from the Middle East between 1980 and 1991.[30] Surely not all these deaths were attributable to Libya; many were the responsibility of Iran, Iraq, or Syria, or of independent organizations. So as an absolute outer estimate of Qaddafi's terrorist toll during these years we have a figure of 2,000. More realistically, we can go through State Department chronologies of Libyan-backed terrorism and take every suspicion or hint as a confirmed Libyan involvement; the total comes to fewer than 1,000 dead.[31]

This is a horrendous figure. But compare it with the record of the Contras in Nicaragua. That they are a terrorist organization is undeniable; as the independent and respected human rights group America's Watch put it in a 1985 report, the Contras "practice terror as a deliberate policy."[32] Likewise undeniable are the facts that the United States created, funded, armed, trained, and directed the Contras (linking sponsor and terrorist far more closely than, for example, Libya and Abu Nidal). In 1989, the State Department noted that "despite Libya's extensive support" for Abu Nidal, "we have no proof that Qaddafi ordered or participated directly" in any Abu Nidal attacks of the previous year.[33] In the case of Nicaragua on the other hand, there is the clear evidence of a manual prepared by the CIA for the Contras urging terrorist acts.[34] This single U.S.-supported terrorist organization, operating in just one small country, was responsible for some 3,000 civilian deaths.[35] Abu Nidal's organization, called by the State Department in 1989 "the world's most dangerous terrorist group," is said by the U.S. government to have been responsible for 280 deaths—one-tenth as many as the Contras—during its entire career.[36]

To take another example, consider RENAMO, a guerrilla organization whose horrific assault on Mozambique was publicly described by a U.S. official in early 1988 as "a systematic brutal war of terror against innocent civilians through forced labor, starvation, physical abuse and wanton killing...one of the most cruel holocausts against ordinary human beings since World War II."[37] Between 1980 and 1988, some 900,000 people died as a result of RENAMO's policies;[38] at least 100,000 civilians were murdered by RENAMO between 1986 and 1988.[39]

RENAMO was originally set up in 1977 by Rhodesian military intelligence in an effort to destabilize newly independent Mozambique. When the white minority regime in Rhodesia passed from the scene, RENAMO was adopted by South Africa. Pretoria provided aid and training to enable RENAMO to carry out its terror campaign: a clear-cut case of state-supported international terrorism. But there were no U.S. air-strikes in retaliation for these murders equivalent to 50,000 La Belle discotheque bombings, no U.S. pressure to push a resolution through the United Nations denouncing South Africa for supporting terrorism. On the contrary, some of the financial support for RENAMO reportedly came from a slush-fund set up by the United States and Saudi Arabia. A secret CIA base was one of the trans-shipment points for some of the arms going to RENAMO.[40] Abu Nidal may be headquartered in Libya, but RENAMO had an office in Washington at the Heritage Foundation headquarters,[41] and the White House Communications Director, Pat Buchanan, received RENAMO officials in his office in 1987.[42] Needless to say, neither South Africa nor the United States appear on the State Department's list of state sponsors of terrorism.

The United States charged that Qaddafi was responsible for laying mines in the Gulf of Suez in 1984, a potentially terrorist attack on civilian sailors. The U.S. charge is probably true.[43] What is certainly true is that any

Libyan action was preceded by U.S. mine-laying in the harbors of Nicaragua.[44]

The United States currently charges Libya with responsibility for blowing up two civilian airliners in 1988-89. These specific incidents will be discussed below; nevertheless there is other evidence linking Qaddafi to attacks on airliners.[45] But U.S.-backed terrorists have also targeted passenger planes. In Afghanistan, U.S.-armed rebels fired on civilian airliners.[46] The leader of UNITA, another U.S.-supported rebel group, has boasted of shooting down civilian planes.[47] CIA-trained Cuban exiles blew up a Cuban airliner, killing 73; one of the perpetrators later worked for the United States on supplying the Contras.[48] And two of the Sikh terrorists who blew up the Air India flight in 1985 killing 329 people were trained at a mercenary school in Alabama tolerated by the U.S. government. (The school's policy, explained the director, was to allow graduates to "pick their own sides.")[49]

Washington also charged Qaddafi with planning the assassination of foreign leaders. In fact, in late 1981, the Reagan administration announced that there was a Libyan plot to kill the U.S. president and other high officials. The members of the Libyan hit squad listed by the U.S. government consisted of individuals associated with the virulently anti-Libyan Amal Shi'ite organization ("a computer error," officials told *Time* magazine[50]). It turned out that the reports were all disinformation, originating either with the Israelis, or with Manucher Ghorbanifar of Iran-Contra fame, or with CIA chief William Casey himself.[51] Even if the reports had been 100 percent true, however, the reaction was ludicrous. *Time* magazine charged that Qaddafi

> may have launched a frightful new era in modern-day terrorism. To be sure, the 20th century does not lack for examples of political murder. But the threat of assassination of a head of government may now have been elevated by Qaddafi, in an era of worldwide terrorism, to a conscious act of statecraft by a sovereign nation. "For years after World War II, heads of state were considered off-limits to assassination teams," observes Paul Wilkinson, professor of international relations at Aberdeen University, Scotland. "If the reports are true, we are being faced with a sinister new development."[52]

It was as if the eight admitted U.S. plots to assassinate Castro had never been revealed,[53] or Lumumba had never been murdered. But, of course, this sort of comparison between U.S. behavior and that of Qaddafi is deemed inappropriate. As State Department spokesperson Margaret D. Tutwiler said when the United States was caught doing something for which it was self-righteously denouncing Nicaragua, "We don't do comparisons."[54]

There *was* a new development in international politics spawned by U.S.-Libyan relations, though it actually didn't occur until 1986. In April of that year the United States tried to assassinate not just Qaddafi but members of his family. This was quite likely the first recorded instance in modern times in which family members (who neither held government position nor were part of any line of succession) were explicitly targeted. According to Seymour Hersh, "One aide recalls a CIA briefing in which it was argued that 'if you really get at Qaddafi's house—and by extension, his family—you've destroyed an important connection for the people in terms of loyalty.'" Pilots were shown reconnaissance photographs indicating, according to one air force intelligence officer, "where Qaddafi was and where his family was."[55] Only one family member was killed in the attack, Qaddafi's "alleged" adopted daughter, as the press put it, suggesting that perhaps some waif had just wandered through eighteen layers of security guards to take a snooze with the Qaddafi clan.

If terrorism is defined as politically motivated violence perpetrated against non-combatant targets, then one of the most serious incidents of international terrorism of the year was precisely this U.S. raid on Libya. Dozens of civilians were killed in what Washington called a surgical strike, leading a British commentator to remark "if this was a 'surgical strike' I would not care to have my appendix removed by the U.S. Air Force."[56]

The targets that the Pentagon claims it intended to hit in the raids are remarkable for how little they had to do with terrorism. Listed were Qaddafi's barracks in Tripoli and Benghazi (on the grounds that these were the command and control centers for Qaddafi's worldwide terrorist program); a military airfield (where transport planes "used to support Qaddafi's export of terrorism were the primary targets," though of course terrorists, Libyan-sponsored or otherwise, don't use transport planes); another military airfield "not directly related to terrorism"; and a "combat swimmer and naval commando school in the Tripoli area where PLO and other terrorist organization frogmen were trained"—perhaps because the La Belle discotheque bomber swam into Berlin?[57]

Stray Dogs and Foreign Plots

During the first seven years of Qaddafi's rule, although dissent was outlawed, no civilian, so far as is known, was executed in Libya, not even those accused of plotting against the regime. In 1977, the first executions were recorded.[58] By 1980, repression and internal unrest had grown considerably. Additionally, in response to growing opposition among the Libyan exile community, Qaddafi called for these "stray dogs" to be eliminated. Eleven exiles living in Europe were killed in 1980-81 by Libyan agents. These were heinous acts, and countries in which these acts occurred were quite justified in condemning Libya; even the usual rationalization for human rights violations (namely, that they were internal matters) could not be invoked when the crimes were committed on foreign soil. A similar, but failed, assassination attempt against a Libyan exile in the United States was quite properly protested by Washington. Six Libyan diplomats were expelled from the United States and, under Reagan, the Libyan embassy in Washington was ordered closed.[59] But the U.S. reaction was very different when similar assassinations or attempted assassinations were carried out by "friendly" governments.

For example, in 1982 the Reagan administration removed Iraq from its list of nations supporting international terrorism, even though the State Department's human rights report that year noted that "there were creditable reports of government-directed assassinations of Iraqi dissidents in other countries."[60]

According to a 1979 Senate report, U.S. officials were aware that since 1973 Philippine agents had been operating in the United States, infiltrating, monitoring, and possibly using violence against groups of exiles opposed to the rule of Philippine dictator Ferdinand Marcos. On at least one occasion, the CIA blocked an FBI investigation of suspicious activities by Filipino agents.[61] On June 1, 1981, two outspoken anti-Marcos Filipino-American labor activists were murdered in their union hall in Seattle. Prosecutors refused to look for a Marcos link to the killings, and so supporters of the dead unionists had to bring a civil suit for damages against the Philippine and U.S. governments. In January 1990, a Federal court finally determined that Marcos had been behind the slayings, but the judge disallowed on national security grounds any consideration of the U.S. role, specifically its toleration of the Marcos government's intelligence operations and its efforts to hide Marcos's responsibility for the murders.[62] In 1983, a Defense Intelligence Agency document substantiated U.S. awareness of continuing harassment of Filipino dissidents in the United States.[63] No Philippine diplomats were expelled, no embassies were closed, and indeed, U.S. diplomatic and military support for the Marcos regime flourished (until a few years later, when U.S. officials determined that the Philippine dictator had outlived his usefulness).

To take one final example, President Jimmy Carter had declared at the end of 1977 that "no nation on Earth" was closer to the United States in military planning than the Shah's Iran. There was no leader, Carter swooned, with whom he had "a deeper sense of personal gratitude and personal friendship" than with the Shah.[64] Accordingly, when an agent of the Shah's notorious secret police, the SAVAK, was dispatched to kill Iranian exiles in the United States and Paris, not only did Washington fail to break diplomatic relations with Iran, but it tried to hide the facts of the plot (the killer had gotten cold feet and confessed), allowed SAVAK to continue operating in the United States, provided SAVAK with intelligence information gathered by the FBI, and persisted in training SAVAK personnel in the United States.[65]

None of these instances justify Qaddafi's behavior in the least. But they do show that principled opposition to killing dissidents abroad was not behind Washington's pious denunciations of Libyan actions.

Qaddafi has also called for death to be meted out to rulers of many African and Middle Eastern nations and he has organized plots (usually unsuccessful) to overthrow them. But again he has hardly been unique in this regard.

In 1971, Qaddafi cheered a thwarted coup attempt (in which he was not involved) against King Hasan of Morocco. After crushing the Moroccan dissidents, Hasan's top general met with anti-Qaddafi plotters and arranged an assassination attempt on the Libyan leader. The general, however, got greedy and decided to do in Hasan as well. His scheme failed and he was killed, so nothing came of the plot.[66] In 1976, Libya was implicated in an abortive attempt to overthrow President Nimieri of the Sudan, "while Egypt, Saudi Arabia, and Sudan were reportedly undertaking a coordinated effort to topple Qaddafi's regime," according to one authority on Libyan foreign policy.[67] In 1977, Egypt launched an actual, though limited, invasion of Libya.[68] In 1979, an organization in Cairo calling itself the "Revolutionary Council of the Prophet of God" announced that Qaddafi and other Libyan leaders had been sentenced to death.[69] In August 1980, French and Egyptian intelligence initiated an unsuccessful anti-Qaddafi plot.[70] In 1981, Qaddafi and Nimieri each publicly declared that the other should be put to death by his own people.[71] Nimieri also called upon Libya's neighbors to "overthrow or kill" Qaddafi.[72] A Libyan exile in Egypt, Mohammed Youssef Magarieff, set up the National Front for the Salvation of Libya, "dedicated to assassinating Qaddafi and overthrowing his regime." In 1983, Nimieri met with Magarieff in Washington and promised him every form of support short of direct military participation: training facilities, weapons, travel documents, and carte blanche to conduct any type of activity against Libya from Sudan.[73] Opposition Libyan exiles were also receiving support from Morocco, Saudi Arabia, and Iraq.[74] In 1984, an anti-Qaddafi hit squad, trained in Sudan under French direction, was infiltrated into Libya from Tunisia.[75]

The United States, of course, has been involved in organizing coups against countless regimes, in many cases against elected governments,[76] and U.S. plotting targeted Libya well before the air-strikes of 1986. During the Ford administration, the United States gave Egyptian President Anwar Sadat a commitment to deter the Soviet Union from intervening in the event of an Egyptian attack on Libya.[77] The Carter administration withdrew the Ford pledge, fearing the United States would lose control of policy, though journalist John Cooley reports that the CIA encouraged the Egyptian attack on Libya in July 1977.[78] Particularly after Camp David, Washington was concerned that an Egyptian invasion might upset the Israeli-Egyptian rapprochement.[79] U.S. officials did not miss the opportunity to remind Sadat, however, that a major advantage of the Camp David accords would be that Egypt could move its armed forces to the Libyan border.[80]

Under the Reagan administration, the CIA drew up a plan to remove Qaddafi from power. The campaign was to use a combination of disinformation, the creation of a counter-government, and paramilitary operations.[81] Tunisian and Saudi officials told journalist Claudia Wright that they were informed by the Reagan administration that Qaddafi would be eliminated by the end of 1981.[82] Reagan renewed Ford's commitment to deter a Soviet intervention if Egypt went to war against Libya. This was not just a hypothetical arrangement: Egypt and Sudan had specific plans to attack Libyan forces in Chad in October 1981, but Sadat's assassination (unrelated to Qaddafi) aborted the prepared operation.[83]

In February 1983, the United States announced that its swift deployment of naval vessels and AWACs had prevented an impending Libyan attack on the Sudan. Strangely, Egypt stated that there was no such threat and the U.S. forces withdrew the next month.[84] At the Security Council, Washington replied to Libyan charges of provocative U.S. military actions, declaring that "the United States had never engaged and did not now engage in acts of provocation" and that Libyan adventurism had been deterred.[85]

We now know, however, what actually happened. The whole thing was a joint U.S.-Egyptian-Sudanese scheme to entrap Libya. Sudanese undercover agents acting as a pro-Libyan group in Khartoum were to request Libyan air intervention, at which time the Egyptian air force, guided by AWACs and refueled by U.S. planes, would unleash devastating counterattacks on Qaddafi's planes. Egypt's only condition for the plan was that the U.S. role had to be kept secret. Once word leaked out about the movement of the AWACs, the plot had to be aborted.[86]

In 1984, the CIA reported that disaffected elements in the Libyan military "could be spurred to assassination attempts."[87] France planned an operation to assassinate or overthrow Qaddafi, and Washington approved sharing intelligence information with Paris.[88]

The next year, the U.S.-authorized operation "Flower," a program to oust Qaddafi. One of the plan's components, "Tulip," involved U.S. support for Libyan exiles. Another component, "Rose," was to be a preemptive military strike on Libya jointly with U.S. allies, particularly Egypt. Rose called for targeting Qaddafi's barracks, and a speech announcing a strike on Libya was secretly written for the chief flower-child, Ronald Reagan.[89]

U.S. officials made a secret trip to Egypt in mid-1985 to coordinate military operations against Qaddafi.[90] In January 1986 Reagan approved expanded covert efforts to subvert Qaddafi and authorized another high official to travel to Cairo to continue the military planning.[91] This time, however, the investigative reporters of the *Washington Post* found out about the secret mission. National Security Adviser John Poindexter asked the *Post* to kill the story. Here we get to see how the newspaper that had exposed Watergate responded to a plea from the U.S. government to help hide a U.S. plan to violate international law. Editor Ben Bradlee decided that the mission would be mentioned, but in a passing oblique reference down in paragraph five.[92]

By the end of March, various stories had reached the press regarding U.S. military plans against Libya in concert with Egypt. One plan that was described "involved an Egyptian ground attack followed by a request for United States assistance," a pattern "similar to the one in the Suez crisis of 1956...." The semi-official Egyptian newspaper *Al-Ahram* reported that there had been three U.S. efforts to get Egypt to attack Libya, all rejected by Cairo.[93] The U.S. ambassador to Egypt informed Washington, however, that Egyptian leader Mubarak secretly vowed to continue the anti-Libyan military planning with the United States.[94]

So when the La Belle bomb went off on April 4, it was hardly the case that the reluctant warriors in the White House had to be coerced into action. Nor, for that matter, did it take much convincing to bring the Congress along. Only three members of the legislative branch (two of them Republicans) publicly challenged the U.S. air raids.[95] So much for checks and balances.

Those who believe that governments should not plot against other governments will quite properly condemn Qaddafi for his foreign policy. But such condemnations coming from Washington or Cairo are shameless hypocrisy.

An Eye for An Eye

Qaddafi is a great believer not just in an eye for an eye, but in two or more eyes for an eye. Like many other leaders—and many citizens—Qaddafi's gut response to violence, real or perceived, is to respond in kind.

In February 1973, the Israelis shot down a Libyan civilian airliner that had strayed over the Israeli-occupied Sinai, killing over 100 people. Israeli claims that they thought the plane might be intending a terrorist kamikaze attack were not credible, given that the airliner was flying *away* from Israel when it was blasted out of the sky; their assertions that they had provided the airliner's pilot with ample warning were simply false.[96] Qaddafi was—understandably—outraged. Anwar Sadat and former Egyptian Minister of Information Mohamed Heikal claim that in retaliation Qaddafi tried to get an Egyptian submarine which was docked in Tripoli to sink the Queen Elizabeth II loaded with American and other Jews celebrating the 25th anniversary of the founding of the State of Israel. According to the story, Sadat blocked the submarine captain from acting.[97] Despite the obvious hostility of the sources to Qaddafi, the account has a certain plausibility.[98]

If true, the incident betrays a moral thuggery on the part of Qaddafi; notice, however, that the same logic is not generally applied to Israeli "reprisal" raids on refugee camps, where hundreds of civilians are killed for every Israeli victim (in keeping with the Israeli policy of "an eye for an eyelash"[99]); nor to the U.S. raid on Libya, which probably killed in a single day more civilians than the number of U.S. victims of every alleged Libyan terrorist attack of the previous six years.[100] Israeli and U.S. attacks, rather than evoking moral outrage, are usually justified with the racist rationalization that massive retaliation seems to be the only language those Arabs understand.

Qaddafi's penchant for reacting to attacks by upping the ante provided the Reagan administration with a powerful tool. In 1978, Jimmy Carter responded in a restrained way to information that Qaddafi was planning to assassinate the U.S. ambassador in Cairo: he sent Qaddafi a letter telling him he knew of the plan and that he had better cut it out; the plan was called off.[101] (Carter's caution was at least partly out of concern not to upset the Egyptian-Israeli negotiations, the disruption of which was Qaddafi's motivation for the plot in the first place.)

The Reagan administration, on the other hand, came to office determined to restore the U.S. reputation for ruthlessness. What was needed was an enemy that could be easily defeated, that was not too closely allied with Moscow, and whom the American people could hate. Libya seemed like an appropriate candidate. The only problem was that though Americans detested Qaddafi, they weren't necessarily in favor of military action. In 1985-86 the National Security Council conducted secret polls to ascertain when Americans would back an armed confrontation.[102] To build support for a military strike, Qaddafi would have to be provoked into taking some action. A Special National Intelligence Estimate on Libya in 1985 concluded that "Qaddafi would directly target U.S. personnel or installations" if he believed he could get away with it and/or (the document is ambiguous) if he "believed the U.S. was engaging in a direct threat to his person or was actively trying to overthrow his regime."[103]

From its first days in office, the Reagan administration was determined to provoke Qaddafi. In August 1981, the United States sent its naval fleet and air force into waters and airspace claimed by Libya. Washington declared that it was merely asserting its right to use international waters and that the resulting clash with Libyan planes was totally unintended and unexpected. The U.S. position was phony on each count.

Back in 1974 the United States had sent Libya a formal note rejecting Libya's claim to the Gulf of Sidra.[104] Under international law this was sufficient to establish that Washington did not accept the claim; there was no legal necessity for the United States to enforce its note with a naval and air armada.[105] In Reagan's first month in office an intelligence estimate concluded that the "chances for an incident off Libya involving the U.S. are relatively high."[106] Five days before the clash, Libya announced that it intended to hold its own air and naval exercises in the Gulf.[107] Thus the feigned surprise at Libya's response on the part of Reagan administration officials was pure posturing for public consumption.

So too were the assurances that the military maneuvers were non-provocative. "I couldn't consider it a provocation," asserted Defense Secretary Caspar Weinberger, "because they are international waters…."[108] Others were not convinced. The Gulf Cooperation Council—a group of pro-Western oil-producing states—condemned U.S. behavior as a "provocative trap," "medieval piracy on the high seas," and "cowboy politics."[109] Tunisian and Saudi newspapers accused the United States of acting like a bully.[110] And privately, U.S. officials admitted as much: "We went ahead because the principle of the open seas is important," said one high-ranking policymaker, "—and because we wanted to tweak Qaddafi's nose."[111]

U.S. naval maneuvers, noted the director of Yale's Center for International and Area Studies, "featured air attack runs toward Libyan targets with the airplanes veering off just short of national airspace."[112] The United States maintained that such maneuvers were permissible under international law, but in fact the matter is not so clear cut. At least twelve nations claim Air Defense Identification Zones extending many miles over the ocean, within which the actions of foreign aircraft may be restricted. The United States, in fact, was the first nation to proclaim such a zone and its claim is the most extensive.[113] Since 1973, Libya has declared a 100-mile restricted zone around Tripoli.[114] The status of such zones under international law is hazy,[115] but attack runs to the 12-mile limit are unambiguously provocative—and the UN Charter prohibits not just the use of force, but the threat of force as well.

The provocation may have worked. According to a State Department "Chronology of Libyan Support for Terrorism 1980-85," almost every terrorist act attributed to Libya between January 1980 and August 1981, the date of the Gulf of Sidra clash, targeted Libyan exiles.[116] But in October 1981, the United States claims that Qaddafi tried to assassinate the U.S. ambassador to Italy, Maxwell Rabb.[117] And the next month, Washington claimed to uncover a Libyan plot to plant explosives in the American Embassy Club in Khartoum.[118]

The U.S. entrapment scheme of 1983 has already been mentioned. In 1985, the House and Senate intelligence committees approved a CIA plan, authorized by the president, one aim of which was, according to the *Washington Post,* to "lure" Qaddafi "into some foreign adventure or terrorist exploit that would give a growing number of Qaddafi opponents in the Libyan military a chance to seize power, or…give one of Qaddafi's neighbors, such as Algeria or Egypt, a justification for responding to Qaddafi militarily."[119]

In early January 1986, Reagan broke all economic relations with Libya. At a White House meeting, according to one participant, a decision was explicitly reached to provoke Qaddafi by again sending naval vessels and aircraft to the Gulf of Sidra. Any Libyan response would be used to justify military action.[120] For four days in January, U.S. war planes flew in the region covered by Libyan radar. In February, two carrier battle groups and their planes conducted exercises in the same region, though not in waters claimed by Libya.[121]

Then, in March, joined by a third carrier, the U.S. military officers moved across the line drawn by Qaddafi, his "Line of Death." U.S. forces were instructed by the White House to "be disproportionate" in responding to any Libyan action.[122] *Newsweek* and *Time* quoted White House aides confiding that "we wanted to provoke Qaddafi into responding so we could stick it to him, and we knew he would oblige us," that "of course we're aching for a go at Qaddafi," and that if Qaddafi "sticks his head up, we'll clobber him; we're looking for an excuse."[123]

Again, according to the Navy, U.S. air sorties "probed" up to the twelve-mile limit of Libyan territorial waters.[124] But a British radar engineer

who worked for the Libyans has stated: "I watched the planes fly approxi-
mately eight miles into Libyan airspace," adding "I don't think the Libyans
had any choice but to hit back."[125]

The Libyans didn't quite hit back: they fired a couple of missiles that
landed so far from any U.S. targets that the Pentagon was not even sure
what they were aiming at.[126] But this was enough for the United States,
which proceeded to attack Libyan missile sites, sink a patrol boat, and
declare that any Libyan military vessel or plane departing Libyan territorial
waters or airspace would be regarded as hostile. An additional Libyan patrol
boat was sunk "as she entered international waters" and another was
severely damaged.[127] Seventy-two Libyan sailors drowned in the confrontation.[128]

The U.S. Senate and House were virtually unanimous in cheering on
Reagan,[129] not even minding that the administration had seen fit to brief the
Kremlin but not the U.S. Congress.[130] (Poindexter claimed he had intended
to brief congressional leaders, but it had "slipped his mind."[131]) Again, world
opinion was rather less sanguine. The delegate from the pro-western
United Arab Emirates, for example, declared during the Security Council
debate:

> The American maneuvers in the Gulf of Sidra were designed to provoke,
> the attack against Libya was premeditated, the entire action was unlawful,
> illegal and unjustifiable, and the use of force was totally out of proportion
> to the situation. The problem was one of arbitrary use of force by a major
> Power against a small State.[132]

The administration made no secret of what it was hoping the result
of the clash would be. "The question now is what will Qaddafi do to save
his manhood."[133] And the effect of the provocation was precisely what the
United States intended: three weeks after the confrontation, the *Washington Post* quoted a source as stating that intelligence reports now showed
that terrorism was "the clear policy of Tripoli" in place of its previous passive
support or occasional expressions of sympathy with radical Arabs.[134] (In
addition to revealing the effects of U.S. incitement, these comments are a
striking admission that, contrary to U.S. claims, terrorism had not been
Qaddafi's "clear policy" in the past.)

As mentioned above, the evidence linking Qaddafi to the La Belle
bombing is not conclusive. But if Qaddafi *had* been responsible, all that
this would have shown was that with sufficient provocation, Qaddafi could
be pushed into terror. U.S. officials claim that the April air-strikes on Libya
were a success because they deterred Qaddafi from some 35 further acts of
terrorism that he was planning.[135] There is no reason to take this figure

seriously, but if it were true, then it would demonstrate again the effects of U.S. provocation. In 1985, by U.S. count, Libya was responsible for fifteen terrorist acts, almost all of them against Libyan exiles.[136] The only specific acts with non-Libyan victims charged to Libya before April 1986, according to the State Department chronology, were a hijacking of an Egyptian plane by Abu Nidal, which "may have involved Libyan support," and the Rome and Vienna Abu Nidal attacks.[137] By comparison, in 1986 Libya was alleged to have been involved in nineteen incidents.[138]

Immediately following the raids, a Libyan ship launched missiles against a U.S. Coast Guard station on Italy's island of Lampedusa.[139] A U.S. Embassy employee in Khartoum was shot and wounded (the first such attack there since 1973).[140] Attacks in Ankara and Madrid were reportedly foiled.[141] In addition, three hostages in Lebanon, two Britons and an American, were killed in retaliation for the raids.[142]

U.S. officials accused European nations of appeasement for condemning the air-strikes. The Europeans, however, knew who the likely victims of any retaliation would be. According to the *Washington Post,* most U.S. officials "said that any new terrorism almost certainly will occur overseas." Because U.S. embassies were, by that time, well protected, "the chances of staging successful actions will be greater against so-called 'civilian targets.'" Observed one State Department official: "This summer is going to be an open season on Americans in Europe."[143]

In August 1986, U.S. officials met again to consider what they might do about Qaddafi. Reagan, remarking on the Libyan leader's penchant for ostentatious clothing, chuckled, "Why not invite Qaddafi to San Francisco, he likes to dress up so much." Secretary of State Shultz then chimed in, "Why don't we give him AIDS." Everyone laughed.[144]

The plan that these jokers came up with was a program of disinformation against Qaddafi that, U.S. officials acknowledged, might provoke new terrorist acts. False reports of impending Libyan terror were to be fed to the press along with stories of imminent U.S. military moves. The State Department proposed electronic signals deception to make it appear that U.S. planes were flying over the line of death. And U.S.-Egyptian military exercises were conducted in a "particularly provocative manner," according to *Washington Post* sources.[145] Whether any of the terrorist acts in the next months were the fruits of this program is unknown.[146]

U.S. officials proudly announced that the decline in Libyan terrorism in the next few years was attributable to the U.S. strike on Libya. Experts who thought the U.S. raid would provoke more Libyan terrorism "were dead wrong," declared the U.S. Ambassador at Large for Counterterrorism.[147] But U.S. officials ignored inconvenient evidence showing the lack of success of their policies. In mid-1987, when Abu Nidal was ejected from Syria, Washington hailed the event as "a major victory for our counterterrorism policies,"[148] neglecting to point out that he relocated to Libya,[149] which would suggest that the non-terroristic pressures on Syria were more efficacious than the killing of civilians in Libya.

In October and November 1991, Libyans were charged with responsibility for two horrendous terrorist acts. The United States and Britain announced the indictment of two men said to be Libyan intelligence agents for blowing up Pan Am flight 103 over Lockerbie, Scotland, in December 1988, killing 270 people. And France indicted four Libyans for the destruction of a French airliner, UTA 772, over Niger in September 1989, killing 171.

One would think that those who pointed the finger at Libya would be interested in examining the relationship between these crimes and the U.S. provocation campaign against Qaddafi. Most commentators were satisfied to note that the presumed Libyan quiescence after the 1986 U.S. air-strike against Tripoli was actually just Qaddafi being smarter and hiding his hand better.[150] Only William Buckley confronted the issue head-on: the 1986 air-strike, he wrote:

> was justified when undertaken, and unmistakably had the effect desired of cooling down Qaddafi, who limited his frustration to knocking down here and there one passenger plane, American and French. The wave of terror it was widely predicted he would initiate in reaction to the bombing never happened.[151]

More U.S. civilians died "here and there" on these two planes than in every incident of international terrorism of the decade.[152] So if Libya were responsible, it is hard to accept Buckley's reassurance that the 1986 military strike on Libya was an effective way to "cool down" Qaddafi. On the contrary, the 1986 raid may possibly have provoked the plane bombings.

The United States, Britain, and France took the issue of Libyan terrorism to the UN Security Council. It makes perfect sense to have an international body deal with questions of international terrorism. A world of peace and law should not allow acts of terrorism to go unchallenged; nor should it allow the powerful to be the unilateral arbiters of justice. However, the three western states used their disproportionate clout to force through the Security Council resolutions representing their private imperial interests. Their actions cheapened the world body and made it less capable of credibly resolving international disputes.

Resolution 731, passed on January 21, 1992, called on Libya to "provide a full and effective response" to the requests by Washington,

London, and Paris to turn over the 2 Pan Am suspects and cooperate in the French investigation of the UTA downing. The United States has stated that the resolution requires that the Pan Am suspects be turned over to the United States or Britain for trial, though in fact the resolution does not specify how Libya must provide its full and effective response. Given U.S. animus toward Libya and thus the serious doubts that a fair trial would be possible in the United States (see Chapter 8 below for a discussion of Noriega's trial),[153] a reasonable person might well judge an offer by Libya to turn the suspects over to various neutral third parties for trial as a full and effective response. This Libya has offered to do—there have been proposals from Libya, the lawyer for the suspects, or third parties for a trial before the United Nations, the World Court, the Arab League, Malta, Switzerland, or indeed any country except the United States or Britain. Washington has rejected all of these possibilities.[154] As one western official explained, "We won't accept attempts at diversion by accepting some other kind of trial that has no precedent in international law and no credibility in the U.S."[155]—somehow ignoring the fact that it is precisely the U.S. demand that Libyan government officials be tried in the United States which has no precedent in international law.

The Libyan response to the indictments has been "precisely as mandated by international law," commented one specialist.[156] The Arab League took note of the "response, flexibility, and rationality of the Libyan position toward all the initiatives intended to solve the crisis...."[157] But the United States declared the Libyan response unacceptable and, while the World Court was still hearing Libya's appeal, got the Security Council to call for sanctions if Tripoli didn't comply with resolution 731 by April 15, 1992. The Security Council acted despite pleas for a delay from the Arab League, the Organization of Islamic States, and the Maghreb Union.[158] The vote was 10 for and 5 abstentions, just one over the required minimum, with the five Third World states abstaining. China's abstention (a "no" vote would have vetoed the resolution) was reportedly obtained by threatening it with the loss of trade preferences and damaged relations.[159]

Vigorous prosecution of alleged crimes has not always prevailed in disputes between the United States and Libya. A few years earlier, suit was brought in U.S. federal court against the U.S. and British governments on behalf of those who suffered losses in the 1986 U.S. air raid on Libya. The court dismissed the case on the grounds that President Reagan and Prime Minister Thatcher could not be sued for war crimes because they had sovereign immunity. A prominent conservative international lawyer, Anthony D'Amato, noted that under this doctrine there could be no such thing as a war crime at all. An appeals court—all of whose justices had been appointed by Reagan—upheld the decision and further ruled that the plaintiffs had to pay the defendants' court costs for bringing a frivolous suit. As D'Amato commented, "The imposition of sanctions casts a serious chilling effect upon all attorneys who engage in international human rights litigation."[160]

In the Security Council, the United States interpreted resolution 731 as requiring Libya to pay compensation for blowing up the planes.[161] This is quite a remarkable demand: suspects are demanded turned over for trial, yet before the trial is held Libya is told it must acknowledge its guilt by paying compensation. What is all the more striking about this is that there remains considerable doubt as to whether Libya is in fact guilty.

The evidence in the case is extremely complex and much of it has not been made public. The United States claims to have a defector from Libyan intelligence and a diary from one of the suspects. The evidence may yet prove compelling, but the Security Council was pressured into accepting the U.S. judgment before seeing that evidence. And there are some reasons for skepticism regarding the U.S. claims.

For years all investigators believed that a Palestinian group, the Popular Front for the Liberation of Palestine - General Command (PFLP-GC), based in Damascus, was responsible for the Pan Am bombing, done at the behest of Iran in retaliation for the U.S. downing of the Iranian civilian airliner in July 1988 (see Chapter 4). PFLP-GC agents were caught in Germany a few months before the bombing with tape-recorders rigged with explosives, similar to the device that destroyed flight 103. U.S. officials suggest that the PFLP-GC may have passed on the operation to the Libyans after the arrests in Germany, but Washington also claims to have intelligence information showing that a meeting at which the bombings were planned took place in Tripoli a month before the arrests.[162] Some have speculated that maybe Iran funded two cells to carry out the bombing: the PFLP-GC and Libya; but intelligence sources have found no evidence of direct contact between Libya and Iran.[163]

The United States claims that one of the Libyan suspects has been identified by a Maltese shop-owner as the person who bought the clothing in which the lethal tape-recorder was wrapped.[164] But earlier it was reported that ingenious detective work, complete with a positive identification by the same shopkeeper, had established that the clothing had been purchased by a PFLP-GC member arrested in Sweden in May 1989.[165] Washington maintains that the diary of the other suspect—clandestinely obtained—includes entries consistent with a plot to switch airline tags on a bag in Malta that would travel to Frankfurt and then London. The *New York Times* account reported that a diary entry a week before the bombing read: "bring the taggs (sic) from the Airport" (sic by the *Times).*[166] But do Libyan intelligence agents keep diaries of their bombing plots in English? Malta claims that it has been able to confirm that no unaccompanied bag was sent to Frankfurt that day,[167] and an FBI investigator acknowledged in an internal October 1989 report that "there remains the possibility that no luggage was transferred from Air Malta 180 to Pan Am 103."[168]

Israel, the PLO, ABC Senior correspondent Pierre Salinger, and *Time* magazine's Roy Rowan all are skeptical of the Libyan connection.[169] There is some evidence lending credence to alternative hypotheses; for example, the view that the bomb was placed on board in Frankfurt is supported by the fact that Frankfurt baggage handlers failed repeated lie detector tests when asked whether they switched bags.[170] Moreover, a suitcase matching the one that contained the bomb arrived in New York the day after the bombing, having been mysteriously left behind in Frankfurt.[171] On the other hand, there are problems as well with the alternative theories: for example, if flight 103 was blown up to get at the CIA agents aboard in order to protect a drug channel, wouldn't it have been easier to kill them in Beirut?[172]

In short, anyone who claims to know for certain what happened with regard to Pan Am flight 103 is probably lying. This doesn't mean that the facts might not ultimately confirm the U.S. case. But in forcing through sanctions against Libya, the United States has not been pursuing the truth or justice, but its own agenda against Libya. A United Nations that would disinterestedly examine charges of terrorism, whether the terrorist acts were allegedly sponsored by Tripoli or Pretoria or Washington, would be a major contribution to global justice. Unfortunately, the attitude of the Bush administration to such a development was demonstrated when Washington pressured the Chamorro government in Nicaragua to drop its claim for reparations against the United States, imposed by the World Court in response to U.S.-sponsored terrorist acts.[173]

Adventureland

If the U.S. condemnation of Libyan terrorism has been hypocritical, U.S. criticism of Qaddafi for his foreign adventurism has been equally so. Some of the allegations can be dismissed out of hand. For example, one U.S. official charged that the Libyan leader had "provided budgetary support to certain African governments"[174]—hardly a subversive activity. Sometimes neighboring countries—such as the Sudan in October of 1981—have warned of imminent Libyan invasion, but expert testimony before Congress has noted "the palpable absurdity of such claims—their real purpose being to divert attention from the very serious economic and political crises now confronting Nimieri's government, and at the same time gain leverage on U.S. policy-makers."[175]

In 1980, a small group of Libyan-trained Tunisians invaded Tunisia, but U.S. government statements were carefully hedged to acknowledge that Libya may not have been responsible.[176] Qaddafi gave support to the loathsome Idi Amin regime in Uganda, but he certainly has not been the only leader to support established governments that are despicable, and at least Qaddafi has had the decency to apologize for backing Amin,[177] something that Washington has never done with regard to the countless tyrants it has supported. Incidentally, Amin was at first given asylum in Libya, but he was later asked to leave and ended up in Saudi Arabia[178]—a nation denounced in the United States rather less vigorously than Libya.

The most serious charge regarding Libyan intervention in the affairs of another nation involves Chad, and here there is no doubt that Qaddafi has behaved in an imperial manner. But the story casts little credit on two other imperial nations, the United States and France.

France had granted independence to Chad in 1960, but French troops were frequently called on to defend the oppressive government against its domestic foes.[179] When Qaddafi took power in Libya in 1969, the first coup attempt against him came from Chadian territory.[180] In 1971, the Libyan leader supported an unsuccessful coup in Chad, whereupon the latter broke diplomatic relations, invited anti-Qaddafi groups to base themselves in the Chadian capital, and claimed the Fezzan region of Libya. Qaddafi retaliated by officially recognizing the rebel organization in northern Chad, FROLINAT, and providing it with training camps.[181]

In 1972 the two nations re-established relations. Apparently there was also a secret understanding allowing Libya to occupy a contested sliver of territory between the two countries known as the Aouzou strip.[182] Whether the Chadian leader was paid off for this territorial adjustment is unknown, but Libya did proceed to occupy the strip and no protest was raised.[183] Libya's claim to Aouzou was not invented out of whole cloth. In 1935, the colonial rulers, France and fascist Italy, had agreed that the strip should be made part of Libya. The agreement, however, was never ratified by the French parliament. Libyans considered the territory theirs, and in the 1950s King Idris sent a motorized column to try to take it from the French.[184]

In March 1979, despite support from French troops, the Chadian government collapsed. With Nigerian mediation, a Transitional Government of National Unity was established and endorsed by the Organization of African Unity (OAU). Goukouni Oueddei and Hissene Habré—leaders of two FROLINAT factions—were made president and defense minister, respectively. Habré, however, with Egyptian and Sudanese help,[185] tried to take total power for himself. Finding himself threatened, Goukouni signed a defense pact with Libya and in October, 1980, Libyan troops entered the country in support of the recognized head of the government.

There has been an effort to disguise the fact that Libyan intervention at this time came at the request of a duly constituted government. The consistent anti-interventionist, of course, will oppose the sending of troops to participate in internal conflicts regardless of who does the inviting, but this has not been the U.S. position with respect to French troops in Chad and in many other African nations.[186] And, needless to say, even an invitation has not been an essential requirement for U.S. interventions, as in Grenada and Panama.

On October 30, 1981, Goukouni—having been promised an OAU peace-keeping force and French aid—asked the Libyan forces to leave Chad. Four days later, Qaddafi agreed. Given a deadline of December 31, Libyan troops actually were out of Chad (though not the Aouzou strip) within two weeks.[187]

The United States provided some of the funding for the OAU peace-keeping force, but covertly was doing everything possible to subvert the government of Chad. Beginning in early 1981, the Reagan administration had started providing arms to Habré's forces which were regrouping in Sudan. Additional support was being provided by Egypt, Morocco, and France.[188] Significantly, even after Libyan forces withdrew from Chad, U.S. aid to Habré continued.[189] Habré proceeded to march into the country, maneuver around the OAU peace-keepers who wanted to avoid combat, and take over the government.

Thus, Washington worked to undermine the recognized government of Chad, despite the fact that Libyan troops had gone. This may seem bizarre, given that the United States was also funding the peace-keeping force, but there was perhaps method to this madness. The U.S. funding was far less than originally considered necessary to support a seven-nation force; the United States provided only enough for the logistical support for Zairian and Nigerian units.[190] And Zaire, whose corrupt ruler had close ties to Washington, had no intention of providing a truly neutral peace-keeping force, let alone one committed to the recognized government of Chad. As Zairian officials admitted, they were aiding Habré all along.[191]

In June 1983, Goukouni tried to make a comeback. His forces, assisted by Libyan troops, moved into northern Chad. (This was the first major Libyan deployment without the request of the Chadian government.) French and Zairian troops came to Habré's aid, and the United States provided military equipment, a few advisers, and AWACs guidance for

French aircraft.[192] In 1984, Libya and France agreed to withdraw their troops, but Libya, having been burned in 1981, apparently did not keep its side of the bargain. In early 1986, French troops returned to southern Chad and there was a de facto partition of the country. At the end of the year, however, Qaddafi and Goukouni had a falling out, whereupon the Libyans found themselves opposed by all Chadian factions. The Libyans were promptly routed by the Chadians, who were aided by new U.S. military aid, French air cover, French special forces and advisers,[193] and U.S. and French intelligence.[194]

Paris would not, however, provide air cover for a Chadian attack on the Aouzou strip, believing that the status of the territory should be determined by peaceful means. Washington, on the other hand, was enthusiastic about aiding Chad's efforts to retake the disputed strip.[195] Using as a pretext an alleged Libyan attack (that French sources consider to have been a complete fabrication), Habré seized Aouzou.[196] Libya retook it a few weeks later and a Chadian ground unit attacked an air base 60 miles inside Libya.[197] U.S. officials denied that they had advised Habré to go north, but they refused to criticize the cross-border raid.[198]

At the end of 1988 the CIA organized 600 Libyans who had been captured in Chad into a commando force to overthrow Qaddafi. In December 1990 another Chadian insurgent overthrew Habré and the CIA commandos were told to leave. Two hundred and fifty of them chose to return to Libya; Kenya was bribed with military aid to accept the other 350, with U.S. officials falsely claiming the money was granted because of Kenya's improved human rights record, which in fact had not changed at all.[199]

To repeat, Libya's behavior with respect to Chad has been reprehensible. But criticism coming from Washington is extremely hypocritical. More generally, Qaddafi has engaged in many shameful actions. But the motives of U.S. officials who condemn Qaddafi are well revealed by their distortions of the record, their exaggerations of his crimes, and their willful neglect of the far more serious crimes that the United States has committed, supported, or tolerated. Moreover, many of Qaddafi's egregious actions were themselves provoked—and knowingly provoked—by U.S. policies.

Qaddafi is one of the foreign devils who will be used to rationalize U.S. intervention in the new, post-Cold War world. The real devils, however, and the real sources of Washington's interventionism, are to be found in the structures of U.S. society.

Chapter 8

Drugs and U.S. Foreign Policy

Eager to justify the Pentagon budget, Defense Secretary Dick Cheney warned in his January 1990 annual report that the United States had to be prepared for—among other dangers—the growing threat of narcotics trafficking.[1] This might seem like a relatively minor foreign policy issue, but Cheney was in fact tapping into a real public concern. Before the Iraqi invasion of Kuwait, polls showed that two-thirds of the U.S. population rated drugs the most serious issue facing the country.[2]

There is no doubt that the drug problem is taking a terrible toll on the American people, particularly in the inner cities. But there is a great deal of doubt whether the Bush administration's war on drugs is the way to deal with the problem. Indeed, the foreign policy of the drug war is fundamentally rooted in hypocrisy.

Merchants of Death

Illegal narcotics are far from the only harmful substances pushed on innocent victims around the world. U.S. firms have exported to the Third World vast quantities of pesticides that have been banned for use in the United States. One government study found that 30 percent of U.S. pesticide exports were not approved by the Environmental Protection Agency for use in this country, and one-fifth had actually had their approval canceled or suspended by the EPA. Ironically, food products grown in the Third World with the aid of these unsafe pesticides are then imported into the United States. The Food and Drug Administration estimated that some 5 percent of U.S. food imports contained illegal pesticide residues, a figure likely to underestimate the threat to U.S. consumers' health given that there were more than 170 pesticides for which the FDA didn't test.[3] This "circle of poison"—in which harmful U.S. pesticides show up on the American dinner table—finally moved liberals in Congress to act in 1990. They tried to amend a farm bill to include a ban on the export of pesticides not approved for use in the United States. Chemical companies argued that since the FDA inspected so little of the food entering the United States,

foreign farmers would simply buy the banned pesticides from manufacturers in other countries, costing U.S. jobs. The amendment did not make it
into the final bill.[4]

An even bigger trade in dangerous substances is the export of unsafe
medicinal drugs to the Third World. Pharmaceutical companies, of course,
try to make a profit everywhere, and they push drugs that have serious
side-effects in any country they can. For example, Hoffman-La Roche
marketed the sedative Versed in the United States, which (according to
internal company documents) was known to be unsafe; and Upjohn, the
manufacturer of the sleeping pill Halcion, has been charged with hiding
evidence of the drug's dangers.[5] But it is in the Third World, with their
weaker regulatory structures, where the multinational drug companies
have run rampant. Drugs that in the United States are banned or severely
restricted have been pushed on poor countries by U.S. firms.[6] The pain-
killer Dipyrone, for example, sometimes causes severe hemorrhaging, yet
it has been advertised in Mexico for the relief of menstrual pain. In 1977
the drug was banned in the United States even for the terminally ill, yet it
continued to be sold by U.S. and other firms in Malaysia and Singapore for
the treatment of headache and flu.[7] More generally, the warnings and
contra-indications routinely distributed with prescription drugs in the
United States are sanitized or omitted entirely when U.S. firms sell their
products in the Third World.[8]

The pharmaceutical companies claim they are doing nothing illegal.
Prescription drug laws and regulations in the Third World do tend to be
relatively weak, but some countries have laws requiring disclosure of drug
hazards and contra-indications; the laws may not be enforced, but they are
on the books and the U.S. firms are often in violation of them.[9] Most Latin
American countries now have laws allowing the sale of imported drugs only
if the drugs are approved for marketing in the country of origin. But U.S.
firms have gotten around this requirement by setting up plants to produce
(or put the finishing touches on) the drug in some third country which has
no restrictions so that this third country can be counted as the country of
origin.[10]

U.S. drug marketing has also been helped along by lavish bribery. In
1976, 22 U.S. pharmaceutical and health product companies reported
making more than $30 million in what were delicately termed "questionable
overseas payments."[11] In 1977 a U.S. law made it illegal for U.S. firms to
bribe foreign officials, but there is no reason to suspect that such payments
have ended. In any case, it is still legal under U.S. law to bribe foreign
doctors,[12] and this is widely done. A Nigerian expert estimated that perhaps
one-third of the total wholesale cost of all prescription drugs went for bribes

and graft, and in other parts of Africa the situation may be even worse.[13] A television documentary in the Philippines revealed that a multinational drug firm in that country ran seminars for doctors complete with prostitutes and pornographic films to entertain the physicians at night.[14]

Modern medicine undoubtedly is beneficial, but each year at least one million people in the Third World die from adverse reactions to medical drugs. Some of these deaths are the inevitable result of the primitive state of our medical knowledge, but many must be attributed to the reckless marketing practices of multinational firms, practices tolerated by the U.S. government.[15]

Another million Third World citizens—these exclusively children—are estimated to have died each year from malnutrition and diarrhea resulting from the use of infant formula.[16] Experts agree that mother's milk is by far the healthiest food for infants, particularly in poor countries where nutritional deficits are common. Human milk is also the cheapest source of nutrients. Mothers who bottle feed are frequently forced by financial hardship to dilute the formula with water, often contaminated, with grim results. The international companies that sell infant formula don't make money when mothers breast-feed, and so they have invested heavily in encouraging Third World women to switch to formula. Among the marketing techniques favored by the companies for securing their multi-billion dollar market have been slick advertising campaigns associating bottle-feeding with modernity, free samples given out in hospitals (if the mother can be kept from breast-feeding long enough, her milk will dry up), and the use of "milk nurses," employees of the infant-formula firms disguised as health professionals.[17]

The dominant firm in the Third World infant-formula business has been the Swiss-based Nestlé company, but three U.S. corporations have also been major exporters of the product and have engaged in hard-sell marketing.[18] An international consumer boycott of Nestlé products helped to mobilize public opinion, and in May 1981 the World Health Organization voted to adopt a non-binding code restricting the promotion of infant-formula products. The code prohibited giving free samples to pregnant women, having salespeople contact mothers, and advertising infant formula to the general public (as opposed to doctors). The vote was 118-1. The lone dissenting vote was that of the United States. The State Department's Elliott Abrams explained that the U.S. government considered the code to violate First Amendment guarantees of free speech.[19]

Narco-traffickers

There are other lethal exports. The United States, for example, has become the major source for assault weapons used by drug cartels in Central and South America. High-powered weaponry purchased under the lax gun-control laws in force in Miami are smuggled to drug gangs in countries like Brazil, where the laws are far more stringent.[20] Even more harmful than weapons, pesticides, prescription drugs, and infant formula, however, has been the trade in tobacco. Some two and a half million people die worldwide each year from the health effects of smoking, accounting for perhaps 5 percent of all deaths.[21] In addition, tobacco growing has added to the problems of deforestation and global warming and, by replacing edible crops on scarce arable land, has driven up food costs in the Third World.[22]

The global tobacco epidemic is not simply the result of people choosing to smoke. It is an epidemic driven by the unparalleled greed of tobacco companies. Many nations have domestic, government-owned tobacco monopolies, but six giant transnational corporations—four of them U.S.-based—dominate the international trade in tobacco products.[23] These firms use every stratagem of modern advertising to sell their lethal product and have been able to enlist the help of the U.S. government in pushing their drug.

Dope pushers are well aware that the best time to hook addicts is when they're young. As U.S. Assistant Secretary of Health James Mason put it: "Anyone who thinks cigarette makers aren't after the youth market—in America or worldwide—must live in a cave."[24] Thus, in the United States, cigarette companies advertise in such magazines as *Sports Illustrated, Rolling Stone, TV Guide,* and *Glamour* with their large teenaged readerships; give out free magazines full of cigarette ads in movie theaters; pay to get their products shown in movies like "Superman"; feature cartoon camels; offer cartoon posters; and sponsor countless sporting events.[25] Smoking, however, has been on the decline in the United States, and to make up for their diminishing domestic market, the U.S. cigarette companies have been expanding overseas. In the developing countries particularly, smoking has been on the increase, "fueled mainly," as the World Health Organization noted in January 1986, "by intensive and ruthless promotional campaigns on the part of the transnational tobacco companies."[26]

In Kenya, Guatemala, and Mexico children wear Marlboro clothing.[27] In Thailand, cigarette logos have appeared on kites, t-shirts, pants, notebooks, earrings, and chewing gum packages.[28] In Japan, attractive young women are hired to give out free Larks on the streets[29] and U.S. firms have dominated the TV advertisements, many of which have been shown during children's programs.[30] In South Korea, U.S. companies have held promotional beach concerts.[31] And in Taiwan, U.S. transnationals have distributed free cigarettes at discos and nightclubs frequented by young people.[32] In February 1988, R.J. Reynolds sponsored a rock concert in Taipei featuring Hong Kong teen-idol Hsow-Yu Chang, with admission offered only in exchange for five empty packs of Winstons (ten for a souvenir sweat shirt).[33]

One tobacco marketing executive explained:

> Nobody is stupid enough to put it in writing, or even in words, but there is always the presumption that your marketing approach should contain some element of market expansion and market expansion in this industry means two things, kids and women. I think that governs the thinking of all the companies.[34]

In countries where women's smoking rates have traditionally been very low, aggressive marketing by U.S. firms has been especially pernicious. In Hong Kong, where only 1 percent of women under 40 smoke, Philip Morris recently launched Virginia Slims with a flood of "women's liberation" ads.[35] Despite rules and voluntary industry codes in Japan prohibiting the targeting of women in cigarette ads, U.S. companies have run TV commercials aimed at women and one company placed a billboard outside the entrance to a Tokyo women's college.[36]

Many countries have laws banning cigarette ads, but the tobacco companies are rarely bound by such legal niceties. In Thailand, a cabinet resolution prohibited all cigarette ads, but the U.S. firms refused to comply, claiming that a cabinet resolution was not a law. When an official law was passed in February 1989, the U.S. companies continued to advertise.[37] In Malaysia and China, where cigarette advertising is banned, ads appear for trips to "Marlboro country," illustrated with scenes of the Marlboro man riding around, though without a cigarette in his mouth.[38]

The tobacco companies are not content to push their products by themselves. To help them in the task, they have recruited—or, more precisely, bought through their campaign contributions—the U.S. government. On the domestic front, the cigarette lobby has been able to chalk up such accomplishments as getting the U.S. taxpayer to subsidize the growing of tobacco leaf or getting Congress to delete funds from the federal budget for anti-smoking education programs in the schools.[39] But the government has also given powerful support to the cigarette companies in their overseas efforts.

It must be emphasized that Washington's exertions on behalf of the tobacco companies has not been for lack of knowledge of the adverse health effects of cigarettes. As far back as the mid-'50s a Virginia Senator wrote to the State Department urging its help in preventing foreign nations from imposing tariffs that would hurt the U.S. tobacco industry, already imperiled as it was by "the rapid increase in lung cancer" that "has cast a cloud upon cigarette smoking as a possible contributing, if not a major, factor in that dread disease."[40]

In 1954, tobacco was included in the U.S. Food for Peace program, under which the government would buy domestic crops and distribute them abroad in an effort to win friends for the Pentagon and win markets for U.S. agriculture. Over the next 25 years, almost $1 billion in tobacco exports were financed through this program.[41] In the early 1960s, the Agriculture Department spent hundreds of thousands of dollars to advertise cigarettes overseas, including the production of a 23-minute promotional color movie called "The World of Pleasure" designed for free foreign distribution.[42] Other federally-funded market development programs continue to assist the export of U.S. tobacco products.[43] In the current year, the Agriculture Department is providing $3.5 million to promote the foreign sale of U.S. tobacco leaf.[44]

During the Carter administration, Secretary of Health, Education, and Welfare Joseph Califano became a vigorous critic of smoking. Among other actions, he asked cigarette companies to devote 10 percent of their advertising budget to a campaign to discourage children and teenagers from smoking, an idea rejected by the companies on the grounds that "the mothers and fathers of this nation, whether smokers or non-smokers, should continue to have freedom of choice in the education and training of their children."[45] Warned that Califano's position was going to cost him political support in North Carolina, Carter went on the stump, joined by his Commerce Secretary Juanita Kreps (a director of R.J. Reynolds), to sing the praises of the tobacco industry. In 1979 Carter fired Califano.[46] During the 1980 presidential campaign, Reagan sent a letter to tobacco farmers declaring:

> Tobacco—no less than corn, wheat, or soybeans—should be viewed as a valuable cash crop with an important role to play in restoring America's balance of trade. I can guarantee that my own Cabinet members will be far too busy with substantive matters to waste their time proselytizing the dangers of cigarette smoking.[47]

Indeed, Reagan administration officials were able to find the time to actively promote the export of cigarettes. Many East Asian nations prohib-

ited the importation and advertising of foreign cigarettes, leaving all tobacco sales to government-run monopolies which did minimal advertising.
In 1985, Reagan directed the U.S. Trade Representative to coerce Japan,
under threat of trade retaliation, to open its market to U.S. cigarettes,
including the right to advertise. (Such actions by the Trade Representative
actually began under Carter, when Japan was pressed in 1979 to remove
restrictions on the sale and advertising of U.S. cigar and pipe tobacco.) The
Trade Representative brought similar pressure on behalf of U.S. cigarettes
against Taiwan in 1986, South Korea in 1988, and Thailand in 1989.[48]

The impact was seen almost immediately. In Japan, cigarette ads rose
from fortieth to second place in total television air time by 1987, and
two-thirds of the ads were for U.S. brands.[49] As U.S. companies went after
Japanese women and teenagers, the government tobacco firm responded
with its own products appealing to these same groups.[50] Japan had had a
20-year decline in smoking rates, but there was a 3 percent increase after
U.S. companies entered the market.[51] In Taiwan and South Korea, a similar
pattern was seen—U.S. pressure to remove restrictions on advertising, U.S.
insistence that print ads be allowed to appear without the Surgeon
General's health warnings, U.S. cigarettes becoming one of the most heavily
advertised products—with an attendant increase in cigarette consumption.[52]

Threats of trade retaliation from the U.S. Trade Representative were
supplemented by lobbying efforts from private citizens who had served in
the Reagan administration: Michael Deaver, Richard Allen, and Alexander
Haig. Additional threats were delivered by Senator Jesse Helms and other
U.S. legislators.[53]

The profits from this narco-trafficking have been immense. In 1986,
the United States exported 64 billion cigarettes; by 1989, the figure was 142
billion. Fifty-five percent of the increase was attributable to imports by
Japan, Taiwan, and South Korea.[54] Philip Morris had $1 billion in overseas
sales in 1986, which grew to $8 billion four years later.[55] Tobacco and
tobacco products produced a trade surplus in 1989 of $4.3 billion, up from
$2 billion in 1986.[56]

At an international conference on Tobacco and Health held in Australia in April 1990, a resolution was approved urging nations not to use
trade leverage to compel other nations to repeal restrictions on the sale,
import, or advertising of tobacco products; the United States was specifically called upon "to cease pro-tobacco trade actions against Thailand and
other countries."[57] The U.S. Assistant Secretary of Health James Mason told
the conference that it was "unconscionable for the mighty transnational
tobacco companies...to be peddling their poison abroad."[58] But by the next

month the Department of Health and Human Services had backed away from its criticisms of efforts to open markets for U.S. cigarettes around the world, and HHS Secretary Louis Sullivan refused to allow Mason to testify before Congress on the issue of tobacco exports.[59] The administration position on the issue was ably put by Vice-President Dan Quayle: "Tobacco exports should be expanded aggressively because Americans are smoking less."[60] C. Everett Koop, Reagan's Surgeon General, expressed a different view after he left office:

> At a time when we are pleading with foreign governments to stop the export of cocaine, it is the height of hypocrisy for the United States to export tobacco. Consider these figures. Last year [1988] in the United States, 2,000 people died from cocaine. In that same year, cigarettes killed 390,000 people.[61]

He urged U.S. citizens to refuse to tolerate the export of "disease, disability and death."[62]

The Washington Connection

Koop, however, understated U.S. hypocrisy. It is not that Washington has been consistently fighting the cocaine and heroin trade while pushing nicotine. It has in fact given support to and cooperated with the illicit drug traffickers when doing so would help other U.S. foreign policy goals, particularly its global crusade against indigenous nationalist and Left forces.

This sordid history has been meticulously documented by Alfred McCoy. In 1947 and again in 1950, the CIA provided arms and money to the Corsican syndicates who controlled the heroin trade in Marseilles. The gangsters were paid to break strikes by Communist-led unions. Washington claimed to see a threatened Communist attempt to take over the French government, but in fact the State Department was secretly reporting that Communist leaders "could no longer hold back the discontent of the rank and file" in the face of wages that were lower than during the depths of the Depression. With U.S. backing, the syndicates came to dominate Marseilles, and from 1948 to 1972 they were responsible for 80 percent of the heroin entering the United States.[63]

U.S. involvement with drug dealers was far more extensive in Southeast Asia. Beginning in 1950, remnants of Chiang Kai-shek's Kuomintang army in Burma were organized by the CIA to conduct raids into China. These KMT units supported themselves by appropriating the opium harvest that grew in the Burmese highlands and shipping it to northern Thailand.

There it was purchased by Thai General Phao Siyanan. The KMT units remained in Burma with U.S. support until 1961 when they moved into Laos and Thailand, still in control of the opium traffic.[64] General Phao was head of the Thai police and the CIA's most important Thai client. The CIA provided him with naval vessels, armored vehicles, aircraft, and hundreds of overt and covert advisers; in 1954 he was awarded the Legion of Merit for "exceptionally meritorious service" by the U.S. Secretary of the Army. His police force was also the largest opium trafficking syndicate in Thailand.[65]

When the French controlled Indochina, their intelligence agencies participated in the opium trade in order to fund covert operations.[66] When Washington replaced the French in 1954, it installed its own puppet, Ngo Dinh Diem, who for three years cracked down on the opium trade. By 1958, however, in the face of growing insurgency in southern Vietnam, the opium trade was revived by Diem's brother Nhu, head of the secret police, as a way to finance counter-insurgency operations.[67]

In neighboring Laos, leading rightist politicians whom the United States backed against the leftist Pathet Lao and often against neutralists as well were key figures in the drug trade.[68] In 1960, the CIA began organizing a secret army among the Hmong tribespeople which, at its peak, numbered some 30,000 guerrillas under General Vang Pao. The Hmong's main cash crop was opium, so to keep its anti-communist army in business, the United States first winked at the opium trade and then in the late 1960s provided CIA aircraft—Air America—to carry the opium to market. The proceeds from the opium gave Vang Pao the clout to round up from the war-weary and impoverished Hmong villagers the young boys who made up his army.[69]

Through the mid-'60s, most of the opium grown in Southeast Asia was consumed locally. But with the huge build-up of U.S. forces in Vietnam, shrewd entrepreneurs realized the extraordinary market provided by these soldiers from the wealthy United States. Heroin laboratories sprang up in Burma and Laos, many of them in areas controlled by paramilitary groups at one time or another supported by the CIA. Hmong army commander General Vang Pao was reported by the U.S. Bureau of Narcotics to be operating a heroin lab at Long Tien, the CIA's headquarters for covert operations in Laos. By 1971, some 10 to 15 percent of GI's were using high purity heroin. In South Vietnam the heroin traffic was controlled by three groups associated with the key political figures in the country: the air force, especially its transport wing, under Vice-President Nguyen Cao Ky; the civil bureaucracy under Premier Tran Thien Khiem; and the army, navy, and National Assembly which answered to President Nguyen Van Thieu.[70] Both

Thieu and Ky financed their 1971 election campaigns from the drug trade. Thieu won the election and by 1973 the South Vietnamese army was responsible for distributing heroin to U.S. troops.[71] Primed by the GI market, Southeast Asia became the leading source for the world's illicit opium.

U.S. officials knew what their allies were doing and covered up for them. In an internal report the CIA's inspector general explained how the agency got involved in the drug trade: "The war has clearly been our overriding priority in Southeast Asia, and all other issues have taken second place in the scheme of things."[72]

A decade later Washington repeated its policy of complicity with drug traffickers, this time in South*west* Asia. Even before the Soviet invasion of Afghanistan, the Carter administration had been providing covert assistance to Afghan guerrilla groups battling the pro-Moscow central government. U.S. aid grew rapidly after Soviet troops entered the country at the end of 1979 and the aid was concentrated on those mujaheddin units recommended by Pakistani intelligence. Washington's favored recipient became Gulbuddin Hekmatyar, who headed a guerrilla force that had been created by the Pakistani military to invade Afghanistan in 1975. Hekmatyar himself had earlier organized a fundamentalist group in Afghanistan whose activities included throwing vials of acid into the faces of female Afghani students who refused to wear veils; in Pakistan he had been associated with a fundamentalist and quasi-fascist political party. Hekmatyar was brutal and corrupt, terrorizing refugees to support him. He also used his U.S.-supplied arms to become Afghanistan's number one heroin trafficker.[73] By the mid-1980s, Afghanistan was the largest single exporter of opium in the world and the source for half of the heroin consumed in the United States. In 1988, there were 100 to 200 heroin refineries in the single Pakistani district bordering Afghanistan.[74]

A White House drug adviser recalled warning in 1979 that "we were going into Afghanistan to support the opium growers in their rebellion against the Soviets. Shouldn't we try to avoid what we had done in Laos?" He was ignored.[75] In 1983, an official of the Drug Enforcement Administration (DEA) returned from a fact-finding trip to Southwest Asia reporting, "You can say the rebels make their money off the sale of opium." He added, "There's no doubt about it. The rebels kept their cause going through the sale of opium."[76] The reaction of the Reagan administration to this revelation was to continue supporting the drug dealers, both in Afghanistan and Pakistan. The *New York Times* reported in 1988 that "The Reagan administration has done little to press the guerrillas to curb the drug trade, according to senior State Department and intelligence analysts."

"We're not going to let a little thing like drugs get in the way of the political situation," said an administration official who follows Afghanistan closely, emphasizing that narcotics are relatively a minor issue in the context of policy toward the Afghan guerrillas.[77]

Contra-Indications

Also during the 1980s, Washington was working with other drug traffickers closer to home, in this case as a way to facilitate the war of the U.S.-created and controlled Contras against the Sandinista government in Nicaragua. The Contra war was one of the few foreign policy issues during the Reagan years to which the Democrats occasionally offered some resistance, and Senator John Kerry's subcommittee on Terrorism, Narcotics, and International Operations did more digging into the unsavory alliances surrounding U.S. Nicaragua policy than was usual for the Congress. On the basis of extensive testimony and documentary evidence, the subcommittee reported:

> it is clear that individuals who provided support for the Contras were involved in drug trafficking, the supply network of the Contras was used by drug-trafficking organizations, and elements of the Contras themselves knowingly received financial and material assistance from drug traffickers. In each case, one or another agency of the U.S. government had information regarding the involvement either while it was occurring, or immediately thereafter.
>
> The Subcommittee found that the Contra drug links included:
> * Involvement in narcotics trafficking by individuals associated with the Contra movement.
> * Participation of narcotics traffickers in Contra supply operations through business relationships with Contra organizations.
> * Provision of assistance to the Contras by narcotics traffickers, including cash, weapons, planes, pilots, air supply services and other materials, on a voluntary basis by the traffickers.
> * Payments to drug traffickers by the U.S. State Department of funds authorized by the Congress for humanitarian assistance to the Contras, in some cases after the traffickers had been indicted by Federal law enforcement agencies on drug charges, in others while traffickers were under active investigation by these same agencies.[78]

The role of the United States in this Contra link to narco-traffickers remains murky, but there is no doubt that U.S. officials knew about it, winked at it, and helped to cover it up. Oliver North's notebook and memos from North's assistant, Robert Owen, contain references to the drug connection.[79] When the General Accounting Office decided to look into the issue of drugs and foreign policy, the White House ordered the CIA and the Defense and State Departments not to cooperate.[80] Attorney General Ed Meese told the U.S. Attorney in Miami to suspend his inquiry into drug trafficking in Central America.[81] And the indictment against a major drug smuggler, Michael Palmer, was dropped as "not being in the interest of the United States."[82]

The Honduran military was a major U.S. ally in its war against Nicaragua. "Without the support of the Honduran military, there would have been no such thing as the Contras," acknowledged a former high-ranking U.S. diplomat.[83] The Contras used Honduras as their northern base and worked with Honduran death squads set up by Argentine and CIA advisers.[84] The Honduran military was also a key participant in the narcotics trade, and the country became a significant transshipment point for drugs headed to the United States.[85] The response of Washington to Honduras's growing role in the drug trade was to close down the DEA station in Tegucigalpa in 1983, just two years after it opened, ensuring that no evidence could be produced linking the military to narco-trafficking.[86] In 1986, Honduran General José Bueso-Rosa was arrested in the United States by the FBI in a plot to assassinate the Honduran president in order to facilitate drug trafficking. The Justice Department called the plot "the most significant case of narco-terrorism yet discovered." Key administration officials, however, privately urged that Bueso-Rosa receive a lenient sentence because, as a deputy assistant secretary of state later explained, "He has been a friend to the U.S....involved in helping us with the Contras."[87]

On the southern front of the anti-Sandinista war, a key figure was John Hull, an American rancher who owned property on the Nicaraguan border and who was paid $10,000 a month by the Contra command at the direction of Oliver North. Five different witnesses told Kerry's subcommittee that Hull was involved in drug trafficking,[88] and the Costa Rican government has been trying, despite U.S. obstructionism, to investigate Hull's activities.[89]

Gen. Paul F. Gorman, former head of U.S. Southern Command acknowledged that "if you want to go into the subversion business, collect intelligence and move arms," you have to deal with drug traffickers.[90] One of the "transport" firms that the United States hired to get supplies to the Contras was an outfit that Customs had earlier reported had been set up by narcotics traffickers linked to Ramon Matta Ballesteros, a major drug figure among whose other credits was involvement in the killing of a DEA agent in Mexico. Only after the situation was revealed in the *New York Times* did Washington try to bring Matta to justice.[91] The Kerry subcommittee identified four companies owned and operated by narcotics traffickers who were hired by the State Department to supply the Contras. "In each case, prior to the time that the State Department entered into contracts with the company, federal law enforcement had received information that the individuals controlling these companies were involved in narcotics."[92]

The subcommittee reported that although there was "substantial evidence of drug smuggling through the war zones on the part of individual Contras, Contra suppliers, Contra pilots, mercenaries who worked with the Contras, and Contra supporters throughout the region," it "did not find that the Contra leaders personally were involved in drug trafficking."[93] This conclusion, however, represents a considerable sanitizing of the actual evidence gathered by the subcommittee. As Kerry himself put it in a closed session statement, later released: "It is clear that there is a networking of drug trafficking through the contras, and it goes right up to Calero, Mario Calero, Adolpho Calero, Enrique Bermudez. And we have people who will so testify and who have." And, presumably, the evidence would have been even stronger had higher-ups not called off a government sting operation against Bermudez, the Contra commander.[94]

The Invasion of Panama

The U.S. invasion of Panama in December 1989 was the first military intervention in modern times rationalized primarily as an effort to bring a drug trafficker to justice. But neither the drug pretext nor the other justifications advanced by U.S. propagandists were the real reasons for this, the twentieth U.S. intervention in the isthmus since the turn of the century.[95] The invasion was actually motivated by the particular needs of the Bush administration and the national security apparatus.

For George Bush, Panamanian General Manuel Noriega was a special problem. When Noriega was indicted on drug charges in early 1988, Vice-President Bush was vulnerable to the charge that he had previously ignored the Panamanian's wrongdoing. The issue was raised by Michael Dukakis in the 1988 election campaign. When economic sanctions and covert operations (some secretly funded by Panamanian government funds held in escrow by the United States) failed to dislodge Noriega, it seemed as if the General was thumbing his nose at the U.S. president. Then, when Bush failed to support a coup attempt against Noriega in October 1989 Bush was roundly denounced in the press and in Congress as being a wimp, with Democrats playing a leading role in the criticism. "It's hard to imagine Lyndon Johnson or Ronald Reagan hesitating," said one; Bush "makes

Jimmy Carter look like a man of resolve," declared another. For the Bush administration, then, invading Panama was a way to put to rest these doubts. "You've got to wonder," commented political analyst Kevin Phillips, "to what extent Bush's Texas psychology figures into this, and to what extent he needs a hunting trophy."[96]

Bush's problem with his reputation was a problem too for the U.S. government more generally. If the leader of a small Third World country wouldn't follow U.S. orders, then who would? The Pentagon itself was being accused (on the Op-Ed page of the *New York Times,* among other places) of unseemly hesitancy to use force.[97] If U.S. military power was not used to bring Noriega to heel, then how was U.S. superpower status—based as it was on military might—to be maintained?

For the Pentagon, the invasion of Panama also provided an opportunity to demonstrate the capabilities and utility of its new, expensive, stealth fighter-bomber, desperate to find a mission as the Cold War wound down. And for the Republican Right, which had never gotten over the fact that the Panama Canal treaties give away "our" canal and "our" military bases, Noriega served as the excuse for reasserting Washington's former direct colonial role in Panama.[98]

These were the real motivations behind the U.S. invasion, not the drug issue. Before examining the drug rationale, it is worth briefly considering some of the other bogus justifications put forward by U.S. policy-makers. According to Washington, Noriega was a threat to U.S. citizens, a threat to the Panama Canal, dictatorial and corrupt, and a notorious abuser of human rights.

A few days before the invasion, a U.S. soldier was killed, and a naval officer and his wife were roughed up. George Bush waxed indignant: "If they kill an American Marine, that's real bad. And if they threaten and brutalize the wife of an American citizen, sexually threatening the lieutenant's wife while kicking him in the groin over and over again—then,…please understand, this president is going to do something about it."[99] But the background to these events exposes the hypocrisy of Bush's outrage.

Tensions between U.S. personnel and the Panama Defense Forces (PDF) had been quite high since the previous summer when U.S. military personnel were ordered to undertake all sorts of provocations. In one particular act of incitement, 1,000 U.S. soldiers conducted an exercise that appeared to be a rehearsal for kidnapping a Panamanian government official, and Noriega's brother was actually taken into custody. The local U.S. commander warned Washington that U.S. military posturing would get an American killed, so the White House had the commander replaced by someone with a more can-do attitude. The new commander ordered off-duty U.S. officers in their civilian clothes to carry out visual reconnaissance of potential targets, including PDF headquarters.[100] Noriega discovered these operations, and so when a car of four off-duty soldiers genuinely got lost near the headquarters and then tried to run a road block, it was not surprising that shots were fired at the car and a soldier killed. The PDF sent word to the United States that the shooting was an isolated incident and unintended,[101] but Washington ignored the message. And little publicity was given to the fact that two days later an off-duty U.S. soldier fired two shots from an illegal gun at a Panamanian traffic cop who had not drawn his weapon.[102]

Bush's concern for American womanhood was also singularly selective. There was only indifference from the White House when four lay church women were raped and murdered in El Salvador in 1980. A month before the U.S. invasion of Panama, a U.S. nun was kidnapped and tortured in Guatemala by individuals apparently under police protection; again there was no action from the White House.[103] And a month after the invasion, another U.S. nun was killed in Nicaragua; evidence implicated the Contras, but the State Department covered up for the U.S.-backed terrorists.[104] It's hard to disagree with former Pentagon official Fred Hoffman, who was privy to planning documents: Washington had a plan to invade Panama and "they were just waiting for an excuse to use it."[105]

The threat to the Panama Canal was even less credible a justification than the threat to U.S. citizens. Nothing Noriega did interfered in any way with the functioning of the Canal. It was only the U.S. invasion itself that resulted in the closing of the waterway for two days, the first time in its history that the Canal was shut down for reasons other than landslides.[106] And it was Ronald Reagan, not Manuel Noriega, who had suggested in 1989 that serious consideration be given to renouncing the Panama Canal treaties.[107]

The other U.S. charges against Noriega were similarly hypocritical. He did indeed steal the 1989 Panamanian elections as U.S. officials claimed (ignoring the $10 million in covert U.S. funds going to the opposition).[108] But this was not the first time that Noriega was responsible for election fraud. In 1984, Noriega, as head of the Panamanian military, picked Nicolas Barletta to be the country's president. An election was held, featuring stuffed ballots, falsified documents, and a rigged vote count, and Barletta won. Washington knew all about the fraud, but no word of protest was raised.[109] In fact, the U.S. government overtly and covertly funneled money to Barletta's campaign,[110] and after his tainted victory, he was invited to the White House to be congratulated by Ronald Reagan.[111] U.S. aid to Panama jumped from $12 million to $75 million,[112] suggesting a less than principled opposition to vote fraud.

The U.S. charges regarding Noriega's corruption were also accurate, but here too the corruption did not begin in 1989. Accepting and extorting money in return for favors was a way of life for the Panama Defense Forces and Noriega as its leader, but probably the most serious violation of his trust of office was taking money from foreign intelligence agencies—the CIA and the U.S. military—to spy on Panamanian military cadets, workers, and students, and to pass on to Washington secret information regarding the Panamanian negotiating position during the Canal talks in the 1970s.[113] Needless to say, the United States had no complaints about this sort of corruption, nor about any of Noriega's other well-documented malfeasance before 1987.

Noriega's human rights record was deplorable, though much exaggerated by U.S. officials. In August 1989, the U.S. ambassador told the UN Security Council that the "Noriega regime's notoriety now rivals that of some of the worst dictatorships of this century,"[114] conjuring up images of Hitler and Stalin. In fact, as the State Department later acknowledged, "People in Panama seldom disappeared permanently under the Noriega regime." Repression of massive anti-regime demonstrations in 1987, 1988, and 1989 resulted in fewer than a dozen deaths.[115] This record might be compared with that of the U.S.-backed government of El Salvador which was responsible for perhaps a thousand times as many killings as Noriega was.

In 1985, a prominent Noriega opponent, Hugo Spadafora, was murdered, almost certainly under Noriega's orders. But the Reagan administration opposed congressional efforts at the time to cut back on U.S. support for the Panamanian strongman; Human Rights Watch claimed that the CIA aided in a cover-up of the Spadafora murder by providing a false witness who blamed the crime on leftist Salvadoran guerrillas.[116] Noriega was also probably involved in the murder of an oppositionist priest in the 1970s and U.S. intelligence agencies believed he was responsible for the plane crash that killed his predecessor, Omar Torrijos.[117] But these crimes did not prevent the United States from establishing warm relations with Noriega.

Why did the United States support Noriega until 1987? Because despite his authoritarianism, his corruption, and his brutality, he supported U.S. interests. Aside from his intelligence activities on behalf of Washington, Noriega was also a crucial ally in the Contra war. He allowed U.S. bases in Panama to be used as the command center for the wars in Nicaragua and El Salvador;[118] he permitted the CIA to train at least 250 Contras at Panamanian military facilities;[119] he provided money for the Contras at a time when Congress prohibited U.S. funding;[120] he allowed Contra leaders to enter and leave Panama freely; he conducted espionage operations on the Sandinistas; he facilitated arms shipments to the Contras; and he carried out sabotage within Nicaragua.[121] When Nicaragua agreed to sign the Contadora treaty that Panama among others had put forward as a way to end the Contra war, the United States got Panama to withdraw the treaty and thus thwart the peace process.[122] In August 1986, Noriega offered to assassinate the Sandinista leadership in return for U.S. help in cleaning up his image; told that U.S. law barred assassination, Noriega then offered to conduct further sabotage operations in Nicaragua. Oliver North met Noriega a month later to discuss targets. The U.S. public relations firm that was doing Contra fund-raising was then hired to promote Noriega.[123] The General's image, however, needed no promotion in the White House, where he was considered a valued ally.

But by 1987 things had changed. Noriega had lost his usefulness to U.S. officials. Exposés in the U.S. press and congressional hearings sponsored by right-wing Senator Jesse Helms weakened Noriega's reputation. And the fact that he had removed his second-in-command (and thus his probable successor), who Washington considered a dangerous leftist, made Noriega suddenly expendable.[124] When federal prosecutors in Florida told the White House that they wanted to indict the Panamanian on drug-trafficking charges, the White House went along,[125] knowing that Bush was going to be vulnerable in the upcoming election to the charge that as CIA director he had quashed an investigation of a Noriega intelligence operation against the United States in the 1970s.[126] But the administration did block any move by the prosecutors to indict the PDF as an institution, making clear that its objection was not to the structures of corruption and dictatorship, but to Noriega as an individual. Secretary of State Shultz even called on the PDF to "maintain its integrity," which was like urging the Reagan administration to maintain its commitment to human rights.[127]

A year and a half after the indictments, Washington still insisted that it was committed to a "peaceful and democratic solution to Panama's problems." The State Department declared that the composition of Panama's government and the future of Panama "were issues to be decided by Panamanians—perhaps with Latin American mediation—but certainly not by the United States."[128] Less than four months later, 26,000 U.S. troops invaded Panama.

At a minimum, hundreds of civilians were killed in the U.S. assault.[129] But no matter. Manuel Noriega was captured and brought to Miami for trial on drug charges.

In April 1992, after long delays, Noriega was found guilty on most counts. The trial, however, left much to be desired. Of the six people who had testified against Noriega at the grand jury hearings three and a half years earlier, only one was considered sufficiently credible by prosecutors to be presented at the trial.[130] Every one of the other witnesses who in 1991-92 tied Noriega directly to drug trafficking was a convicted drug dealer, offered a reduced sentence or the right to keep illicit drug profits.[131] And the witnesses often contradicted each other.[132] The trial also featured widespread prosecutorial misconduct,[133] and the judge disallowed evidence regarding Noriega's cooperation with the CIA and other intelligence agencies, or discussion of how he came to be in Miami.[134]

That there were legal improprieties does not mean that Noriega was innocent of involvement in drug trafficking. But the trial did make clear that Noriega was not a major kingpin in the drug trade, but a middle level player. His profits from drugs and drug money laundering did not exceed $10-15 million, which by the standards of the drug trade isn't very much.[135] A telling summary of Noriega's role was put forward by the chief prosecutor when he explained in his opening statement in October 1991 how one prospective witness, Medellín cartel co-founder Carlos Lehder, would describe the Panamanian: "From Lehder's perspective, Manuel Noriega was a nobody.... In his words, 'he was just another crooked cop.' The cartel was paying off hundreds of crooked cops throughout Colombia, Panama, even Florida."[136] It is one thing to reduce the sentences of low-level criminals in order to get testimony against a major crime boss; in the Noriega trial, however, the individual whom the Department of Justice once called "the No. 1 drug man in the U.S." was granted immunity from prosecution and allowed to keep his yachts and planes; and one of the biggest drug smugglers had his sentence reduced from life plus 245 years to nine years, while receiving $500,000 from the U.S. government in legal fees. According to a congressional report, fifteen of the witnesses against Noriega were excused of crimes worse than those for which the General stood trial.[137] This prosecutorial behavior made no sense in order to convict "just another corrupt cop," but it was necessary to provide an after-the-fact justification for the U.S. invasion.

Evidence at the trial and independent research implicate Noriega in the drug trade in two different time periods: one in the early 1970s, and the other in the early 1980s.[138] Significantly, the U.S. government certainly knew about this involvement while it was supporting Noriega before 1988.[139] In the mid-1970s CIA chief George Bush approved covert funds for Noriega and, after the General was cut off for a brief period under Carter, the Reagan administration restored the funding in the '80s. As the State Department's

Frank McNeil testified before the Kerry subcommittee, the U.S. government was "coddling…Noriega beyond any time when one could reasonably doubt Noriega's involvement in drug trafficking to the United States" because he was helping with the Contras.[140]

Panama's importance to the drug trade was not so much as a trans-shipment point as a center for laundering the profits. Noriega got his share of this business (as he did of other illegal activities: smuggling coffee, selling visas, transporting arms to any side in a guerrilla war[141]) but in fact the entire Panamanian financial sector had essentially been set up as a haven for illicit funds. The traditional Panamanian elite who controlled the banking industry was thus up to its neck in servicing the drug trade. This elite had been forced to accept political rule by Noriega and the PDF and to cut these upstarts in on its profits. The U.S. invasion put the traditional elite, and thus the drug money launderers, back in power. The new President Guillermo Endara, his attorney general, his treasury minister, one of his vice-presidents, and the Chief Justice of the Supreme Court had all served as directors of banks and corporations tied to drug trafficking.[142] Ironically, in 1985 the U.S. government had tried to get Panama to agree to a banking treaty that would clamp down on drug-money laundering. Noriega supported the treaty, while the commercial elite which was reinstalled in power following the invasion opposed it.[143]

With Noriega out of power and the PDF in disarray, money laundering of drug profits continued and more cocaine bound for the United States than ever before passed through Panama.[144] The *New York Times* reported that U.S. diplomats and drug enforcement officials said they "would have no comment on" Panama's "internal drug enforcement efforts"[145]—no doubt because the United States doesn't like to interfere in other country's internal affairs.

The new Panamanian government, as the *New York Times* put it, "has been exceptionally dependent on American aid and advice." "The President, his key aides and the American ambassador, Deane R. Hinton, have breakfast together once a week in a meeting that many Panamanians view as the place where important decisions are made."[146] There has been some economic growth in the aftermath of the invasion, possibly drug-related, but unemployment stood at 15.7 percent, a third higher than in 1987 under Noriega.[147] And while U.S. aid to the Panamanian banking industry has been plentiful, most of the assistance intended for the poor or to promote democracy has yet to be disbursed.[148]

High in the Andes

Panama has been the one case of U.S. invasion rationalized by drug policy, but combating narcotics is the explanation as well for ongoing U.S. interventions in three South American countries. The standard U.S. view portrays Colombia, Peru, and Bolivia as nations terrorized by powerful drug-trafficking cartels, often working in alliance with left-wing guerrillas. According to this view, the hard-pressed Andean governments may need U.S. support in order to protect their populations and prevail against the narco-terrorists. This standard view is almost totally incorrect.

The real problem facing the people of these countries is grueling poverty caused by the astounding greed of local elites and the grim workings of the international economic system, maintained by equally greedy elites in the industrialized nations.

In Bolivia in the first half of the 1980s, gross national product declined 2.3 percent per year, official unemployment went from 5.7 percent to 20 percent, and inflation stood at 10,000 percent in 1985. The world price of tin declined 57 percent between 1980 and 1988; over the five-year period 1983-87, Bolivian exports shrank 38 percent. The government closed most state-owned tin mines, throwing thousands of miners out of work.[149] More than one out of every six Bolivian children die before their fifth birthday.[150]

Peru too faces desperate conditions. In the mid-1980s, its economic crisis surpassed the Great Depression of the 1930s; according to the World Bank, "The overwhelming majority of Peruvians are markedly worse off than in 1970."[151] Under the country's new president, Alberto Fujimori, Peru has adopted unhindered free market policies (despite his campaign promises to the contrary[152]) in order to reintegrate itself into the world capitalist system. The result of "Fuji-shock," the *New York Times* reported, has been "increased unemployment and poverty," with estimates of the number of Peruvians living in extreme poverty nearly doubling in three years. Fully 80 percent of the workforce is either unemployed or underemployed. Gross national product fell 20 percent in a single year. One quarter of the country's population live in urban slums. Schoolteachers' children are not eating three meals a day any more, tuberculosis is up, and cholera—a characteristic disease of poverty—claimed 2,540 lives last year.[153] In the highlands, peasants have a standard of living "closer to that of sub-Saharan Africa than coastal Peru."[154]

A guerrilla army, Sendero Luminoso (Shining Path), today controls an estimated 40 percent of the country. Sendero is a Maoist organization, highly authoritarian and extremely ruthless—it has killed hundreds of leftists, and regularly executes homosexuals—but is considered by many

Peruvians the country's only salvation.[155] One-sixth of Peruvians are willing to admit to pollsters that conditions in their country justify subversion.[156]

The government's response has been to wage a counter-insurgency campaign of incredible brutality. Peru topped the list of "disappearances" reported to the United Nations four out of the last five years.[157] In April 1991, the Organization of American States identified 86 documented cases of human rights abuses by the military in South America; 50 of them took place in Peru.[158] And the victims of military terror are rarely guerrillas, but rather community activists and the civilian population more generally, which is routinely subjected to bombing, strafing, murder, and rape, thus generating more recruits for Sendero.[159] The military exercised absolute authority in emergency zones covering two-thirds of the country; no member of the armed forces has yet been punished for a human rights violation. The Fujimori government sharply increased the authority of the military, while denouncing human rights organizations as "the legal arm of the subversives."[160] And the Bush administration recently declared that Peru had improved its human rights record enough to justify the release of millions of dollars of military aid, despite the fact that human rights groups insisted the situation remained as bad as ever.[161]

In April 1992, Fujimori dissolved the Congress and suspended the constitution. He claimed that his assumption of absolute power was necessary in order to fight Sendero and corruption. In fact, however, the coup has played right into Sendero's strategy. Democratic niceties had never restrained the armed forces in their counter-insurgency campaign, and the main target of the military crackdown seems to be legal opposition groups.[162] As for corruption, Fujimori's own family has recently been implicated in a scheme to misappropriate charitable donations,[163] and one of the president's closest aides is thought to be tied to drug traffickers.[164]

Colombia has one of most skewed income distributions in Latin America, with 40 percent of the population living in absolute poverty. Two factions of the elite fought a bloody civil war from 1948 to 1958 in which several hundred thousand people (mostly not members of the elite) were killed; the agreement ending the fighting provided for the two factions to alternate turns at the presidency, thus continuing the historic exclusion of the mass of the population from power.[165] Over the years, opposition groups developed, some of them waging guerrilla war and others trying to pursue legal means of struggle. The repression has been monstrous, and concentrated most viciously against the legal Left. More than 100 right-wing death squads exist, many of whose members are active or retired military and police personnel. Military collaboration with these death squads may not be centrally coordinated, but the national government has not made much effort to curtail the terror. In March 1990, for example, the Interior Minister charged that the legal left-wing Patriotic Union (UP) was the "political arm" of a guerrilla group; the UP's presidential candidate warned that this was a death sentence for his party's leaders and sure enough he himself was murdered a few days later. More than 1,000 UP activists were killed between 1985 and 1990. And these were not the only victims: from 1981-86 some 3,500 journalists, students, trade unionists, and opposition party members were assassinated, and from 1986-90 8,000 members of the legal Left were killed.[166] The right-wing paramilitary groups that cooperate with the military also have ties to the drug cartels.[167]

The economic crisis in the Andean nations has been exacerbated by a staggering foreign debt owed to U.S. and other banks, and by an increasingly inhospitable market for their exports in the industrialized world. The United States, for example, placed non-tariff barriers on about a quarter of its commodity imports in the mid-'60s, but on more than half of them by the mid-'80s.[168] In 1989 Washington scuttled an international agreement on coffee prices, causing significant harm to the Colombian economy.[169] According to a UN report: "The decline of prices for commodities like sugar (by 64 percent), coffee (30 percent), cotton (32 percent) and wheat (17 percent) between 1980 and 1988 motivated farmers to turn to cash crops like the coca bush and the opium poppy to avoid economic ruin."[170] In Peru and Bolivia in particular, many poor peasants have been forced to turn to coca cultivation in order to survive. There is simply no crop as profitable.[171] The campesinos, however, earn very little from their coca growing; the great bulk of the profits go to the major drug-trafficking organizations.

In Bolivia, the traffickers come from the rural elite.[172] In 1980 in the "cocaine coup"—the 189th coup in Bolivia's history[173]—the country's leading drug kingpin took over the government. Although the Carter administration refused to recognize the new government and cut almost all aid,[174] a key DEA agent believes that the CIA supported the coup and thwarted an undercover operation against the drug lord.[175] A witness told Kerry's subcommittee of funneling money on behalf of Argentine military intelligence to support the coup, with CIA knowledge.[176] In March 1991, the head of the country's anti-drug police resigned amid charges of drug trafficking; he had been appointed to his post despite having served in the cabinet during the cocaine coup regime.[177]

In Peru, major government officials have been involved in the drug trade. When the military was sent into the coca-growing Upper Huallaga Valley region to fight guerrillas in 1984, drug traffickers experienced what one observer called a "golden age," with individual military officers making bonanza profits.[178] Today, officers bribe their superiors to get assigned to the lucrative coca areas.[179]

Most of the Andean drug trade, however, has been dominated by Colombian traffickers, particularly associated with two cartels, one based in Medellín and the other in Cali. The Medellín cartel was formed in 1981 when leftist guerrillas kidnapped the sister of a major drug lord; Medellín traffickers banded together to form right-wing death squads to terrorize the Left. In 1983, the Colombian Attorney General asserted that 59 active military personnel were members of these assassination teams.[180] But the Medellín cartel fought the government too, killing many judges and politicians, and the government responded with intermittent crackdowns. Ultimately, the government and the cartel called a truce, with the drug lords accepting prison, built to their own specifications and from which they could continue their drug operations.[181] The Cali cartel, however, has come to control 75 percent of the cocaine trade. These traffickers do not target the state and are far better integrated into the Colombian elite than were those from Medellín and as such the government is disinclined to interfere with them.[182] The Cali cartel is particularly thought to have the support of those sections of the military who collaborate with far-right paramilitary groups in killing leftists.[183]

Some Colombian guerrilla groups operate in coca-growing regions, taxing and at times even managing coca cultivation and processing of their own; occasionally guerrillas and traffickers opportunistically cooperate; but generally those who control the cocaine refining—the most profitable part of the drug trade—are the cartel lords who have acquired a great deal of rural property and behave like other rich landlords, that is, they try to smash the Left. As one mainstream expert put it, relations between Colombian guerrillas and traffickers "have involved far more bloodshed than cooperation."[184]

In Peru, Shining Path is the dominant political force in the coca-growing Upper Huallaga Valley. U.S. officials claim the guerrillas are in partnership with the drug traffickers, but in fact they are allied to the peasant coca-growers, helping them get a better price for their crop, and protecting them from the lawless violence of the traffickers and the government.[185] Sendero thus plays a role with respect to the drug trade similar to the legal trade unions in Bolivia that represent the coca-growers, while it is the military and government officials who are linked to the traffickers.[186] Shining Path makes money from the drug trade by taxing the peasants, but if the guerrillas were making the $100 million a year that some U.S. analysts have claimed,[187] they would probably have far more expensive weaponry.[188]

A few years ago, CIA director William Casey ordered a study of the links between drug traffickers and leftist guerrillas. The study concluded that there were no significant links. Casey then ordered a second study, which found that the two groups "fed at the same trough," that is, they sometimes operated in the same areas, and sometimes shared landing strips.[189] Less compromised experts have summarized the evidence this way: "Although there are linkages between the cocaine industry and revolutionary organizations, these linkages do not add up to an alliance. Indeed, cocaine traffickers and guerrillas have usually been competitors and sometimes mortal enemies."[190]

Uncle Sam to the Rescue

The U.S. government has taken a number of approaches to dealing with Andean drug trafficking, all based on the premise that the U.S. drug problem can be solved abroad.

First, it has pressured Latin American countries to undertake—or, more typically, to allow the United States to undertake—aerial spraying to eradicate the coca crop. Since the coca plant is so hardy, highly toxic herbicides must be used, with consequent danger to the environment and humans. The head of the Agriculture Department's Narcotics Laboratory quit in protest over the government's reckless attitude toward ecological hazards,[191] and Eli Lilly and Dow Chemical—no friends of the earth—refused to supply the U.S. government with their herbicides unless they were held blameless for any environmental damage. (Washington said no.) But, in any event, spraying cannot overcome the economic realities; less than 1 percent of coca land is eradicated annually and far more new acreage comes under coca cultivation each year than is sprayed.[192]

What little eradication has taken place has largely been counter-productive. In Bolivia, rather than discouraging peasant growers, eradication has operated like farm price supports that stabilize prices by keeping marginal land out of use.[193] Worse, Peruvian peasants whose livelihood is destroyed by eradication campaigns become eager recruits for Shining Path.[194] The Peruvian military is well aware of this problem, but some U.S. policy-makers seem oblivious to the consequences. As one State Department official put it: "If you are saying that coca farmers won't be able to make a living after spray[ing], that's right. That is the point of the exercise."[195]

A second U.S. approach to the South American drug problem has been trying to promote crop substitution. This approach, however, is doomed to failure. For starters, the United States is not really interested in

creating economic competitors. For example, when U.S. foreign aid officials tried to foster Bolivian soybean exports as an alternative to coca, the
U.S. Department of Agriculture objected that this would compete with U.S.
products, and the idea was dropped.[196] But in any case the scale of U.S. aid
is woefully inadequate: as one Latin American scholar asked, "How could
a crop-substitution investment of $5.3 million per annum conquer an
economy that brings Peru some $2 billion each year?"[197] Without govern-
ment solvency, crop substitution has no chance of success; likewise, highly
unequal land distribution patterns make it suicidal for peasants to give up
the lucrative coca plant.[198] The United States provides Peruvian peasants
with loans to encourage crop substitution, but the interest rates are over
100 percent because of Peru's economic crisis; the only crop that brings in
enough money to pay back such loans is coca; so peasants use the money
to plant coca.[199] Those farmers who do plant alternative crops clear additional jungle lands to expand coca production as well.[200] An international
agricultural expert who works on promoting alternative crops in Peru
summed up the dilemma: "We could spend $1 billion to turn around the
Upper Huallaga, and then two years later there would be a new Upper
Huallaga somewhere else."[201] In February 1992, Bush told Latin American
leaders that they would have to deal with the drug problem without any
new U.S. funds to create alternatives to the drug trade.[202]

The third U.S. approach to the drug problem—and the one increasingly being emphasized—is the military approach. This involves training,
funding, and arming the Andean armed forces and police, with some direct
participation by U.S. personnel. Starting in 1985, armed DEA agents were
operating in the Upper Huallaga Valley of Peru.[203] The following year, 160
U.S. soldiers played a supporting role in Operation Blast Furnace, a large-
scale anti-drug raid in Bolivia; the U.S. troops stayed for four months, and
when they pulled out, army trainers remained behind. As the State Department boasted in 1988, "U.S. border patrol agents, U.S. military trainers and
DEA personnel in the [coca-growing] regions are providing constant supervision over Bolivian interdiction operations."[204] In 1989, U.S. Marines were
secretly authorized to train Peruvian Marines, and Green Berets began
providing instruction to Peruvian police.[205] By January 1992, some 200 U.S.
military personnel were stationed in South America on anti-drug missions,
and the United States was providing $150 million in counter-narcotics
military aid.[206]

The Andean governments have very little interest in pursuing the war
on drugs. Their own links to the traffickers, their fear of pushing peasants
into the arms of guerrillas, and the dependence of their economies—espe-

cially in Bolivia and Peru—on the drug trade make them reluctant participants in the U.S. crusade.[207]

But in Peru and Colombia the governments are willing to accept U.S. military aid because this can be used—and is used—against guerrillas. In Colombia, military officials told U.S. congressional staff investigators that more than 95 percent of their 1990 anti-drug aid would support a major counter-insurgency operation in an area not involved in narcotics trafficking.[208] Rural communities are subjected to aerial bombing by the Colombian armed forces, using planes provided by U.S. military aid.[209] As human rights analyst Coletta Youngers has remarked, U.S. military aid which is supposed to protect Colombia's democracy from narco-terrorism is in fact "facilitating one of the most brutal counter-insurgency campaigns in Latin America."[210] The General Accounting Office reported that U.S. oversight was unable to tell whether anti-drug aid was being used against drugs or primarily against insurgents and to abuse human rights.[211] The point, however, has become moot, as the Bush administration has decided—at least in the case of Peru—to explicitly support both the anti-drug and the anti-guerrilla wars on the grounds that the two problems are "inextricably bound together."[212] In fact, the opposite is the case: the drug war alienates the peasantry and augments the ranks of Shining Path. And the strategy of providing more aid to the Peruvian military strengthens the forces of the status quo that are the greatest obstacle to the social, economic, and political reforms that are prerequisites for ending the insurgency.

The U.S. military has failed miserably in combating drug trafficking in the Andes. In the 1986 Operation Blast Furnace in Bolivia a grand total of one person was arrested, a teenaged boy; as soon as U.S. forces pulled out, the traffickers returned and business resumed as before.[213] Not only has the drug war been unable to suppress the cocaine trade in Colombia, Peru, and Bolivia, but Colombian cartels are now branching out into heroin,[214] and trafficking is spreading to Venezuela, Ecuador, Brazil, Argentina, Surinam, Chile, and elsewhere.[215] In 1989 the Bush administration announced as its goal a reduction of 15 percent in cocaine availability by the fall of 1991; but cocaine production in South America increased 28 percent in 1990 and another 8 percent in 1991.[216]

The U.S. military has been equally unsuccessful in stopping the flow of drugs at the U.S. border. Although the Pentagon budget for counter-narcotics operations jumped from zero before fiscal year 1989 to more than a billion dollars in 1991,[217] the Defense Department's efforts "have not had a significant impact on the national goal of reducing drug supplies," in the words of the General Accounting Office.[218] The failure has not been due to Pentagon incompetence (though the proposal to have National Guard members dress up as cactuses so they could sneak up on smugglers left something to be desired).[219] The Rand Corporation, the GAO, the Congressional Office of Technology Assessment, and the Inter-American Commission on Drug Policy all agree that the economics of drug smuggling guarantee that even a more effective interdiction effort would have negligible impact on the availability of cocaine in the United States.[220]

Why then does the U.S. government pursue this futile drug war? It does so because the drug war serves a functional role for many important sectors in U.S. society.

For the Pentagon, counter-narcotics operations provide a rationale for continued bloated budgets. "It's their new meal ticket now that the commies are not their big threat," a congressional staffer told *Newsweek*.[221] The war on drugs, commented a *New York Times* correspondent, is "one of the few growth areas the Pentagon has left."[222] Some years ago the military—afraid of getting stuck in a quagmire—had resisted taking on an anti-drug mission, but, as one general confessed, "With peace breaking out all over, it might give us something to do."[223] Particularly for the Panama-based U.S. Southern Command, the Latin American drug war was "the only war we've got."[224]

Drug wars also are functional for those who want to legitimate U.S. interventionism in the Third World. Army Colonel John Waghelstein, former chief of U.S. military advisers in El Salvador, has written that fighting the combination of leftist guerrillas and narco-terrorists would allow the United States to "regain the high moral ground" lost to religious and academic groups who oppose U.S. intervention in Latin America.[225]

For the Bush administration, fighting drug wars represents a way to *appear* to be dealing with a problem that is wracking American society—without having to admit the ugly truth, that drug abuse is not forced on the United States from the outside, but is the result of lives made desperate by the poverty, the unemployment, and the alienation of American society.

The war on drugs cannot be won in the Upper Huallaga Valley or on the Mexican border. It cannot be won in the urban centers of the United States by jailing or shooting those most victimized by U.S. capitalism. It can be won only when our national priority becomes the rebuilding of our cities, our schools, our hospitals, and the very lives of our people.

Conclusion

For at least half a century, the Soviet threat admirably served the needs of U.S. policy-makers, providing the defining enemy that rationalized massive military spending, constant interventions abroad, and repression at home. With the disintegration of the Soviet Union, the managers of the U.S. state are already trying to concoct new rationalizations to achieve the same ends. In the preceding chapters, I have examined many of these new arguments for U.S. intervention and have tried to show in each case that the declared justification has been a sham. This returns us to the question of what then have been the real reasons for U.S. interventions?

U.S. troops did not land in Grenada or the Dominican Republic in order to save American citizens in distress. The intervention is far better explained by the fact that the government of the former and the constitutionalists contending for power in the latter were both nationalistically-inclined and thus a challenge to U.S. economic hegemony in the Caribbean. In Nicaragua, U.S. economic interests were also challenged; and in its effort to crush the Sandinistas, Washington resorted to terrorism and cooperated with narcotics-traffickers. Alliances of convenience were forged as well with drug dealers in Southeast Asia in an effort to defeat the Vietnamese revolution.

Controlling the world's oil resources has always been a fundamental goal of the U.S. government. In the Middle East, radical nationalist regimes in Libya, Iran, and Iraq have threatened this control. The United States has worked to demonize Libya (often for actions that U.S. allies have conducted on a far larger scale), to destabilize it, and even to attack it. Washington has also used supplies of arms and intelligence, covert operations, and occasional military force in order to minimize the independence of the governments in Baghdad and Teheran. And when Saddam Hussein went too far (not in massacring Kurds, but in threatening U.S. control over the petroleum supplies of the Persian Gulf) enormous military force was applied.

In promoting the interests of corporate America, the U.S. government has helped to provide markets, regardless of the social consequences of the products sold. Weapons sales to the Shah of Iran in the 1970s led to a regional arms race costly in human as well as financial terms. Continuing U.S. arms sales to the Middle East today stoke tensions in that region while boosting the corporate balance sheets. Washington has also facilitated the sale of tobacco and other legal but harmful products overseas.

Foreign corpses evoke little sympathy from U.S. policy-makers, particularly when the victims are considered racial inferiors. Jews during the holocaust, Africans in Biafra or Burundi, Asians in Bangladesh—all were expendable to the larger interests of U.S. foreign policy. Sometimes the United States ignored the deaths of these *Untermenschen,* sometimes it collaborated with their killers, as in Indonesia or Guatemala. When Third World people fought and died in the Iran-Iraq war, Washington covertly armed both sides.

Lack of sentimentality for dark-skinned people has been part of an approach to foreign policy that prizes masculine toughness and disparages any human empathy as feminine weakness. Kissinger called for "a tough, even abrasive foreign policy" in the aftermath of the Vietnam War to reclaim U.S. virility. The pounding of Cambodia in the Mayaguez affair did not save American lives, but, in Barry Goldwater's words, showed "we still got some balls in this country." The Reagan administration was particularly determined to restore the U.S. reputation for manly ruthlessness. Accordingly, Grenada was invaded, as White House aides admitted, so that the United States wouldn't be seen as a paper tiger. And U.S. policy-makers openly spoke of challenging Qaddafi's "manhood" to provoke him into an act that would give Washington a chance to "stick it to him." Testosterone poisoning has been a long-standing ailment of U.S. officials, who have frequently invoked military responses to problems that were susceptible to more pacific solutions.

Militarism and interventionism have also served the political needs of U.S. presidents. When domestic policies are routinely pursued that reduce the living standards of the average citizen and redistribute wealth to the rich, a distraction that can get the public to rally 'round the flag will provide a healthy boost to presidential approval ratings. A quagmire like Vietnam can be an administration's undoing, but there is nothing like a short military operation against a hopelessly outclassed opponent to enhance a president's popularity: witness the attacks on Grenada, Libya, Panama, or Iraq.

The recent changes in the Soviet Union and Eastern Europe have been dramatic and profound, but they have had a negligible impact on the fundamental roots of U.S. foreign policy. The capitalist system functions essentially as before, and the prevailing ideology of racism, sexism, and heterosexism is basically intact. Thus the social forces that have driven U.S. interventionism in the past will continue to spawn interventions in the aftermath of the Cold War. But the changed international environment will likely alter the pattern of U.S. interventionism.

In the past, the Soviet Union provided radical movements in many U.S. client states with the material support they needed to seriously challenge the regime in power. Moscow did this not out of a deep commitment to radical ideals, but as a way to weaken its global adversary—the United States. (The Kremlin did not come to the aid of even pro-Soviet Communist parties who were ruthlessly suppressed in Turkey in the 1920s or Egypt in the 1960s or Iraq in the 1970s, because the regimes doing the suppressing were deemed sufficiently anti-western.[1]) Soviet support for some of the popular insurgencies within the U.S. empire has often meant that the local gendarme alone has been unable to maintain the status quo. And when U.S. economic and military aid and U.S. covert operations have not been enough to keep down popular unrest, more direct forms of U.S. intervention have been employed. With the demise of the Soviet Union, there will be fewer serious threats to the survival of repressive regimes, and thus less need for direct U.S. interventionism.

On the other hand, the Soviet Union also played a role in inhibiting U.S. interventions during the Cold War. The presence of Soviet naval vessels off the coast of India or in the Mediterranean or the Persian Gulf raised the specter that the landing of U.S. Marines in some Third World country might broaden into a superpower confrontation. During the Cold War, the Pentagon sought to achieve military superiority over the Soviet Union at every level of the escalatory scale as a way to maintain U.S. freedom of action (that is, freedom to intervene). Ship-board nuclear missiles and similar weapons systems had no real military utility in an all-out U.S.-Soviet conflict, but they were useful for discouraging Moscow from intervening in Washington's interventions. Nevertheless, given that U.S. military action against a Third World nation carried with it the risk of a wider war, there is no doubt that the existence of a powerful Soviet Union constrained U.S. interventions. This constraint is now gone.

The Cold War served the needs of the capitalist system in Western Europe and Japan as well as in the United States. In Europe and Japan, the U.S.-led anti-Soviet crusade helped to undermine the appeal of the Communist Party and the Left more generally. More importantly, U.S. action against those who would threaten U.S. foreign investment often also protected the investment opportunities of Japanese and European corporations. Only the United States had the military ability to project force globally and only the United States had the power to deter a Soviet counter-intervention. So the European and Japanese allies deferred to U.S.

leadership in the Cold War, though they often had to go along with policies that benefitted Washington far more than themselves.

Japanese and European subordination to the United States also reflected the global preeminence of the U.S. economy in the years following World War II. But U.S. economic primacy has declined since the 1960s, and the allies have grown correspondingly independent. The final end of the Cold War coincided with the end of U.S. economic dominance. And thus, in the new post-Cold War world, U.S. allies in Europe and Japan will be far less willing to accept Washington's lead. The French government, for example, recently warned the United States not to try to rule the world.[2] For its part, the U.S. government understands the new international realities. Recent Pentagon planning documents (revised into more diplomatic language after much criticism) defined the key U.S. objective to be preventing the emergence of a new superpower. In the Middle East, the overall goal was to "remain the predominant outside power in the region."[3]

Does this mean that the United States will soon be going to war with the Europeans or Japan? No, but nor did the Cold War mean that the United States went to war with Moscow. Nevertheless, conflicts of interest among the capitalist powers may well result in different ones of them supporting opposite sides in a civil or local war. It will be difficult to invest these conflicts with the same level of popular backing that the global campaign against the Soviet Union enjoyed, but economic stagnation may yet provide fertile ground for xenophobia. Anti-Japanese racism in the United States and Japanese racism against minority groups in the United States reflect and add to the growing tensions.

Because the capitalist nations do have more interests in common than did the United States and the Soviet Union, U.S. interventions in the future are more likely to be under the guise of collective action. The U.S.-led coalition war against Iraq in 1991 was in some ways the archetypical case of collective action in the post-Cold War era. But the United Nations Security Council which Washington was able to dominate during the Gulf War situation will come under increasing pressure to more accurately reflect the actual power distribution, if not the population distribution, of the world. With Germany and Japan on the Council, that body will be less susceptible to U.S. control. Unless Third World representation is increased as well, the United Nations will become a front for the interests of the rich countries in situations where the interests of the capitalist states coincide. Where these interests do not coincide, interventions will be undertaken on a unilateral basis, most often by the most powerful nation: the United States.

The focus on domestic issues in the U.S. presidential campaign may suggest that foreign policy just isn't that important anymore, that U.S.

intervention no longer matters very much. But U.S. intervention aims to maintain the global status quo, a status quo that consigns much of the Earth's population, mostly people of color, to poverty and misery. The eastern gulag may be gone, but millions of people in the western empire live in literal slavery—in such nations as the Dominican Republic, Haiti, Pakistan, India, Mauritania, and South Africa.[4] In sub-Saharan Africa and Latin America, living standards declined in absolute terms during the decade of the 1980s.[5] Children have been particularly victimized: in many poor countries the average weight-for-age of those under five has been falling, spending on education has been declining, primary school enrollments have dropped, and child prostitution is growing.[6]

This is suffering on a massive scale. And it is perpetuated by the interventions on behalf of the status quo on the part of the United States and other rich nations. An end to these interventions will not suddenly eliminate global poverty. But it would create the space within which popular movements throughout the world could confront the systemic roots of that poverty.

Stopping U.S. interventionism thus constitutes a continuing moral imperative for those in the United States concerned with peace and social justice. The U.S. government will try to build public support for its interventionist policies by claiming it is defending vital resources, human rights, or Americans in distress, or preventing weapons proliferation, terrorism, or drug-trafficking. But, as I have tried to show in this book, these are just covers for policies motivated by the dynamics of U.S. capitalism and a racist, sexist, and heterosexist ideology.

Notes

The following abbreviations are used in the notes and bibliography.

AP	Associated Press
Comm.	Committee
Cong. Rec.	U.S. *Congressional Record*
CQ	Congressional Quarterly
D/S	U.S. Department of State, Washington, D.C.
DoD	U.S. Department of Defense, Washington, D.C.
FBIS	Foreign Broadcast Information Service
GAO	U.S. General Accounting Office, Washington, D.C.
HR	U.S. House of Representatives
LAT	*Los Angeles Times*
NACLA	*NACLA: Report on the Americas*
NYT	*New York Times*
Sen.	U.S. Senate
SL	Newark *Star Ledger*
subcomm.	subcommittee
UP	University Press
UPI	United Press International
USGPO	U.S. Government Printing Office
WP	*Washington Post*
WSJ	Wall Street Journal

Introduction

1. Richard Nixon, *The Real War,* New York: Warner Books, 1981, pp. 2-3.
2. Ronald Reagan during 1980 campaign, quoted in Ronald Steel, "Cold War, Cold Comfort," *New Republic,* 11 April 1981, pp. 15-17.
3. See Clyde Haberman, "Challenge in the Pacific," *NYT Magazine,* 7 Sept. 1986, p. 104; William T. Tow, "American Interests in the Southwest Pacific During A 'Post-ANZUS' Era," *SAIS Review,* vol. 7, no. 2, Summer/Fall 1987, pp. 156-57.
4. Thomas L. Friedman, "Rethinking Foreign Affairs: Are They Still A U.S. Affair?" *NYT,* 7 Feb. 1992, p. A10.
5. Elaine Sciolino, "CIA Chief Says Threat By Ex-Soviets Is Small," *NYT,* 23 Jan. 1992, p. A8.
6. Dick Cheney, speech to National Newspaper Association, Washington, D.C., 16 March 1990 (DoD News Release), p. 5.
7. U.S. Army, *Trained and Ready in An Era of Change: Posture Statement, FY 1991,* statement of Michael P.W. Stone and General Carl E. Vuono before Comms. and subcomms. of Sen. and HR, [1990], p. I-6.
8. Patrick E. Tyler, "7 Hypothetical Conflicts Foreseen by the Pentagon," *NYT,* 17 Feb. 1992, p. A8.

9. Leslie H. Gelb, "They're Kidding," *NYT,* 9 March 1992, p. A17.

10. Morton Kondracke, "Punch-Puller," *New Republic,* 16 March 1992, p. 15.

11. Fred Barnes, "Washington Diarist," *New Republic,* 17 Feb. 1992, p. 42.

12. Charles Krauthammer, "The Curse of Legalism," *New Republic,* 6 Nov. 1989, p. 49; Charles Krauthammer, "The Lonely Superpower," *New Republic,* 29 July 1991, p. 24; Charles Krauthammer, "Don't Cash the Peace Dividend," *Time,* 26 March 1990, p. 88.

1: The Sources of U.S. Foreign Policy

1. Quoted in Noam Chomsky, *At War with Asia,* New York: Pantheon, 1969, p. 111.

2. James C. Thomson, Jr., Peter W. Stanley, and John Curtis Perry, *Sentimental Imperialists. The American Experience in East Asia,* New York: Harper & Row, 1981. Henry Pachter ("The Problem of Imperialism," *Dissent,* Sept.- Oct. 1970, p. 462) uses the term "imperialism" to describe U.S. foreign policy but specifies that he is referring to an imperialism that results from folly or from "the willful extravaganza of idealistic dreamers" rather than from the inherent structures of U.S. capitalism.

3. Hans Morgenthau, *In Defense of the National Interest,* New York: Alfred Knopf, 1951, p. 23.

4. General James Rusling, "Interview With President William McKinley," *The Christian Advocate* (New York), 22 Jan. 1903, p. 17, in *The Philippines Reader,* ed. Daniel B. Schirmer and Stephen R. Shalom, Boston: South End Press, 1987, p. 22.

5. HR, Select Comm. on Intelligence, 19 Jan. 1976 (Pike Report) in *Village Voice,* 16 Feb. 1976, pp. 85, 87n465, 88n471. The Pike Report attributes the last quote only to a "senior official"; William Safire (*Safire's Washington,* New York: Times Books, 1980, p. 333) identifies the official as Kissinger.

6. Transcript, Cuban Missile Crisis Meetings, 16 Oct. 1962, p. II:27 (Papers of John F. Kennedy, President's Office Files, John F. Kennedy Library, Boston, MA).

7. Abram Chayes, *Proceedings of the American Society of International Law,* 57th meeting (25-27 April 1963), p. 11. Chayes is not some right-wing fanatic; in the 1980s he represented Nicaragua in its claim against the United States before the World Court. For a critique of Chayes's view of the role of law in the Cuban missile crisis, see Stephen R. Shalom, "International Lawyers and Other Apologists: The Case of the Cuban Missile Crisis," *Polity,* vol. 12, no. 1, Fall 1979.

8. Michael R. Gordon, "Legal Advisor Leaves a Trail of Furious Debate," *NYT,* 1 March 1988, p. A14.

9. Daniel Patrick Moynihan, *Loyalties,* San Diego: Harcourt Brace Jovanovich, 1984, p. 65. In November 1983, Moynihan presented the conference committee report on the Intelligence Authorization Act and argued that Nicaragua had violated international law by providing arms and other military support to groups seeking to overthrow the government of El Salvador "and other Central American governments." He explained that he and his colleagues had pressed the administration to redefine its covert program to accord with international law and that the goal of Reagan's program, "as it should be," was to bring Nicaragua into conformity with international law (Daniel Patrick Moynihan, *On the Law of Nations,* Cambridge, MA: Harvard UP, 1990, p. 138). Moynihan charges that the Reagan administration went on to ignore this congressional view by mining Nicaraguan harbors. But the World Court did not just find the mining illegal; the whole U.S. covert war against Nicaragua was found to violate international law.

10. *Cong. Rec.,* 20 Mar. 1990, p. S2802. For background, see Fred Khouri, *The Arab-Israeli Dilemma,* 2nd ed., Syracuse: Syracuse UP, 1976, pp. 114, 116.

11. Henry Cabot Lodge, "The Philippine Islands," in *American Imperialism in 1898,* ed. Theodore P. Greene, Boston: D.C. Heath & Co., 1955, p. 72. This was a common theme

among those who favored annexation of the Philippines; thus Sen. Beveridge: "The Declaration of Independence applies to all men? How dare we, then, deny its application to the American Indians?" (Quoted in Claude G. Bowers, *Beveridge and the Progressive Era,* Cambridge, MA: Houghton Mifflin, 1932, p. 121.)

12. Douglas Little, "Cold War and Covert Action: The United States and Syria, 1945-1958," *Middle East Journal,* vol. 44, no. 1, Winter 1990, pp. 55-57.

13. Jonathan Kwitny, *Endless Enemies,* New York: Penguin, 1984, p. 75.

14. Seymour M. Hersh, *The Price of Power: Kissinger in the Nixon White House,* New York: Summit, 1983, p. 265. Needless to say, Salvador Allende was not a Communist.

15. *NYT,* 1 July 1981, p. 13.

16. Thomson, Stanley, & Perry, *Sentimental Imperialists,* pp. 103-04.

17. V.I. Lenin, *Imperialism: The Highest Stage of Capitalism,* New York: International Publishers, 1939, p. 79.

18. D.K. Fieldhouse, "'Imperialism': An Historical Revision," in *Economic Imperialism: A Book of Readings,* ed. Kenneth E. Boulding and Tapan Mukerjee, Ann Arbor: University of Michigan Press, 1972, p. 106.

19. Pachter, "Problem of Imperialism," p. 475.

20. Benjamin J. Cohen, *The Question of Imperialism,* New York: Basic Books, 1973, p. 251, citing Robert W. Tucker, *The Radical Left and American Foreign Policy,* Baltimore: Johns Hopkins Press, 1971, p. 52. Whether Tucker is giving his view here or simply stating the position of the radical Left is unclear; but Cohen accepts it. For extensive documentation regarding the importance of foreign markets in the worldview of U.S. policy-makers, see William Appleman Williams, *The Tragedy of American Diplomacy,* rev. ed., New York: Delta, 1962; Richard J. Barnet, *The Roots of War,* Baltimore: Penguin, 1972, pp. 137-205; Joyce and Gabriel Kolko, *The Limits of Power,* New York: Harper & Row, 1972, chap. 1.

21. Frederic S. Pearson, "American Military Intervention Abroad: A Test of Economic and Noneconomic Explanations," in *The Politics of Aid, Trade and Investment,* ed. Satish Raichur and Craig Liske, New York: Halsted, 1976, pp. 37-62.

22. In Richard M. Pfeffer, ed., *No More Vietnams? The War and the Future of American Foreign Policy,* New York: Harper Colophon, 1968, p. 269.

23. Official public statements: *Public Papers of the Presidents of the United States: Dwight D. Eisenhower, 1954,* Washington, D.C.: USGPO, 1960, pp. 382-83; HR, Foreign Affairs Comm., *The Mutual Security Program,* Hearings, 1951, p. 916; *Mutual Security Act of 1956,* Hearings, 1956, p. 243; *Mutual Security Act of 1958,* Hearings, 1958, p. 1198; Sen., Foreign Relations Comm., *Japanese Peace Treaty and Other Treaties Relating to Security in the Pacific,* Hearings, 1952, pp. 11-12, 28; *Mutual Security Act of 1954,* Hearings, 1954, p. 219.

Prestigious study groups: Staff of the International Studies Group of the Brookings Institution, *Major Problems of United States Foreign Policy, 1952-53,* Washington: 1952, p. 289; *Staff Papers Presented to the U.S. Commission on Foreign Economic Policy,* Washington, D.C.: Feb. 1954, pp. 251-54; Study Group Sponsored by the Woodrow Wilson Foundation and the National Planning Association, *The Political Economy of American Foreign Policy,* New York: Henry Holt & Co., 1955, p. 135.

Private statements: DoD, *The Pentagon Papers, Sen. Gravel Edition,* Boston: Beacon Press, 1971, vol. 1, pp. 375, 386, 436, 450; Council on Foreign Relations, Study Group Reports, Japanese Peace Treaty Problems, digest of discussion, 23 Oct. 1950, in John Foster Dulles Papers, Princeton University; "Opening Statement by Secretary Dulles before the First Closed Session of the Bangkok Conference, February 23, 1955," in Dulles Papers; Dean Acheson to all Diplomatic and ECA Far East Missions (including South Asia), 21 Dec. 1951, Subject: Relationship with Japan and Production of Essential

Materials, in Myron M. Cowen Papers, Truman Library, Independence, MO; D/S, "Urgency of Tariff Negotiations to Increase Japan's Trade," 18 June 1954, p. 3, in Dwight D. Eisenhower Papers, Eisenhower Library, Abilene, KS (Official File, OF 149-B-2, Apr. 1955).

For many additional citations and further discussion, see Gabriel Kolko, *The Roots of American Foreign Policy,* Boston: Beacon Press, 1969, pp. 99-100, 105; John W. Dower, "The Superdomino in Postwar Asia: Japan In and Out of the Pentagon Papers," in *The Pentagon Papers, Sen. Gravel Edition,* vol. 5, *Critical Essays,* ed. Noam Chomsky and Howard Zinn, Boston: Beacon Press, 1972; Noam Chomsky, *For Reasons of State,* New York: Vintage, 1973, pp. 39-42; Frederick S. Dunn, et al., *Peace-Making and the Settlement with Japan,* Princeton: Princeton UP, 1963, pp. 145, 149; Jerome B. Cohen, *Economic Problems of Free Japan,* Princeton: Center for International Studies, Princeton University, Memorandum No. 2, 1952, p. 84; Carl Oglesby in Carl Oglesby and Richard Schaull, *Containment and Change,* New York: Macmillan, 1967, pp. 123-29; Chomsky, *At War with Asia,* pp. 33-36; Kolko and Kolko, *The Limits of Power,* p. 795n22; Hernando J. Abaya, *The Untold Philippine Story,* Quezon City: Malaya Books, 1967, pp. 54-55; Robert Pringle, *Indonesia and the Philippines: American Interests in Island Southeast Asia,* New York: Columbia UP, 1980, pp. 134-38.

24. Thomson, Stanley, & Perry, *Sentimental Imperialists,* p. 102, state that the argument that overseas markets were needed to solve the problems of the U.S. economy, both "as an analysis of the economy and as a prescription for its future" was "wrong," and "was widely understood, or at least suspected, to be wrong at the time." Walter LaFeber, *The New Empire: An Interpretation of American Expansion, 1860-1898,* (Ithaca: Cornell UP, 1963), and Thomas J. McCormick, *The China Market: America's Quest for Informal Empire, 1893-1901,* (Chicago: Quadrangle, 1967), provide a great deal of evidence that government and business leaders thought the argument to be correct; Thomson, Stanley, & Perry give none to support their contrary view.

25. For example, Charles P. Kindleberger writes, "Nor is neo-imperialism proof against confiscation of foreign properties in the host countries, witness Mexico, Iran, Ceylon, Indonesia, Peru and so on." (*Power and Money,* New York: Basic Books, 1970, p. 81.) This shows no more, however, than that U.S. power is not unlimited (leaving aside the fact that at least in the case of Iran the United States did help topple a government that nationalized foreign assets).

26. Charles T. Goodsell, *American Corporations and Peruvian Politics,* Cambridge, MA: Harvard UP, 1974, pp. 46-47, 55, 85, 130-31, 134-37.

27. James R. Kurth, "Testing Theories of Economic Imperialism," in *Testing Theories of Economic Imperialism,* ed. Steven J. Rosen and James R. Kurth, Lexington, MA: Lexington Books, 1974, p. 13.

28. Sen., Select Comm. on Intelligence Activities, *Alleged Assassination Plots Against Foreign Leaders,* Sen. Report No. 94-465, Nov. 1975, pp. 139-48.

29. It is sometimes suggested that U.S. intervention in Chile was supported only by that rogue elephant of the corporate world, ITT (e.g., Bruce M. Russett and Elizabeth C. Hanson, *Interest and Ideology: The Foreign Policy Beliefs of American Businessmen,* San Francisco: W.H. Freeman, 1975, p. 43). But in 1970 the chairperson of the board of Anaconda and the Council for Latin America—whose "member companies control 85 percent of United States private investments in Latin America and have wide influence in Washington"—urged the U.S. government to actively intervene to prevent Allende's election. Anaconda and other concerns offered to funnel money to a right-wing candidate, but Washington declined the offer, preferring to use taxpayers' money. (Seymour Hersh, *NYT,* 24 Dec. 1976, p. A3.)

30. Harold Macmillan, *Riding the Storm, 1956-1959,* New York: Harper & Row, 1971, p. 522; Dwight D. Eisenhower, *Waging Peace, 1956-1961,* Garden City, NY: Doubleday, 1965, pp. 271, 278, 286. According to a study for the Council on Foreign Relations, Washington and London "knew that an armed venture in Iraq might be the one thing that would bring Soviet forces into the Middle East. It could unite the whole Arab world against them, making impossible any future position there for the West except one based on force alone.... If a real civil struggle had developed in Iraq, that might have put a different face on the matter. But no part of the Iraqi army took up arms in defense of the Hashemite dynasty...or of the old regime, whose demise was greeted with general rejoicing." The new government of Abdul Karim Qassim "seemed to be popular and in full control," was not joining the UAR, was not a foreign puppet, and "gave assurances that oil would continue to be shipped westward." (John C. Campbell, *Defense of the Middle East: Problems of American Policy,* New York: Praeger, 1960, p. 147.) Even an analyst who argues that the U.S. intervention in Lebanon did not aim to stage a counter-revolution in Iraq, acknowledges that Eisenhower "wanted to have some forces in the area in case events took an unexpected turn," for example, if pro-west officers in Iraq called for help. U.S. goals, he says, included being prepared to act "in or against Iraq should circumstances require." (William B. Quandt, "Lebanon, 1958, and Jordan, 1970," in *Force Without War: U.S. Armed Forces as a Political Instrument,* ed. Barry M. Blechman and Stephen S. Kaplan, Washington, D.C.: Brookings Institution, 1978.)

31. George W. Stocking, *Middle East Oil: A Study in Political and Economic Controversy,* Nashville: Vanderbilt UP, 1970, pp. 215-16. *NYT* quoted in Micah L. Sifry, "U.S. Intervention in the Middle East: A Case Study," in *The Gulf War Reader,* ed. Micah L. Sifry and Christopher Cerf, New York: Times Books, 1991, p. 32.

32. Thomas Powers, *The Man Who Kept the Secrets: Richard Helms and the CIA,* New York: Knopf, 1979, p. 130; John Ranelagh, *The Agency: The Rise and Decline of the CIA,* New York: Simon & Schuster, 1986, p. 345.

33. Edith and E.F. Penrose, *Iraq: International Relations and National Development,* Boulder: Westview, 1978, p. 288; Hanna Batatu, *The Old Social Classes and the Revolutionary Movements of Iraq,* Princeton: Princeton UP, 1978, pp. 985-86.

34. Richard Drinnon, *Facing West: The Metaphysics of Indian-Hating and Empire Building,* New York: Schocken Books, 1990, pp. 55 (Pequots), 65 (Washington), 199†, 502 (nits), 329 (Sherman).

35. Roosevelt quoted in Oscar M. Alfonso, *Theodore Roosevelt and the Philippines, 1897-1909,* Quezon City: University of the Philippines Press, 1970, p. 20.

36. John W. Dower, *War Without Mercy: Race and Power in the Pacific War,* New York: Pantheon, 1986, p. 151. It has been argued that Roosevelt's views were not true "racism" because he "attributed differences of 'race' to acquired characteristics and to the effect of geographic environment" and "he did not regard the 'backward people' as permanently or inherently inferior" (Howard K. Beale, *Theodore Roosevelt and the Rise of America to World Power,* Baltimore: Johns Hopkins Press, 1956, pp. 30-31) and thus he was "anything but racist in the anthropological sense" (James A. Field, Jr., "American Imperialism: The Worst Chapter in Almost Any Book," *American Historical Review,* vol. 83, no. 3, 1978, p. 649). That Roosevelt was willing to rationalize genocide, however, would seem to make the question of whether he was racist "in the anthropological sense" rather beside the point.

37. Walter L. Williams, "United States Indian Policy and the Debate over Philippine Annexation: Implications for the Origins of American Imperialism," *Journal of American History,* vol. 66, March 1980, p. 820.

38. Michael H. Hunt, *Ideology and U.S. Foreign Policy,* New Haven: Yale UP, 1987, p. 163.

39. Hersh, *Price of Power,* pp. 110-11.

40. Rubin Francis Weston, *Racism in U.S. Imperialism: The Influence of Racial Assumptions on American Foreign Policy, 1893-1946,* Columbia: University of South Carolina Press, 1972, pp. 208-09.

41. Weston, *Racism in U.S. Imperialism,* p. 46.

42. Hunt, *Ideology and U.S. Foreign Policy,* p. 127.

43. Drinnon, *Facing West,* p. 299.

44. Drinnon, *Facing West,* p. 314.

45. Williams, "...Indian Policy...," pp. 827-29.

46. Dower, *War Without Mercy,* p. 152.

47. See Williams, "...Indian Policy...," p. 822; and Daniel B. Schirmer, *Republic Or Empire,* Boston: Schenkman, 1972.

48. Weston, *Racism in U.S. Imperialism,* pp. 125-26 (Vardaman), 101-02, 95 (Tillman), 169 (Newlands), 201-03 (Puerto Rico), 33-34, 74 (Wilson).

49. Dower, *War Without Mercy,* pp. 8, 61-71, 11, 53-55.

50. Hunt, *Ideology and U.S. Foreign Policy,* p. 162.

51. Hunt, *Ideology and U.S. Foreign Policy,* p. 162.

52. Douglas Little, "Cold War and Colonialism in Africa: The United States, France, and the Madagascar Revolt of 1947," *Pacific Historical Review,* vol. 59, no. 4, Nov. 1990, pp. 540-41.

53. Jack O'Dell, "Racism: Fuel for the War Machine," in *Beyond Survival,* ed. Michael Albert and David Dellinger, Boston: South End Press, 1983, pp. 139-40.

54. Little, "Cold War and Colonialism in Africa," p. 528.

55. Hunt, *Ideology and U.S. Foreign Policy,* p. 165.

56. Anthony Lake, *The "Tar Baby" Option,* New York: Columbia UP, 1976. For more on the logic of the Nixon administration's Africa policy, see M.A. El-Khawas and Barry Cohen, *The Kissinger Study of Southern Africa,* Westport, CT: Lawrence Hill, 1976.

57. Hersh, *Price of Power,* p. 110.

58. Quoted in Selig Harrison, *The Widening Gulf: Asian Nationalism and American Policy,* New York: Free Press, 1978, p. 429.

59. Barnet, *Roots of War,* p. 133†, citing Parenti, *The Anti-Communist Impulse.*

60. Harrison, *Widening Gulf,* p. 428.

61. Drinnon, *Facing West,* pp. 456-57.

62. Drinnon, *Facing West,* p. 449. A Vietcong defector who claimed he changed his political views was reported to have given himself away by crying at the end of a movie when the Indians lost. He was said to have been turned over to the South Vietnamese army for internment as a prisoner of war. Reuters, "Vietcong Captives Cheer for Indians in Movies," *NYT,* 23 Jan. 1967.

63. Loren Baritz, *Backfire,* New York: Ballantine, 1985, p. 37.

64. Hunt, *Ideology and U.S. Foreign Policy,* p. 166.

65. David K. Shipler, "The Arab-American Counts His Stereotypes," *NYT,* 31 Dec. 1985, p. B6.

66. Rael Jean Isaac, "Arab 'Lies That Lead to Good Results'" (letter), *NYT,* 23 Feb. 1979, p. A26.

67. Cited in Edward W. Said, *Covering Islam: How the Media and the Experts Determine How We See the Rest of the World,* New York: Pantheon, 1981, p. xxviii. This book and Said's *Orientalism* (New York: Vintage, 1978) contain many further examples of racist views of Arabs and Muslims.

68. See Nabeel Abraham, "The Gulf Crisis and Anti-Arab Racism in America," in *Collateral Damage: The 'New World Order' At Home and Abroad,* ed. Cynthia Peters, Boston: South End Press, 1992, for discussion and many examples of anti-Arab incidents.

69. Dower, *War Without Mercy,* pp. 99-111.

70. Henry Kissinger, *White House Years*, Boston: Little, Brown & Co., 1979, p. 6.
71. Peter G. Filene, *Him/Her/Self: Sex Roles in Modern America*, 2nd ed., Baltimore: Johns Hopkins UP, 1986, p. 70.
72. Hunt, *Ideology and U.S. Foreign Policy*, p. 128.
73. Theodore Roosevelt, "Fear God and Take Your Own Part (1916) in *War: An International Anthology*, ed. Melvin Small and J. David Singer, 2nd ed., Chicago: Dorsey Press, 1989, p. 106.
74. Barnet, *Roots of War*, p. 109.
75. Marc Feigen Fasteau, *The Male Machine*, New York: Delta, 1975, p. 164.
76. Fasteau, *Male Machine*, p. 163.
77. Fasteau, *Male Machine*, p. 172.
78. Barnet, *Roots of War*, p. 115.
79. *Newsweek*, 22 April 1991, p. 54, citing Robert Caro, *The Years of Lyndon Johnson*.
80. Gloria Steinem, "The Myth of Masculine Mystique," in *Men and Masculinity*, ed. Joseph H. Pleck and Jack Sawyer, Englewood Cliffs, NJ: Prentice Hall, 1974, p. 136.
81. Quoted in Fasteau, *Male Machine*, p. 173.
82. Fasteau, *Male Machine*, p. 174.
83. Kissinger, *White House Years*, p. 74.
84. Kissinger, *White House Years*, p. 491.
85. Steinem, "Myth of Masculine Mystique," p. 137.
86. Fasteau, *Male Machine*, p. 184.
87. Kissinger, *White House Years*, p. 191.
88. Hersh, *Price of Power*, p. 100n.
89. Bruce Mazlish, *Kissinger: The European Mind in American Policy*, New York: Basic Books, 1976, pp. 134, 145.
90. Kissinger, *White House Years*, p. 318.
91. Hersh, *Price of Power*, pp. 108-09, 113.
92. Susan Griffin, "Ideologies of Madness," in *Exposing Nuclear Phallacies*, ed. Diana E.H. Russell, New York: Pergamon, 1989, pp. 119-20.
93. Cynthia Enloe, *Bananas, Beaches, and Bases: Making Feminist Sense of International Politics*, Berkeley: University of California Press, 1990, pp. 74-75.
94. Naomi Weisstein, *Nation*, 15/22 July 1991, p. 131.
95. Lloyd S. Etheredge, *A World of Men: The Private Sources of American Foreign Policy*, Cambridge, MA: MIT Press, 1978, pp. 60-62.
96. Diana E.H. Russell, "Sexism, Violence, and the Nuclear mentality," in Russell, ed., *Exposing Nuclear Phallacies*, pp. 69-70.
97. Quoted in Herbert Mitgang's review of Jean Edward Smith, *George Bush's War* (Holt, 1992), *NYT*, 18 March 1992, p. C19.
98. Joan Hoff-Wilson, "Conclusion: Of Mice and Men," in *Women and American Foreign Policy, Lobbyists, Critics, and Insiders*, ed. Edward P. Crapol, Westport, CT: Greenwood Press, 1987, p. 174, also pp. 175-76; GAO, *Minorities and Women Are Underrepresented in the Foreign Service*, GAO/NSIAD-89-146, June 1989.
99. Wilson, who was head of General Motors before being made Secretary of Defense, said, "What was good for the United States was good for General Motors and vice versa." Eisenhower complained that critics erroneously interpreted Wilson as meaning that what was good for General Motors was good for the U.S., but since Wilson said "and vice versa" this interpretation is entirely correct. See Dwight D. Eisenhower, *Mandate for Change, 1953-1956*, Garden City, NY: Doubleday, 1963, pp. 110-11.

2: The Soviet Threat

1. Robert Rudolph, "The Schoolboy Suspect," *SL,* 24 May 1988, p. 8; Robert Rudolph, "FBI Defends Its Probe of Jersey Schoolboy, Denies 'Intrusive' Conduct," *SL,* 27 May 1988, p. 28; *WSJ,* 15 Jan. 1990, pp. B2, B6.

2. On the domestic sources of the Soviet threat, see Alan Wolfe, *The Rise and Fall of the Soviet Threat,* Boston: South End Press, 1984.

3. For example, DoD officials have claimed that the Pentagon's $50 million computing initiative can help the "Star Wars" project, but "is based on a much broader concept of defense: By strengthening the civilian computer industry, they contend, the Pentagon will help insure that the United States does not fall behind in developing sophisticated technologies that are necessary not only for military defense but also for economic survival." Warren E. Leary, "The Battle To Mechanize The Military Mind," *NYT,* 15 May 1988, p. 7E.

4. Kissinger and Brzezinski quoted in Theodore Draper, "American Hubris," in *The Gulf War Reader,* ed. Micah L. Sifry and Christopher Cerf, New York: Times Books, 1991, p. 55.

5. Boren speech to National Press Club, 3 April 1990, quoted in Gabriel Kolko, "The Gulf and Afterwards: The Future of American Foreign Policy," *Studies in Political Economy,* no. 34, Spring 1991, p. 9.

6. Quoted in Ronald Steel, "Cold War, Cold Comfort," *New Republic,* 11 April 1981, pp. 15-17.

7. Quoted in Ronald Steel, *Walter Lippmann and the American Century,* New York: Vintage, 1980, p. 237.

8. Frank Kellogg, "Bolshevik Aims and Policies in Mexico and Latin America," *Cong. Rec.,* Sen., 14 Jan. 1927, p. 1649, quoted in Philip Brenner, "Waging Ideological War: Anti-Communism and U.S. Foreign Policy in Central America," in *Socialist Register, 1984: The Uses of Anti-Communism,* ed. Ralph Miliband, John Saville, & Marcel Liebman, London: Merlin, 1984, p. 230.

9. Melvyn P. Leffler, "Adherence to Agreements: Yalta and the Experiences of the Early Cold War," *International Security,* vol. 11, no. 1, Summer 1986, p. 89.

10. Leffler, "Adherence to Agreements," p. 112.

11. Quoted in Jose W. Diokno, *A Nation for Our Children,* ed. Priscila S. Manalang, Quezon City: Jose W. Diokno Foundation and Claretian Publications, 1987, p. 186.

12. Joseph M. Jones, *The Fifteen Weeks,* New York: Viking Press, 1955, pp. 139-42, 151. See also Dean Acheson, *Present at the Creation,* New York: New American Library, 1969, p. 293; Lawrence S. Wittner, "The Truman Doctrine and the Defense of Freedom," *Diplomatic History,* vol. 4, no. 2, Spring 1980.

13. Matthew A. Evangelista, "Stalin's Postwar Army Reappraised," (1982/83) in *Soviet Military Policy,* ed. Sean M. Lynn-Jones, Steven E. Miller, and Stephen Van Evera, Cambridge, MA: MIT Press, 1989, p. 294. To quote hawk Adam Ulam: "quite apart from the atom bomb," war with the United States over Western Europe was "simply inconceivable to a man as realistic and cautious as Stalin" (*Expansion and Coexistence: The History of Soviet Foreign Policy, 1917-67,* New York: Praeger, 1968, p. 414). See concurring views of George Kennan and Bernard Brodie quoted in John Mueller, "The Essential Irrelevance of Nuclear Weapons," *International Security,* vol. 13, no. 2, Fall 1988, p. 60n11.

14. Acheson, *Present at the Creation,* pp.375-76; Paul Y. Hammond, "NSC-68: Prelude to Rearmament," in *Strategy, Politics, and Defense Budgets,* ed. Warner Schilling, New York: Columbia UP, 1962, p. 309, cited in Alan Wolfe, "The Irony of Anti-Communism: Ideology and Interest in Post-War American Foreign Policy," in Miliband, et al., eds., *Socialist Register, 1984,* p. 217.

15. Walter LaFeber, *America, Russia, and the Cold War, 1945-1980,* 4th ed., New York: John Wiley, 1980, p. 132.

16. Dulles, 9 May 1958, quoted in LaFeber, *America, Russia,...,* p. 207.

17. Lloyd S. Etheredge, *Can Governments Learn?* New York: Pergamon, 1985, pp. 28n22, 29n29. Shortly before the coup, Guatemala's Foreign Minister charged that U.S. policy amounted to "cataloguing as 'Communism' every manifestation of nationalism or economic independence, any desire for social progress, any intellectual curiosity, and any interest in progressive or liberal reforms...." Quoted in Noam Chomsky, *Turning the Tide,* Boston: South End Press, 1985, p. 52.

18. *Cong. Rec.,* 1954, pt. 1, p. 249, quoted in Richard H. Immerman, *The CIA in Guatemala,* Austin: University of Texas Press, 1982, pp. 102-03.

19. Quoted in D.F. Fleming, *The Cold War and Its Origins, 1917-1960,* Garden City, NY: Doubleday, 1961, p. II:1052, citing *Nation,* 17 Aug. 1957, p. 62.

20. Sen., Select Comm. on Intelligence Activities, *Alleged Assassination Plots Against Foreign Leaders,* Sen. Report No. 94-465, Nov. 1975, p. 93.

21. McNamara interview in Robert Scheer, *With Enough Shovels,* New York: Vintage, 1983, pp. 214-15.

22. Alain C. Enthoven and K. Wayne Smith, *How Much Is Enough?* New York: Harper Colophon, 1971, pp. 133, 135, 153-54.

23. Quoted in Arthur Macy Cox, *Russian Roulette,* New York: Times Books, 1982, pp. 110-111.

24. See Franklyn D. Holzman, "Soviet Military Spending: Assessing the Numbers Game," *International Security,* vol. 6, no. 4, Spring 1982. CIA number-juggling continued into the 1980s. See Franklyn D. Holzman, "Politics and Guesswork: CIA and DIA Estimates of Soviet Military Spending," *International Security,* vol. 14, no. 2, Fall 1989; and Holzman's exchange with James E. Steiner of the CIA, "CIA Estimates of Soviet Military Spending," *International Security,* vol. 14, no. 4, Spring 1990.

25. Richard Ned Lebow, "The Soviet Offensive in Europe: The Schlieffen Plan Revisited?" (1985) in Lynn-Jones, et al., eds., *Soviet Military Policy,* p. 328.

26. Andrew Cockburn, *The Threat: Inside the Soviet Military Machine,* New York: Vintage, 1983, pp. 57-58, citing interviews conducted by the DoD.

27. Cockburn, *Threat,* p. 63.

28. Cockburn, *Threat,* pp. 263-64.

29. Robert W. Komer, "What 'Decade of Neglect'?" *International Security,* vol. 10, no. 2, Fall 1985, pp. 73, 75.

30. Alarmist assessments are collected in Michael Salman, Kevin J. Sullivan, and Stephen Van Evera, "Analysis or Propaganda? Measuring American Strategic Nuclear Capability, 1969-88," in *Nuclear Arguments: Understanding the Strategic Nuclear Arms and Arms Control Debates,* ed. Lynn Eden and Steven E. Miller, Ithaca: Cornell UP, 1989, pp. 173-5; Jones is quoted on p. 174n4. The authors show that the claims of Soviet superiority were false both in the early and the late 1980s. For more enlightenment from T. K. Jones, see Scheer, *With Enough Shovels,* pp. 18-26.

31. E.g., DoD, *Soviet Military Power, 1985,* 1985, pp. 24-25.

32. Cockburn, *Threat,* pp. 407-08.

33. James Cable, "Gunboat Diplomacy's Future," *Proceedings,* U.S. Naval Institute, Aug. 1986, pp. 38-39.

34. U.S. officials asserted that they had to do so in order to establish their right to sail in international waters. This legal argument is false (see Charles Maechling, Jr., "Crisis at the Turkish Straits," *Proceedings,* U.S. Naval Institute, Aug. 1988, pp. 69-70) and if, as the press reported, U.S. ships were engaged in intelligence gathering while in Soviet waters, then their presence was illegal (W.E. Butler, "Innocent Passage and the 1982

Convention: The Influence of Soviet Law and Policy," *American Journal of International Law,* vol. 81, 1987, p. 345).

35. Frank Elliott, "The Navy in 1987," *Proceedings,* U.S. Naval Institute, May 1988, p. 146-147.

36. Bryan Ranft and Geoffrey Till, *The Sea in Soviet Strategy,* Annapolis: Naval Institute Press, 1983, pp. 197-98.

37. Richard Sharpe, ed., *Jane's Fighting Ships, 1988-89,* London: Jane's Publishing, 1988, p. 111.

38. Raymond Bonner, *Weakness and Deceit: U.S. Policy and El Salvador,* New York: Times Books, 1984, pp. 256-60.

39. *Jacobsen Report,* quoted in Holly Sklar, *Washington's War on Nicaragua,* Boston: South End Press, 1988, pp. 209-10.

40. Noam Chomsky, *The Culture of Terrorism,* Boston: South End Press, 1988, p. 156, citing report in the *Boston Globe.*

41. Bill Keller, *NYT,* 10 May 1987, p. 3E. The *Times* headlined this story "Kremlin Reinterprets and Re-emphasizes the Legacy of Lenin"; much more accurate would have been "Reagan Lies," but the U.S. press largely accepts the worldview of the U.S. government.

42. *NYT,* 13 Jan. 1988, p. A9. I omit here the issue of what the Korean airliner was actually doing over Soviet airspace. For reasons to doubt the official explanation, see Richard Witkin, "Study Says Korean Airliner Was On Its Intended Course When Downed in '83," *NYT,* 20 Feb. 1992, p. A12.

43. William J. Broad, "CIA Disputes White House on Soviet Antimissile Gains," *NYT,* 29 May 1986, p. B5.

44. HR, Foreign Affairs Comm., subcomm. on Asian and Pacific Affairs, *Situation and Outlook in the Philippines,* Hearings, Oct. 1984, p. 191.

45. Sen., Foreign Relations Comm., subcomm. on U.S. Security Agreements and Commitments Abroad, *United States Security Agreements and Commitments Abroad: The Republic of the Philippines,* Hearings, Sept.-Oct. 1969, p. 245.

46. Leif Rosenberger, "Philippine Communism and the Soviet Union," *Survey,* Spring 1985, p. 137.

47. Richard J. Kessler, *WP,* 26 July 1987, pp. B1, B4.

48. All the materials available at the Soviet embassy in Manila when I was there in June 1988 were in English.

49. Robert Shaplen, "The Thin Edge," *New Yorker,* 21 Sept. 1987, p. 74.

50. U.S. Navy, "Admiral Lyons Press Conference Transcript," Naval Message 090754Z, Feb. 1987, section 2:2.

51. See the sources cited in Stephen R. Shalom, "Trading Off Foreign Military Bases in the Philippines and Vietnam: The Strategic Implications," *Pilipinas,* no. 10, Spring 1988, pp. 27-28.

52. Hamish McDonald, "The Cam Ranh Bugbear," *Far Eastern Economic Review,* 18 June 1987, pp. 34-35.

53. See Shalom, "Trading Off…," pp. 29-30.

54. DoD, *Soviet Military Power: An Assessment of the Threat, 1988,* 1988, p. 85.

55. David Wood, "Navy Battens Down Hatches Against Potential 'Threat' of Arms Control," *SL,* 13 Aug. 1989, p. I:65.

56. Reuters, *SL,* 25 Mar. 1988, p. 6.

57. C.A.H. Trost, "The Morning of the Empty Trenches: Soviet Politics of Maneuver and the U.S. Response," *Proceedings,* U.S. Naval Institute, Aug. 1988, p. 14.

58. Joseph K. Woodard, "The Soviet Navy and Command of the Seas," *Global Affairs,* Spring 1989, pp. 46-47.

3: Stopping the Spread of Weapons of Mass Destruction

1. *Newsweek,* 3 Dec. 1990, p. 22; "Taking Out Iraq's Nukes," *NYT,* 25 Nov. 1990, p. E10; Michael R. Gordon, "U.S. Aides Press Iraqi Nuclear Threat," *NYT,* 26 Nov. 1990, p. A13.
2. Barry Rubin, *Paved With Good Intentions,* New York: Penguin, 1980, p. 133; Amin Saikal, *The Rise and Fall of the Shah,* Princeton: Princeton UP, 1980, p. 165.
3. Andrew J. Pierre, *The Global Politics of Arms Sales,* Princeton: Princeton UP, 1982, pp. 48, 145-49.
4. Pierre, *Global Politics of Arms Sales,* pp. 150-51.
5. Seymour M. Hersh, *The Price of Power: Kissinger in the Nixon White House,* NY: Summit, 1983, p. 542n.
6. See Chapter 1, note 5.
7. Henry Kissinger, *White House Years,* Boston: Little, Brown, 1979, p. 1265; Henry Kissinger, *Years of Upheaval,* Boston: Little, Brown, 1982.
8. Stephen C. Pelletiere, Douglas V. Johnson II, and Leif R. Rosenberger, *Iraqi Power and U.S. Security in the Middle East,* Carlisle Barracks, PA: Strategic Studies Institute, U.S. Army War College, 1990, p. 16.
9. Efraim Karsh, "Military Power and Foreign Policy Goals: The Iran-Iraq War Revisited," *International Affairs,* vol. 64, no. 1, Winter 1987/88, p. 84. Likewise: "The destabilization of the regional balance of power in the Middle East was produced by a series of arms-export drives.... The first radical destabilization of this balance occurred when the Shah was armed to the teeth by Kissinger and Nixon." This allowed the Shah to unilaterally renounce the frontier treaty with Iraq which in turn "fueled Iraqi arms purchases and drove the communist-exterminating Saddam into the arms of the Soviet Union" (Frederic P. Smoler, "The Arming of Saddam Hussein," *Dissent,* Summer 1991, pp. 350-51).
10. Pierre, *Global Politics of Arms Sales,* p. 49.
11. Pierre, *Global Politics of Arms Sales,* p. 49.
12. Christian Catrina, *Arms Transfers and Dependence,* New York: Taylor & Francis for UNIDIR, 1988, pp. 378-79.
13. Cyrus Vance, *Hard Choices,* New York: Simon & Schuster, 1983, p. 319. Another policy-maker, however, states that Israel and Saudi Arabia were denied exclusion from the ceiling. William B. Quandt, *Decade of Decisions,* Berkeley: University of California Press, 1977, p. 118.
14. Pierre, *Global Politics of Arms Sales,* pp. 47, 57-8, 61.
15. Zbigniew Brzezinski, *Power and Principle: Memoirs of the National Security Adviser, 1977-1981,* New York: Farrar, Straus, Giroux, 1983, pp. 144-45. For a discussion of the problems in measuring arms transfers (does one count agreements or deliveries, are small arms included, etc.?) see Catrina, *Arms Transfers and Dependence,* pp. 18-26, 51-56, 363-77.
16. Pierre, *Global Politics of Arms Sales,* pp. 286-89.
17. Barry M. Blechman, Janne E. Nolan, and Alan Platt, "Pushing Arms," *Foreign Policy,* no. 46, spring 1982, p. 147; see also Raymond L. Garthoff, *Détente and Confrontation,* Washington, D.C.: Brookings, 1985, p. 761.
18. Blechman, et al., "Pushing Arms," pp. 140-41.
19. Karsh, "Military Power...," p. 89.
20. Pelletiere, et al., *Iraqi Power...,* p. 93n166.
21. Douglas Frantz and Murray Waas, "Bush Secret Effort Helped Iraq Build its War Machine," *LAT,* 23 Feb. 1992, p. A1; Douglas Frantz and Murray Waas, "U.S. Loans Indirectly Financed Iraq Military," *LAT,* 25 Feb. 1992, p. A1.
22. William D. Hartung, "Relighting the Mideast Fuse," *NYT,* 20 Sept. 1991, p. A27; Eric Schmitt, "U.S. To Sell Saudis $20 Billion In Arms; Weapons Deal Is Largest In History,"

NYT, 15 Sept. 1990, p. 5; AP, "U.S. Helps To Rearm In Mideast As It Talks Peace," *SL,* 6 March 1991, p. 10; Patrick E. Tyler, "Cheney Wants No Limit On Arms For Gulf Allies," *NYT,* 20 Mar. 1991; Robert Pear, "U.S. Ranked No. 1 in Weapons Sales," *NYT,* 11 Aug. 1991, p. I:10; Eric Schmitt, "Cheney Says U.S. Plans New Arms Sale to the Middle East," *NYT,* 5 June 1991, p. A3; Michael T. Klare, "It's Business As Usual," *Nation,* 3 Feb. 1992, p. 120. Naturally, the tax-payer was asked to help subsidize U.S. arms exports: see Clyde H. Farnsworth, "White House Seeks to Revive Credits for Arms Exports," *NYT,* 18 March 1991, p. A1, D6. In 1991, U.S. arms sales to the Middle East were six times as large as sales from the next largest supplier, Yugoslavia (AP, "U.S. Arms Sales to Mideast Are 'Towering,'" *SL,* 13 March 1992, p. 14).

23. David B. Ottaway, "Middle East Weapons Proliferate," *WP,* 19 Dec. 1988, p. A4.

24. Edward M. Spiers, *Chemical Warfare,* Urbana: University of Illinois Press, 1986, p. 13.

25. Leonard A. Cole, *Clouds of Secrecy,* Savage, MD: Littlefield, Adams, 1990, pp. 11-12.

26. Spiers, *Chemical Warfare,* p. 14.

27. Charles Piller and Keith R. Yamamoto, *Gene Wars: Military Control Over the New Genetic Technologies,* New York: William Morrow, 1988, p. 30.

28. David E. Omissi, *Air Power and Colonial Control: The Royal Air Force, 1919-1939,* Manchester: Manchester UP, 1990, pp. 14, 21, 160, 182. Churchill quoted in *WESPAC Newsletter,* June-July 1991, p. 7.

29. See HR, Foreign Affairs Comm., subcomm. on National Security Policy and Scientific Developments, *U.S. Chemical Warfare Policy,* Hearings, May 1974, pp. 365-66.

30. Spiers, *Chemical Warfare,* pp. 89-97.

31. Spiers, *Chemical Warfare,* pp. 97-104.

32. John W. Powell, "Japan's Germ Warfare: The U.S. Cover-up of a War Crime," *Bulletin of Concerned Asian Scholars,* vol. 12, no. 4, Oct.-Dec. 1980; John W. Powell, "A Hidden Chapter in History," *Bulletin of the Atomic Scientists,* vol. 37, no. 8, Oct. 1981.

33. Spiers, *Chemical Warfare,* pp. 80-84.

34. John Ellis van Courtland Moon, "Project SPHINX: The Question of the Use of Gas in the Planned Invasion of Japan," *Journal of Strategic Studies,* vol. 12, no. 3, 1989, pp. 303-323.

35. Powell, "Japan's Germ Warfare."

36. Jaap van Ginneken, "Bacteriological Warfare," *Journal of Contemporary Asia,* vol. 7, no. 2, 1977, p. 134.

37. Powell, "Japan's Germ Warfare," pp. 2-3, 15n1.

38. See van Ginneken, "Bacteriological Warfare"; Stephen L. Endicott, "Germ Warfare and 'Plausible Denial': The Korean War 1952-1953," *Modern China,* vol. 5, no. 1, Jan. 1979; Jeanne McDermott, *The Killing Winds,* New York: Arbor House, 1987, pp. 158-69.

39. Richard D. McCarthy, *The Ultimate Folly,* New York: Knopf, 1970, p. 24.

40. Piller and Yamamoto, *Gene Wars,* p. 47.

41. Cole, *Clouds of Secrecy,* p. 33.

42. Cole, *Clouds of Secrecy,* pp. 45-46.

43. Cole, *Clouds of Secrecy,* pp. 68-69.

44. McCarthy, *Ultimate Folly,* p. 66.

45. Thomas Powers, *The Man Who Kept the Secrets: Richard Helms and the CIA,* New York: Knopf, 1979, p. 130; John Ranelagh, *The Agency: The Rise and Decline of the CIA,* New York: Simon & Schuster, 1986, p. 345.

46. See Fred A. Wilcox, *Waiting for an Army to Die: The Tragedy of Agent Orange,* New York: Vintage, 1983, pp. 59-78.

47. Elisa D. Harris, "The Biological and Toxin Weapons Convention," in *Superpower Arms Control: Setting the Record Straight,* ed. Albert Carnesale and Richard N. Haass, Cambridge, MA: Ballinger, 1987, pp. 196-97. For the resolution, see HR, *U.S. Chemical Warfare Policy,* pp. 372-73.

48. Clergy and Laity Concerned, *In the Name of America,* Annandale, VA: Turnpike Press, 1968, p. 121.

49. Clergy and Laity Concerned, *In the Name of America,* p. 124; John Duffett, ed., *Against the Crime of Silence: Proceedings of the Russell International War Crimes Tribunal,* New York: O'Hare Books, 1968, p. 344.

50. HR, Foreign Affairs Comm., subcomm. on National Security Policy and Scientific Developments, *Chemical and Biological Warfare: U.S. Policies and International Effects,* Hearings, Nov.-Dec. 1969, pp. 151, 225, 228; and the press reports quoted in Duffett, *Against the Crime of Silence,* pp. 345-46; Clergy and Laity Concerned, *In the Name of America,* p. 125.

51. HR, *Chemical and Biological...,* p. 196. Compare this view with a front-page *NYT* story headlined "UN Team Finds Chemical Arms 4 Times Greater Than Iraq Claims" (Frank J. Prial, 31 July 1991, pp. A1, A6). The head of the UN inspection team was quoted as saying that "a large number" of the Iraqi weapons "had turned out to contain 'relatively harmless' tear gas. But he emphasized that they were military weapons, to be used in combat, rather than riot-control weapons normally used by the police."

52. HR, *Chemical and Biological...,* p. 215.

53. Ralph Littauer and Norman Uphoff, eds., *The Air War in Indochina,* rev. ed., Boston: Beacon Press, 1972, p. 96.

54. Harris, "Biological and Toxin...," pp. 191-92. In 1975, President Ford issued an executive order renouncing the "first use of riot control agents in war except in defensive military modes to save lives." In the 1991 war against Iraq, the Pentagon gave the U.S. commander the authority to initiate use of non-lethal riot-control gases. The *NYT* reporter noted that it was "unclear" whether the U.S. would be able to use such gases in offensive military operations. Patrick E. Tyler, "Pentagon Said to Authorize U.S. Use of Nonlethal Gas," *NYT,* 26 Jan. 1991.

55. Littauer and Uphoff, *Air War in Indochina,* p. 243.

56. Drew Fetherston and John Cummings (*Newsday*), "CIA Linked to 1971 Swine Virus in Cuba," *WP,* 9 Jan. 1977, p. A2. See also re an apparently unconsummated 1962 operation: Drew Fetherston and John Cummings (*Newsday*), "Canadian Says U.S. Paid Him $5,000 to Infect Cuban Poultry," *WP,* 21 March 1977, p. A18.

57. Sen., Select Comm. to Study Governmental Operations on Intelligence Activities, *Unauthorized Storage of Toxic Agents,* Hearings, Sept. 1975.

58. This was not the first controversy regarding Soviet compliance with the Biological and Toxin Weapons Convention. In 1979, an outbreak of anthrax occurred in the Soviet city of Sverdlovsk. On March 17, 1980, the Carter administration privately asked Moscow to explain what happened. The next day, before any chance for a Soviet reply, the administration publicly announced its suspicion that there had been an accident at a biological warfare facility. Washington was quite right to make an inquiry, but, as unidentified officials acknowledged to the *NYT,* the decision to go public was "part of an anti-Soviet campaign" and the timing was "no accident," coming as the Cold War was heating up again following the Soviet invasion of Afghanistan.

Whether the Soviet Union was engaged in proscribed biological warfare activity (or even "defensive" research permitted under the 1972 Convention) is unknown. Moscow claimed that the outbreak was due to tainted meat sold on the black market. The Soviet explanation, noted Elisa Harris after a careful study in 1987, was plausible and "supported by more of the evidence available in the public domain than [was] the U.S. explanation." More recently, a number of articles in the Soviet and Russian press suggest that the Soviet explanation was false, but many questions still remain. (Elisa D. Harris, "Sverdlovsk and Yellow Rain: Two Cases of Soviet Noncompliance?" *International Security,* vol. 11, no. 4, Spring 1987, pp. 45-46, 93n211, 56, 55n58 [a draft of this article was submitted to the CIA for security review]; Milton Leitenberg, "Anthrax in Sverdlovsk: New Pieces to the Puzzle," *Arms Control Today,* April 1992, pp. 10-13.)

59. Kenneth Adelman quoted in Lois R. Ember, "Worldwide Spread of Chemical Arms Receiving Increased Attention," *Chemical & Engineering News,* 14 April 1986, p. 9.

60. McDermott, *Killing Winds,* p. 66.

61. Robert L. Bartley and William P. Kucewicz, "'Yellow Rain' and the Future of Arms Agreements," *Foreign Affairs,* vol. 61, no. 4, Spring 1983, p. 814.

62. Bartley and Kucewicz, "Yellow Rain...," pp. 815-16, 821.

63. Julian Robinson, Jeanne Guilleman, and Matthew Meselson, "Yellow Rain: the Story Collapses," *Foreign Policy,* no. 68, Fall 1987, p. 103.

64. See Grant Evans, *The Yellow Rainmakers,* London: Verso, 1983; Lois R. Ember, "Yellow Rain," *Chemical & Engineering News,* 9 Jan. 1984; Jacqui Chagnon and Roger Rumpf, "Search for Yellow Rain," *Southeast Asia Chronicle,* no. 90, June 1983.

65. Robinson, et al., "Yellow Rain..."; Ember, "Yellow Rain."

66. Harris, "Sverdlovsk and Yellow Rain," p. 90-91.

67. No. 90, June 1983.

68. Robinson, et al., "Yellow Rain...," pp. 108-09, 112-13, 115; Philip M. Boffey, "Declassified Cables Add to Doubts About U.S. Disclosures on 'Yellow Rain'," *NYT,* 31 Aug. 87, p. A14.

69. Wayne Biddle, "Restocking the Chemical Arsenal," *NYT Magazine,* 25 May 1981, p. 38.

70. McDermott, *Killing Winds,* p. 76.

71. Kenneth Adelman, "Chemical Weapons: Restoring the Taboo," *Orbis,* Fall 1986, pp. 453-54.

72. Ember, "Worldwide Spread...," p. 10.

73. Adelman, "Chemical Weapons: Restoring the Taboo," p. 454.

74. U.S. Arms Control and Disarmament Agency, *Documents on Disarmament, 1984,* Washington, D.C.: 1986, pp. 135-36.

75. R.P.H. King, "The United Nations and the Iran-Iraq War, 1980-1986," in Brian Urquhart and Gary Sick, eds., *The United Nations and the Iran-Iraq War,* New York: Ford Foundation, August 1987, pp. 19-20; Elaine Sciolino, "How the U.S. Cast Off Neutrality in Gulf War," *NYT,* 24 Ap. 1988, p. 2E.

76. Pelletiere, et al., *Iraqi Power...,* p. ix.

77. See Sen., Foreign Relations Comm., *Chemical Weapons Use in Kurdistan: Iraq's Final Offensive,* staff report, Sept. 1988; Edward Mortimer, letter, *New York Review of Books,* 22 Nov. 1990, p. 53. The primary means of delivering the lethal chemicals was by helicopters purchased from the United States for crop dusting. Steve Fetter, "Weapons of Mass Destruction: What Is The Threat? What Should Be Done?" *International Security,* vol. 16, no. 1, Summer 1991, p. 19.

78. CQ, *CQ Almanac, 1988,* Washington, D.C.: 1989, pp. 510-11; *CQ Weekly Report,* 28 April 1990, pp. 1281-82.

79. Frantz and Waas, "Bush Secret Effort...," p. A1; Frantz and Waas, "U.S. Loans...," p. A1; Richard Hornik, "With A Little Help from Friends," *Time,* 11 June 1990, p. 34.

80. GAO, *Chemical Warfare: Many Unanswered Questions,* GAO/IPE-83-6, 29 April 1983, pp. 26, 35, 49, 52. U.S. intelligence agencies later acknowledged that their estimates of the Soviet chemical weapons stockpile were far too high. See R. Jeffrey Smith, "Estimate of Soviet Arms Is Cut," *WP,* 9 Nov. 1989, p. A71.

81. Jonathan B. Tucker, "Gene Wars," *Foreign Policy,* no. 57, Winter 1984/1985, p. 60; Cole, *Clouds of Secrecy,* 128-32.

82. Cole, *Clouds of Secrecy,* pp. 124-25.

83. Cole, *Clouds of Secrecy,* p. 17.

84. R. Jeffrey Smith, "U.S. Ushers in New Era of Chemical Weapons," *WP*, 15 Jan. 1989, pp. A1, A18. The legislative history can be followed in CQ, *CQ Almanac*, esp. 1983, pp. 175, 178, 186-87, 189-90, 480, 489, 491; 1984, pp. 42-43; 1985, pp. 140, 149, 157, 379, 386, 391-92; 1986, p. 17.

85. Edward Cody, "149 Nations Vow to Shun Poison Gas," *WP*, 12 Jan. 1989, pp. A1, A32.

86. R. Jeffrey Smith, "U.S. to Keep Producing Poison Gas," *WP*, 9 Oct. 1989, pp. A1, A8. Bush had not mentioned his decision when he told the United Nations two weeks earlier that he favored immediate steps to "halt and reverse" the scourge of chemical weapons. Nor had Bush shared with the UN the fact that his offer to cut the U.S. chemical stockpile by 80 percent, if Moscow would agree to do the same, was, as Senator Nunn put it, making "a virtue of necessity," given that Congress had already ordered the destruction of 90 percent of all the Pentagon's pre-1969 chemical stockpile. CQ, *CQ Almanac, 1989*, Washington, D.C.: 1990, pp. 500-01.

87. John Felton, "Approval Seen on Chemical Weapons," *CQ Weekly Report*, 9 June 1990, p. 1800.

88. AP, "Bush Offers To Destroy All U.S. Chemical Weapons," *SL*, 14 May 1991, pp. 1, 6; Michael R. Gordon, "U.S. Weighs A Plan For Arms Control In The Middle East," *NYT*, 14 May 1991, pp. A1, A11.

89. Paul Lewis, "U.S. Now Prefers Limited Inspection of Chemical Arms," *NYT*, 14 Aug. 1991, pp. A1, A6; GAO, *Arms Control: U.S. and International Efforts to Ban Chemical Weapons*, GAO/NSIAD-91-317, Sept. 1991, p. 18.

90. Edward Cody, "Talks Show Growing Arab Consensus That Chemical Arms Balance Nuclear," *WP*, 13 Jan. 1989, p. A24; Fetter, "Weapons of Mass Destruction," p. 33n55.

91. H.W. Brands, Jr., "Testing Massive Retaliation: Credibility and Crisis Management in the Taiwan Strait," *International Security*, vol. 12, no. 4, Spring 1988, p. 149n93.

92. Gordon H. Chang, "To the Nuclear Brink: Eisenhower, Dulles, and the Quemoy-Matsu Crisis," *International Security*, vol. 12, no. 4, Spring 1988, pp. 106-08.

93. Brands, "Testing Massive Retaliation," pp. 126, 128, 142; Chang, "To the Nuclear Brink," pp. 98-99.

94. Chang, "To the Nuclear Brink," p. 121.

95. Joseph S. Nye, "The Superpowers and the Non-proliferation Treaty," in Carnesale and Haass, eds., *Superpower Arms Control*, p. 167, citing William B. Bader, *The United States and the Spread of Nuclear Weapons*, New York: Pegasus, 1968, p. 26.

96. Nye, "Superpowers and Non-proliferation Treaty," p. 168.

97. Garthoff, *Détente and Confrontation*, p. 984n46. Garthoff was involved in these internal deliberations.

98. Seymour M. Hersh, *The Samson Option*, New York: Random House, 1991, pp. 149-50.

99. Nye, "Superpowers and Non-proliferation Treaty," p. 171.

100. Text is in HR, Foreign Affairs Comm. subcomm.; Sen., Governmental Affairs Comm. subcomm.; and Congressional Research Service of the Library of Congress, *Nuclear Proliferation Factbook*, August 1985, pp. 68-73.

101. Ground Zero, *Nuclear War: What's In It For You?* New York: Pocket Books, 1982, p. 267.

102. Garthoff, *Détente and Confrontation*, p. 335.

103. Garthoff, *Détente and Confrontation*, pp. 336-37.

104. Sean M. Lynn-Jones, "Lulling and Stimulating Effects of Arms Control," in Carnesale and Haass, eds., *Superpower Arms Control*, p. 239.

105. HR, *Nuclear Proliferation Factbook*, p. 69.

106. Alva Myrdal, *The Game of Disarmament: How the United States and Russia Run the Arms Race*, New York: Pantheon, 1976, pp. 95, 222.

107. William Epstein, "The Proliferation of Nuclear Weapons," in *Progress in Arms Control?* ed. Bruce M. Russett and Bruce G. Blair, San Francisco: Freeman, 1979, p. 192.

108. Pat Towell, "Senate Ratifies Two Pacts Limiting Nuclear Tests," *CQ Weekly Report,* 29 Sept. 1990, p. 3137. Bush did not sign the instrument of ratification until December 10 (Reuters, "Bush Signs 2 Pacts Limiting Underground Nuclear Tests" *NYT,* 11 Dec. 1990, p. A13). In 1977, Carter had shelved the treaty in order to negotiate a comprehensive test ban accord. But, U.S. obstruction—motivated by the Pentagon belief that testing should continue—prevented any agreement (Garthoff, *Détente and Confrontation,* pp. 756-59). Reagan refused to resubmit the Threshold Test Ban Treaty to the Senate unless it was amended to enhance the verification provisions (Pat Towell, "Senate Committee Takes Up Pair of '70s-Era Treaties," *CQ Weekly Report,* 21 July 1990, p. 2335).

109. Myrdal, *Game of Disarmament,* p. 174. The Soviet Union conducted a test just before the conference began. William Epstein, *The Last Chance: Nuclear Proliferation and Arms Control,* New York: Free Press, 1976, p. 253.

110. Nye "Superpowers and Non-proliferation Treaty," p. 182.

111. Reuters, "Deadlock Threatens Future of Nuclear Treaty," *NYT,* 16 Sept. 1990, p. I:5; Jerome Weisner, "Why Don't We Stop Testing the Bomb?" *NYT,* 23 Dec. 1990, p. E11.

112. Jennifer Scarlott, "Nuclear Proliferation After the Cold War," *World Policy Journal,* vol. 8, no. 4, Fall 1991, p. 697. In November 1989, nonaligned nations had gotten the U.S. and Britain to agree to call a conference in 1991 to discuss converting the partial test ban treaty into a comprehensive test ban. U.S. and British officials, reported the *NYT,* "accuse the nonaligned movement of irresponsibility, saying its attempt to strengthen the partial test ban treaty will weaken support for the nuclear nonproliferation treaty and encourage the spread of dangerous technology." Washington and London abruptly called the conference for January 1991, without a planned preparatory meeting, and said all signatories had to pay equal shares of the conference costs, instead of the usual method of allocating costs by national wealth. (Paul Lewis, "Nonaligned Nations Seek Total Nuclear Test Ban," *NYT,* 15 Nov. 1989, p. A17.) The U.S. ultimately backed off from its financial blackmail, but at the January conference it continued to oppose a comprehensive test ban and an overwhelmingly-endorsed follow-up conference.

113. Michael R. Gordon, "Why Bush Was Worried," *NYT,* 28 Sept. 1991, p. 1.

114. R.W. Apple, "Bush's New Strategy: Seizing The Initiative And Avoiding Deeper Arms Cuts," *NYT,* 28 Sept. 1991, p. 4.

115. Text of Bush speech, *NYT,* 28 Sept. 1991, p. 4.

116. Morton H. Halperin, "What's The Use Of 'First Use'?" *NYT,* 1 Oct. 1991, p. A23.

117. Hersh, *Price of Power,* p. 148.

118. HR, *Nuclear Proliferation Factbook,* p. 78.

119. Richard H. Ullman, "The Covert French Connection," *Foreign Policy,* no. 75, Summer 1989.

120. Leonard S. Spector, *Nuclear Proliferation Today,* New York: Vintage, 1984, pp. 85-86.

121. Nye, "Superpowers and Non-proliferation Treaty," p. 181.

122. Spector, *Nuclear Proliferation Today,* pp. 90-92.

123. Michael R. Gordon, "U.S. Reported to Seek Waiver of Arms Ban to Aid Pakistan," *NYT,* 2 Oct. 1990, p. A8; Neil A. Lewis, "Key Congressman Urges Halt in Pakistan Aid," *NYT,* 3 Oct. 1990, p. A7.

124. J.D.L. Moore, *South Africa and Nuclear Proliferation,* New York: St. Martin's, 1987, p. 143; Jane Hunter, *Israeli Foreign Policy: South Africa and Central America,* Boston: South End Press, 1987, p. 37.

125. Spector, *Nuclear Proliferation Today,* pp. 296-97.

126. John Maxwell Hamilton and Leonard S. Spector, "Congressional Counterattack: Reagan and the Congress," in *The Nonproliferation Predicament,* ed. Joseph F. Pilat, New

Brunswick, NJ: Transaction Books, 1985, pp. 63-64; Spector, *Nuclear Proliferation Today*, p. 217.

127. Michael Wines, "U.S. Explores New Strategies To Limit Weapons Of Mass Destruction," *NYT*, 30 Sept. 1990, p. I:20.

128. Michael Wines, "Supercomputers Backed for Brazil," *NYT*, 19 Oct. 1990, p. A6; Michael Wines, "Brazil Won't Sign Atom Pact But Plans Curbs, Aide Says," *NYT*, 17 Oct. 1990, p. A10. For details on Brazil's nuclear program, the role of supercomputers in that program, and Brazilian cooperation with Iraq, see *Cong. Rec.*, 30 July 1990, pp. S11044-48.

129. Gary Milhollin, "Building Saddam Hussein's Bomb," *NYT Magazine*, 8 March 1992, p. 32; Evan Thomas, et al., "Saddam's Nuclear Secrets," *Newsweek*, 7 Oct. 1991, p. 34.

130. Spector, *Nuclear Proliferation Today*, pp. 117, 375n40.

131. Steve Weissman and Herbert Krosney, *The Islamic Bomb*, New York: Times Books, 1981, p. 11.

132. Hersh, *Samson Option*, pp. 39-40.

133. Hersh, *Samson Option*, p. 205.

134. Spector, *Nuclear Proliferation Today*, pp. 123-25; Dan Raviv and Yossi Melman, *Every Prince A Spy*, Boston: Houghton Mifflin, 1990, pp. 191, 197-9. Seymour Hersh argues that the company and its president were not guilty (Hersh, *Samson Option*, pp. 241-57), but he ignores all the other suspicious activity that the company was involved in (Andrew and Leslie Cockburn, *Dangerous Liaison: The Inside Story of the U.S.-Israeli Covert Relationship*, New York: HarperCollins, 1991, pp. 81-88). For other examples of Israeli theft of military technology, see Cockburn and Cockburn, *Dangerous Liaison*, pp. 194, 197.

135. Hersh, *Samson Option*, p. 64.

136. *Newsweek*, 9 April 1990, p. 28; Hersh, *Samson Option*, pp. 213-14; Raviv and Melman, *Every Spy A Prince*, pp. 304-05.

137. Hersh, *Samson Option*, p. 111.

138. Hersh, *Samson Option*, p. 11.

139. Shai Feldman, *Israeli Nuclear Deterrence*, New York: Columbia UP, 1982, p. 217. See also Hersh, *Samson Option*, pp. 58, 186; Cockburn and Cockburn, *Dangerous Liaison*, p. 75.

140. Feldman, *Israeli Nuclear Deterrence*, pp. 218-26; Hersh, *Samson Option*, p. 262.

141. Hersh, *Samson Option*, p. 119.

142. Hersh, *Samson Option*, p. 199.

143. Cockburn and Cockburn, *Dangerous Liaison*, p. 97. See also Hersh, *Samson Option*, pp. 285-86.

144. Feldman, *Israeli Nuclear Deterrence*, p. 218.

145. Spector, *Nuclear Proliferation Today*, p. 126; see also Quandt, *Decade of Decision*, p. 67.

146. Mahmoud Karem, *A Nuclear-Weapon-Free Zone in the Middle East: Problems and Prospects*, New York: Greenwood Press, 1988, pp. 92-96, 137-39.

147. Karem, *Nuclear-Weapon-Free Zone*, p. 97.

148. Karem, *Nuclear-Weapon-Free Zone*, pp. 99-100, 103, 139-48. Egypt sponsored the resolution alone in 1979.

149. Karem, *Nuclear-Weapon-Free Zone*, pp. 104-08.

150. Paul F. Power, "Preventing Nuclear Conflict in the Middle East: The Free-Zone Strategy," *Middle East Journal*, vol. 37, Autumn 1983, p. 623n12.

151. Hersh, *Samson Option*, pp. 8-9.

152. Power, "Preventing Nuclear Conflict...," p. 623.

153. Power, "Preventing Nuclear Conflict...," p. 624.

154. Spector, *Nuclear Proliferation Today*, p. 138; Power, "Preventing Nuclear Conflict...,"
p. 624; Hunter, *Israeli Foreign Policy*, pp. 33-34, citing David Horovitz, *Jerusalem Post*
Foreign Service, in *Northern California Jewish Bulletin*, 27 Feb. 1987; my colleague
Maya Chadda has spoken to Indian officials who confirm the reports.

155. 8 June 1981, D/S, *American Foreign Policy: Current Documents, 1981,* 1984, pp. 684-85.

156. 16 June 1981, D/S, *American Foreign Policy: Current Documents, 1981,* p. 686.

157. Alan Cowell, "Rights Group Assails Iraq for 'Ruthless' Repression," *NYT,* 11 Feb. 1990,
p. I:13; *NYT,* 13 Aug. 1990, p. A11. For U.S. de facto support of Saddam Hussein in the
aftermath of the 1991 Gulf War when he slaughtered Kurds, see Chapter 6 below.

158. Zachary Lockman and Joel Beinin, eds., *Intifada: The Palestinian Uprising Against
Israeli Occupation*, Boston: South End Press, 1989, pp. 324-25. See also Louis Wolf,
"Israel Wages Chemical Warfare With American Tear Gas," *Covert Action Information
Bulletin*, no. 30, Summer 1988, p. 26.

159. For documentation, with comparison to Iraqi practice, see Norman G. Finkelstein,
"Israel and Iraq: A Case Study in Hypocrisy," *New Politics,* vol. 3, no. 2 (new series),
whole no. 10, Winter 1991.

160. See Noam Chomsky, *The Fateful Triangle,* Boston: South End, 1983, pp. 213-42.

161. David B. Ottaway, "Middle East Weapons Proliferate," *WP,* 19 Dec. 1988, p. A4.

162. Peter Pry, *Israel's Nuclear Arsenal,* Boulder: Westview, 1984, p. 92.

163. Leonard S. Spector, *Going Nuclear,* Cambridge, MA: Ballinger, 1987, 140-41.

164. Elaine Sciolino, "Documents Detail Israeli Missile Deal With the Shah," *NYT,* 1 April 1986,
p. A17; Karem, *Nuclear-Weapon Free Zone,* p. 71; Raviv and Melman, *Every Spy A
Prince,* p. 345; Pry, *Israel's Nuclear Arsenal,* p. 37; A.M. Rosenthal, "Missile-Mongering,"
NYT, 10 April 1992, p. A37.

165. "Israel Reported Selling Secret Military Data," *SL,* 2 April 1992, pp. 1, 14; Patrick E. Tyler,
"U.S. Said to Ignore Reports Israel Broke Law," *NYT,* 2 April 1992, p. A7.

166. Kevin Toolis, "The Man Behind Iraq's Supergun," *NYT Magazine,* 26 Aug. 1990, p. 46.

167. Moore, *South Africa and Nuclear Proliferation,* p. 125; Hunter, *Israeli Foreign Policy,*
pp. 39-40. See also Toolis, "The Man Behind Iraq's Supergun," p. 50.

168. I say this notwithstanding the post-war UN investigations of the Iraqi nuclear program.
Logically, of course, even if later facts were to show that Iraq was just a day away from
developing a nuclear weapon, this would not lessen the Bush administration's deceit in
making claims unsupported by the evidence available at the time the claims were made.
In any event, however, although UN investigations have revealed that Baghdad's
nuclear effort had been more elaborate and advanced than previously believed by
informed observers, the investigations did not support—despite much hype—the
charge by Secretary of Defense Dick Cheney in November 1990 that Hussein could have
a nuclear bomb within six months. (Cheney admitted that "it wouldn't be anything you
could deliver from an airplane" or "anything that would be weaponized in the sense of
a nuclear weapon.") (Michael R. Gordon, "U.S. Aides Press Iraqi Nuclear Threat," *NYT,*
26 Nov. 1990, p. A13; Reuters, "Cheney Sees Nukes Ahead," *SL,* 26 Nov. 1990, p. 5.) The
Financial Times of London on October 4, 1991 quoted David Kay, head of the UN team,
as saying that "Iraq could have been as little as two months away from starting a nuclear
arsenal" if a regular supply of enriched uranium was available. The next day, Kay
changed his estimate to 12 to 18 months. Kay and others suggested that Iraq was on the
way to possessing hydrogen bombs, but UN officials backed off this claim shortly
afterwards (David Albright and Mark Hibbs, "Hostages, Headlines, and Hype," *Bulletin
of the Atomic Scientists,* Jan.-Feb. 1992, p. 32.) Gary Milhollin wrote that according to
UN estimates Saddam Hussein was 18 to 24 months from building a bomb when the
Gulf War started. The Iraqis, he stated, "had a workable and mostly tested bomb design,"
but yet he notes that the design was "highly unstable," always "on the verge of going

off—even while sitting on the workbench" (Milhollin, "Building Saddam Hussein's Bomb," pp. 30, 32), suggesting that some more testing had yet to be done. None of these estimates are likely to be accurate. The best guess is that Iraq might have produced enough highly enriched uranium for a nuclear weapon "in two or three years if the war had not occurred—but it would have been far from certain." After producing its first weapon, it would probably have been able to produce one weapon a year, so that by the middle of the decade it could have had a small nuclear arsenal. (David Albright and Mark Hibbs, "Iraq's Bomb: Blueprints and Artifacts," *Bulletin of the Atomic Scientists*, Jan.-Feb. 1992, p. 31; see also p. 37.) A secret meeting of UN experts has now concluded that Iraq was at least three years away and maybe more from acquiring even a crude bomb. (Paul Lewis, "UN Experts Now Say Baghdad Was Far From Making an A-Bomb Before Gulf War," *NYT*, 20 May 1992, p. A6.) Baghdad was also several years away from developing a missile capable of carrying a nuclear warhead (Albright and Hibbs, "Iraq's Bomb...," p. 36).

169. Ann Lewis, "Squelch Iraq's Nuclear Ambitions," *NYT*, 20 Dec. 1990, p. A31.

170. Elaine Sciolino, "Word of Iraqi Nuclear Effort is a Mixed Blessing for Bush," *NYT*, 10 July 1991, p. A9. An administration official noted that atom bomb technology "does not depend on procuring materials abroad." "If you have the scientists, the electricity, and a metal-working foundry, you can do it indigenously." Even if current Iraqi facilities were all destroyed, "what's to stop anyone from doing this again in 1995?" (Elaine Sciolino, "U.S. Doubts Iraq's Accounting of Nuclear Material," *NYT*, 9 July 1991, p. A11.) And the head of the CIA testified that Iraq could rebuild its nuclear infrastructure in a few years. (Elaine Sciolino, "Iraqis Could Pose a Threat Soon, CIA Chief Says," *NYT*, 16 Jan. 1992, p. A9). These comments likely exaggerate the imminence of any rebuilding in order to justify tougher supervision over Iraq.

171. For an incisive discussion of this matter, see Scarlott, "Nuclear Proliferation After the Cold War," pp. 704-06.

172. Gordon, "U.S. Weighs...," pp. A1, A11; Andrew Rosenthal, "Bush Unveils Plan For Arms Control In The Middle East," *NYT*, 30 May 1991, pp. A1, A19. "By leaving intact Israel's 100-200 weapon nuclear arsenal, while stripping the Arab countries of their ability to produce chemical weapons, the proposal would return to the status quo ante in which Israel held a monopoly on weapons of mass destruction" (Scarlott, "Nuclear Proliferation After the Cold War," p. 701).

173. "U.S. Reportedly Let Pakistan Buy Arms From Private Sellers," *NYT*, 7 March 1992, p. I:7.

174. John Noble Wilford, "Agency Seeking Soviet Advances For 'Star Wars'," *NYT*, 8 Feb. 1992, pp. 1, 4. The U.S. shopping list includes particle beam technologies for space weapons and prototypes of a nuclear power system that would orbit in space.

175. Eric Schmitt, "U.S. Says There Are No Plans To Cut Back Nuclear Testing," *NYT*, 27 May 1992, p. A6.

4: Protecting Resources

1. Joe Stork, *Middle East Oil and the Energy Crisis,* New York: Monthly Review Press, 1975, p. 26.

2. Quoted in William B. Quandt, *Saudi Arabia in the 1980s: Foreign Policy, Security, and Oil,* Washington, D.C.: Brookings Institution, 1981, p. 48.

3. See Michael J. Cohen, *Palestine: Retreat from the Mandate,* New York: Holmes & Meier, 1978, pp. 154-55; Stork, *Middle East Oil...,* pp. 34-35.

4. George W. Stocking, *Middle East Oil: A Study in Political and Economic Controversy,* Nashville: Vanderbilt UP, 1970, pp. 103-06.

5. Quoted in Stork, *Middle East Oil...,* p. 74.

6. Kennett Love, *Suez: the Twice-Fought War,* New York: McGraw Hill, 1969, p. 651.

7. Love, *Suez,* p. 387.

8. Henry Kissinger, *Years of Upheaval,* Boston: Little Brown, 1982, p. 858.

9. Michael Renner, "Restructuring the World Energy Industry," *MERIP Reports,* no. 120, Jan. 1984, p. 13.

10. Edith Penrose, "The Development of Crisis," in *The Oil Crisis,* ed. Raymond Vernon, New York: Norton, 1976, p. 49.

11. V.H. Oppenheim, "Why Oil Prices Go Up; The Past: We Pushed Them," *Foreign Policy,* no. 25, Winter 1976-77, pp. 30, 32-33.

12. Oppenheim, "Why Oil Prices…," pp. 24-25.

13. Kissinger, *Years of Upheaval,* p. 863.

14. Robert B. Stobaugh, "The Oil Companies in the Crisis," in Vernon, ed., *Oil Crisis,* p. 185.

15. Quoted in Mira Wilkins, "The Oil Companies in Perspective," in Vernon, ed., *Oil Crisis,* p. 173.

16. Kissinger, *Years of Upheaval,* p. 873.

17. Stobaugh, "Oil Companies…," p. 193, table 3.

18. Romano Prodi and Alberto Clô, "Europe," in Vernon, ed., *Oil Crisis,* p. 101.

19. Yoshi Tsurumi, "Japan," in Vernon, ed., *Oil Crisis,* p. 123.

20. Horst Menderhausen, *Coping with the Oil Crisis,* Baltimore: Johns Hopkins UP, 1976, pp. 60-61.

21. HR, Merchant Marine and Fisheries Comm., subcomm. on Panama Canal/Outer Continental Shelf, *Offshore Oil and Gas Oversight,* Hearings, 1984, pp. 469-74.

22. Richard Halloran, "What Price U.S. Patrols in the Gulf?" *NYT,* 21 Feb. 1988, p. 2E.

23. Edward B. Atkeson, "The Persian Gulf: Still A Vital Interest?" *Armed Forces Journal International,* vol. 124, no. 9, April 1987, p. 54.

24. Frank Church, "The Impotence of Oil Companies," *Foreign Policy,* no. 27, Summer 1977, p. 49.

25. Anthony H. Cordesman, *The Gulf and the Search for Strategic Stability,* Boulder: Westview, 1984, p. 264.

26. Casualty figures are uncertain: see Anthony H. Cordesman, *The Iran-Iraq War and Western Security, 1984-87,* London: Jane's Publishing Co., 1987, p. 9; *NYT,* 10 Aug. 1988, p. A8; in 1982 the D/S estimated that the war had created 2 million refugees: Cordesman, *The Gulf and the Search for Strategic Stability,* p. 671; health spending from Ruth Leger Sivard, *World Military and Social Expenditures, 1987-88,* Washington, D.C.: World Priorities, 1988, table II.

27. Diana Johnstone, "'Little Satan' Stuck in the Arms Export Trap," *MERIP Reports,* no. 148, Sept.-Oct. 1987, pp. 8-9. French aid included expert help to improve the guidance system of Scud missiles, and the loan of 5 Super-Etendarde aircraft and 30 military personnel, including 7 pilots who even flew combat missions (Fredric Smoler, "The Arming of Saddam Hussein," *Dissent,* Summer 1991, pp. 347-48). France also arranged some covert arms supplies to Iran to help ensure the safety of its citizens working there (Gary Sick, *October Surprise: America's Hostages in Iran and the Election of Ronald Reagan,* New York: Times Books, 1991, p. 109).

28. Steven A. Emerson and Cristina Del Sesto, *Terrorist,* New York: Villard Books, 1991, pp. 216-17.

29. Mansour Farhang, "The Iran-Iraq War: The Feud, the Tragedy, the Spoils," *World Policy Journal,* vol. 2, Fall 1985, p. 668; see also Cordesman, *Iran-Iraq War…,* pp. 23-36; Nita M. Renfrew, "Who Started the War?" *Foreign Policy,* no. 66, Spring 1987, pp. 104-06. Michael T. Klare claims 28 countries supplied weapons to both sides ("Who's Arming Who?: The Arms Trade in the 1990s," *Technology Review,* Spring 1991, p. 31).

30. *Time,* 25 July 1983, p. 28, quoted in Mansour Farhang, "The Iran-Israel Connection," in *Consistency of U.S. Foreign Policy: The Gulf War and the Iran-Contra Affair,* ed. Abbas Alnasrawi and Cheryl Rubenberg, Belmont, MA: AAUG, 1989, p. 96.

31. John W. Amos II, "The Iraq-Iran War: Conflict, Linkage, and Spillover in the Middle East," in *Gulf Security into the 1980s: Perceptual and Strategic Dimensions,* ed. Robert G. Darius, John W. Amos II, Ralph H. Magnus, Stanford: Hoover Institution Press, 1984, p. 65. However, Moscow did not prevent its East European allies from supplying Baghdad. Carol R. Saivetz, *The Soviet Union and the Gulf in the 1980s,* Boulder: Westview, 1989, pp. 35-36.

32. Cordesman, *The Gulf and the Search for Strategic Stability,* p. 717; Robert O. Freedman, "Soviet Policy Toward the Persian Gulf from the Outbreak of the Iran-Iraq War to the Death of Konstantin Chernenko," in *U.S. Strategic Interests in the Gulf Region,* ed. Wm. J. Olson, Boulder: Westview, 1987, p. 55.

33. Freedman, "Soviet Policy...," p. 55.

34. Emerson and Del Sesto, *Terrorist,* p. 112.

35. See Chapter 7, note 60, below.

36. Douglas Frantz and Murray Waas, "Bush Secret Effort Helped Iraq Build Its War Machine," *LAT,* 23 Feb. 1992, p. A1.

37. Seymour M. Hersh, "U.S. Secretly Gave Aid To Iraq Early In Its War Against Iran," *NYT,* 26 Jan. 1992, p. I:1, 12.

38. Frantz and Waas, "Bush Secret Effort...," p. A1.

39. Seymour M. Hersh, "U.S. Secretly Gave...," p. I:1, 12; Murray Waas, "What We Gave Saddam for Christmas," *Village Voice,* 18 Dec. 1990, p. 27.

40. Sen., Foreign Relations Comm., *War in the Persian Gulf: The U.S. Takes Sides,* staff report, Committee Print S. Prt. 100-60, Nov. 1987 pp. 21-22.

41. Between 1985 and 1990, the U.S. approved $1.5 billion in exports of dual-use equipment to Iraq, of which $.5 billion was shipped. See Clyde H. Farnsworth, "Military Exports To Iraq Come Under Scrutiny," *NYT,* 25 June 1991, p. A11; AP, "U.S. Exports To Iraq Totaled $1.5 Billion," *SL,* 8 Feb. 1991, p. 15. Shipments were made directly to Iraq's Ministry of Defense, its Atomic Energy Commission, and its missile research facility. Twenty shipments of biological agents—the raw material of germ warfare—were approved for export to Baghdad's Atomic Energy Commission (Emerson and Del Sesto, *Terrorist,* pp. 219-21).

42. Steve Fetter, "Weapons of Mass Destruction: What Is The Threat? What Should Be Done?" *International Security,* vol. 16, no. 1, Summer 1991, p. 19.

43. Murray Waas and Douglas Frantz, "Bush Had Long History of Support For Iraq Aid," *LAT,* 24 Feb. 1992, p. A1.

44. Frantz and Waas, "Bush Secret Effort...," p. A1.

45. Los Angeles Times Wire Service, "U.S. Had Secret Hand in the Rise of Saddam," *SL,* 8 Aug. 90, p. 15.

46. Michael T. Klare, "The RDF: Newest 'Fire Brigade' for U.S. Intervention in the Third World," in *U.S. Strategy in the Gulf: Intervention Against Liberation,* ed. Leila Meo, Belmont, MA: AAUG, 1981, pp. 99-100, 104.

47. Harold Brown, *Thinking About National Security,* Boulder: Westview, 1983, p. 157.

48. For examples from policy-makers and the press, see Maya Chadda, *Paradox of Power: the United States in Southwest Asia, 1973-1984,* Santa Barbara: ABC-Clio, 1986, pp. 111-12.; and for a particularly gross example, *Business Week,* 19 Nov. 1979, p. 190, quoted in James F. Petras and Roberto Korzeniewicz, "U.S. Policy Towards the Middle East," in Meo, ed., *U.S. Strategy in the Gulf,* p. 84.

49. A point made by Chadda, *Paradox of Power,* p. 112.

50. Brown, *Thinking About National Security,* p. 157.

51. Zbigniew Brzezinski, *Power and Principle: Memoirs of the National Security Adviser, 1977-1981,* New York: Farrar, Straus, Giroux, 1987, p. 450.
52. Cordesman, *The Gulf and the Search for Strategic Stability,* p. 847.
53. Deborah Shapley "The Army's New Fighting Doctrine," *NYT Magazine,* 28 Nov. 1982, p. 47.
54. Klare, "RDF...," p. 107.
55. *Public Papers of the Presidents of the United States, Ronald Reagan, 1981,* Washington, D.C.: USGPO, 1982, pp. 870-71.
56. Stephen Engelberg, "Iran and Iraq Got 'Doctored' Data, U.S. Officials Say," *NYT,* 12 Jan. 1987, p. A1, A6.
57. Brown, *Thinking About National Security,* makes this point, p. 149.
58. *NYT,* 25 Sept. 1982, quoted in Christopher Paine, "On the Beach: The Rapid Deployment Force and the Nuclear Arms Race," *MERIP Reports,* no. 111, Jan. 1983, p. 11.
59. CQ, *U.S. Defense Policy,* 3rd ed., Washington, D.C.: 1983, p. 193. The quote is CQ's summary.
60. James P. Wooten, *Rapid Deployment Force,* CRS Issue Brief No. IB80027, updated 16 July 1984, p. 4, quoted in Martha Wenger, "The Central Command: Getting to the War on Time," *MERIP Reports,* no. 128, Nov.-Dec. 1984, p. 20; see also Richard Halloran, "Pentagon Draws Up First Strategy for Fighting A Long Nuclear War," *NYT,* 20 May 1982, pp. 1, 12.
61. Quoted in CQ, *U.S. Defense Policy,* pp. 195-96.
62. Cordesman, *The Gulf and the Search for Strategic Stability,* p. 62.
63. Wenger "Central Command," p. 22, citing James P. Wooten, *Rapid Deployment Force.*
64. Judith Miller and Jeff Gerth, "U.S. Is Said to Develop Oman As Its major Ally in the Gulf," *NYT,* 25 Mar. 1985, pp. A1, A8.
65. Bernard Gwertzman, "Saudis To Let U.S. Use Bases in Crisis," *NYT,* 5 Sept. 1985, pp. A1, A10.
66. (*The Tower Commission Report*), *President's Special Review Board,* New York: Bantam Books/Times Books, 1987, pp. 294-95. Hereafter cited as Tower Commission.
67. Farhang, "Iran-Israel Connection," p. 95; Bob Woodward, *Veil: The Secret Wars of the CIA, 1981-1987,* New York: Simon & Schuster, 1987, p. 480.
68. Leslie H. Gelb, "U.S. Said to Aid Iranian Exiles in Combat and Political Units," *NYT,* 7 Mar. 1982, pp. A1, A12.
69. David Binder, "U.S. Concedes It Is Behind Anti-Khomeini Broadcasts," *NYT,* 29 June 1980, p. 3; Woodward, *Veil,* p. 480.
70. Gelb, "U.S. Said to Aid...," pp. A1, A12.
71. Tower Commission, p. 398; Farhang, "Iran-Israel Connection," p. 95.
72. Farhang, "Iran-Israel Connection," p. 92.
73. Seymour M. Hersh, "The Iran Pipeline: A Hidden Chapter," *NYT,* 8 Dec. 1991, pp. I:1, 16; Sick, *October Surprise,* p. 198.
74. Sick, *October Surprise,* p. 202.
75. Sick, *October Surprise.*
76. Tower Commission, pp. 103-04.
77. Quoted in Jonathan Marshall, Peter Dale Scott, and Jane Hunter, *The Iran-Contra Connection,* Boston: South End Press, 1987, pp. 160-61.
78. Tower Commission, p. 271.
79. Tower Commission, p. 194.
80. Tower Commission, p. 388.
81. Tower Commission, p. 65.
82. Tower Commission, p. 113.
83. Tower Commission, p. 261.

84. Tower Commission, p. 299.
85. See, in addition to the sources in notes 73 and 74 above, Leslie H. Gelb, "Iran Said to Get Large-Scale Arms From Israel, Soviet and Europeans," *NYT*, 8 Mar. 1982, pp. A1, A10; Cordesman, *Iran-Iraq War…*, p. 31.
86. Sen., *War in the Persian Gulf*, p. 21.
87. Tower Commission, p. 27.
88. *Public Papers of the Presidents of the United States, Ronald Reagan, 1986,* Washington, D.C.: USGPO, 1988-89, p. 1546.
89. Tower Commission, p. 48; see also p. 398.
90. Tower Commission, p. 427.
91. Joe Stork and Martha Wenger, "U.S. Ready to Intervene in the Gulf War," *MERIP Reports,* no 125/126, July-Sept. 1984, pp. 47-48, citing *Newsday,* 20 May 1984.
92. Tower Commission, pp. 239-40.
93. Cordesman, *Iran-Iraq War…*, p. 38.
94. Tower Commission, pp. 239-40.
95. Tower Commission, p. 279.
96. Tower Commission, p. 73; see also Cordesman, *Iran-Iraq War…*, p. 38.
97. Engelberg, "Doctored Data…," pp. A1, A6.
98. Woodward, *Veil,* p. 480.
99. Woodward, *Veil,* p. 480; Stephanie G. Neuman, "Arms, Aid and the Superpowers," *Foreign Affairs,* vol. 66, no. 5, Summer 1988, p. 1052.
100. Engelberg, "Doctored Data…," pp. A1, A6.
101. Sen., *War in the Persian Gulf*, p. 37.
102. Sen., *War in the Persian Gulf*, p. 37.
103. D/S, *U.S. Policy in the Persian Gulf,* Special Report No. 166, July 1987, p. 11.
104. Freedman, "Soviet Policy…," p. 52; Michael Lenker, "The Effect of the Iran-Iraq War on Soviet Strategy in the Persian Gulf," in *Gulf Security and the Iran-Iraq War,* ed. Thomas Naff, Washington, D.C.: National Defense UP, 1985, p. 95.
105. James Weinrauch, "Iran's Response to UN Resolution 598: The Role of Factionalism in the Negotiation process," *American Arab Affairs,* no. 31, Winter 1989-90, p. 17.
106. Norman Higby, oil consultant, letter, *NYT,* 11 Feb 1991, p. A18.
107. John Simpson, *From the House of War,* cited by Christopher Hitchens, "Tilting Democracy," *Middle East Report,* Jan.-Feb. 1992, p. 33.
108. *NYT,* 7 June 1987, quoted in Theodore Draper, "American Hubris," in *The Gulf War Reader,* ed. Micah L. Sifry and Christopher Cerf, New York: Times Books, 1991, p. 49, 51.
109. *WP,* 7 June 1987, quoted in Draper, "American Hubris," p. 51.
110. *WP,* 16 Aug. 1987, p. A23.
111. Sen., *War in the Persian Gulf*, p. ix.
112. D/S, *U.S. Policy in the Persian Gulf,* pp. 1-2.
113. Sen., *War in the Persian Gulf*, p. 2.
114. Sen., *War in the Persian Gulf*, p. 4.
115. Sen., *War in the Persian Gulf*, p. vii.
116. Ronald O'Rourke, "The Tanker War," *Proceedings,* U.S. Naval Institute, May 1988, p. 34.
117. Ronald O'Rourke, "Gulf Ops," *Proceedings,* U.S. Naval Institute, May 1989, pp. 42-43.
118. Sen., *War in the Persian Gulf*, p. 3.
119. O'Rourke, "Tanker War," p. 32; O'Rourke, "Gulf Ops," p. 43.
120. Sen., *War in the Persian Gulf*, p. ix.
121. Fox Butterfield, "Soviets in UN Council Ask for U.S. Pullout From Gulf," *NYT,* 16 July 1988, p. 2.
122. "What If Iran Attacks Again?" *NYT,* 20 Oct. 1987, p. A34.

123. O'Rourke, "Tanker War," p. 30.

124. O'Rourke, "Tanker War," p. 32; O'Rourke, Gulf Ops," p. 43.

125. O'Rourke, "Gulf Ops," p. 47.

126. Sen., *War in the Persian Gulf,* p. 37. "The pretense that Kuwait was neutral was sheer humbug; Kuwait was Iraq's foremost ally." Draper, "American Hubris," p. 46.

127. Robert L. Bambarger and Clyde R. Mark, *Escalation of the Conflict in the Persian Gulf,* CRS, May 30, 1984, printed in HR, *Offshore Oil...,* p. 593. Of 181 Iraqi attacks in the tanker war from 1981 to October 12, 1987, only 48 were aimed at vessels flying the Iranian flag. Anthony H. Cordesman, *The Gulf and the West,* Boulder: Westview, 1988, p. 398.

128. Ross Leckow, "The Iran-Iraq Conflict in the Gulf: The Law of War Zones," *International and Comparative Law Quarterly,* vol. 37, July 1988, pp. 636-38, 644.

129. Gary Sick, "Failure and Danger in the Gulf," *NYT,* 6 July 1988, p. A23.

130. Sen., *War in the Persian Gulf,* p. 29.

131. O'Rourke, "Gulf Ops," p. 44.

132. Steve Lohr, *NYT,* 20 Ap. 1988, p. A16.

133. John Barry "The Secret War," *Newsweek,* 13 July 1992, p. 37; John Barry and Roger Charles, "Sea of Lies," *Newsweek,* 13 July 1992, p. 39.

134. D/S, *U.S. Policy in the Persian Gulf,* p. 5.

135. O'Rourke, "Tanker War," p. 30.

136. Francis Fukuyama, *Gorbachev and the New Soviet Agenda in the Third World,* R-3634-A, Santa Monica, CA: Rand Corporation, June 1989, pp. viii, 43.

137. Fukuyama, *Gorbachev...,* pp. 60, 47, 28-29, 53, 45.

138. O'Rourke, "Tanker War," p. 33.

139. Commdr. David R. Carlson, "The *Vicennes* Incident," letter, *Proceedings,* U.S. Naval Institute, Sept. 1989, pp. 87-88.

140. John Barry and Roger Charles, "Sea of Lies," *Newsweek,* 13 July 1992, pp. 29, 33, 39. The Vicennes attacked the gunboats after they fired on a U.S. helicopter that flew over them in Iranian waters (p. 32).

141. This and subsequent quotes from Bush's UN remarks are from George Bush, "The Persian Gulf Conflict and Iran Air 655," D/S, *Current Policy,* no. 1093, 1988, p. 2. *Newsweek* states that the Pentagon failed to inform Bush what actually happened, but a D/S official warned the Vice-President's chief of staff that the facts were in doubt (John Barry and Roger Charles, "Sea of Lies," *Newsweek,* 13 July 1992, pp. 38-39). This did not stop Bush from including specific charges in his speech.

142. Steven Emerson and Brian Duffy, *The Fall of Pan Am 103,* New York: G.P. Putnam's Sons, 1990, p. 59.

143. Emerson and Duffy, *Fall of Pan Am 103,* p. 59; John Barry and Roger Charles, "Sea of Lies," *Newsweek,* 13 July 1992, pp. 37-38.

144. AP, "U.S. Wins Arab Respect with Gulf Ship Escorts," *SL,* 19 Oct. 1988, p. 4; see also Richard Halloran, *NYT,* 4 Dec. 1988, p. 32.

145. "Why the U.S. Navy is in the Gulf," *NYT,* 6 July 1988, p. A22.

146. "What If Iran Attacks Again?" *NYT,* 20 Oct. 1987, p. A34.

147. "In Captain Rogers's Shoes" *NYT,* 5 July 1988, p. A16.

148. Not until Oct. 20, did the U.S. officially refer to the Iraqi attack as an invasion; at the same time it called for Iraq to withdraw (Sick, *October Surprise,* p. 160). Moorhead Kennedy, one of the U.S. diplomats held hostage in Iran, has told me that his 1988 book says "Iran and Iraq had gone to war," rather than "Iraq invaded Iran," at the insistence of his co-author who was still well-connected to the D/S. See Terrell E. Arnold and Moorhead Kennedy, *Think About Terrorism: The New Warfare,* New York: Walker and Co., 1988, p. 68.

149. R.P.H. King, "The United Nations and the Iran-Iraq War, 1980-1986," in *The United Nations and the Iran-Iraq War*, ed. Brian Urquhart and Gary Sick, New York: Ford Foundation, August 1987, pp. 10, 14-16, 23.

150. Brzezinski, *Power and Principle*, p. 453.

151. King, "The United Nations...," p. 10.

152. Farhang, "Iran-Iraq War...," p. 673; King, "The United Nations...," p. 18.

153. Farhang, "Iran-Iraq War...," pp. 673-75.

154. Gary Sick, "Trial By Error: Reflections on the Iran-Iraq War," *Middle East Journal*, vol. 43, no. 2, Spring 1989, p. 236.

155. Dilip Hiro, *Iran Under the Ayatollahs*, London: Routledge & Kegan Paul, 1985, p. 211; Efraim Karsh and Inari Rautsi, *Saddam Hussein: A Political Biography*, New York: Free Press, 1991, p. 165; Emerson and Del Sesto, *Terrorist*, pp. 115-16; Noam Chomsky, *The Fateful Triangle*, Boston: South End Press, 1983, 197n; Judith Miller and Laurie Mylroie, *Saddam Hussein and the Crisis in the Gulf*, New York: Times Books, 1990, p. 115; and sources given in Scott MacLeod, "The Terrorist's Terrorist," *New York Review of Books*, 28 May 1992, p. 9.

156. Hiro, *Iran Under the Ayatollahs*, p. 211.

157. Farhang, "Iran-Iraq War...," pp. 675-76.

158. Alexander M. Haig, Jr., *Caveat*, New York: Macmillan, 1984, p. 334n.

159. King, "The United Nations...," p. 17.

160. Leckow, "The Iran-Iraq Conflict...," p. 640.

161. Elaine Sciolino, "How the U.S. Cast Off Neutrality in Gulf War," *NYT*, 24 Ap. 1988, p. 2E.

162. King, "The United Nations...," pp. 19-20.

163. King, "The United Nations...," p. 18.

164. King, "The United Nations...," p. 19.

165. Tower Commission, pp. 117-118.

166. Tower Commission, pp. 49-50.

167. Sick, "Trial By Error," p. 240.

168. Sen., Foreign Relations Comm., subcomm. on Europe and the Middle East, *Developments in the Middle East, September 1987*, Hearings, Sept. 1987, p. 19; Sick, "Trial By Error," p. 241.

169. Kuwait KUNA, 19 Sept. 1987, in FBIS-NES-87-183, 22 Sept 1987, pp. 45-47.

170. Sick, "Failure and Danger...," p. A23.

171. Sick, "Trial By Error," p. 241.

172. Sick, "Trial By Error," pp. 242-43.

173. Miller and Mylroie, *Saddam Hussein and the Crisis in the Gulf*, p. 143.

174. Frantz and Waas, "Bush Secret Effort...," p. A1; AP, "Documents Show U.S. Gave 'Secrets' To Iraq," *SL*, 10 March 1992, p. 4.

175. The Iraqi-issued transcript, not denied by Washington, is in *NYT*, 23 Sept. 1990, p. I:19.

176. Louis Uchitelle, "Gulf Victory May Raise U.S. Influence in OPEC," *NYT*, 5 March 1991, pp. D1, D17.

5: Protecting Americans Abroad

1. William D. Rogers in *Humanitarian Intervention and the United Nations*, ed. Richard B. Lillich, Charlottesville: UP of Virginia, 1973, pp. 10-11.

2. Franck in Lillich, ed., *Humanitarian Intervention...*, p. 63.

3. Ian Brownlie, *International Law and the Use of Force By States*, London: Oxford UP, 1963, p. 99; Rogers in Lillich, ed., *Humanitarian Intervention...*, p. 24.

4. Jerome Slater, *Intervention and Negotiation: The United States and the Dominican Republic*, New York: Harper & Row, 1970, pp. 24n, 24.

5. Theodore Draper, *The Dominican Revolt,* New York: Commentary, 1968, p. 61.
6. Abraham F. Lowenthal, *The Dominican Intervention,* Cambridge, MA: Harvard UP, 1972, p. 83.
7. Lowenthal, *Dominican Intervention,* p. 84.
8. Slater, *Intervention...,* pp. 33-34.
9. Lyndon Baines Johnson, *The Vantage Point,* New York: Holt, Rinehart and Winston, 1971, p. 191.
10. Slater, *Intervention...,* p. 33.
11. Lowenthal, *Dominican Intervention,* pp. 95-96.
12. Lowenthal, *Dominican Intervention,* p. 101.
13. Lowenthal, *Dominican Intervention,* p. 102.
14. Lowenthal, *Dominican Intervention,* pp. 102-03; Draper, *Dominican Revolt,* p. 115.
15. Lowenthal, *Dominican Intervention,* p. 104.
16. McGeorge Bundy, Bill Moyers, and Adlai Stevenson convinced LBJ to delete the anti-communist rationale from his speech. Lowenthal, *Dominican Intervention,* p. 105.
17. Lowenthal, *Dominican Intervention,* p. 204n27.
18. Slater, *Intervention...,* p. 33.
19. Draper, *Dominican Revolt,* pp. 91-93; Lowenthal, *Dominican Intervention,* p. 207n50.
20. Slater, *Intervention...,* pp. 33-34.
21. Lowenthal, *Dominican Intervention,* p. 116.
22. Slater, *Intervention...,* p. 38; Draper, *Dominican Revolt,* pp. 66-71.
23. Draper, *Dominican Revolt,* pp. 159-68.
24. Slater, *Intervention...,* p. 204.
25. Slater, *Intervention...,* p. 203.
26. Lowenthal, *Dominican Intervention,* p. 212n10.
27. For a critique of the elections, see Edward S. Herman and Frank Brodhead, *Demonstration Elections: U.S.-Staged Elections in the Dominican Republic, Vietnam, and El Salvador,* Boston: South End Press, 1984, pp. 17-54. Slater notes that U.S. officials privately admit that their decision to seek elections was strongly influenced by polls prior to April 1965 showing that Balaguer would beat Bosch. Slater, *Intervention...,* p. 49.
28. Slater, *Intervention...,* p. 171.
29. Noam Chomsky and Edward S. Herman, *The Washington Connection and Third World Fascism,* Boston: South End Press, 1979, pp. 243-51.
30. Quoted in Gabriel Kolko, *Confronting the Third World,* New York: Pantheon, 1988, p. 164.
31. The crew is often erroneously numbered 39, a confusion attributable to maritime jargon which sometimes uses the word "crew" to refer to sailors other than the captain. As the skipper of the Mayaguez explained: "I am not a crew member. I am the man that signs the agreement with the crew that I will live up to certain regulations of the maritime law with the crew.... I am on the official crew list of the ship, but I am not a member" (HR, International Relations Comm. and its subcomm. on International Political and Military Affairs, *Seizure of the Mayaguez,* Hearings, parts 1-3, May-Sept. 1975; part 4, Committee Print, Oct. 1976, pp. II:200-01). Remarkably for a mission whose sole alleged purpose was the recovery of the sailors, U.S. policy-makers didn't know how many there were, even on May 16 after their recovery (HR, *Seizure of the Mayaguez,* p. I:101; see also pp. II:238, 241). And writing a few years later both Gerald Ford and his press secretary get the number wrong (Gerald R. Ford, *A Time to Heal,* New York: Harper & Row, 1979, p. 276; Ron Nessen, *It Sure Looks Different from the Inside,* New York: Simon & Schuster distributor for Playboy Press, 1978, p. 130).

32. Thomas B. Ross, "Kissinger Pushing for Tough Foreign Policy to Combat Post-Viet Weakness," *Boston Globe*, 11 May 1975, p. 15.
33. *Time*, 26 May 1975, p. 9.
34. HR, *Seizure of the Mayaguez*, p. I:44.
35. William Shawcross, *Sideshow: Kissinger, Nixon and the Destruction of Cambodia*, New York: Pocket Books, 1979, p. 432.
36. HR, Appropriations Comm. subcomm., *Department of Defense Appropriations for 1976*, Hearings, part 3, 1975, p. 614; HR, *Seizure of the Mayaguez*, p. IV:17; *Time*, 26 May 1975, p. 10; Roy Rowan, *The Four Days of Mayaguez*, New York: Norton, 1975, p. 67.
37. HR, *Seizure of the Mayaguez*, p. I:91; *Boston Globe*, 17 May 1975, p. 4.
38. Nessen, *Sure Looks Different...*, p. 120.
39. HR, *Seizure of the Mayaguez*, p. II:191. Cambodia claimed the ship was two to three miles from the island (HR, *Seizure of the Mayaguez*, p. II:233). Shawcross states the ship was within two miles (*Sideshow*, p. 432).
40. HR, *Seizure of the Mayaguez*, p. II:213.
41. Rowan, *Four Days of Mayaguez*, p. 68.
42. Nessen, *Sure Looks Different...*, p. 118.
43. Nessen, *Sure Looks Different...*, p. 118.
44. Ford, *Time to Heal*, p. 276.
45. HR, *Seizure of the Mayaguez*, p. II:237. For testimony that air strikes were conducted from Thailand, see HR, *DoD Appropriations 1976*, pp. 608, 613.
46. Text in HR, *Seizure of the Mayaguez*, p. I:61.
47. *Boston Globe*, 18 May 1975, p. 66.
48. Jordan J. Paust, "The Seizure and Recovery of the *Mayaguez*," *Yale Law Journal*, vol. 85, 1976, pp. 783n47, 797n102.
49. Paust, "Seizure," p. 778. Paust cites D/S lawyers acknowledging that the legality of the seizure was open to controversy (p. 778) and himself concludes that Cambodia acted "lawfully" in its seizure and search of the Mayaguez (p. 795).
50. Text in HR, *Seizure of the Mayaguez*, p. I:61.
51. HR, *Seizure of the Mayaguez*, p. I:95. See also Rowan, *Four Days of Mayaguez*, p. 92.
52. *Time*, 26 May 1975, p. 12; Shawcross, *Sideshow*, p. 432; Paust, "Seizure," p. 914.
53. HR, *Seizure of the Mayaguez*, p. IV:67.
54. HR, *Seizure of the Mayaguez*, p. I:95.
55. Rowan, *Four Days of Mayaguez*, p. 141.
56. HR, *Seizure of the Mayaguez*, pp. I:8. Later another DoD official claimed he was certain no Americans were aboard, but when pressed he acknowledged, "There is always a risk" (p. I:55).
57. *Time*, 26 May 1975, p. 11; HR, *Seizure of the Mayaguez*, p. II:189, 250.
58. HR, *Seizure of the Mayaguez*, p. II:189; Rowan, *Four Days of Mayaguez*, pp. 134-36.
59. *Time*, 26 May 1975, p. 11.
60. Ford, *Time to Heal*, p. 279; see also Rowan, *Four Days of Mayaguez*, pp. 141-42.
61. HR, *Seizure of the Mayaguez*, pp. IV:60, 69, 122.
62. HR, *Seizure of the Mayaguez*, p. II:230, III:275, IV:66.
63. HR, *Seizure of the Mayaguez*, p. II:246, III:274.
64. Rowan, *Four Days of Mayaguez*, p. 176; see also Shawcross, *Sideshow*, p. 433.
65. Nessen, *Sure Looks Different...*, pp. 121-22.
66. Rowan, *Four Days of Mayaguez*, p. 178.
67. Rowan, *Four Days of Mayaguez*, pp. 179-80.
68. HR, *Seizure of the Mayaguez*, pp. II:230-31.
69. HR, *Seizure of the Mayaguez*, p. II:240.
70. HR, *Seizure of the Mayaguez*, p. I:92.

71. This point is made by the GAO. See HR, *Seizure of the Mayaguez*, p. IV:67.

72. Actually the first wave of U.S. planes did not drop any bombs, a fact that Ford had not realized and was later annoyed about. See Ford, *Time to Heal*, p. 284; HR, *Seizure of the Mayaguez*, p. IV:125.

73. HR, *Seizure of the Mayaguez*, p. IV:96; Ford, *Time to Heal*, p. 282.

74. The U.S. message was communicated only in a White House press release issued at Nessen's 9:15 press conference (Rowan, *Four Days of Mayaguez*, pp. 204-05; Nessen, *Sure Looks Different...*, pp. 121-22). Other methods aside from the press release were considered for delivering the U.S. message, but "for some reason" never used (Nessen, *Sure Looks Different...*, p. 126n; HR, *Seizure of the Mayaguez*, p. IV:68.

75. HR, *Seizure of the Mayaguez*, p. IV:97.

76. HR, *Seizure of the Mayaguez*, p. IV:97.

77. Shawcross, *Sideshow*, p. 433; Fred S. Hoffman, AP, *Boston Globe*, 18 May 1975, p. 66; Rowan, *Four Days of Mayaguez*, p. 219.

78. HR, *Seizure of the Mayaguez*, p. IV:97.

79. HR, *Seizure of the Mayaguez*, pp. IV:95, 97.

80. Nessen, *Sure Looks Different...*, pp. 128-29.

81. Ford, *Time to Heal*, pp. 283-84.

82. HR, *Seizure of the Mayaguez*, p. IV:94.

83. See Rowan, *Four Days of Mayaguez*, p. 90; HR, *Seizure of the Mayaguez*, pp. I:127, II:153n1; Thomas D. Des Brisay, *Fourteen Hours at Koh Tang*, monograph 5, USAF Southeast Asia Monograph Series, volume 3, ed. A.J.C. Lavalle, Washington, D.C.: USGPO, [1975?], p. 149. Ford acknowledged 41 deaths: Ford, *Time to Heal*, p. 284.

84. *Time*, 26 May 1975, p. 9.

85. Shawcross, *Sideshow*, p. 433.

86. *Time*, 26 May 1975, p. 17. For corroboration that the Cambodian captors ate only what was left after the Americans had eaten, see Captain Miller's testimony: HR, *Seizure of the Mayaguez*, p. II:251.

87. Rowan, *Four Days of Mayaguez*, p. 218.

88. The GAO reports that the DoD put Cambodian casualties at 47 killed, 55 wounded, and an unknown number missing (HR, *Seizure of the Mayaguez*, p. IV:65), but this latter category means that essentially any number could have died.

89. Shawcross, *Sideshow*, p. 434.

90. HR, *Seizure of the Mayaguez*, p. III:282.

91. *Time*, 26 May 1975, p. 18.

92. Quoted in Noam Chomsky, *Towards A New Cold War*, New York: Pantheon, 1982, p. 149.

93. CQ, *CQ Almanac, 1975*, Washington, D.C.: 1976, p. 311.

94. Hugh O'Shaughnessy, *Grenada*, New York: Dodd, Mead & Co., 1984, p. 151.

95. O'Shaughnessy, *Grenada*, p. 148.

96. William C. Gilmore, *The Grenada Intervention: Analysis and Documentation*, New York: Facts on File, 1984, p. 19.

97. For a careful review, see Tony Thorndike, *Grenada: Politics, Economics, and Society*, Boulder: L. Rienner, 1985. A November 1984 poll found 86.2 percent of Grenadians favorably disposed toward Bishop. Jorge Heine, "The Hero and the Apparatchik: Charismatic Leadership, Political Management, and Crisis in Revolutionary Grenada," in *A Revolution Aborted: The Lessons of Grenada*, ed. Jorge Heine, Pittsburgh: University of Pittsburgh Press, 1991, p. 251.

98. O'Shaughnessy, *Grenada*, p. 81; Kai P. Schoenhals and Richard A. Melanson, *Revolution and Intervention in Grenada: The New Jewel Movement, the United States, and the Caribbean*, Boulder: Westview, 1985, p. 115.

99. Patrick Tyler, "U.S. Tracks Cuban Aid to Grenada," *WP,* 27 Feb. 1983, p. A1, cited in Gregory Sandford and Richard Vigilante, *Grenada: The Untold Story,* Lanham, MD: Madison Books, 1984, pp. 120-21n69.

100. Gordon K. Lewis, *Grenada: The Jewel Despoiled,* Baltimore: Johns Hopkins UP, 1987, p. 87; Robert Pastor, "The United States and the Grenada Revolution: Who Pushed First and Why?" in Heine, ed., *Revolution Aborted,* pp. 198, 213n42. In August 1983, the U.S. also tried unsuccessfully to oppose Grenada's application for a $14.1 million IMF loan. James Ferguson, *Grenada: Revolution in Reverse,* London: Latin American Bureau, 1991, p. 18.

101. Sandford and Vigilante, *Grenada,* pp. 102-03.

102. Pastor, "U.S. and Grenada Revolution," p. 199; Gilmore, *Grenada Intervention,* p. 29; EPICA, *The Caribbean: Survival, Struggle and Sovereignty,* 2nd ed., Boston: South End Press, 1988, p. 124.

103. Gilmore, *Grenada Intervention,* p. 29.

104. Schoenhals and Melanson, *Revolution,* p. 135.

105. O'Shaughnessy, *Grenada,* pp. 194-95.

106. Schoenhals and Melanson, *Revolution,* p. 132.

107. O'Shaughnessy, *Grenada,* p. 88. A year earlier, the World Bank called the lack of a major airport "the most limiting single factor in achieving the island's growth possibilities." Jorge Heine, "Introduction: A Revolution Aborted," in Heine, ed., *Revolution Aborted,* p. 19.

108. Schoenhals and Melanson, *Revolution,* p. 188n69.

109. Schoenhals and Melanson, *Revolution,* p. 57.

110. O'Shaughnessy, *Grenada,* p. 252.

111. Some vague statements by Grenadian leaders have been cited by the U.S. government to try to prove the intention to use the airport for military purposes (see, e.g., D/S and DoD, *The Soviet-Cuban Connection in Central America and the Caribbean,* March 1985, p. 13; Sandford and Vigilante, *Grenada,* p. 104). But in October 1982 Bishop and Bernard Coard told former National Security Council member Robert Pastor that the airport would not play any military role; Pastor passed this on to the D/S, suggesting that it try to get private and public assurances to this effect. To Pastor's knowledge, there was no such D/S follow up (Pastor, "U.S. and Grenada Revolution," p. 204), indicating the real level of Washington's concern about the airport.

112. HR, Foreign Affairs Comm, subcomms. on International Security and Scientific Affairs and Western Hemisphere Affairs, *U.S. Military Actions in Grenada: Implications for U.S. Policy in the Eastern Caribbean,* Hearings, Nov. 1983, p. 34; Sen., Foreign Relations Comm., *Situation in Grenada,* Hearings, Oct. 1983, p. 46.

113. Sandford and Vigilante, *Grenada,* p. 103.

114. HR, *Military Actions in Grenada,* p. 44; see also pp. 73, 81.

115. Gilmore, *Grenada Intervention,* p. 61; O'Shaughnessy, *Grenada,* p. 167.

116. Philip Taubman, "U.S. Reports Evidence of Island Hostage Plan," *NYT,* 28 Oct. 1983, p. A14.

117. Stuart Taylor, Jr., "In Wake of Invasion, Much Official Misinformation By U.S. Comes to Light," *NYT,* 6 Nov. 1983, p. 20.

118. John Norton Moore, "Grenada and the International Double Standard," *American Journal of International Law,* vol. 78, 1984, p. 150.

119. Taylor, "In Wake of Invasion...," p. 20.

120. HR, *Military Actions in Grenada,* p. 176.

121. HR, *Military Actions in Grenada,* p. 188.

122. Maurice Waters, "The Invasion of Grenada, 1983, and the Collapse of Legal Norms," *Journal of Peace Research,* vol. 23, no. 3, 1986, p. 238.

123. Hedrick Smith, "Ex-U.S. Official Cites Ease in Leaving Grenada Day Before Invasion," *NYT,* 29 Oct. 1983, p. I:7; Gilmore, *Grenada Intervention,* p. 34.

124. O'Shaughnessy, *Grenada,* p. 161.

125. Lewis, *Grenada,* p. 111.

126. HR, *Military Actions in Grenada,* pp. 73, 80.

127. HR, *Military Actions in Grenada,* p. 81.

128. Lewis, *Grenada,* p. 104.

129. Waters, "Invasion of Grenada…," p. 243; Jonathan Kwitny, *Endless Enemies,* New York: Penguin, 1984, pp. 413-14.

130. HR, *Military Actions in Grenada,* p. 193.

131. House of Commons, Second Report from the Foreign Affairs Comm., *Grenada,* Session 1983-84, London: HMSO, 1984, p. xiv, ¶ 33; Gilmore, *Grenada Intervention,* pp. 35, 3; Waters, "Invasion of Grenada…," p. 243.

132. Bourne and Solin quoted in HR, *Military Actions in Grenada,* p. 83; Modica quoted : Anthony Payne, Paul Sutton, and Tony Thorndike, *Grenada: Revolution and Invasion,* New York: St. Martin's, 1984, p. 155.

133. HR, *Military Actions in Grenada,* pp. 177, 193-94.

134. Text in Gilmore, *Grenada Intervention,* pp. 93-94.

135. Gilmore, *Grenada Intervention,* p. 62.

136. Bernard Gwertzman, "Steps to the Invasion: No More 'Paper Tiger'," *NYT,* 30 Oct. 198 p. 20; O'Shaughnessy, *Grenada,* p. 170; HR, *Military Actions in Grenada,* pp. 73, 8 Smith, "Ex-U.S. Official…," p. I:7.

137. Gilmore, *Grenada Intervention,* p. 63n136.

138. Gilmore, *Grenada Intervention,* pp. 62-63, 63n135.

139. HR, *Military Actions in Grenada,* p. 47.

140. Gilmore, *Grenada Intervention,* p. 63n136.

141. HR, *Military Actions in Grenada,* p. 73. Barbara Crossette transmitted a remarkable piece of disinformation: "An Administration official familiar with American planning regarding Grenada…reiterated the Administration's contention that the decision invade was not made definitively until the night of Oct. 24, after the imposition of shoot-on-sight curfew and the closing of the island's commercial airport underc General Austin's assurances of the safety of American citizens in Grenada." (Barba Crossette, "The Caribbean After Grenada," *NYT Magazine,* 18 March 1984, p. 66). Th curfew was *lifted,* not imposed, on Oct. 24, and the airport was opened.

142. O'Shaughnessy, *Grenada,* p. 26.

143. B. Drummond Ayres, Jr., "Grenada Invasion: A Series of Surprises," *NYT,* 14 Nov. 198 p. A6.

144. HR, *Military Actions in Grenada,* pp. 178, 195.

145. An eyewitness report counted at least 30 corpses, despite U.S. claims that there we only 18 dead (O'Shaughnessy, *Grenada,* p. 208).

146. Robert D. McFadden, "From Rescued Students, Gratitude and Praise," *NYT,* 28 Oct. 198 p. A1.

147. A *NYT*/CBS News Poll conducted on October 26 and 27 showed 51 percent approve of the invasion, but less than a third believed sending troops was the best response the crisis. 58 percent of respondents said they believed that Americans were in dange David Shribman, "Poll Shows Support for Presence of U.S. Troops in Lebanon ar Grenada," *NYT,* 29 Oct. 1983, p. I:9.

148. Text is in Gilmore, *Grenada Intervention,* pp. 79, 81, 83.

149. House of Commons, *Grenada,* p. xiii, ¶ 30.

150. Gwertzman, "Steps to Invasion," p. 20.

151. O'Shaughnessy, *Grenada,* p. 9.

152. Gilmore, *Grenada Intervention,* p. 34.
153. Gilmore, *Grenada Intervention,* p. 20.
154. House of Commons, *Grenada,* p. xvi, ¶ 37.
155. Quoted in Michael J. Levitin, "The Law of Force and the Force of Law: Grenada, the Falklands, and Humanitarian Intervention," *Harvard International Law Journal,* vol. 27, no. 2, Spring 1986, p. 646, who disagrees; until records are made available, he writes, "the United States is entitled to the benefit of the doubt here" since "our government shades and interprets, but it does not fabricate out of thin air."
156. Moore, "Grenada and International Double Standard," p. 148. The text of his alleged letter of 24 Oct. requests that "a peace-keeping force should be established."
157. Lewis, *Grenada,* pp 96-97.
158. "Transcript of Address by President on Lebanon and Grenada," *NYT,* 28 Oct. 1983, p. A10.
159. Nor was there any evidence that Cuba was going to intervene to restore Bishop supporters to power; Castro explicitly ruled out such interference (see his speech of November 14 in O'Shaughnessy, *Grenada,* p, 236). But if Cuba *had* done so, and if, as is entirely possible, there was popular support among Grenadians, one wonders whether Washington and its apologists would have declared this a case of justified humanitarian intervention?
160. Large extracts from the documents have been published. See D/S and DoD, *Grenada Documents: An Overview and Selection,* Sept. 1984; Paul Seabury and Walter A. McDougall, eds., *The Grenada Papers,* San Francisco: Institute for Contemporary Studies, 1984; D/S and DoD, *Grenada: A Preliminary Report,* Dec. 16, 1983; Jiri Valenta and Herbert J. Ellison, eds., *Grenada and Soviet/Cuban Policy: Internal Crisis and U.S./OECS Intervention,* Boulder: Westview, 1986.
161. Jiri Valenta, "Findings and Recommendations," in Valenta and Ellison, eds., *Grenada and Soviet/Cuban Policy,* p. 243.
162. Colin Legum, "Grenada: Linkage and Impact on the Third World," in Valenta and Ellison, eds., *Grenada and Soviet/Cuban Policy,* p. 158.
163. Sandford and Vigilante, *Grenada,* p. 177; HR, *Military Actions in Grenada,* p. 92; Michael T. Kaufman, "Head of Caribbean Troops Discounts Grenada Threat," *NYT,* 7 Nov. 1983, p. A14.
164. Lewis, *Grenada,* p. 101.
165. O'Shaughnessy, *Grenada,* p. 187.
166. O'Shaughnessy, *Grenada,* p. 177.
167. Michael J. Bazyler, "Reexamining the Doctrine of Humanitarian Intervention in Light of the Atrocities in Kampuchea and Ethiopia," *Stanford Journal of International Law,* vol. 23, Summer 1987, p. 587n174.
168. See Fernando Teson, *Humanitarian Intervention; An Inquiry Into Law And Morality,* Dobbs Ferry, NY: Transnational Pub., 1988, pp. 188-200; Levitin, "Law of Force...."
169. Crossette, "Caribbean After Grenada," p. 66.
170. Lewis, *Grenada,* p. 111.
171. Lewis, *Grenada,* p. 98.
172. House of Commons, *Grenada,* p. lxv.
173. HR, *Military Actions in Grenada,* p. 88.
174. HR, *Military Actions in Grenada,* pp. 73-74; Lewis, *Grenada,* p. 97.
175. O'Shaughnessy, *Grenada,* pp. 222-23.
176. I am using Walzer's paraphrase of Mill's argument. Michael Walzer, *Just and Unjust Wars,* New York: Basic Books, 1977, pp. 87-89.

177. William C. Adams, "Grenada Update: The Public's Attitudes," *Public Opinion,* Feb.-March 1984, p. 54; Selwyn Ryan, "The Restoration of Electoral Politics in Grenada," in Heine, ed., *Revolution Aborted,* p. 266.

178. Grenada "has become increasingly dependent on U.S. assistance to service its debt." (GAO, *Caribbean Basin Initiative: Impact on Selected Countries,* GAO/NSIAD-88-177 July 1988, p. 20.) U.S. aid in 1984 was $57 million, more than $500 per person in a country where annual per capita income was less than $1,000. Ferguson, *Grenada,* pp. 9, 19.

179. Ryan, "Restoration...," pp. 277, 288n27; Ferguson, *Grenada,* p. 48; EPICA, *Caribbean,* pp. 132-33.

180. Ferguson, *Grenada,* pp. 24, 31-32, 94-96, 105-08, 112; Ryan, "Restoration...," pp. 284-85.

181. Ferguson, *Grenada,* pp. 23-24; GAO, *Caribbean Basin,* pp. 42-43.

182. Ferguson, *Grenada,* pp. 9, 31, 78.

183. Ferguson, *Grenada,* pp. 7, 77, 81-84, 87-88, 78; Ryan, "Restoration...," p. 285. For pre-1984 migration figures, see Wallace Joefield-Napier, "Macroeconomic Growth Under the People's Revolutionary Government: An Assessment," in Heine, ed., *Revolution Aborted,* p. 99.

184. Ferguson, *Grenada,* pp. 33-35, 53. See also Alexander Cockburn, "After the Press Bus Left: Grenada Four Years After," *In These Times,* Oct. 14-20, 1987, p. 17; Martin Burcharth, "Grenada Today," *Nation,* 1 March 1986, p. 228.

185. Richard A. Haggerty and John F. Hornbeck, "Grenada," in *Islands of the Commonwealth Caribbean: A Regional Study,* ed. Sandra W. Meditz and Dennis M. Hanratty, Washington, D.C.: Federal Research Division, Library of Congress, for the Dept. of the Army 1989, p. 357.

186. Gwertzman, "Steps to Invasion," p. 20.

6: The U.S. Response to Humanitarian Crises

1. Ian Brownlie, "Thoughts on Kind-Hearted Gunmen," in *Humanitarian Intervention and the United Nations,* ed. Richard B. Lillich, Charlottesville: UP of Virginia, 1973, p. 143.

2. Michael Reisman with Myres S. McDougal, "Humanitarian Intervention to Protect the Ibos," in Lillich, ed., *Humanitarian Intervention...,* pp. 182-83. On the Platt Amendment, see Robert F. Smith, *The United States and Cuba,* New Haven: College and UP, 1960, pp. 187-88.

3. Ian Brownlie, *International Law and the Use of Force By States,* London: Oxford UP, 1963, p. 340.

4. Quoted in Thomas M. Franck and Nigel S. Rodley, "After Bangladesh: The Law of Humanitarian Intervention by Military Force," *American Journal of International Law* vol. 67, 1973, p. 282.

5. Falk in Lillich, ed., *Humanitarian Intervention...,* p. 11.

6. Nayan Chanda, *Brother Enemy,* New York: Collier, 1986, pp. 80, 439n25.

7. Earlier years too saw horrendous carnage; among the many victims were the native peoples of North America and Australia, African slaves, the Hereros of South-West Africa, the Armenians, and the people of the Soviet Union. For discussion, see Frank Chalk and Kurt Jonassohn, *The History and Sociology of Genocide,* New Haven: Yale UP, 1990; and Edward S. Herman, "Politically Correct Holocausts," *Z Magazine,* April 1992, pp. 54-56.

8. Calculated from United Nations, *Demographic Yearbook, 1962,* New York: 1963, pp. 508-09, 513; *Demographic Yearbook, 1963,* New York: 1974, pp. 257, 259; *Demographic Yearbook, 1988,* New York: 1990, pp. 397, 399.

9. D/S, *Foreign Relations of the United States, 1902,* pp. 42, 44, quoted in Franck and Rodley, "After Bangladesh," p. 291. For more on Hay's anti-Semitism and on the irony that the U.S. Jewish community considered him a champion, see Richard Drinnon, *Facing West: The Metaphysics of Indian-Hating and Empire Building,* New York: Schocken Books, 1990, pp. 257, 512-13.

10. John Higham, *Strangers in the Land: Patterns of American Nativism, 1860-1925,* New York: Atheneum, 1963, p. 309.

11. David S. Wyman, *Paper Walls: America and the Refugee Crisis, 1938-1941,* New York: Pantheon, 1968, p. 59.

12. Wyman, *Paper Walls,* p. 50, 61.

13. Wyman, *Paper Walls,* p. 146.

14. David S. Wyman, *The Abandonment of the Jews,* New York: Pantheon, 1984, p. 72.

15. Wyman, *Abandonment of the Jews,* pp. x, 136.

16. Wyman, *Abandonment of the Jews,* p. 126n.

17. Wyman, *Abandonment of the Jews,* p. x.

18. Quoted in Lenni Brenner, *Zionism in the Age of Dictators,* Westport, CT: Lawrence Hill, 1983, p. 228.

19. Wyman, *Abandonment of the Jews,* p. 189n.

20. Wyman, *Abandonment of the Jews,* p. 29.

21. Wyman, *Abandonment of the Jews,* p. 8.

22. Wyman, *Abandonment of the Jews,* pp. 264, 266-67, 269.

23. Wyman, *Abandonment of the Jews,* pp. 204, x, 220, 285.

24. Wyman, *Abandonment of the Jews,* p. 296. The War Department rejected appeals to bomb Auschwitz four different times: see Martin Gilbert, *Auschwitz and the Allies,* New York: Holt, Rinehart and Winston, 1981, pp. 255-56, 303, 321, 327-28.

25. Wyman, *Abandonment of the Jews,* pp. 297-300, 304, 305, 306, 95n; Gilbert, *Auschwitz and the Allies,* pp. 249, 301, 307, 309, 311, 318, 322.

26. Wyman, *Abandonment of the Jews,* pp. 173, 200, 175.

27. Suzanne Cronje, *The World and Nigeria,* London: Sidgwick & Jackson, 1972, p. 79.

28. "The Nigeria-Biafra Conflict," ed. Michael A. Samuels, CSIS study, Georgetown University, Washington D.C., 1969, printed in Sen., Judiciary Comm., subcomm. to Investigate Problems with Refugees and Escapees, *Relief Problems in Nigeria-Biafra,* Hearings, July 1969, Jan. 1970, p. I:118.

29. John J. Stremlau, *The International Politics of the Nigerian Civil War, 1967-1970,* Princeton: Princeton UP, 1977, p. 70.

30. Charles R. Nixon, "Self-Determination: The Nigeria/Biafra Case," *World Politics,* vol. 24, no. 4, July 1972, pp. 477-82.

31. A pro-Lagos journalist claims that there were at most 10,000 deaths (John de St. Jorre, *The Brothers' War: Biafra and Nigeria,* Boston: Houghton Mifflin, 1972, pp. 85-86); a conference report from the mainstream Center for Strategic and International Studies of Georgetown University gives the figure as 10,000-30,000 ("The Nigeria-Biafra Conflict," ed. Michael A. Samuels, CSIS study, Georgetown University, Washington D.C., 1969, printed in Sen., *Relief... in Nigeria-Biafra,* p. I:99.

32. St. Jorre, *Brothers' War,* pp. 84-87.

33. Dan Jacobs, *The Brutality of Nations,* New York: Knopf, 1987, p. 20.

34. Zdenek Cervenka, *The Nigerian War, 1967-1970,* Frankfurt am Main: Bernard & Graefe, Verlag fur Wehrwesen, 1971, p. 109; St. Jorre, *Brothers' War,* pp. 298-99.

35. Jacobs, *Brutality of Nations,* p. 173.

36. Roger Morris, *Uncertain Greatness: Henry Kissinger and American Foreign Policy,* New York: Harper & Row, 1977, p. 122; St. Jorre, *Brothers' War,* p. 216.

37. Cronje, *The World and Nigeria,* p. 225.

38. St. Jorre, *Brothers' War,* pp. 179, 302n11.
39. Cronje, *The World and Nigeria,* pp. 242-43; Sen., *Relief...in Nigeria-Biafra,* p. II:184.
40. Cronje, *The World and Nigeria,* p. 370n44.
41. Nicholas deB. Katzenbach, "The Tragedy of Nigeria," 3 Dec. 1968, in *Documents of American Foreign Relations, 1968-69,* ed. Richard P. Stebbins and Elaine P. Adam, New York: Simon & Schuster for the Council on Foreign Relations, 1972, p. 366.
42. Katzenbach, "Tragedy of Nigeria," p. 366; Jacobs, *Brutality of Nations,* p. 116; Stremlau, *International Politics...,* p. 312n157.
43. Jacobs, *Brutality of Nations,* p. 92.
44. Stremlau, *International Politics...,* p. 336. See also Jacobs, *Brutality of Nations,* pp. 31 35; St. Jorre, *Brothers' War,* p. 244. The latter author himself considers starvation a "legitimate" wartime killer (St. Jorre, *Brothers' War,* pp. 285-86).
45. C. Paul Vincent, *The Politics of Hunger: The Allied Blockade of Germany, 1915-1919,* Athens: Ohio UP, 1985, pp. 42, 159.
46. Vincent, *Politics of Hunger,* p. 58n72.
47. Vincent, *Politics of Hunger,* pp. 49, 58n80, 145. Vincent notes that the deaths were estimated by the German government in December 1918 and may be too high, but they exclude the 1918 influenza epidemic.
48. Vincent, *Politics of Hunger,* p. 79.
49. Vincent, *Politics of Hunger,* p. 85.
50. Vincent, *Politics of Hunger,* p. 81.
51. Vincent, *Politics of Hunger,* pp. 81, 97, 108.
52. Vincent, *Politics of Hunger,* pp. 90, 112.
53. Vincent, *Politics of Hunger,* pp. 93, 97, 114.
54. Morris, *Uncertain Greatness,* p. 122; see also Jacobs, *Brutality of Nations,* pp. 261, 361n
55. Morris, *Uncertain Greatness,* p. 122.
56. Jacobs, *Brutality of Nations,* pp. 74, 146-47.
57. Morris, *Uncertain Greatness,* p. 19.
58. The text of his statement is in A.H.M. Kirk-Greene, ed., *Crisis and Conflict in Nigeria. A Documentary Sourcebook 1966-1970,* vol. 2, London: Oxford UP, 1971, pp. II:334-35
59. Morris, *Uncertain Greatness,* p. 42.
60. Seymour M. Hersh, *The Price of Power: Kissinger in the Nixon White House,* New York Summit Books, 1983, p. 111.
61. Morris, *Uncertain Greatness,* p. 131.
62. Morris, *Uncertain Greatness,* p. 121.
63. Stremlau, *International Politics...,* pp. 292-93. See also Richardson's testimony in Sen., *Relief...in Nigeria-Biafra,* p. I:29.
64. Hersh, *Price of Power,* p. 111.
65. Morris, *Uncertain Greatness,* p. 123.
66. Sen., *Relief...in Nigeria-Biafra,* pp. I:12, II:169.
67. Jacobs, *Brutality of Nations,* pp. 226, 230.
68. Andrew Borowiec, "Death, Not Food, Is Awaiting Many Biafran Refugees," *Washington Star,* Jan. 21, 1970, in Sen., *Relief...in Nigeria-Biafra,* p. II: 274.
69. Ibid.
70. Sen., *Relief...in Nigeria-Biafra,* pp. II:177, 179; Jacobs, *Brutality of Nations,* pp. 256, 258; St. Jorre, *Brothers' War,* pp. 405-07.
71. Andrew Borowiec, "Death, Not Food..." p. II:274.
72. Sen., *Relief...in Nigeria-Biafra,* p. II:172.
73. Morris, *Uncertain Greatness,* pp. 129-30.
74. Morris, *Uncertain Greatness,* pp. 125-29.
75. Jacobs, *Brutality of Nations,* pp. 287-88.

76. St. Jorre, *Brothers' War*, p. 404. The one million figure is on pp. 304, 412. Roger Morris states that classified D/S figures put the toll at 20,000, but that many put the figure far higher (Morris, *Uncertain Greatness*, p. 130). For an estimate that considerably more than two million died of starvation all together, see Jacobs, *Brutality of Nations*, p. 326.

77. Cervenka, *Nigerian War...*, p. 125; Sen., *Relief...in Nigeria-Biafra*, p. I:14, 33.

78. Speech of 16 May 1969, in Kirk-Greene, ed., *Crisis and Conflict in Nigeria*, p. II:403.

79. *Time*, 3 May 1971, in Sen., Judiciary Comm., subcomm. to Investigate Problems with Refugees and Escapees, *Relief Problems in East Pakistan and India*, Hearings, June, Sept. 1971, p. I:105.

80. See news reports reprinted in Sen., *Relief...in East Pakistan...*, pp. I:104-05.

81. Morris, *Uncertain Greatness*, p. 216.

82. Sen., *Relief...in East Pakistan...*, p. I:212.

83. *Le Monde*, 10 June 1971; *NYT*, 14 July 1971 (Sydney H. Schanberg); *WP*, 23 Aug. 1971 (Stephen Klaidman), reprinted in Sen., *Relief...in East Pakistan...*, pp. I:180, 163, II:342.

84. Interview with *Le Figaro* reported in *NYT*, 29 Sept. 1971, quoted in U Thant, *View from the UN*, Garden City, NY: Doubleday, 1978, p. 426. General Tikka Khan, the military governor of East Bengal, when reminded he was administering a majority province of Pakistan, replied, "I will reduce this majority into a minority" (Quoted in Chalk and Jonassohn, *History and Sociology of Genocide*, p. 396).

85. John P. Lewis testimony in Sen., *Relief...in East Pakistan...*, p. II:242.

86. Richard Sisson and Leo E. Rose, *War and Secession: Pakistan, India, and the Creation of Bangladesh*, Berkeley: University of California Press, 1990, p. 259.

87. Lawrence Lifschultz, *Bangladesh: The Unfinished Revolution*, London: Zed Press, 1979, p. 158.

88. Christopher Van Hollen, "The Tilt Policy Revisited: Nixon-Kissinger Geopolitics and South Asia," *Asian Survey*, vol. 20, no. 4, April 1980, p. 342.

89. Van Hollen, "Tilt Policy Revisited...," p. 341.

90. Henry Kissinger, *White House Years*, Boston: Little, Brown, 1979, p. 852.

91. Van Hollen, "Tilt Policy Revisited...," p. 341; Nixon usually referred to Gandhi as "that bitch" and sometimes used more derogatory epithets.

92. Kissinger, *White House Years*, p. 854.

93. Van Hollen, "Tilt Policy Revisited...," p. 343.

94. Kissinger, *White House Years*, pp. 724, 740.

95. Morris, *Uncertain Greatness*, p. 214.

96. Kissinger, *White House Years*, p. 853.

97. Sisson and Rose, *War and Secession*, pp. 222, 307n3.

98. Kissinger, *White House Years*, p. 857.

99. Van Hollen, "Tilt Policy Revisited...," p. 342. Nixon's level of humanitarian concern is indicated by his memoirs. His full account of the atrocities reads as follows: "Eight months earlier there had been a rebellion in East Pakistan against the government of President Yahya Khan. Indian officials reported that nearly 10 million refugees fled from East Pakistan into India" (Richard Nixon, *RN: The Memoirs of Richard Nixon*, New York: Grosset and Dunlap, 1978, p. 525).

100. Sen., *Relief...in East Pakistan...*, pp. I:23-24; Sisson and Rose, *War and Secession*, pp. 256-57.

101. Tad Szulc, *NYT*, 27 June 1971, in Sen., *Relief...in East Pakistan...*, p. I:206. See also Benjamin Welles, "U.S. Acknowledges Sales of Ammunition to Pakistan," *NYT*, 14 April 1971, in Sen., *Relief...in East Pakistan...*, p. I:199.

102. Sen., *Relief...in East Pakistan...*, p. III:356.

103. Sen., *Relief...in East Pakistan...*, p. III:372.

104. Sen., *Relief...in East Pakistan...*, pp. III:374-76, 394-95.

105. Flora Lewis, "The Isolationism Toward Pakistan," *WP*, 11 July 1971, in Sen., *Relief…in East Pakistan…*, p. I:159.

106. Kissinger, *White House Years*, p. 878. Kissinger states that the U.S. got Yahya's permission to make this announcement, but says that it took two months for the Pakistanis to agree to let the pipeline run out (p. 865); earlier, however, he said the pipeline was due to run out on its own by October (p. 861).

107. Sen., *Relief…in East Pakistan…*, p. I:24. See also Tad Szulc, "U.S. Says It Will Continue Aid to Pakistan Despite Cutoff Urged By Other Nations," *NYT*, 29 June 1971, in Sen., *Relief…in East Pakistan…*, p. I:206.

108. Sydney H. Schanberg, "U.S. Rift Widens In India, Eases In Pakistan," *NYT*, 6 Sept. 1971, in Sen., *Relief…in East Pakistan…*, pp. III:465-66.

109. Malcolm W. Browne, "Fear Seen Bringing Washington and Yahya Closer," *NYT*, 6 Sept. 1971, in Sen., *Relief…in East Pakistan…*, p. III:466.

110. Sisson and Rose, *War and Secession*, p. 258.

111. Kissinger, *White House Years*, p. 856.

112. Van Hollen, "Tilt Policy Revisited…," p. 346.

113. Van Hollen, "Tilt Policy Revisited…," p. 347.

114. Sisson and Rose, *War and Secession*, p. 211.

115. Sisson and Rose, *War and Secession*, pp. 212-14.

116. Sisson and Rose state that it is difficult to establish who formally started the war on December 3 (*War and Secession*, p. 307n1), but most other sources (e.g., Kissinger, *White House Years*, p. 896; Robert Jackson, *South Asian Crisis: India, Pakistan and Bangla Desh*, New York: Praeger, 1975, p. 111), including Sisson and Rose elsewhere (pp. 212-14) indicate Pakistan struck first on December 3. Sisson and Rose also date the "realistic" beginning of the war as November 21, when Indian military units moved into Pakistani territory (pp. 212-14), but one should note that: (1) Kissinger recommended against cutting aid to India in late November because the situation was ambiguous (Van Hollen, "Tilt Policy Revisited…," p. 350); and (2) that the crisis was brought to the United Nations only in December.

117. Michael J. Bazyler, "Reexamining the Doctrine of Humanitarian Intervention in Light of the Atrocities in Kampuchea and Ethiopia," *Stanford Journal of International Law*, vol. 23, Summer 1987, p. 589.

118. Leo Kuper, *The Prevention of Genocide*, New Haven: Yale UP, 1985, p. 54.

119. Bazyler, "Reexamining…," p. 589n187.

120. Sen., *Relief…in East Pakistan…*, pp. II:241, 255-56, 276, 347, III:358, 459-61; Sisson and Rose, *War and Secession*, p. 178.

121. Sisson and Rose, *War and Secession*, pp. 206-07, 303-04n2; Lifschultz, *Bangladesh*, p. 25; Sen., *Relief…in East Pakistan…*, pp. II:281-82 (John P. Lewis), p. I:174 (Lee Lescaze, *WP*, 4 June 1971), I:192 (Nayan Chanda, "Double-Think?" *Far Eastern Economic Review*, 19 June 1971), I:167-68 (Peter R. Kann, *WSJ*, 28 April 1971), I:206 (Tad Szulc, *NYT*, 27 June 1971).

122. Lifschultz, *Bangladesh*, pp. 130, 139; see also Donald F. McHenry and Kai Bird, "Food Bungle in Bangladesh," *Foreign Policy*, no. 27, Summer 1977, p. 73.

123. McHenry and Bird, "Food Bungle…," pp. 73-75.

124. McHenry and Bird, "Food Bungle…," p. 76.

125. Jack Anderson with George Clifford, *The Anderson Papers*, New York: Random House, 1973, p. 220.

126. Kissinger, *White House Years*, p. 853.

127. Jackson, *South Asian Crisis*, p. 213.

128. Kissinger, *White House Years*, p. 865.

129. Kuper, *Prevention of Genocide*, p. 55.

130. Anthony Astrachan, "Pakistani Plight 'Desperate'," *WP,* 17 Oct. 1971, in Sen., *Relief... in East Pakistan...,* p. II:319; Thant, *View from the UN,* pp. 422, 436; Jackson, *South Asian Crisis,* pp. 184-87. See also Kissinger, *White House Years,* p. 894.

131. Fernando R. Teson, *Humanitarian Intervention: An Inquiry into Law and Morality,* Dobbs Ferry, NY: Transnational Publishers, 1988, p. 186n194. In his memoirs, Kissinger used similar characterizations for the Pakistani bloodbath, calling it an "error" and "worse than a crime; it was a blunder" (Kissinger, *White House Years,* pp. 875, 871).

132. Minutes of meeting in Jackson, *South Asian Crisis,* p. 218.

133. Sydney H. Schanberg, "India—Will Words Yield To Bullets?" *NYT,* 8 Aug. 1971, in Sen., *Relief... in East Pakistan...,* p. II:347.

134. Sisson and Rose, *War and Secession,* p. 172.

135. Kissinger, *White House Years,* p. 910.

136. David K. Hall, "The Laotian War of 1962 and the Indo-Pakistan War of 1971," in *Force Without War: U.S. Armed Forces As A Political Instrument,* ed. Barry M. Blechman and Steven S. Kaplan, Washington, D.C.: Brookings Institution, 1978, p. 187; Jackson, *South Asian Crisis,* pp. 222-24, 226-28; Anderson and Clifford, *Anderson Papers,* p. 252. A month earlier, the *WP* had urged the U.S. to cut off the direct supply of arms to Pakistan, pointing out that "the amount of arms affected would be trivial; whatever supplies might still be deemed necessary could be routed through third countries" (2 Nov. 1971, in Sen., *Relief... in East Pakistan...,* p. III:473).

137. Van Hollen, "Tilt Policy Revisited...," pp. 351, 351n27.

138. Jackson, *South Asian Crisis,* p. 141.

139. Thant, *View From the UN,* p. 432.

140. Jackson, *South Asian Crisis,* pp. 144-45.

141. Jackson, *South Asian Crisis,* p. 223. (Kissinger's comments are in the words of the minute-taker.)

142. McHenry and Bird, "Food Bungle...," p. 82.

143. Lifschultz, *Bangladesh,* p. 100.

144. Sisson and Rose, *War and Secession,* pp. 246, 312n15; Lifschultz, *Bangladesh,* pp. 109-10.

145. René Lemarchand and David Martin, *Selective Genocide in Burundi,* London: Minority Rights Group, Report No. 20, 1974, pp. 5, 14-15. Some speculate that the government knew about the intended Hutu uprising but did not try to prevent it, wanting an excuse for massacre; and one source has suggested that the Tutsis provoked the Hutu revolt. See Stanley Meisler, "Burundi," in Chalk and Jonassohn, *History and Sociology of Genocide,* p. 387.

146. Thomas Patrick Melady, *Burundi: The Tragic Years,* Maryknoll, NY: Orbis Books, 1974, p. 15; Michael Bowen, Gary Freeman, and Kay Miller, *Passing By: The United States and Genocide in Burundi, 1972,* Washington, D.C.: Carnegie Endowment for International Peace, 1973, p. 6.

147. Melady, *Burundi,* p. 10. Melady's claim that the "Belgian government was the second government to urge moderation and an end to the killings, the first having been the United States government on May 5, when I saw Micombero" (Melady, *Burundi,* p. 16) obscures the fact that the Belgian meeting was *after* the Belgian government had characterized events in Burundi as amounting to "veritable genocide"; Melady's meeting was before it was clear what was happening. See also Bowen, et al., *Passing By,* p. 1, which reports that a later internal review by the D/S expressed doubt "that a private diplomatic expression of Washington's 'displeasure' had been conveyed honestly to the Burundian authorities."

148. Melady, *Burundi,* pp. 16-18.

149. Melady, *Burundi,* p. 18.

150. Melady, *Burundi,* pp. 107-08.
151. Melady, *Burundi,* p. 34; Bowen, et al., *Passing By,* pp. 27, 49.
152. Bowen, et al., *Passing By,* p. 11; Melady, *Burundi,* p. 32.
153. Melady, *Burundi,* p. 24.
154. Melady, *Burundi,* p. 82.
155. Meisler, "Burundi," pp. 390-91.
156. Melady, *Burundi,* p. 83.
157. Jonathan Kwitny, *Endless Enemies,* New York: Penguin, 1984, p. 75.
158. Bowen, et al., *Passing By,* p. 8.
159. Bowen, et al., *Passing By,* pp. 3-4, 25.
160. Melady, *Burundi,* p. 83; Lemarchand and Martin, *Selective Genocide in Burundi,* p. 20.
161. Bowen, et al., *Passing By,* pp. 4, 16.
162. Bowen, et al., *Passing By,* pp. 3-4.
163. Bowen, et al., *Passing By,* p. 23.
164. Jack Anderson, "Burundi's Nickel Makes U.S. Forget," *Boston Evening Globe,* 14 March 1974, p. 39.
165. D/S, *American Foreign Policy: Basic Documents, 1977-1980,* 1983, p. 1044.
166. Zbigniew Brzezinski, *Power and Principle: Memoirs of the National Security Adviser, 1977-1981,* New York: Farrar, Straus, Giroux, 1983, p. 212.
167. William Shawcross, *The Quality of Mercy: Cambodia, Holocaust and Modern Conscience,* New York: Touchstone, 1985, p. 78.
168. Shawcross, *Quality of Mercy,* pp. 70-71.
169. Shawcross, *Quality of Mercy,* pp. 56-57.
170. Chanda, *Brother Enemy,* p. 85.
171. Quoted by Strobe Talbott, *Time,* February 6, 1989, p. 40.
172. Joel Charny and John Spragens, Jr., *Obstacles to Recovery in Vietnam and Kampuchea: U.S. Embargo of Humanitarian Aid,* Boston: Oxfam America, 1984, p. 2.
173. Justus M. van der Kroef, "Delaying Peace: The Case of Cambodia," *Bulletin of Peace Proposals,* 17:1 (1986), pp. 63-64.
174. Shawcross, *Quality of Mercy,* p. 356.
175. Chanda, *Brother Enemy,* pp. 390-91; Grant Evans and Kelvin Rowley, *Red Brotherhood At War,* London: Verso, 1984, p. 264.
176. Jeremy J. Stone, "Secret U.S. War In Cambodia," *NYT,* 16 Nov. 1989, p. A31.
177. Quoted in Robert Pear, "Congress Curbing Bush's Ability To Aid the Cambodian Guerrillas," *NYT,* 15 Nov. 1989, p. A8. See also Steven Erlanger, "Cambodia Factions Said to Link Armies," *NYT,* 4 Feb. 1990, p. 25.
178. GAO, *Cambodia: U.S. Non-lethal Assistance and Status of the Cambodian Seat at the United Nations,* testimony, GAO/T-NSIAD-90-6319, Sept. 1990, pp. 2-4.
179. Paul Lewis, "Europeans Warn Sihanouk on UN Seat," *NYT,* 15 April 1990, p. I:3.
180. Thomas L. Friedman, "U.S. Shifts Cambodia Policy; Ends Recognition of Rebels; Agrees to Talks with Hanoi," *NYT,* 19 July 1990, pp. A1, A10.
181. Stephen J. Solarz, "What New Policy Toward Cambodia?" *NYT,* 26 July 1990, p. A19. Solarz supported U.S. policy.
182. Clifford Krauss, "Congress Still Uneasy on Cambodia," *NYT,* 12 April 1991, p. A3; Don Oberdorfer, "U.S. to Resume Aid to Cambodian Rebels," *WP,* 30 April 1991, p. A17.
183. Clifford Krauss, *Inside Central America,* New York: Summit Books, 1991, pp. 18, 20, 33. See also Noam Chomsky, *Turning the Tide,* Boston: South End Press, 1985, pp. 154-57; Michael McClintock, *The American Connection,* vol. 2, *State Terror and Popular Resistance in Guatemala,* London: Zed Books, 1985.
184. Noam Chomsky and Edward S. Herman, *The Washington Connection and Third World Fascism,* Boston: South End Press, 1979, pp. 205-17.

185. See Noam Chomsky, "'A Gleam of Light in Asia,'" *Z Magazine*, Sept. 1990.

186. Noam Chomsky, "Preface," to José Ramos-Horta, *FUNU: The Unfinished Saga of East Timor*, Trenton, NJ: Red Sea Press, 1987.

187. Samuel Decalo, *Psychoses of Power: African Personal Dictatorships*, Boulder: Westview, 1989, p. 100.

188. Tony Avirgan and Martha Honey, *War in Uganda: The Legacy of Idi Amin*, Westport, CT: Lawrence Hill & Co., 1982, pp. 9-10; Mahmood Mamdani, *Imperialism and Fascism in Uganda*, Trenton, NJ: Africa World Press, 1984, p. 30; Thomas Melady and Margaret Melady, *Idi Amin Dada: Hitler in Africa*, Kansas City: Sheed Andrews and McMeel, 1977, pp. 57-58; George Ivan Smith, *Ghosts of Kampala*, New York: St. Martin's, 1980, pp. 57-58, 63, 69-70, 75-76, 80-81.

189. Melady and Melady, *Idi Amin Dada*, pp. 9-12; Decalo, *Psychoses of Power*, p. 9.

190. Melady and Melady, *Idi Amin Dada*, p. 5.

191. Avirgan and Honey, *War in Uganda*, p. 15.

192. Mamdani, *Imperialism and Fascism in Uganda*, pp. 78-79; Avirgan and Honey, *War in Uganda*, pp. 17-19; John de St. Jorre, "The Ugandan Connection," *NYT Magazine*, 9 April 1978, pp. 27-28. This support is in addition to that provided by former CIA operative Frank Terpil (Avirgan and Honey, *War in Uganda*, p. 21), who was likely acting without U.S. government approval.

193. Decalo, *Psychoses of Power*, pp. 114, 117, 196.

194. Suzanne Jolicoeur Katsikas, *The Arc of Socialist Revolutions: Angola to Afghanistan*, Cambridge, MA: Shenkman, 1982, p. 126.

195. See, for example, U.S. War Department, *The Chinese Communist Movement*, ed. Lyman P. Van Slyke, Stanford: Stanford UP, 1968, pp. 20-21, 23, 31.

196. Aryeh Neier, "Watching Rights," *Nation*, 16 March 1992, p. 331; Dennis Hevesi, "2 Rights Groups Indict Iraqis for Attacks on Kurds in 80's," *NYT*, 2 Mar. 1992, p. A6; Chris Hedges, "Kurds Unearthing New Evidence of Iraqi Killings," *NYT*, 7 Dec. 1991, pp. 1, 7; *NYT*, 13 Aug 1990, p. A11.

197. Michael Wines, "Kurd Gives Account of Broadcasts to Iraq Linked to the CIA," *NYT*, 6 April 1991, pp. 1, 5; Clifford Krauss, "U.S. Urges Turkey to Open Borders to Fleeing Kurds," *NYT*, 5 April 1991, p. 1.

198. See Chapter 3 for details. U.S. bombing at the end of the Gulf War concentrated on the conscript units of the Iraqi army who were to play a vital role in the anti-Saddam uprising in southern Iraq, while the Republican Guard had already been withdrawn to safety. Apparently the rebels were denied access to Iraqi weapons and ammunition under U.S. control. See Faleh Abd al-Jabbar, "Why the Uprisings Failed," *Middle East Report*, May-June 1992, pp. 9, 12-13.

199. Edward Mortimer, "Iraq: The Road Not Taken," *New York Review of Books*, 16 May 1991, p. 3.

200. Andrew Rosenthal, "U.S., Fearing Iraqi Breakup, Is Termed Ready to Accept a Hussein Defeat of Rebels," *NYT*, 27 March 1991, pp. A1, A9. This is not to deny that there were many revenge killings by the opposition, particularly in the south, which may have been one factor causing Ba'athists to rally behind Saddam Hussein (al-Jabbar, "Why the Uprisings Failed," pp. 10, 13).

201. Not by pressuring Turkey to open its borders to fleeing refugees, which would have saved many lives but offended Washington's Turkish ally, but by establishing a safe haven zone inside Iraq. See Bill Frelick, "The False Promise of Operation Provide Comfort," *Middle East Report*, May-June 1992, p. 26.

202. Chris Hedges, "Kurds in Turkey Seem To Be Nearing Full-Scale Revolt," *NYT*, 30 March 1992, pp. A1, A6. "Complete silence" is not quite correct. In fact, the Bush administration did issue a condemnation—of the Kurdish Workers Party for "acts of terrorism" against

Turkey. Germany, on the other hand, cut off arms to Ankara. John Tagliabue, "Defending Kurds, Bonn Cuts Arms Flow to Turkey," *NYT*, 27 March 1992, p. A10.

203. AP, "Turks Attack Separatist Kurds in North Iraq," *NYT*, 8 Aug. 1991, p. A12; AP, "Turkish Planes Pummel Iraq Villages As They Try to Rout Kurdish Rebels," *SL*, 13 Oct. 1991, p. I:4; Reuters, "Turkish Troops Attack Kurds' Bases in Iraq," *NYT*, 13 Oct. 1991, p. 19. Re security zone: Frelick, "False Promise of Operation Provide Comfort," p. 27.

204. Christine Moss Helms, *Iraq: Eastern Flank of the Arab World*, Washington, D.C.: Brookings Institution, 1984, p. 190n31; Jabr Muhsin, George Harding, and Fran Hazelton, "Iraq in the Gulf War," in *Saddam's Iraq: Revolution or Reaction?* ed. Committee Against Repression and For Democratic Rights In Iraq, London: Zed Books, 1989, p. 232.

205. Lois Whitman, deputy director of Helsinki Watch, "Kurdish Oppression in Turkey Goes On," (letter), *NYT*, 7 April 1991, p. E18.

206. Clyde Haberman, "The Kurds in Flight Once Again," *NYT Magazine*, 5 May 1991, p. 52.

207. During the Gulf War, political pundit William Safire, in a column ironically entitled "Remember the Kurds," urged Turkey to attack Iraq and to equip Kurds to join in the fray; he held out the possibility that Turkey could be rewarded for such loyal service by getting a piece of Iraq after the war (*NYT*, 28 Jan. 1991, p. A23). What made this offer especially cynical was that it is precisely the Kurdish region of Iraq that Turkey has claimed for 70 years, so paying off Turkey would come at the expense of the Kurds. During the Gulf War, Turkey had warned that it would intervene militarily to prevent the rise of an independent Kurdistan (Haberman, "Kurds in Flight...," p. 54).

208. Obviously, Saddam Hussein's troops were directly doing the killing, but this does not warrant the conclusion of Michael Walzer that Kurdish deaths are not the result "of any American decisions" (*Dissent*, Summer 1991, p. 425).

7: Terrorism—The Case of Libya

1. For a summary of the historical record, see Stephen R. Shalom, "The United States and Libya. Part I: Before Qaddafi," *Z Magazine*, May 1990, pp. 67-74.

2. See chapter 3 above.

3. See Noam Chomsky, *The Fateful Triangle*, Boston: South End, 1983, pp. 39-88.

4. Mahmoud G. ElWarfally, *Imagery and Ideology in U.S. Policy Toward Libya, 1969-1982*, Pittsburgh: University of Pittsburgh Press, 1988, p. 155.

5. Quoted in René Lemarchand, "Beyond the Mad Dog Syndrome," in *The Green and the Black: Qadhafi's Policies in Africa*, ed. René Lemarchand, Bloomington: Indiana UP, 1988, p. 2.

6. For background on these two, see Edward Herman and Gerry O'Sullivan, *The "Terrorism" Industry*, New York: Pantheon, 1989, especially pp. 146-48, 170-73.

7. Sterling says Qaddafi provided "the funds, arms, and training" (*The Terror Network*, New York: Berkeley, 1982, p. 242); she also states that Qaddafi "donated his first $50 million to the PLO shortly after the Olympic Games massacre (throwing in a five-million dollar bonus for those particular hit-men)." The latter would be consistent with Qaddafi's praise for the terrorists after the fact, without indicating Libyan sponsorship. Alexander's assertions are in Sen., Judiciary Comm., subcomm. on Security and Terrorism, *Libyan Sponsored Terrorism: A Dilemma for Policy-makers*, Hearings, Feb. 1986, pp. 85-86, 97.

8. D/S, *The Libyan Problem*, Special Report No. 111, Oct. 1983, p. 2.

9. David Blundy and Andrew Lycett, *Qaddafi and the Libyan Revolution*, Boston: Little, Brown, 1987, p. 78.

10. *American Journal of International Law*, vol. 80, 1986, p. 635; Sen., *Libyan Sponsored...*, p. 17; D/S, *Syrian Support for International Terrorism: 1983-86*, Special Report No.

157, Dec. 1986, p. 2. See also Ronald Reagan, "Libyan Sanctions," D/S, *Current Policy,* No. 780, 1986, p. 1; Sen., *Libyan Sponsored...,* p. 55.

11. Sen., *Libyan Sponsored...,* p. 35.

12. Sen., *Libyan Sponsored...,* p. 55. Iklé was asked why the U.S. doesn't attack terrorist training bases; he explained: "their training may be long behind them. They may have been trained years ago in Prague or someplace." (Sen., *Libyan Sponsored...,* p. 23) In fact, the Rome and Vienna terrorists had been recently trained in Syrian-controlled areas of Lebanon. Syria, however, was a serious military power, with real Soviet ties, and hence inappropriate for demonstrating U.S. toughness.

13. Sen., *Libyan Sponsored...,* pp. 38, 55-56. The January 1986 U.S. White Paper on Libya, however, said only that "there are reliable press reports" that Abu Nidal's headquarters has been moved to Libya (D/S, *Libya Under Qadhafi: A Pattern of Aggression,* Washington, D.C.: Special Report No. 138, Jan. 1986, p. 2) and that "Abu Nidal himself and many of the group's operations *may* have moved" to Libya within the last 12 months (p. 4, emphasis added).

14. L. Paul Bremer III, "Terrorism: Its Evolving Nature," D/S, *Current Policy,* No. 1151, 1989, p. 2. Abu Nidal lived in Syria on and off for 17 months from Oct. 22, 1985 to March 28, 1987. Patrick Seale, *Abu Nidal: A Gun for Hire,* New York: Random House, 1992, p. 294. Seale also comments somewhat confusingly that Abu Nidal latched on to Qaddafi "with great eagerness" in 1984-85 (p. 139); that in 1985 a key Abu Nidal aide moved to Libya, signaling that Abu Nidal had now made Libya his principal base (p. 149); and that "from the summer of 1986, Abu Nidal started quietly moving his organization out of Syria" (255).

15. Sen., *Libyan Sponsored...,* p. 13.

16. See sources in Noam Chomsky, *Pirates and Emperors,* New York: Claremont Research, 1986, p. 169n12-13.

17. Bernard Gwertzman, "U.S. Presses Bonn and Other Allies to Expel Libyans," *NYT,* 9 April 1986, p. A12.

18. Seale, *Abu Nidal,* pp. 243-45. Seale also recounts suspicions that Mossad may have penetrated and been manipulating the Abu Nidal organization (the governments of both Libya and Israel had an interest in discouraging Italy and Austria from attempting to broker a PLO-Israeli peace). It's unlikely, Seale concludes, that Israel would maneuver an attack on Jewish passengers; on the other hand, Israel's failure to retaliate against Abu Nidal has been strangely uncharacteristic (Seale, *Abu Nidal,* pp. 171, 211, 246). I am not persuaded that Mossad controls (as opposed to having penetrated) the Abu Nidal organization. More convincing is Scott MacLeod's comment: "Mossad officials did not have to invent or sponsor Abu Nidal in order to decide their strategic interests were served by not killing a terrorist who discredits the PLO while also causing extreme violence within Palestinian ranks" ("The Terrorist's Terrorist," *New York Review of Books,* 28 May 1992, p. 10). Thus, for their own reasons, both Abu Nidal and Israel go after moderate Palestinians instead of each other.

19. Seale, *Abu Nidal,* pp. 307-10, 327.

20. Anthony D'Amato, "The Imposition of Attorney Sanctions for Claims Arising from the U.S. Air Raid on Libya," *American Journal of International Law,* vol. 84, 1990, pp. 705, 705n2; Robert J. McCartney, "Police Arrest Woman in '86 Berlin Bombing," *WP,* 12 Jan. 1988, pp. A16, A18; Seymour M. Hersh, "Target Qaddafi," *NYT Magazine,* 22 Feb. 1987, pp. 74-76. See also citations in Noam Chomsky, "International Terrorism: What is the Remedy?" *Third World Affairs,* Jan. 1988, p. 9.

21. Interview by journalist working for *Stars and Stripes* in Germany, quoted in Chomsky, *Pirates and Emperors,* pp. 149-50. Particularly odd is the claim by Emerson and Duffy that the conclusive intercepts were obtained by West German electronic intelligence

and passed on to the U.S. National Security Agency, and that other confirming evidence was gathered by the German Interior intelligence agency. If this were so, why were West German officials so unconvinced by the U.S. evidence? See Steven Emerson and Brian Duffy, *The Fall of Pan Am 103,* New York: G.P. Putnam's Sons, 1990, p. 180. Even if Bonn were annoyed at Reagan's disclosing the intercepts, this would be no reason to dispute that there was firm evidence of Libyan involvement—if such evidence existed.

22. Hersh, "Target Qaddafi," pp. 19, 74.

23. Craig R. Whitney, "East's Archives Reveal Ties To Terrorists," *NYT,* 15 July 1990, p. I:6; Joel Bleifuss, *In These Times,* Sept. 26-Oct. 2, 1990, p. 5; Jonas Bernstein, "When in Need, Terrorist Groups Turned Eastward," *Insight/Washington Times,* 21 Jan. 1991 (*Newsbank,* 1991 INT 21:F9-10); *Die Welt,* 12 July 1990, p. 1, in FBIS-WEU-90-135, 13 July 1990, pp. 2-3; "Bomben von Derwisch," *Der Spiegel,* no. 29, 1990, pp. 22-25; Hamburg DPA, 27 July 1990, and *Frankfurter Allgemeine,* 30 July 1990, p. 2, in FBIS-WEU-90-146, pp. 3-4; Hamburg DPA, 7 Aug. 1990, citing *Stern,* in FBIS-WEU-90-152, p. 9. Bleifuss and Bernstein mention that the alleged agent was arrested.

24. Martin Sicker, *The Making of a Pariah State: the Adventurist Politics of Muammar Qaddafi,* New York: Praeger, 1987, p. 110. It is possible, though, given the tensions between Moscow and the East German regime at the time, that the latter wanted to embarrass Gorbachev.

25. AP, "U.S. Reportedly Had Warning of '86 Bombing," *WP,* 15 July 1990; Joel Bleifuss, *In These Times,* Sept. 26-Oct. 2, 1990, p. 5; "Bomben von Derwisch," *Der Spiegel,* no. 29, 1990, pp. 22-25.

26. D'Amato, "Attorney Sanctions...," pp. 705, 705n2.

27. Leslie H. Gelb, "U.S. Aides Think Libya Was Linked To At Least One Bombing Last Week," *NYT,* 8 April 1986, p. A8.

28. See Edward S. Herman, *The Real Terror Network,* Boston: South End Press, 1982; Chomsky, *Pirates and Emperors;* Noam Chomsky, *The Culture of Terrorism,* Boston: South End Press, 1988; Herman and O'Sullivan, *"Terrorism" Industry;* Alexander George, ed., *Western State Terrorism,* New York: Routledge, 1991.

29. See Herman and O'Sullivan, *"Terrorism" Industry,* for discussion.

30. Data provided by Joseph Reap of the Office of Counter-Terrorism, D/S, June 1992. 1,482 deaths were recorded in the Middle East and another 782 worldwide casualties of Middle East spillover.

31. See D/S, *Libya Under Qadhafi,* pp. 5-8, for 1980-85; D/S, *Libya's Continuing Responsibility for Terrorism,* Nov. 1991, pp. 9-12, for incidents since 15 April 1986. For incidents alleged between these dates: see John Whitehead, "Counterterrorism Policy," D/S, *Current Policy,* No. 823, 1986, p. 1; D/S, *Patterns of Global Terrorism: 1986,* January 1988, pp. 5-8. The totals come to 99 from 1980-April 15, 1986 (including five dozen killed when Egyptian troops stormed a hijacked airliner), and 525 from April 15, 1986 to 1991 (including 441 on Pan Am 103 and UTA 772 and 5 terrorists killed) for a grand total of 624 from 1980-91. On the Egyptian airliner, see D/S, *Patterns of Global Terrorism: 1985,* Oct. 1986, p. 40.

32. America's Watch, *Violations of the Laws of War By Both Sides in Nicaragua 1981-85,* March 1985, p. vi, quoted in Michael J. Glennon, letter, *American Journal of International Law,* vol. 81, no. 2, April 1987, p. 393.

33. D/S, *Patterns of Global Terrorism: 1988,* Washington, D.C.: March 1989, p. 46. In this and subsequent quotes, I have changed the many different spellings of the Libyan leader's name to Qaddafi.

34. See Holly Sklar, *Washington's War on Nicaragua,* Boston: South End Press, 1988, esp. pp. 177-87.

35. Sklar, *Washington's War on Nicaragua,* p. 393.

36. D/S, *Libya's Continuing Responsibility for Terrorism*, p. 5. D/S: Youssef M. Ibrahim, "New Unraveling Is Seen For Abu Nidal Group," *NYT*, 17 May 1990, p. A9. In a single terrorist incident orchestrated by Saudi Arabia with CIA approval in a failed effort to assassinate a Shi'ite leader in March 1985, more than a fifth as many people were killed as the Abu Nidal organization killed over two decades. See Bob Woodward, *Veil: The Secret Wars of the CIA, 1981-1987*, New York: Simon & Schuster, 1987, pp. 396-97.

37. Sean Gervasi and Sybil Wong, "The Reagan Doctrine and the Destabilization of Southern Africa," in George, ed., *Western State Terrorism*, pp. 244-45.

38. Gervasi and Wong, "Reagan Doctrine and Southern Africa," p. 240, citing UN report.

39. Herman and O'Sullivan, *"Terrorism" Industry*, p. 257n57. The *NYT* account of the State Department-sponsored report that used this figure omits the fact that it refers to the years after 1985. A State department official is quoted as saying that, if anything, the figure understates the scope and magnitude of the problem. Robert Pear, "Mozambicans Fled Rebels, U.S. Says," *NYT*, 21 April 1988, p. A11.

40. Gervasi and Wong, "Reagan Doctrine and Southern Africa," p. 228.

41. Michael Maren, "U.S. Callousness and Mozambique Massacres," *NYT*, 22 Aug. 1987, p. 27. In the Summer of 1991, Egypt let Abu Nidal open an office in Cairo—to punish Arafat for opposing the war against Iraq (Seale, *Abu Nidal*, p. 319).

42. Steve Askin, "Massacre in Mozambique," *Progressive*, Dec. 1988, p. 27.

43. See Scott C. Truver, "Mines of August: an International Whodunit," *Proceedings*, U.S. Naval Institute, Naval Review, May 1985.

44. Sklar, *Washington's War on Nicaragua*, pp. 165-68.

45. See, for example, John Cooley, *Libyan Sandstorm*, New York: Holt, Rinehart & Winston, 1982, pp. 179-80.

46. UPI, "Afghan Airliner Lands After Rebel Fire Hits It," *NYT*, 26 Sept. 1984, p. A9.

47. Anthony Lewis, "Don't We Care?" *NYT*, 31 July 1986, p. A21.

48. Noam Chomsky, "International Terrorism: Image and Reality," in George, ed., *Western State Terrorism*, p. 23. See also chapter 8, note 89, below. In one case where there were many U.S. victims—the crash of a plane in Gander, Canada, carrying U.S. soldiers home from Europe—Washington was singularly uninterested in pursuing the matter out of concern that the illegal Iran-Contra network might have been exposed. See Roy Rowan, "Gander: Different Crash, Same Questions," *Time*, 27 April 1992, pp. 33-34.

49. Peter Carlson and Joyce Leviton, "Two suspected Sikh terrorists honed their combat skills at an Alabama war school," *People*, 5 Aug. 1985, pp. 47-48. A.M. Rosenthal writing in 1990 ("The League of Terror," *NYT*, 27 May 1990, p. E13) commented that in the previous 5 years alone terrorist attacks against planes of half a dozen countries had killed 1,030 people. "Not one nation has taken retaliatory action." Presumably he wishes India had taken retaliatory action against the United States, whose tolerance of the mercenary training school Indian Prime Minister Rajiv Gandhi found incredible.

50. James Kelly, "Searching for Hit Teams," *Time*, 21 Dec. 1981, pp. 17-19. See also Duncan Campbell and Patrick Forbes, "Tale of Anti-Reagan Hit Team Was Fraud," *New Statesman*, 16 Aug. 1985, p. 6.

51. Edward Haley, *Qaddafi and the United States since 1969*, New York: Praeger, 1984, p. 266, citing the *LAT* (Israel); Woodward, *Veil*, New York: Simon & Schuster, 1987, pp. 186, 413 (Ghorbanifar); Hersh, "Target Qaddafi," p. 19 (Casey). Former Jack Anderson associate Ron McRae claims that he started the misinformation with an intentionally false story that a gullible press corps lapped up. See Ron McRae, "Beyond Gonzo," *Spy*, June 1992, pp. 55-56.

52. James Kelly, "Searching for Hit Teams," *Time*, 21 Dec. 1981, p. 22.

53. Herman, *Real Terror Network*, p. 64.

54. Robert Pear, "CIA Crash Called Problem in Angola," *NYT*, 1 Dec. 1989, p. 9.

55. Hersh, "Target Qaddafi," p. 20.

56. Malcolm Spaven, "A Piece of the Action: The Use of U.S. Bases in Britain," in *Mad Dogs: The U.S. Raids on Libya,* ed. E.P. Thompson, et al., London: Pluto Press, 1986, p. 17. Libya announced that 36 civilians and one soldier died; other estimates put the number of deaths at 50-100, mostly military. Edward Schumacher, "The United States and Libya," *Foreign Affairs,* vol. 65, Winter 1986-87, p. 335.

57. W. Hays Parks, "Crossing the Line," *Proceedings,* U.S. Naval Institute, Nov. 1986, pp. 47-48. Claire Sterling, writing five years before the U.S. air-strike, mentions another Libyan naval commando training camp; she then adds: "Whether a coincidence or not, the IRA used frogmen to blow up Lord Mountbatten on his fishing boat" (Sterling, *Terror Network,* p. 246). But, as Connor Cruise O'Brien has commented: "It is neither a coincidence nor not a coincidence; it is just plain wrong. Frogmen were not used for that murder" (Quoted in Herman, *Real Terror Network,* p. 57).

58. Cooley, *Libyan Sandstorm,* p. 168; John Wright, *Libya: A Modern History,* Baltimore: Johns Hopkins UP, 1982, p. 197; Lisa Anderson, "Libya and American Foreign Policy," *Middle East Journal,* vol. 36, no. 4, Autumn 1982, p. 521.

59. D/S, *American Foreign Policy: Basic Documents, 1977-1980,* 1983, p. 604; D/S, *American Foreign Policy: Current Documents, 1981,* 1984, pp. 787-88.

60. D/S, *Country Reports on Human Rights Practices for 1981,* Report submitted to HR, Foreign Affairs Comm. and Sen., Foreign Relations Comm. by the D/S, Joint Comm. Print, Feb. 1982, p. 984. On Iraq's removal from the list of terrorist states, see D/S, *American Foreign Policy: Current Documents, 1982,* 1985, p. 784n5. The removal was published in the *Federal Register,* but no announcement was made (Steven A. Emerson and Cristina Del Sesto, *Terrorist,* New York: Villard Books, 1991, p. 113). That the U.S. was aware of Iraq's continuing support for terrorism, see Douglas Frantz and Murray Waas, "Bush Secret Effort Helped Iraq Build Its War Machine," *LAT,* 23 Feb. 1992, p. A1; Emerson and Del Sesto, *Terrorist,* pp. 207-08; Judith Miller and Laurie Mylroie, *Saddam Hussein and the Crisis in the Gulf,* New York: Times Books, 1990, p. 144.

61. Fred Poole and Max Vanzi, *Revolution in the Philippines,* New York: McGraw Hill, 1984, pp. 269-71.

62. Daniel Junas, "Verdict in Political Slayings Holds Implications for U.S.," *In These Times,* Jan. 17-23, 1990, p. 16.

63. Bernard Gwertzman, "Filipinos in U.S. Were Harassed, Ex-aides Assert," *NYT,* Aug. 26, 1983, pp. A1, A4.

64. D/S, *American Foreign Policy, 1977-80,* pp. 723-24.

65. "The Iran File," *60 Minutes,* transcript, March 2, 1980, pp. 6-10. See also "Activities of Foreign Spies in U.S. Revealed in Report," *Boston Globe,* Aug. 9, 1979, pp. 1, 7.

66. Patrick Seale and Maureen McConville, *The Hilton Assignment,* New York: Praeger, 1973, pp. 224-32.

67. Ronald B. St. John, *Qadhafi's World Design: Libyan Foreign Policy, 1969-1987,* London: Saqi Books, 1987, p. 60.

68. William J. Foltz, "Libya's Military Power," in Lemarchand, ed., *Green and Black,* pp. 59-60.

69. Wright, *Libya: A Modern History,* p. 276.

70. Diana Johnstone, "Muammar Khadafy's Three-ring Circus," *In These Times,* 12-18 Feb. 1986, p. 7; Jeff McConnell, "Libya: Propaganda and Covert Operations," *CounterSpy,* vol. 6, no. 1, Nov. 1981-Jan. 1982, p. 30.

71. Cooley, *Libyan Sandstorm,* p. 209.

72. Haley, *Qaddafi and the United States,* p. 210.

73. Woodward, *Veil,* pp. 302-03.

74. Woodward, *Veil,* p. 95.

75. Francois Burgat, "Qadhafi's 'Unitary' Doctrine," in Lemarchand, ed., *Green and Black,* p. 27; Hersh, "Target Qaddafi," p. 48; Bonnie Cordes, *Qaddafi: Idealist and Revolutionary Philanthropist,* P-7209, Santa Monica: Rand Corporation, March 1986, p. 7.

76. For some examples, see chapter 1 above.

77. Haley, *Qaddafi and the United States,* pp. 5, 282.

78. Cooley, *Libyan Sandstorm,* p. 192. Israel's attitude is unclear: Begin told Carter in 1979 of Israel's readiness to join Egypt in an attack on Libya (Jimmy Carter, *Keeping Faith,* New York: Bantam, 1982, p. 414); on the other hand, Cooley claims that Israel opposed Egypt's 1977 invasion for fear it would strengthen Sadat in his negotiations with Israel (Cooley, *Libyan Sandstorm,* p. 192). See also McConnell, "Libya: Propaganda and Covert Operations," p. 29.

79. Haley, *Qaddafi and the United States,* pp. 5, 23-24, 282-83.

80. Carter, *Keeping Faith,* p. 384.

81. *Newsweek,* 3 Aug. 1981, p. 19.

82. Claudia Wright, "Libya and the West: Headlong into Confrontation," *International Affairs,* Winter 1981-82, p. 16.

83. Haley, *Qaddafi and the United States,* pp. 8-9.

84. Lisa Anderson, "Qaddafi and the Kremlin," *Problems of Communism,* vol. 34, Sept.-Oct. 1985, p. 41.

85. *UN Chronicle,* vol. 20, April 1983, p. 12; the quotes are a UN paraphrase of the U.S. statement. See also D/S, *Libyan Problem,* p. 5.

86. Patrick E. Tyler, "U.S. Aborted 1983 Trap Set For Libyan Forces," *WP,* 12 July 1987, pp. A1, A25.

87. Bob Woodward, "CIA Anti-Qaddafi Plan Backed," *WP,* 3 Nov. 1985, p. A19.

88. Hersh, "Target Qaddafi," p. 48.

89. Woodward, *Veil,* pp. 411-12.

90. Hersh, "Target Qaddafi," p. 48.

91. Woodward, *Veil,* p. 432.

92. Woodward, *Veil,* pp. 435-36.

93. R.W. Apple, "U.S. Said To Hope Clashes Prompt Moves in Libya To Oust Qaddafi," *NYT,* 3 April 1986, p. A8.

94. Woodward, *Veil,* p. 444.

95. Michael Rubner, "Antiterrorism and the Withering of the 1973 War Powers Resolution," *Political Science Quarterly,* vol. 102, no. 2, Summer 1987, p. 210.

96. For the most complete account, see Stephen Green, *Living By the Sword,* Brattleboro, VT: Amana, 1988, pp. 63-80.

97. Harold D. Nelson, ed., *Libya: A Country Study,* American University, Washington, D.C., Foreign Area Studies, 1979, p. 53; Mohamed Heikal, *The Road to Ramadan,* New York: Ballantine, 1975, pp. 196-97.

98. It is accepted by Jonathan Bearman, *Qadhafi's Libya,* London: Zed, 1986, p. 115.

99. Seale, *Abu Nidal,* p. 71.

100. Incidents from D/S, *Libya Under Qadhafi,* pp. 5-7; U.S. casualties from D/S, *Patterns of Global Terrorism: 1985,* pp. 15, 17; and D/S, *Patterns of Global Terrorism: 1986,* pp. 16, 18. U.S. deaths in incidents with suspected Libyan involvement were 1 in 1981 (a Libyan dissident in the U.S.), 5 in the Rome/Vienna airport killings, 1 on the hijacked Egyptian airliner in November 1985, and 2 at the La Belle discotheque, for a total of 9. See note 56 above for Libyan deaths.

101. Cooley, *Libyan Sandstorm,* pp. 80-82; Blundy & Lycett, *Qaddafi and the Libyan Revolution,* pp. 152-53; Haley, *Qaddafi and the United States,* pp. 341-42n16. These accounts, and others, may all originate from the same source; however, given that the

Carter administration didn't use the incident to publicly score points against Libya, I am inclined to believe it.

102. Jack Anderson and Dale Van Atta, "The Secret Poll Behind the Libya Raid," *WP*, 28 Feb 1988, p. C7.
103. Woodward, *Veil*, p. 410.
104. Parks, "Crossing the Line," p. 42.
105. See Yehuda Z. Blum, "The Gulf of Sidra Incident," *American Journal of International Law*, vol. 80, July 1986, p. 674; Erik R. Peterson, letter, *NYT*, 10 Sept. 1981, p. A30.
106. Woodward, *Veil*, p. 95.
107. John K. Cooley, "Libya Says Peace Endangered," *WP*, 20 Aug. 1981, p. A21.
108. D/S, *American Foreign Policy: Current Documents, 1981*, p. 789.
109. Haley, *Qaddafi and the United States*, p. 277; "Kaddafi Beats His Drum," *Newsweek*, Sept. 1981, p. 34.
110. Cooley, *Libyan Sandstorm*, p. 268. See also Haley, *Qaddafi and the United States*, pp. 8, 277.
111. John Brecher, et al., "To the Shores of Tripoli," *Newsweek*, 31 Aug. 1981, p. 15. *Newsweek* reported before the clash that "Washington officials are also eager to see how Qaddafi will react to what they insist is a coincidence: Egyptian troops will conduct maneuvers along the border at the same time" as the U.S. naval exercises ("The U.S. Challenge Libya's Kaddafi," 24 Aug. 1981, p. 13). At his press conference on August 19, Secretary of Defense Weinberger denied any knowledge of the Egyptian maneuvers (D/S, *American Foreign Policy: Current Documents, 1981*, p. 790).
112. Foltz, "Libya's Military Power," p. 60.
113. Elizabeth Cuadra, "Air Defense Identification Zones: Creeping Jurisdiction in the Air space," *Virginia Journal of International Law*, vol. 18, 1978, pp. 491-92, 509.
114. Erik R. Peterson, letter, *NYT*, 10 Sept. 1981, p. A30. In 1992, when Syria was considering flying a plane to Libya in violation of the UN sanctions, the *NYT* cited an anonymous U.S. air industry official to the effect that "all of the air over the Mediterranean Sea has been divided up among the coastal countries' air traffic control regions. So a flight from Syria to Libya would need permission from some combination of air traffic controllers in Cyprus, Egypt, Greece, Lebanon or Turkey, depending on the route chosen..." (Chris Hedges, "Syria Trying to Breach Air Embargo on Libya," *NYT*, 21 April 1992, p. A5).
115. See Head, "ADIZ, International Law and Contiguous Airspace," *Harvard International Law Club Bulletin*, vol. 2, 1960, p. 28, reprinted in *Alberta Law Review*, vol. 3, 1964, p 182; Cuadra, "Air Defense Identification Zones...."
116. D/S, *Libya Under Qadhafi*, p. 7.
117. Haley, *Qaddafi and the United States*, p. 262.
118. D/S, *Libyan Problem*, p. 2.
119. Bob Woodward, "CIA Anti-Qaddafi Plan Backed," *WP*, 3 Nov. 1985, p. A1.
120. Hersh, "Target Qaddafi," p. 48.
121. Robert E. Stumpf, "Air War with Libya," *Proceedings*, U.S. Naval Institute, Aug. 1986, pp. 43-45; Parks, "Crossing the Line," p. 44.
122. Hersh, "Target Qaddafi," p. 71.
123. Quoted in Rubner, "Antiterrorism...," p. 200.
124. Stumpf, "Air War with Libya," p. 47; Parks, "Crossing the Line," p. 45.
125. Blundy & Lycett, *Qaddafi and the Libyan Revolution*, pp. 7-8.
126. Parks, "Crossing the Line," p. 45.
127. Parks, "Crossing the Line," p. 45; Stumpf, "Air War with Libya," pp. 46-47.
128. Schumacher, "The United States and Libya," p. 335.
129. Rubner, "Antiterrorism...," pp. 202-03.
130. Rubner, "Antiterrorism...," p. 198.

131. Rubner, "Antiterrorism…," p. 197, quoting *Newsweek*.

132. *UN Chronicle,* vol. 23, April 1986, p. 22; the words are a paraphrase by the UN

133. John Newhouse, "Confrontation," *New Yorker,* 28 April 1986, p. 112.

134. Bob Woodward and Patrick E. Tyler, "U.S. Targeted Qaddafi Compound After Tracing Terror Message," *WP,* 16 April 1986, p. A24.

135. L. Paul Bremer III, "Terrorism: Myths and Reality," D/S, *Current Policy,* No. 1047, 1988, p. 3.

136. Sen., *Libyan Sponsored…,* p. 34; note that these 15 incidents are a rather trivial fraction of the 450 terrorist incidents said to have originated in the Middle East in 1985.

137. D/S, *Libya Under Qadhafi,* p. 5.

138. Bremer, "Terrorism: Its Evolving Nature," p. 2.

139. Lillian Craig Harris, *Libya: Qadhafi's Revolution and the Modern State,* Boulder: Westview, 1986, p. 102.

140. Blaine Harden, "U.S. Embassy Employee Shot and Wounded in Sudan," *WP,* 16 April 1986, p. A24.

141. Schumacher, "The United States and Libya," p. 342.

142. Nora Boustany, "U.S. Hostage In Lebanon Among Murder Victims In Retaliation For Raid," *WP,* 19 April 1986, p. A1.

143. John M. Goshko, "'Soft Targets' For Terror Concern U.S. Officials," *WP,* 16 April 1986, p. A16.

144. Woodward, *Veil,* p. 474.

145. Woodward, *Veil,* pp. 472, 474; Bob Woodward, "Gadhafi Target of Secret U.S. Deception Plan," *WP,* 2 Oct. 1986, pp. A1, A12.

146. The final provocation of the Reagan presidency came in January 1989 when the U.S. Navy again held maneuvers off the Libyan coast. Two Libyan fighter planes were shot down by U.S. F-14s. The Pentagon later acknowledged that the U.S. commander on the scene radioed the Navy jets that they were in a cautionary, not a fire-at-will, situation; and, according to a veteran pilot, the second MiG was running for home when it was shot down. See George C. Wilson, "Decision of F14s to Fire Is Questioned," *WP,* 10 Jan. 1989, pp. A1, A18.

147. Bremer, "Terrorism: Myths and Reality," p. 3.

148. Bremer, "Terrorism: Its Evolving Nature," p. 2.

149. *Facts on File,* Aug. 21, 1987, p. 602.

150. George Lardner, Jr., "French Link Libyans to Bombings," *WP,* 27 June 1991; Andrew Rosenthal, "U.S. Accuses Libya As 2 Are Charged in Pan Am Bombing," *NYT,* 15 Nov. 1991, p. A8.

151. William Buckley, "Ground Libya Until It Surrenders Terrorists," *SL,* 3 Dec. 1991, p. 18.

152. Figures computed from D/S, *Significant Incidents of Political Violence Against Americans, 1988,* May 1989, pp. 2-3; *1989,* June 1990, p. 2; *1990,* July 1991, p. 2.

153. Qaddafi noted that even President Bush had said he was stunned by the verdict of the jury in the Rodney King case (FBIS-NES-92-089, 7 May 1992, p. 12). Qaddafi is being opportunist here, but his point that prejudice can often interfere with justice in the United States is no doubt valid.

154. E.g., Michael Wines, "U.S. Will Try Diplomatic Action Before A Military Strike On Libya," *NYT,* 16 Nov. 1991, p. 4; *NYT* ad, 7 Jan. 1992, p. A13; Barbara Crossette, "U.S. Dismisses Libyan Offer On Neutral Trial Site For Bomb Suspects," *NYT,* 3 March 1992, p. A10; AP, "Qaddafi Rejects UN Demands Con Bomb Suspects," *NYT,* 5 April 1992, p. 13; AP, "Syria May Violate UN Sanctions, Fly Jet To Libya," *SL,* 19 April 1992, p. I:2.

155. Judith Miller, "Moroccan King, A Friend of U.S., Rejects Hard Line Toward Libya," *NYT,* 2 March 1992, p. A7.

156. Marc Weller, "Libyan Terrorism, American Swagger," *NYT,* 15 Feb. 1992, p. 23. See also Alfred P. Rubin, "The U.S. and Britain Should Take Libya to Court," *Christian Science Monitor,* 2 Dec. 1991, p. 19.

157. FBIS-NES-92-064, 1 April 1992, p. 2.

158. Paul Lewis, "Security Council Votes To Prohibit Arms Exports And Flights To Libya," *NYT,* 1 April 1992, p. A1.

159. Paul Lewis, "China Is Warned Not To Veto Plan To Place UN Sanctions On Libya," *NYT,* 28 March 1992, pp. 1, 6.

160. D'Amato, "Attorney Sanctions...," pp. 706-08; Saltany v. Reagan, 702 F. Supp. 319 (D.D.C. 1988); Saltany v. Reagan, 886 F. 2d 438 (D.C. Cir 1989).

161. *U.S. Dept. of State Dispatch,* 6 April 1992, p. 267.

162. George Lardner, Jr., "French Link Libyans to Bombings," *WP,* 27 June 1991.

163. Robin Wright and Ronald J. Ostrow, "Pan Am 103 Clue Leads to Libyans," *WP,* 24 June 1991.

164. D/S, "Fact Sheet: Additional Information on the Bombing of Pan Am Flight 103," *U.S. Dept. of State Dispatch,* 18 Nov. 1991, p. 854.

165. Steven Emerson and Brian Duffy, "The German Connection," *NYT Magazine,* 18 March 1990, p. 87; Emerson and Duffy, *Fall of Pan Am 103,* pp. 232, 245; Roy Rowan, "Pan Am 103: Why Did They Die?" *Time,* 27 April 1992, p. 27.

166. Wines, "U.S. Will Try...," p. 4.

167. ABC News Nightline, "Insufficient Proof of Libyan Bombers in Pan Am 103?" transcript, show #2846, 20 April 1992, p. 2; Ann Leggett, letter, *NYT,* 3 March 1992, p. A22; Rowan, "Why Did They Die?" p. 30; AP, "Pan Am Bombing Suspects," *SL,* 19 Feb. 1992, p. 4.

168. Rowan, "Why Did They Die?" p. 28.

169. Clyde Haberman, "Israelis Remain Convinced Syrians Downed Flight 103," *NYT,* 21 Nov. 1991, p. A14; AP, "PLO Adviser Denies Libya Role In Flight 103 Blast," *SL,* 16 Feb. 1992, p. I:7; ABC News Nightline, "Insufficient Proof...?" p. 2; Rowan, "Why Did They Die?".

170. Rowan, "Why Did They Die?" p. 30; ABC News Nightline, "Insufficient Proof...?" p. 1.

171. Rowan, "Why Did They Die?" p. 30.

172. Emerson and Duffy, *Fall of Pan Am 103,* p. 77.

173. Mark A. Uhlig, "U.S. Urges Nicaragua To Forgive Legal Claim," *NYT,* 30 Sept. 1990, p. I:18.

174. Sen., Foreign Relations Comm., subcomm. on African Affairs and Near Eastern and South Asian Affairs, *Libyan Activities,* Hearings, July 1981, p. 2.

175. HR, Foreign Affairs Comm., subcomm. on Africa, *Libya-Sudan-Chad Triangle: Dilemma for United States Policy,* Hearings, Oct.-Nov. 1981, p. 38.

176. See C. Wright, "Libya and the West...," p. 32; D/S, *American Foreign Policy, Current Documents, 1977-1980,* p. 603; Sen., *Libyan Activities,* p. 3.

177. Harris, *Libya,* p. 105n4.

178. Wright, *Libya: A Modern History,* p. 213.

179. John Wright, *Libya, Chad and the Central Sahara,* Totowa, NJ: Barnes and Noble Books, 1989, pp. 124-29; René Lemarchand, "The Case of Chad," in Lemarchand, ed., *Green and Black,* p. 111.

180. Lemarchand, "Case of Chad," p. 109; Cooley, *Libyan Sandstorm,* pp. 98-99.

181. Wright, *Libya, Chad and the Central Sahara,* p. 129.

182. Lemarchand, "Case of Chad," p. 114.

183. Wright, *Libya, Chad and the Central Sahara,* pp. 130-31; Cooley, *Libyan Sandstorm,* p. 120.

184. Sicker, *Making of a Pariah State,* p. 95; St. John, *Qaddafi's World Design,* pp. 93-94; Lemarchand testimony in HR, *Libya-Sudan-Chad Triangle,* p. 34.

185. Wright, *Libya, Chad and the Central Sahara,* p. 131.

186. See John Darton, "France's Aid in Chad's Civil War Highlights Its Touchy Police Role," *NYT*, 15 May 1978, pp. A1, A8; Richard Bernstein, "In Africa, France Is Still A Military Power," *NYT*, 19 April 1987, p. E3; Francis Terry McNamara, *France in Black Africa*, Washington, D.C.: National Defense University, 1989, pp. 150, 154, 164-66.

187. David S. Yost, "French Policy in Chad: The Libyan Challenge," *Orbis*, vol. 21, no. 1, Winter 1983, pp. 977-78.

188. René Lemarchand, "The Crisis in Chad," in *African Crisis Areas and U.S. Foreign Policy*, ed. Gerald J. Bender, James S. Coleman, Richard L. Sklar, Berkeley: University of California Press, 1985, p. 248; Jay Peterzell, "The Secret War Against Qaddafi," *Nation*, 21 Jan. 1984, p. 49; Yost, "French Policy in Chad," p. 968; Woodward, *Veil*, pp. 96-97; Haley, *Qaddafi and the United States*, pp. 210-11. Neither Paris nor Washington seemed to mind that they were backing someone who not only had been responsible for the massacre of hundreds of Chadians, but had kidnapped several Europeans, refusing to release them after the ransom demands were met, and killing or capturing those who came to negotiate their release. Ironically, it was Goukouni who got the hostages freed. See Peterzell, "Secret War," p. 50; Lemarchand, "Crisis in Chad," p. 252; Lemarchand, "Case of Chad," p. 123n4.

189. Peterzell, "Secret War," p. 51; Haley, *Qaddafi and the United States*, p. 249.

190. Peterzell, "Secret War," p. 52; Yost, "French Policy in Chad," p. 980.

191. Peterzell, "Secret War," p. 52; Nzongola-Ntalaja, "United States Policy toward Zaire," in Bender, et al., ed., *African Crisis Areas*, p. 236.

192. D/S, *Libyan Problem*, p. 4; Oye Ogunbadejo, "Qaddafi and Africa's International Relations," *Journal of Modern African Studies*, (Cambridge) vol. 24, no. 1, 1986, p. 45; Lemarchand, "Crisis in Chad," p. 249.

193. *Facts on File*, Jan. 9, 1987, p. 1; April 17, 1987, p. 258.

194. Bernard Trainor, "France and U.S. Aiding Chadians With Intelligence to Rout Libyans," *NYT*, 3 April, 1987, pp. A1, A5.

195. *Facts on File*, Sept. 11, 1987, pp. 657-58.

196. *Facts on File*, Sept. 11, 1987, p. 657.

197. *Facts on File*, Sept. 11, 1987, p. 657.

198. *Facts on File*, Sept. 11, 1987, p. 658.

199. Clifford Krauss, "Failed Anti-Qaddafi Effort Leaves U.S. Picking Up the Pieces," *NYT*, 12 March 1991, p. A15; Angus Deming, et al., "Have Rebels, Will Travel," *Newsweek*, 25 March 1991, p. 43. Ultimately, Washington decided to bring the 350 Libyans to the U.S. (Neil A. Lewis, "350 Libyans Trained To Oust Qaddafi Are To Come To U.S.," *NYT*, 17 May 1991, p. A8).

8: Drugs and U.S. Foreign Policy

1. Dick Cheney, *Report of the Secretary of Defense to the President and the Congress*, Washington, D.C.: USGPO, Jan. 1990, p. iii.

2. Peter Dale Scott and Jonathan Marshall, *Cocaine Politics: Drugs, Armies, and the CIA in Central America*, Berkeley: University of California Press, 1991, p. 1.

3. Ruth Norris, ed., *Pills, Pesticides & Profits*, Croton-on-Hudson, NY: North River Press, 1982, pp. 7, 26; *CQ Weekly Report*, June 9, 1990, p. 1783; GAO, *Food Safety and Quality: Five Countries' Efforts To Meet U.S. Requirements On Imported Produce*, GAO/RCED-90-55, March 1990, pp. 12, 34-35. The GAO found that of 26 pesticides for which U.S. registration had been canceled or suspended as of 1988, 35 percent were registered for use in at least one of five Latin American countries studied; an additional 110 pesticides for which no U.S. tolerances had been established were registered in one or more of these countries (GAO, *Food Safety and Quality*, pp. 26-27, 32).

4. *CQ Weekly Report,* June 9, 1990, p. 1783; Oct. 13, 1990, p. 3411; CQ, *CQ Almanac, 1990,* Washington, D.C.: 1991, p. 349.

5. Gina Kolata, "Drug Maker Didn't Heed Warning on Deadly Effect," *NYT,* 4 July 1991, pp. A1, A10; Gina Kolata, "Consumer Group Says LaRoche Withheld Data on Drug's Safety," *NYT,* 1 Aug. 1991, p. B7; Robert Cohen, "Hoffman-La Roche Investigated for Alleged Withholding of Safety Data," *SL,* 16 Feb. 1992, p. I:16; Gina Kolata, "Maker of Sleeping Pill Hid Data on Side Effects, Researchers Say," *NYT,* 20 Jan. 1992, pp. A1, B7.

6. Robert J. Ledogar, *Hungry for Profits: U.S. Food and Drug Multinationals in Latin America,* New York: IDOC/North America, 1975, pp. 27-36. Laxness in monitoring drugs is not confined to the Third World: see Warren E. Leary, "Report Says FDA Is Lax On Over-the-Counter Drugs," *NYT,* 27 Feb. 1992, p. A12.

7. Ledogar, *Hungry for Profits,* pp. 31-33, 41-42; Norris, ed., *Pills, Pesticides...,* pp. 42-43.

8. Norris, ed., *Pills, Pesticides...,* pp. 39, 48-49; Milton Silverman, *The Drugging of the Americas: How Multinational Drug Companies Say One Thing about Their Products to Physicians in the United States, and Another Thing to Physicians in Latin America,* Berkeley: University of California Press, 1976, passim; Ledogar, *Hungry for Profits,* p. 51. It is conceivable, of course, that the social benefits and costs of a particular drug may vary from society to society, so that what ought to be banned in the U.S. ought to be legal in some other country. (The birth control drug Depo-Provera is sometimes said to fall in this category. See Norris, ed., *Pills, Pesticides...,* p. 45.) For most of the drugs considered in the studies cited above, this claim cannot be seriously offered.

9. Milton Silverman, Philip R. Lee, and Mia Lydecker, *Prescriptions for Death: The Drugging of the Third World,* Berkeley: University of California Press, 1982, p. 116.

10. Silverman, *Drugging of the Americas,* p. 117.

11. Silverman, et al., *Prescriptions for Death,* p. 125.

12. Silverman, et al., *Prescriptions for Death,* p. 126.

13. Silverman, et al., *Prescriptions for Death,* pp. 121-23.

14. Silverman, et al., *Prescriptions for Death,* pp. 120-21.

15. The one million figure is an extrapolation from U.S. data, which overstates the Third World toll because poor countries have lower per capita drug use rates, and understates it because of the widespread use of drugs considered unsafe in the U.S. See Silverman, et al., *Prescriptions for Death,* p. 86.

16. Norris, ed., *Pills, Pesticides...,* p. 75; Stephen Solomon, "The Controversy Over Infant Formula," *NYT Magazine,* 6 Dec. 1981, p. 94, citing estimate by Dr. Stephen Joseph, an AID official who resigned over the issue.

17. Norris, ed., *Pills, Pesticides...,* p. 78; Solomon, "Controversy Over Infant Formula," pp. 100-02.

18. Norris, ed., *Pills, Pesticides...,* p. 76; Ledogar, *Hungry for Profits,* p. 137.

19. Norris, ed., *Pills, Pesticides...,* pp. 80-81; Solomon, "Controversy Over Infant Formula," p. 94. For Abrams's statement, see D/S, *American Foreign Policy: Current Documents, 1981,* 1984, pp. 249-50. Arthur Hoppe writing in the *San Francisco Chronicle* of May 27, 1981, commented: "Some critics worry that by causing one million deaths a year, the infant formula industry may be curtailing its market. Fortunately, this isn't true. As luck would have it, the breast-feeding mother is unlikely to get pregnant while lactating and thus won't breed again for another year or two. The mother who employs the lethal bottle, on the other hand, can produce another offspring nine months after the birth of her first—thus assuring the industry a constant supply of hungry little customers." Breast-feeding, he noted, "obviously instills in both mother and child the socialistic concept that there is, indeed, such a thing as a free lunch." Quoted in Silverman, et al., *Prescriptions for Death,* p. 118.

20. HR, Select Comm. on Narcotics Abuse and Control, *The Flow of Precursor Chemicals and Assault Weapons from the United States into the Andean Nations,* Hearings, Nov. 1989, pp. 16, 44; James Brooke, "Gun Runners From Miami Give Brazilian Drug Gangs Lead in Arms Race," *NYT,* 23 Feb. 1992, p. I:3.

21. See Council on Scientific Affairs, AMA, "The Worldwide Smoking Epidemic," *JAMA,* vol. 263, no. 24, 27 June 1990, p. 3312. Estimates from 2-3 million are given in Sen., Labor and Human Resources Comm., *Smoking and World Health,* Hearings, May 1990, pp. 1, 3, 7, 27. If current trends continue, in 30 years smoking will become the leading cause of premature death in the world ("Experts at Buenos Aires Conference Predict Pandemic of Tobacco Deaths," *JAMA,* vol. 267, no. 24, 24 June 1992, p. 3255).

22. Council on Scientific Affairs, "Worldwide Smoking Epidemic," pp. 3313-14; Alexander Cockburn, "Beat the Devil," *Nation,* 30 Oct. 1989, p. 482, citing Susan Motley in *Multinational Monitor,* July/Aug. 1987.

23. Council on Scientific Affairs, "Worldwide Smoking Epidemic," p. 3313.

24. Patrick G. Marshall, "Tobacco Industry: On the Defensive, But Still Strong," *Editorial Research Reports,* vol. 1, no. 35, Sept. 21, 1990, p. 541.

25. Larry C. White, *Merchants of Death: The American Tobacco Industry,* New York: William Morrow, 1988, pp. 122-24; Sen., *Smoking and World Health,* p. 36; Morton Mintz, "Marketing Tobacco to Children," *Nation,* 6 May 1991, p. 594; Elizabeth M. Whelan, *A Smoking Gun: How the Tobacco Industry Gets Away With Murder,* Philadelphia: George F. Stickley Co., 1984, p. 186. On the camel cartoons, see Jane E. Brody, "Smoking Among Children Is Linked To Cartoon Camel in Advertisements," *NYT,* 11 Dec. 1991, p. D22; Geoffrey Cowley, "I'd Toddle a Mile for a Camel," *Newsweek,* 23 Dec. 1991, p. 70; and, for the enthusiastic views of advertising executives, Stuart Elliott, "Camel Cartoons Draws Buyers, Too," *NYT,* 12 Dec. 1991, pp. D1, D5.

26. Quoted by William H. Foege in Sen., *Smoking and World Health,* p. 11.

27. Dr. Gregory N. Connolly, Mass. Dept. of Public Health, in Sen., *Smoking and World Health,* p. 16; Joanne Cornbleet, letter, *JAMA,* vol. 267, no. 24, 24 June 1992, p. 3286.

28. Sen., *Smoking and World Health,* pp. 65-66, 72-73.

29. Peter Schmeisser, "Pushing Cigarettes Overseas," *NYT Magazine,* 10 July 1988, pp. 17 (picture), 22.

30. Sen., *Smoking and World Health,* pp. 36-37.

31. GAO, *Trade and Health Issues: Dichotomy Between U.S. Tobacco Export Policy and Antismoking Initiatives,* May 1990, GAO/NSIAD-90-190, p. 26.

32. GAO, *Dichotomy Between Tobacco Export Policy...,* p. 26.

33. After protest, the concert was canceled, but fans were told they could still exchange spent packs for a cassette. Schmeisser, "Pushing Cigarettes Overseas," pp. 22, 62; Sen., *Smoking and World Health,* pp. 10, 35.

34. White, *Merchants of Death,* p. 123.

35. Lori Heise, "Unhealthy Alliance," *World Watch,* Sept.-Oct. 1988, p. 24.

36. Sen., *Smoking and World Health,* p. 39; Philip J. Hilts, "U.S. Tobacco Ads in Asia Faulted," *NYT,* 5 May 1990, p. 35; GAO, *Dichotomy Between Tobacco Export Policy...,* p. 25.

37. Sen., *Smoking and World Health,* pp. 66, 73; Morton Mintz, "Tobacco Roads," *Progressive,* May 1991, pp. 26-27; GAO, *Dichotomy Between Tobacco Export Policy...,* pp. 28-29.

38. Sen., *Smoking and World Health,* pp. 25, 38, 39.

39. Peter Taylor, *The Smoke Ring: Tobacco, Money, and Multinational Politics,* New York: Pantheon, 1984, p. 215.

40. A. Willis Robertson to John Foster Dulles, 24 May 1955, Dwight D. Eisenhower Papers, Eisenhower Library, Abilene Kansas, OF 149-B-2, Tobacco.

41. Whelan, *Smoking Gun*, pp. 167-68; Taylor, *Smoke Ring*, pp. 262-3; Sen., *Smoking and World Health*, p. 100.

42. Whelan, *Smoking Gun*, pp. 97-98; Thomas Szasz, *Ceremonial Chemistry: The Ritual Persecution of Drugs, Addicts, and Pushers*, rev. ed., Holmes Beach, FL: Learning Publications, 1985, p. 205.

43. GAO, *Dichotomy Between Tobacco Export Policy...*, pp. 5, 44-45.

44. AP, "U.S. Aids Promotion of Smoking Overseas," *SL*, 10 Feb. 1992, p. 3.

45. Taylor, *Smoke Ring*, pp. 214-15.

46. Whelan, *Smoking Gun*, pp. 123-24; Taylor, *Smoke Ring*, pp. 216-17, 223. On Kreps, see Bryan Burrough and John Helyar, *Barbarians at the Gate: The Fall of RJR Nabisco*, New York: Harper Perennial, 1990, p. 60. As governor of Georgia, Carter had published a pamphlet on "killers and cripplers" which discussed the causes of heart disease and cancer without any mention of cigarettes or tobacco. Whelan, *Smoking Gun*, p. 123.

47. Taylor, *Smoke Ring*, p. 228.

48. GAO, *Dichotomy Between Tobacco Export Policy...*, pp. 17-18.

49. Sen., *Smoking and World Health*, p. 36.

50. Heise, "Unhealthy Alliance," p. 23; Sen., *Smoking and World Health*, p. 37.

51. Sen., *Smoking and World Health*, pp. 4, 9-10. The smoking rate continues to increase in Japan. See *Newsweek*, 4 May 1992, p. 10.

52. Dr. Gregory N. Connolly in Sen., *Smoking and World Health*, pp. 16, 34-35, 51; Schmeisser, "Pushing Cigarettes Overseas," p. 20; GAO, *Dichotomy Between Tobacco Export Policy...*, pp. 6, 12.

53. GAO, *Dichotomy Between Tobacco Export Policy...*, pp. 22-23; Gregory N. Connolly, "Tobacco and United States Trade Sanctions," in *Smoking and Health 1987: Proceedings of the Sixth World Conference on Smoking and Health*, ed. Masakazu Aoki, et al., New York: Elsevier Science Pub. Co., 1988, pp. 352-53; Gregory N. Connolly in Sen., *Smoking and World Health*, p. 51; Heise, "Unhealthy Alliance," p. 22; Schmeisser, "Pushing Cigarettes Overseas," p. 62.

54. GAO, *Dichotomy Between Tobacco Export Policy...*, p. 39.

55. Sen., *Smoking and World Health*, p. 16.

56. GAO, *Dichotomy Between Tobacco Export Policy...*, p. 5.

57. GAO, *Dichotomy Between Tobacco Export Policy...*, p. 34.

58. Marshall, "Tobacco Industry," p. 541.

59. Philip J. Hilts, "Health Dept. Softens Stance on Cigarette Exports," *NYT*, 18 May 1990, p. A14; Mintz, "Tobacco Roads," p. 26.

60. Mintz, "Tobacco Roads," p. 28.

61. Quoted in Sen., *Smoking and World Health*, pp. 62-63.

62. Schmeisser, "Pushing Cigarettes Overseas," p. 18.

63. Alfred W. McCoy, *The Politics of Heroin: CIA Complicity in the Global Drug Trade*, Westport, CT: Lawrence Hill, 1991, pp. 47-48, 55-57, 60.

64. McCoy, *Politics of Heroin*, pp. 162, 165-178.

65. McCoy, *Politics of Heroin*, pp. 184-86.

66. McCoy, *Politics of Heroin*, pp. 129, 131-46.

67. McCoy, *Politics of Heroin*, pp. 161, 197, 203.

68. McCoy, *Politics of Heroin*, pp. 288-89, 299.

69. McCoy, *Politics of Heroin*, pp. 304, 291, 321. See also the exchange of letters between Richard Helms and Jonathan Mirsky, *New York Review of Books*, 22 Nov. 1990, pp. 52-53.

70. McCoy, *Politics of Heroin*, pp. 284-89, 223, 226.

71. McCoy, *Politics of Heroin*, p. 229.

72. McCoy, *Politics of Heroin*, pp. 254-56, 386.

73. McCoy, *Politics of Heroin*, pp. 449-52.

74. Scott and Marshall, *Cocaine Politics*, p. 187; McCoy, *Politics of Heroin*, p. 447, 454.

75. McCoy, *Politics of Heroin*, pp. 436-37.

76. Scott and Marshall, *Cocaine Politics*, p. 5.

77. Quoted in Scott and Marshall, *Cocaine Politics*, p. 5. See also James Rupert and Steve Coll, "U.S. Declines to Probe Afghan Drug Trade," *WP*, 13 May 1990, p. A1.

78. Sen., Foreign Relations Comm., subcomm. on Terrorism, Narcotics, and International Operations, *Drugs, Law Enforcement and Foreign Policy*, Report, Committee Print S. Prt. 100-165, Dec. 1988, p. 36.

79. Sen., *Drugs...and Foreign Policy*, pp. 60-61; Scott and Marshall, *Cocaine Politics*, p. 106; John Weeks and Phil Gunson, *Panama: Made in the USA*, London: Latin America Bureau, 1991, p. 49.

80. Kevin Buckley, *Panama: The Whole Story*, New York: Simon & Schuster, 1991, p. 165.

81. Andrew Zimbalist and John Weeks, *Panama at the Crossroads: Economic Development and Political Change in the Twentieth Century*, Berkeley: University of California Press, 1991, p. 140.

82. Scott and Marshall, *Cocaine Politics*, p. 165.

83. Scott and Marshall, *Cocaine Politics*, pp. 56-57.

84. Clifford Krauss, *Inside Central America*, New York: Summit Books, 1991, pp. 193-94.

85. Scott and Marshall, *Cocaine Politics*, p. 63.

86. Scott and Marshall, *Cocaine Politics*, pp. 56-57.

87. Sen., *Drugs...and Foreign Policy*, pp. 76, 121-22. See also Scott and Marshall, *Cocaine Politics*, pp. 61-62; Krauss, *Inside Central America*, pp. 198-99.

88. Leslie Cockburn, *Out of Control*, New York: Atlantic Monthly Press, 1987, p. 245; Sen., *Drugs...and Foreign Policy*, p. 54.

89. See, e.g., Christopher Hitchens, *Nation*, 18 Dec. 1989, p. 742; Hitchens, *Nation*, 12/19 Aug. 1991, p. 184; Martha Honey and David Myers, "Hull Shucks Jail," *Village Voice*, 22 Oct. 1991, pp. 20-21. Other support for the southern front during the period that the Boland amendment prohibited official U.S. government assistance to the Contras came from several groups of Miami-based Cuban Americans. Their help, the Kerry subcommittee reported, "was funded in part with drug money" (Sen., *Drugs...and Foreign Policy*, p. 59). Cuban-American criminal organizations controlled the drug trade in Miami in the late 1960s. Seventy percent of the 150 people arrested in June 1970 in the largest-ever bust of major drug smugglers had been part of the Bay of Pigs invasion force: their CIA training and protection had made them the most successful traffickers in the business (Scott and Marshall, *Cocaine Politics*, pp. 26-27). According to the Bureau of Narcotics and Dangerous Drugs, nearly 10 percent of the Bay of Pigs invasion force were eventually arrested for drug charges (Henrik Krüger, *The Great Heroin Coup: Drugs, Intelligence, and International Fascism*, Boston: South End, 1980, p. 145, citing *Newsday*). Two Cuban Americans who played an important role in supplying the Contras were Luis Posada Carriles and Felix Rodriguez. Posada was wanted in Venezuela for blowing up a Cuban airliner and both men were veterans of CIA efforts to assassinate Castro. Vice-President George Bush met with Rodriguez in January 1985, two months after the latter's former business partner was indicted for cocaine-smuggling and attempted assassination. Bush's assistant for national security affairs Donald Gregg kept an autographed picture of Rodriguez on his desk (Cockburn, *Out of Control*, pp. 98-99, 222-23, 274n, 224).

90. Jonathan Marshall, "Drugs and United States Foreign Policy," in *Dealing with Drugs: Consequences of Government Control*, ed. Ronald Hamowy, Lexington, MA: Lexington Books, 1987, p. 166.

91. Sen., *Drugs...and Foreign Policy*, pp. 77-78, 125, 286, 288.

92. Sen., *Drugs...and Foreign Policy*, pp. 42-43.

93. Sen., *Drugs...and Foreign Policy*, p. 2.

94. Sen., *Drugs...and Foreign Policy*, pp. 775, 780.

95. Weeks and Gunson, *Panama: Made in the USA*, p. 1.

96. R.W. Apple, Jr., "Bush's Obsession," *NYT*, 26 Dec. 1989, p. A11; Maureen Dowd, "A Sense of Inevitability in Bush's Decision to Act," *NYT*, 24 Dec. 1989, p. I:9; R.W. Apple, Jr., "Bush and Panama: Chance Lost, Perhaps to Hesitancy," *NYT*, 8 Oct. 1989, p. I:16; Democrat Dave McCurdy, chair of the House Intelligence Committee, quoted in C.S. Manegold, et al., "Amateur Hour," *Newsweek*, 16 Oct. 1989, p. 30; Phillips quoted in R.W. Apple, Jr., "Bush's Obsession," *NYT*, 26 Dec. 1989, p. A11. On escrow: Murray Waas, "There You Go Again," *Village Voice*, 22 Aug. 1989, pp. 20-22.

97. Elliott Abrams, "Noriega Respects Power. Use It," *NYT*, 5 Oct. 1989, p. A31; Edward Luttwack, "Do the Joint Chiefs Fear All Risks?" *NYT*, 27 Oct. 1989, p. A35.

98. AP, "Military Hails Stealth Debut," *SL*, 27 Dec. 1989, p. 13; James Ridgeway, "The Canal Is Ours," *Village Voice*, 14 June 1988, p. 16.

99. John Dinges, *Our Man in Panama*, rev. ed., New York: Random House, 1991, p. 313.

100. Buckley, *Panama: The Whole Story*, pp. 189, 191, 224.

101. Andrew Rosenthal, "President Calls Panama Slaying A Great Outrage," *NYT*, 19 Dec. 1989, p. A12; Buckley, *Panama: The Whole Story*, p. 229.

102. Rosenthal, "President Calls...," p. A12; "Tensions Rise As Yank Shoots Panama Soldier," *SL*, 19 Dec. 1989, p. 20; Dinges, *Our Man In Panama*, p. 307; Buckley, *Panama: The Whole Story*, pp. 232, 286.

103. Alex Cockburn quoted in Weeks and Gunson, *Panama: Made in the USA*, p. 13.

104. David Corn, "Stealth Contras," *Nation*, 26 Feb. 1990, p. 264.

105. Weeks and Gunson, *Panama: Made in the USA*, p. 16, citing *Newsweek*. The editors of the *NYT* further justified the invasion on the grounds that Noriega had declared the existence of a "state of war" with the United States (21 Dec. 1989, p. A30). But U.S. officials had ignored the Panamanian statement at the time (see White House spokesperson Marlin Fitzwater's acknowledgment of this point, "Tensions Rise As Yank Shoots Panama Soldier," *SL*, 19 Dec. 1989, p. 20), which in any event declared that U.S. actions had created the state of war (Buckley, *Panama: The Whole Story*, pp. 225, 231). The U.S. military commander in Panama had announced two months earlier that the United States was literally at war with Noriega (Buckley, *Panama: The Whole Story*, p. 222) without evoking editorial comment from the *Times*.

106. Dinges, *Our Man in Panama*, p. 308.

107. Weeks and Gunson, *Panama: Made in the USA*, p. 70. In July 1986, Oliver North wrote in his notebook under the heading "Noriega," "Objective: Residual U.S. force in Panama after 2000" (Jay Mallin, "Notebooks of North Tantalizing But Tame," *Washington Times*, 9 May 1990). After the invasion, *Newsweek* reported that some Pentagon officials were "quietly debating whether Washington should renegotiate the Panama Canal Treaties to allow a U.S. military presence in Panama after the Dec. 31, 1999, pullout date" ("New Treaty?" *Newsweek*, 14 Jan. 1991, p. 4). And a year later, a senior U.S. official said there was "evidence of interest" by both governments in Washington's keeping at least some bases (Shirley Christian, "Panama Questions U.S. Base Closure," *NYT*, 19 April 1992, p. I:7).

108. Dinges, *Our Man In Panama*, pp. 188-90.

109. Dinges, *Our Man In Panama*, p. 195-98.

110. Dinges, *Our Man In Panama*, p. 366n; Murray Waas, "Made for Each Other: The Secret History of George Bush and Manuel Noriega," *Village Voice*, 6 Feb. 1990, p. 29.

111. Dinges, *Our Man In Panama*, pp. 189, 195.

112. Dinges, *Our Man In Panama*, p. 205.

113. Cadets: Krauss, *Inside Central America*, p. 263; workers: Dinges, *Our Man In Panama*, p. 40; Krauss, *Inside Central America*, p. 264; students: Dinges, *Our Man In Panama*, p. 81; canal: Larry Rohter, "More Than an Ex-dictator's Future at Stake As Trial of Noriega Begins," *NYT*, 5 Sept. 1991, p. D24, chart.

114. Weeks and Gunson, *Panama: Made in the USA*, p. 119.

115. Weeks and Gunson, *Panama: Made in the USA*, pp. 119-20; Buckley, *Panama: The Whole Story*, pp. 95, 132.

116. Weeks and Gunson, *Panama: Made in the USA*, pp. 122-23; see also Waas, "Made for Each Other," p. 33.

117. Seymour Hersh reports quoted in R.M. Koster and Guillermo Sanchez, *In the Time of Tyrants; Panama: 1968-1990*, New York: Norton, 1990, p. 166; Reuters, "U.S. Called 'Blind' To Noriega Crimes," *SL*, 19 Feb. 1990, p. 18.

118. Dinges, *Our Man In Panama*, pp. 147-49.

119. Krauss, *Inside Central America*, p. 278.

120. Sen., *Drugs...and Foreign Policy*, p. 92.

121. Zimbalist and Weeks, *Panama at the Crossroads*, pp. 75, 139.

122. Dinges, *Our Man In Panama*, p. 200.

123. Sen., *Drugs...and Foreign Policy*, pp. 95-96; Dinges, *Our Man In Panama*, pp. 253-54.

124. Andrew Zimbalist, "Why Did the U.S. Invade Panama?" *Radical America*, vol. 23, nos. 2-3 (1989, published Oct. 1990), p. 10; Zimbalist and Weeks, *Panama at the Crossroads*, p. 143; Krauss, *Inside Central America*, p. 281; Weeks and Gunson, *Panama: Made in the USA*, p. 66.

125. Dinges, *Our Man In Panama*, pp. 294-95.

126. Krauss, *Inside Central America*, p. 286.

127. Michael Massing, "The Intervention That Misfired," *Nation*, 21 May 1988, pp. 709-10; Weeks and Gunson, *Panama: Made in the USA*, p. 43; Buckley, *Panama: The Whole Story*, pp. 117-18; Zimbalist and Weeks, *Panama at the Crossroads*, p. 145.

128. Lawrence Eagleburger, "The Case Against Panama's Noriega," D/S, *Current Policy*, no. 1222, speech to OAS, 31 Aug. 1989, pp. 5, 6.

129. Dinges, *Our Man in Panama*, pp. 312-13.

130. AP, "Discrepancies in Testimony, Vanishing Witnesses Delay Noriega Bid," *SL*, 22 Dec. 1991, p. I:55; Larry Rohter, "Judge Grants Delay in Start of Defense at Noriega Trial," *NYT*, 18 Dec. 1991, p. A24. The original indictment (which presumably justified the invasion) was considered weak by the prosecutors, and most of the government's case was developed after Noriega's capture. Larry Rohter, "Victory in Noriega Case Stunned Even Prosecutors," *NYT*, 17 April 1992, p. B16.

131. AP, "Judge Denies Motion To Drop Case Against Noriega But Has Doubts," *NYT*, 19 Dec. 1991, p. B21; Rohter, "More Than Ex-dictator's Future...," p. D24; Larry Rohter, "More Than Drugs Are At Stake in Noriega Trial," *NYT*, 29 Sept. 1991, p. E4; Richard Reeves, "Bad Go Free, Good Pay in Bush America," *SL*, 28 Nov. 1991, p. 36; Larry Rohter, "U.S. Jury Convicts Noriega of Drug-Trafficking Role as the Leader of Panama," *NYT*, 10 April 1992, p. A24.

132. "Many lawyers here say the discrepancies may not make a difference. Miami juries are accustomed to convicting drug defendants and rarely worry about squaring statements of their confederates" (Michael Isikoff, "Case Against Noriega Buffeted By Inconsistency," *WP*, 6 Oct. 1991, p. A5). See also Larry Rohter, "After 7 Months and a Final Skirmish, the Noriega Case Goes to the Jury," *NYT*, 5 April 1992, p. 29. Only one witness said he had seen Noriega accept a bribe from the Medellín cartel, and he had earlier told his lawyer that he had no information that could implicate Noriega (Larry Rohter, "Judge Examines Truthfulness of Noriega Witness," *NYT*, 26 March 1992, p. A16; Rohter, "U.S. Jury Convicts...," p. A24).

133. Michael Massing, "Noriega in Miami," *Nation,* 2 Dec. 1991, p. 698. The government advanced the "novel" argument that the Sixth Amendment right to a fair trial does not protect foreigners "until they are in the jurisdiction of the United States" (Larry Rohter, "After 7 Months...," p. 29). Prosecutors were aided in their misconduct by Panamanian officials, who, for example, detained a defense witness at the airport in Panama to prevent him from testifying (Larry Rohter, "After One Last Witness Dispute, Both Sides Rest in Noriega Trial," *NYT,* 31 March 1992, p. A15).

134. Larry Rohter, "Jury Finally Gets Noriega Drug Case," *NYT,* 4 April 1992, p. 6; Larry Rohter, "U.S. Jury Convicts...," p. A24.

135. Dinges, *Our Man In Panama,* p. 316.

136. Michael Isikoff, "Case Against Noriega Buffeted By Inconsistency," *WP,* 6 Oct. 1991, p. A4; see also AP, "Convicted Drug Baron Testifies Noriega Was Just Another Corrupt Cop," *SL,* 20 Nov. 1991, p. 5.

137. Richard Reeves, "Bad Go Free, Good Pay in Bush America," *SL,* 28 Nov. 1991, p. 36; David Johnston, "No Victory for Panama," *NYT,* 11 April 1992, p. 12; Bob Cohn with Spencer Reiss, "Noriega: How the Feds Got Their Man," *Newsweek,* 20 April 1992, p. 37.

138. Dinges, *Our Man In Panama,* pp. 128, 185-86, 316-17; Massing, "Noriega in Miami," p. 697.

139. Seymour M. Hersh, "U.S. Aides in '72 Weighed Killing Officer Who Now Leads Panama," *NYT,* 13 June 1986, pp. A1, A8; Seymour M. Hersh, "Panama Strongman Said to Trade in Drugs, Arms and Illicit Money," *NYT,* 12 June 1986; Sen., *Drugs...and U.S. Foreign Policy,* pp. 89-92.

140. Sen., *Drugs...and U.S. Foreign Policy,* p. 92.

141. AP, "BCCI Official Tells Drug Jury of Millions of Dollars Deposited by Noriega," *SL,* 10 Dec. 1991, p. 16.

142. Mark Cooper, "Same As It Ever Was," *Village Voice,* 28 May 1991, pp. 36-37; Joseph B. Treaster, "Cocaine Is Again Surging Out of Panama," *NYT* 13 Aug. 1991, p. A9; Zimbalist and Weeks, *Panama at the Crossroads,* p. 199n51; Weeks and Gunson, *Panama: Made in the USA,* p. 98.

143. Cooper, "Same As It Ever Was," p. 38; Dinges, *Our Man In Panama,* p. 204.

144. GAO, *The War on Drugs: Narcotics Control Efforts in Panama,* GAO/NSIAD-91-233, July 1991, pp. 1-3; Michael Massing, "The Salvation of Panama?" *New York Review of Books,* 13 June 1991, p. 23; Treaster, "Cocaine Again Surging...," pp. A1, A9; Shirley Christian, "Central America a New Drug Focus," *NYT,* 16 Dec. 1991, p. A10; Mark A. Uhlig, "Panama Drug Smugglers Prosper As Dictator's Exit Opens The Door," *NYT,* 21 Aug. 1990, p. A1; Cooper, "Same As It Ever Was," p. 34; Weeks and Gunson, *Panama: Made in the USA,* p. 104; Krauss, *Inside Central America,* p. 297; Johnston, "No Victory...," p. 1.

145. Mark A. Uhlig, "Panama Drug Smugglers Prosper As Dictator's Exit Opens The Door," *NYT,* 21 Aug. 1990," p. A2.

146. Shirley Christian, "Despite Distrust, Most Panamanians Seem Friendly to U.S.," *NYT,* 12 June 1992, p. A11.

147. Shirley Christian, "Panama Grows, Reaching Skyward, Yet Down Below Much Pain Remains," *NYT,* 29 April 1992, p. A6.

148. "U.S. Aid Fails To Help Panama, Report Says," *NYT,* 13 June 1992, p. 5.

149. Rensselaer W. Lee III, *The White Labyrinth: Cocaine and Political Power,* New Brunswick: Transaction Publishers, 1989, pp. 6, 36, 39; Alison Jamieson, "Global Drug Trafficking," *Conflict Studies,* no. 234, Sept. 1990, pp. 3, 19; Jo Ann Kawell, "Under the Flag of Law Enforcement," *NACLA: Report on the Americas,* vol. 22, no. 6, March 1989, pp. 26-29.

150. UNICEF, *The State of the World's Children, 1989,* New York: Oxford UP, 1989, p. 94.

151. Carol Wise, "The Perils of Orthodoxy: Peru's Political Culture," *NACLA: Report on the Americas,* vol. 20, no. 3, June 1986, p. 16.

152. Phillip Smith, "Grappling with Shining Path," *New Politics,* vol. 3, no. 4 (new series), whole number 12, winter 1992, p. 88; Jo-Marie Burt and Aldo Panfichi, *Peru: Caught in the Crossfire,* Jefferson City, MO: Peru Peace Network - USA, 1992, p. 19.

153. James Brooke, "Marxist Revolt Grows Strong In The Shantytowns Of Peru," *NYT,* 11 Nov. 1991, p. A6; Michael Massing, "In the Cocaine War...The Jungle Is Winning," *NYT Magazine,* 4 March 1990, p. 92; James Brooke, "Fujimori Aims For A Head-on Collision With 'Shining Path,'" *NYT,* 8 Dec. 1991, p. E3; Smith, "...Shining Path," p. 87. See also Burt and Panfichi, *Peru: Caught in the Crossfire,* pp. 3-4, 52; James Brooke, "A Lethal Army of Insurgents Lima Could Not Stamp Out," *NYT,* 7 April 1992, A1, A16; Nathaniel C. Nash, "Peru's Basic Problems Won't Be Ordered Away," *NYT,* 12 April 1992, p. E2.

154. Robin Kirk, "Shining Path Is Gaining in Peru," *Nation,* 29 April 1991, p. 552.

155. Smith, "...Shining Path," pp. 88-93; Raul Gonzalez, "Coca's Shining Path," *NACLA: Report on the Americas,* vol. 22, no. 6, March 1989, p. 23; Burt and Panfichi, *Peru: Caught in the Crossfire,* p. 39. Sendero does not apologize for killing people from the United Left. See Anita Fokkema, Interview with Luis Arce Borja, *NACLA Report on the Americas,* vol. 24, no. 4, Dec.-Jan 1990-91, pp. 23-24. Ironically, paramilitary death squads in Colombia engage in "social cleansing" campaigns, killing prostitutes, homosexuals, and street children (Ruth Conniff, "Colombia's Dirty War, Washington's Dirty Hands," *Progressive,* May 1992, pp. 24, 26).

156. Brooke, "Marxist Revolt...," p. A6.

157. Juan E. Mendez, "U.S. Joins Peru's Dirty War," *NYT,* 7 May 1990, p. A15; Robin Kirk, "Sowing Violence in Peru," *Progressive,* July 1991, p. 31; Nathaniel C. Nash, "10 Die a Day, or Disappear, and Peru Goes Numb," *NYT,* 14 July 1991, p. E2; Charles Lane, et al., "Peru: Into the Crossfire," *Newsweek,* 19 Aug. 1991, p. 29; Robin Kirk, "Oh! What a Lovely Drug War in Peru," *Nation,* 30 Sept. 1991, pp. 357, 372-76.

158. GAO, *The Drug War: U.S. Programs in Peru Face Serious Obstacles,* GAO/NSIAD-92-36, Oct. 1991, p. 26.

159. Kirk, "Shining Path Is Gaining in Peru," pp. 554-55; Harry Anderson, et al., "The Next Nasty War?" *Newsweek,* 21 May 1990, p. 37; GAO, *...Programs in Peru...,* p. 26.

160. See Lauren K. Saunders, letter, *NYT,* 4 May 1990, p. A34; Nancy Peckenham, "Peru: Ayacucho under Siege," *NACLA: Report on the Americas,* vol. 19, no. 3, May/June 1985, p. 7; Kirk, "Shining Path Is Gaining in Peru," p. 555; Burt and Panfichi, *Peru: Caught in the Crossfire,* pp. 28-29; James Brooke, "Peru's Military Is Granted Broad Powers In Rebel War," *NYT,* 3 Dec. 1991, p. A17; Charles Lane, et al., "Peru: Into the Crossfire," p. 29; Kirk, "...Lovely Drug War...," p. 375; GAO, *...Programs in Peru...,* pp. 21, 26-27; Nash, "10 Die a Day...," p. E2; Smith, "...Shining Path," p. 94; Reuters, "Rights Group Raps Peru's President," *SL,* 13 Oct. 1991, p. 7; Brooke, "Fujimori Aims...," p. E3.

161. Clifford Krauss, "U.S. Will Assist Peru's Army in Fighting Cocaine and Rebels," *NYT,* 25 Jan. 1992, p. 4; Ted Weiss, letter, *NYT,* 1 Aug. 1991, p. A20; Clifford Krauss, "State Dept. Backs Peru Aid Package," *NYT,* 1 Aug. 1991, p. A9; GAO, *...Programs in Peru...,* p. 27; GAO, *The Drug War: Counternarcotics Programs in Colombia and Peru,* testimony, GAO/T-NSIAD-92-9, 20 Feb. 1992, pp. 4-5; Washington Office on Latin America (WOLA), *Clear and Present Danger: The U.S. Military and the War on Drugs in the Andes,* Washington, D.C.: Oct. 1991, pp. 114-15.

162. Nathaniel C. Nash, "Peru's Fugitive Ex-President Tells of Escape from Troops," *NYT,* 24 April 1992, p. A11. On Sendero hopes of provoking a coup: Nelson Manrique, "Time of Fear," *NACLA Report on the Americas,* vol. 24, no. 4, Dec.-Jan 1990-91, p. 36; Eugene Robinson, "Peru's Coup: A Boost to Rebels?" *WP,* 12 April 1992, p. A32; Sarah Kerr,

"Fujimori's Plot: An Interview with Gustavo Gorriti," *New York Review of Books,* 25 June 1992, p. 21.

163. James Brooke, "Peru's Chief: Every Bit the Emperor," *NYT,* 16 April 1992, p. A3; Mario Vargas Llosa, "The Road to Barbarism," *NYT,* 12 April 1992, p. E21.

164. Nathaniel C. Nash, "Fujimori Talks Tough But The Coca Thrives," *NYT,* 26 April 1992, p. E2; Kerr, "…Interview with Gustavo Gorriti," pp. 18-19. Mario Vargas Llosa, Fujimori's opponent in the presidential election, refers to recent explicit charges of collusion between drug traffickers and some of the military officers supporting Fujimori's coup (Vargas Llosa, "Road to Barbarism," p. E21).

165. Bruce Bagley, "Colombia and the War on Drugs," *Foreign Affairs,* Fall 1988, pp. 71-72; Conniff, "Colombia's Dirty War…," p. 24; Jenny Pearce, "The People's War," *NACLA: Report on the Americas,* vol. 23, no. 6, April 1990, p. 15.

166. Bagley, "Colombia and the War on Drugs," p. 72; Michael Massing, "The War on Cocaine," *New York Review of Books,* 22 Dec. 1988, p. 61; Jenny Pearce, "The Dirty War," *NACLA: Report on the Americas,* vol. 23, no. 6, April 1990, pp. 26-28; Ken Dermota, "Dead Left," *Village Voice,* 3 July 1990, p. 18; James Brooke, "Assassins Wiping Out Colombia Party," *NYT* 8 April 1990, p. 10; Clara Ponce De Leon, "Colombia: Another 'Dirty War'?" *NACLA: Report on the Americas,* July-Aug. 1987, p. 4; Pearce, "People's War," p. 13.

167. Conniff, "Colombia's Dirty War…," pp. 24-26; Leslie Wirpsa, "'Leave the Region or Die,'" *Progressive,* May 1992, p. 23; WOLA, *Clear and Present Danger,* pp. 59-60.

168. Clarence Lusane, *Pipe Dream Blues: Racism and the War on Drugs,* Boston: South End Press, 1991, p. 113.

169. Joseph B. Treaster, et al., "Battle Against Drug Trafficking Is Languishing in South America," *NYT,* 1 Jan. 1990, p. 9; Jamieson, "Global Drug Trafficking," p. 15.

170. Jamieson, "Global Drug Trafficking," p. 3.

171. Jamieson, "Global Drug Trafficking," p. 19.

172. Lee, *White Labyrinth,* p. 5.

173. Jamieson, "Global Drug Trafficking," p. 19.

174. Kawell, "Flag of Law Enforcement," pp. 26-27.

175. Michael Levine, *Deep Cover,* New York: Dell, 1990, pp. 6, 91-92.

176. David Corn, "The CIA and The Cocaine Coup," *Nation,* 7 Oct. 1991, pp. 404-406.

177. WOLA, *Clear and Present Danger,* p. 101.

178. Lee, *White Labyrinth,* pp. 177, 89-90; see also Scott and Marshall, *Cocaine Politics,* pp. 84, 191.

179. Peter R. Andreas, Eva C. Bertram, Morris J. Blachman, & Kenneth E. Sharpe, "Dead-End Drug Wars," *Foreign Policy,* no. 85, winter 1991-92, p. 118; James Brooke, "Fighting the Drug War in the Skies Over Peru," *NYT,* 28 March 1992, p. 4.

180. Ponce De Leon, "Colombia: Another 'Dirty War'," p. 6.

181. James Brooke, "Jailed Drug Cartel Chief Still Feared in Colombia," *NYT,* 21 Jan. 1992, p. A12. See also James Brooke, "The Drug War the POW's May Have Won," *NYT,* 23 June 1991, p. E2; Tom Morganthau, et al., "'El Padrino' Cuts a Deal," *Newsweek,* 10 June 1991, p. 23; James Brooke, "Gaviria's Gamble," *NYT Magazine,* 13 Oct. 1991, p. 41; Joseph B. Treaster, "Drug Baron Gives Up In Colombia As End to Extradition Is Approved," 20 June 1991, p. A14; Joseph B. Treaster, "Arrest Called Unlikely to Cut Narcotics Shipments to U.S.," *NYT,* 21 June 1991, p. A8; WOLA, *Clear and Present Danger,* p. 100.

182. Andreas, et al., "Dead-End Drug Wars," pp. 111, 114; James Brooke, "Cali, the 'Quiet' Drug Cartel, Profits by Accommodation," *NYT,* 14 July 1991, p. I:1; Jamieson, "Global Drug Trafficking," p. 15; Marc W. Chernick, "The Drug War," *NACLA: Report on the Americas,* vol. 23, no. 6, April 1990, p. 36; WOLA, *Clear and Present Danger,* p. 100.

183. Jamieson, "Global Drug Trafficking," p. 16.

184. Bagley, "Colombia and the War on Drugs," p. 84. See also Lee, *White Labyrinth*, pp. 118, 158, 170; Elaine Shannon, *Desperados: Latin Drug Lords, U.S. Lawmen, and the War America Can't Win*, New York: Viking Penguin, 1988, p. 145; WOLA, *Clear and Present Danger*, p. 59; Peter Sanchez, "The 'Drug War': The U.S. Military and National Security," *Air Force Law Review*, vol. 34, 1991, p. 114. For the contrary U.S. government view, see GAO, *The Drug War: Observations on Counternarcotics Aid to Colombia*, GAO/NSIAD-91-296, Sept. 1991, pp. 19-20. In Colombia in 1985, the guerrilla group M-19 raided the Supreme Court building, leading to the deaths of 100 people including 11 judges and the destruction of narcotics extradition files (Kerry Report, p. 31). The Reagan administration was quick to use this as proof of narco-guerrilla collaboration (Shannon, *Desperados*, pp. 174-76). In fact, however, two Colombian commissions and independent reporters found no evidence tying traffickers to the incident (Lee, *White Labyrinth*, p. 174; Chernick, "Drug War," p. 31). Lee notes that it cannot be ruled out that drug lord Carlos Lehder, considered reckless by the rest of his Medellín colleagues, was involved, but warns that there is no evidence to support this speculation (Lee, *White Labyrinth*, pp. 174-75). Moreover, the raid may have revealed more about the callousness of the Colombian government than of the guerrillas. No one was killed until the government, ignoring offers to talk, stormed the building. According to the ballistics report, no one was wounded by M-19 weapons; eyewitnesses claimed that some 50 people were killed by a huge cannon shell fired by the army through the top story. (The surviving judges boycotted a memorial mass for their dead colleagues to protest the government's reckless disregard for their safety [Guy Gugliotta and Jeff Leen, *Kings of Cocaine*, New York: Simon & Schuster, 1989, p. 250].) The extradition records were burned in a fire probably started by army artillery, but in any event the files were copies of documents already in the United States, so drug traffickers had no special interest in destroying them (see Lee, *White Labyrinth*, pp. 172-74; Ponce De Leon, "Colombia: Another 'Dirty War'," p. 4; Shannon, *Desperados*, pp. 175-76).

185. Smith, "...Shining Path," pp. 95-96; Jo Ann Kawell, "Going to the Source," *NACLA: Report on the Americas*, vol. 22, no. 6, March 1989, p. 15.

186. Kawell, "Flag of Law Enforcement," pp. 27-29; Simon Strong, "Peru Is Losing More Than the Drug War," *NYT*, 17 Feb. 1992, p. A17.

187. GAO, *...Programs in Peru...*, p. 24.

188. Lee, *White Labyrinth*, pp. 175-76.

189. Shannon, *Desperados*, p. 146.

190. Lee, *White Labyrinth*, p. 157. See also Edmundo Morales, *Cocaine: White Gold Rush in Peru*, Tucson: University of Arizona Press, 1989, p. 172; Chernick, "Drug War," p. 31.

191. Gustavo A. Gorriti, "How to Fight the Drug War," *Atlantic Monthly*, July 1989, p. 74; Robert Neuwirth, "Coca Challenge," *Village Voice*, 12 Nov. 1991, p. 24; Lee, *White Labyrinth*, pp. 91, 206, 210.

192. Lee, *White Labyrinth*, p. 204. Lee also notes the persistent rumors suggesting that coca farmers use cash payments for eradication to underwrite the costs of new coca fields (Lee, *White Labyrinth*, p. 234).

193. Peter Passell, "Coca Dreams, Cocaine Reality," *NYT* 14 Aug. 1991, p. D2.

194. Charles Lane, et al., "Peru: Into the Crossfire," p. 30; Kawell, "Going to the Source," pp. 14-15.

195. Morales, *Cocaine*, p. 167, citing *NYT*, June 1988. As a Bolivian official who led a raid on a small cocaine lab put it, "We know the people hate us. When we do this, we're taking their livelihood away from them" (Nathaniel C. Nash, "In the Drug War, U.S. Sows Dollars, Reaps Hate," *NYT*, 13 March 1992. p. A4).

196. GAO, *Restrictions on U.S. Aid to Bolivia for Crop Development Competing With U.S. Agricultural Exports and their Relationship to U.S. Anti-Drug Efforts*, testimony, GAO/T-NSIAD-90-52, 27 June 1990, pp. 2, 7, 9, 21.

197. Morales, *Cocaine*, p. 166.

198. Kirk, "Sowing Violence in Peru," p. 31; Morales, *Cocaine*, p. 166. In Bolivia, farmers who accepted government payments to switch crops found that the prices paid for their crops were so low that they could not support their families, and that the roads and bridges that the government promised to build to get the produce to market had not been built. "If there were real development all our members would change to another crop," explained one farmer leader (Nash, "In the Drug War…," p. A4).

199. Morales, *Cocaine*, pp. xx, 152.

200. Clifford Krauss, "U.S. Withholding Drug Aid to Peru," *NYT*, 11 Nov. 1991, p. A6.

201. James Brooke, "The Cocaine War's Biggest Success: A Fungus," *NYT*, 22 Dec. 1991, p. I:15.

202. Michael Wines, "Drug War to Widen on Same Budget," *NYT*, 28 Feb. 1992, p. A9.

203. Lane, et al., "Peru: Into the Crossfire," p. 29.

204. Kawell, "Flag of Law Enforcement," p. 26; D/S, *International Narcotics Control Strategy Report*, Sept. 1988, p. 6.

205. Nathaniel Nash, "The Challenge of Peru: Drugs and Disarray," *NYT*, 11 Aug. 1991, p. E3.

206. James Brooke, "Gains Seen in Fight to Cut Drug Trade," *NYT*, 15 Jan. 1992, p. A13. Despite the headline, the article notes that three Americans were killed in Peru a few days earlier and that the drug "flow from Colombia appears to have continued largely unimpeded." Another *NYT* article claims that 500 U.S. soldiers are "working on intelligence and antinarcotics training programs in Latin America." Krauss, "U.S. Will Assist…," p. 4.

207. Dependence: Kawell, "Flag of Law Enforcement," p. 26; Lee, *White Labyrinth*, pp. 3, 37-38. Reluctance: Andreas, et al., "Dead-End Drug Wars," pp. 110, 113; WOLA, *Clear and Present Danger*, pp. 98-100. In Peru, the military has even engaged in armed attacks in order to disrupt DEA operations (Andreas, et al., "Dead-End Drug Wars," pp. 115-16).

208. Andreas, et al., "Dead-End Drug Wars," p. 116. See also Kirk, "…Lovely Drug War…," p. 374; WOLA, *Clear and Present Danger*, pp. 51-52.

209. Coletta Youngers, "Body Count," *Nation*, 2 July 1990, p. 5. The U.S. gave the Colombian Air Force 8 Cessna A-37B Dragonflies from drug war funds; the plane is designed for counter-insurgency, and is inappropriate for anti-drug missions. WOLA, *Clear and Present Danger*, pp. 53-55.

210. Youngers, "Body Count," p. 5. See also Jorge Gómez Lizarazo, "Colombian Blood, U.S. Guns," *NYT*, 28 Jan. 1992, p. A21. Indifference to human rights considerations occurs in Guatemala as well where U.S. officials work with that country's military intelligence division on anti-drug operations. As one U.S. drug expert put it, "As long as they keep doing good work, you don't ask about involvement in the killings and disappearances so often attributed to them" (WOLA, *Clear and Present Danger*, pp. 88, 90).

211. GAO, *…Observations…Colombia*, pp. 2, 5, 19, 21-27; GAO, *The Drug War: Counternarcotics Programs in Colombia and Peru*, testimony, GAO/T-NSIAD-92-9, 20 Feb. 1992, pp. 2-3.

212. Philip Shenon, "Peru Drug Fund Used in War, Aide Says," *NYT*, 21 June 1990, p. A3; James Brooke, "Peru Develops Plan To Work With U.S. To Combat Drugs," *NYT*, 25 Jan. 1991, p. A2.

213. Shannon, *Desperados*, pp. 355-56, 363; Lee, *White Labyrinth*, p. 48; Michael T. Klare, "Fighting Drugs with the Military," *Nation*, 1 Jan. 1990, p. 8; Bagley, "Colombia and the War on Drugs," p. 90.

214. AP, "Drug Barons Branch Out To Heroin," *SL,* 13 Oct. 1991, p. I:7; "Colombian Heroin May Be Increasing," *NYT,* 27 Oct. 1991, p. 15; Joseph B. Treaster, "Colombia's Drug Lords Add New Product: Heroin For U.S.," *NYT,* 14 Jan. 1992, pp. A1, B2.

215. James Brooke, "Colombian Drug Cartels Push Into Venezuela," *NYT,* 1 Sept. 1991, p. I:15; Clifford Krauss, "Anti-Drug Effort Drags Outside U.S.," *NYT,* 25 Nov. 1990, p. 9; Tom Morganthau, et al., "The Widening Drug War," *Newsweek,* 1 July 1991, p. 32; Joseph B. Treaster, "Cocaine Manufacturing Is No Longer Just A Colombian Monopoly," *NYT,* 30 June 1991, p. E5; AP, "Venezuela Town Turns Into Cocaine 'Gateway,'" *SL,* 2 Jan. 1992, p. 27; Nathaniel C. Nash, "Cocaine Invades Chile, Scorning the Land Mines," *NYT,* 23 Jan. 1992, p. A4; Joseph B. Treaster, "Smuggling and Use of Illicit Drugs Are Growing, UN Survey Finds," *NYT,* 13 Jan. 1992, p. A11; WOLA, *Clear and Present Danger,* pp. 105, 129. In March 1991, Assistant Secretary of Defense Henry Rowen could list only one concrete result of the Bush administration's Andean strategy: the "shift in illegal drug trade to other countries" (Quoted in WOLA, *Clear and Present Danger,* p. 97).

216. WOLA, *Clear and Present Danger,* p. 94; Joseph B. Treaster, "Bush Sees Progress, But U.S. Report Sees Surge in Drug Production," *NYT,* 1 March 1992, p. 12. The 1991 figure represents the volume of coca leaf extracted.

217. GAO, *Drug Control: Status Report on DOD Support to Counternarcotics Activities,* GAO/NSIAD-91-117, June 1991, pp. 3, 8, 9.

218. GAO, *Impact of DOD's Detection and Monitoring on Cocaine Flow,* GAO/NSIAD-91-297, Sept. 1991, pp. 5, 24.

219. James Der Derian, "Narco-Terrorism At Home and Abroad," *Radical America,* vol. 23, nos. 2-3 (1989, published Oct. 1990), p. 23.

220. Peter Reuter, Gordon Crawford, and Jonathan Cave, *Sealing the Borders: The Effects of Increased Military Participation in Drug Interdiction,* R-3594-USDP, Santa Monica: Rand Corporation, 1988, pp. xi, 122; GAO, *Impact of DOD's...on Cocaine Flow,* pp. 5, 6, 24, 28, 27.

221. Douglas Waller, et al., "Risky Business," *Newsweek,* 16 July 1990, p. 17.

222. Krauss, "U.S. Will Assist...," p. 4.

223. *LAT,* 15 Dec. 1990, quoted in Scott and Marshall, *Cocaine Politics,* p. 3. See also Klare, "Fighting Drugs...," p. 10; Jo Ann Kawell, "Drug Wars: The Rules of the Game," *NACLA: Report on the Americas,* vol. 23, no. 6, April 1990, p. 9.

224. Gen. Maxwell Thurman quoted in Burt and Panfichi, *Peru: Caught in the Crossfire,* p. 35.

225. Waghelstein quoted in Klare, "Fighting Drugs...," p. 10; and in Mary Jo McConahay and Robin Kirk, "Over There," *Mother Jones,* Feb.-March 1989, p. 38.

Conclusion

1. See Stephen R. Shalom, "Socialism Resurgent?" *Z Magazine,* July-Aug. 1989, for further discussion and examples.

2. Reuters, "France to U.S.: Don't Rule," *NYT,* 3 Sept. 1991, p. A8.

3. *NYT,* 24 May 1992, p. I;14.

4. *Newsweek,* 4 May 1992, pp. 30-39.

5. Robert J. Samuelson, "End of the Third World," *Newsweek,* 23 July 1990, p. 45.

6. UNICEF, *The State of the World's Children, 1989,* New York: Oxford UP, 1989, p. 1; AP, "UN Says Prostitution of Children Is Growing," *NYT,* 19 Feb. 1992, p. A11.

Bibliography

ABC News Nightline, "Insufficient Proof of Libyan Bombers in Pan Am 103?" transcript, show #2846, 20 April 1992.

Acheson, Dean, *Present at the Creation,* New York: New American Library, 1969.

Adelman, Kenneth, "Chemical Weapons: Restoring the Taboo," *Orbis,* Fall 1986.

al-Jabbar, Faleh Abd, "Why the Uprisings Failed," *Middle East Report,* May-June 1992.

Albright, David, and Mark Hibbs, "Iraq's Bomb: Blueprints and Artifacts," *Bulletin of the Atomic Scientists,* Jan.-Feb. 1992.

Anderson, Jack, with George Clifford, *The Anderson Papers,* New York: Random House, 1973.

Andreas, Peter R., Eva C. Bertram, Morris J. Blachman, & Kenneth E. Sharpe, "Dead-End Drug Wars," *Foreign Policy,* no. 85, Winter 1991-92.

Avirgan, Tony, and Martha Honey, *War in Uganda: The Legacy of Idi Amin,* Westport, CT: Lawrence Hill & Co., 1982.

Bagley, Bruce, "Colombia and the War on Drugs," *Foreign Affairs,* Fall 1988.

Barnet, Richard J., *The Roots of War,* Baltimore: Penguin, 1972.

Bartley, Robert L., and William P. Kucewicz, "'Yellow Rain' and the Future of Arms Agreements," *Foreign Affairs,* vol. 61, no. 4, Spring 1983.

Bazyler, Michael J., "Reexamining the Doctrine of Humanitarian Intervention in Light of the Atrocities in Kampuchea and Ethiopia," *Stanford Journal of International Law,* vol. 23, Summer 1987.

Bender, Gerald J., James S. Coleman, & Richard L. Sklar, eds., *African Crisis Areas and U.S. Foreign Policy,* Berkeley: University of California Press, 1985.

Biddle, Wayne, "Restocking the Chemical Arsenal," *NYT Magazine,* 25 May 1981.

Blechman, Barry M., Janne E. Nolan, and Alan Platt, "Pushing Arms," *Foreign Policy,* no. 46, Spring 1982.

Blundy, David, and Andrew Lycett, *Qaddafi and the Libyan Revolution,* Boston: Little, Brown, 1987.

Bowen, Michael, Gary Freeman, and Kay Miller, *Passing By: The United States and Genocide in Burundi, 1972,* Washington, DC: Carnegie Endowment for International Peace, 1973.

This list includes only sources cited at least twice in at least one chapter.

Brands, H.W. Jr., "Testing Massive Retaliation: Credibility and Crisis Management in the Taiwan Strait," *International Security*, vol. 12, no. 4, Spring 1988.

Bremer, L. Paul III, "Terrorism: Its Evolving Nature," D/S, *Current Policy*, No. 1151, 1989.

Bremer, L. Paul III, "Terrorism: Myths and Reality," D/S, *Current Policy*, No. 1047, 1988.

Brooke, James, "Fujimori Aims For a Head-on Collision with 'Shining Path,'" *NYT*, 8 Dec. 1991.

Brooke, James, "Marxist Revolt Grows Strong In The Shantytowns Of Peru," *NYT*, 11 Nov. 1991.

Brown, Harold, *Thinking About National Security*, Boulder: Westview, 1983.

Brzezinski, Zbigniew, *Power and Principle: Memoirs of the National Security Adviser, 1977-1981*, New York: Farrar, Straus, Giroux, 1983.

Buckley, Kevin, *Panama: The Whole Story*, New York: Simon & Schuster, 1991.

Burt, Jo-Marie, and Aldo Panfichi, *Peru: Caught in the Crossfire*, Jefferson City, MO: Peru Peace Network - USA, 1992.

Carnesale, Albert, and Richard N. Haass, eds., *Superpower Arms Control: Setting the Record Straight*, Cambridge, MA: Ballinger, 1987.

Carter, Jimmy, *Keeping Faith*, New York: Bantam, 1982.

Catrina, Christian, *Arms Transfers and Dependence*, New York: Taylor & Francis for UNIDIR, 1988.

Cervenka, Zdenek, *The Nigerian War, 1967-1970*, Frankfurt am Main: Bernard & Graefe, Verlag fur Wehrwesen, 1971.

Chadda, Maya, *Paradox of Power: the United States in Southwest Asia, 1973-1984*, Santa Barbara: ABC-Clio, 1986.

Chalk, Frank, and Kurt Jonassohn, *The History and Sociology of Genocide*, New Haven: Yale UP, 1990.

Chanda, Nayan, *Brother Enemy*, New York: Collier, 1986.

Chang, Gordon H., "To the Nuclear Brink: Eisenhower, Dulles, and the Quemoy-Matsu Crisis," *International Security*, vol. 12, no. 4, Spring 1988.

Chernick, Marc W., "The Drug War," *NACLA: Report on the Americas*, vol. 23, no. 6, April 1990.

Chomsky, Noam, *At War with Asia*, New York: Pantheon, 1969.

Chomsky, Noam, *Pirates and Emperors*, New York: Claremont Research, 1986.

Clergy and Laity Concerned, *In the Name of America*, Annandale, VA: Turnpike Press, 1968.

Cockburn, Andrew, *The Threat: Inside the Soviet Military Machine*, New York: Vintage, 1983.

Cockburn, Andrew and Leslie, *Dangerous Liaison: The Inside Story of the U.S.-Israeli Covert Relationship*, New York: HarperCollins, 1991.

Cockburn, Leslie, *Out of Control,* New York: Atlantic Monthly Press, 1987.

Cole, Leonard A., *Clouds of Secrecy,* Savage, MD: Littlefield, Adams, 1990.

CQ, *U.S. Defense Policy,* 3rd ed., Washington, DC: 1983.

Conniff, Ruth, "Colombia's Dirty War, Washington's Dirty Hands," *Progressive,* May 1992.

Cooley, John, *Libyan Sandstorm,* New York: Holt, Rinehart & Winston, 1982.

Cooper, Mark, "Same As It Ever Was," *Village Voice,* 28 May 1991.

Cordesman, Anthony H., *The Gulf and the Search for Strategic Stability,* Boulder: Westview, 1984.

Cordesman, Anthony H., *The Iran-Iraq War and Western Security, 1984-87,* London: Jane's Publishing Co., 1987.

Council on Scientific Affairs, AMA, "The Worldwide Smoking Epidemic," *JAMA,* vol. 263, no. 24, 27 June 1990.

Cronje, Suzanne, *The World and Nigeria,* London: Sidgwick & Jackson, 1972.

Crossette, Barbara, "The Caribbean After Grenada," *NYT Magazine,* 18 March 1984.

Cuadra, Elizabeth, "Air Defense Identification Zones: Creeping Jurisdiction in the Airspace," *Virginia Journal of International Law,* vol. 18, 1978.

D/S, *American Foreign Policy: Basic Documents, 1977-1980,* 1983.

D/S, *American Foreign Policy: Current Documents, 1981,* 1984.

D/S, *Libya Under Qadhafi: A Pattern of Aggression,* Special Report No. 138, Jan. 1986.

D/S, *The Libyan Problem,* Special Report No. 111, Oct. 1983.

D/S, *Libya's Continuing Responsibility for Terrorism,* Nov. 1991.

D/S, *Patterns of Global Terrorism: 1985,* Oct. 1986.

D/S, *Patterns of Global Terrorism: 1986,* January 1988.

D'Amato, Anthony, "The Imposition of Attorney Sanctions for Claims Arising from the U.S. Air Raid on Libya," *American Journal of International Law,* vol. 84, 1990.

Decalo, Samuel, *Psychoses of Power: African Personal Dictatorships,* Boulder: Westview, 1989.

Dinges, John, *Our Man in Panama,* rev. ed., New York: Random House, 1991.

Dower, John W., *War Without Mercy: Race and Power in the Pacific War,* New York: Pantheon, 1986.

Draper, Theodore, "American Hubris," in Sifry and Cerf, eds., *The Gulf War Reader.*

Draper, Theodore, *The Dominican Revolt,* New York: Commentary, 1968.

Drinnon, Richard, *Facing West: The Metaphysics of Indian-Hating and Empire Building,* New York: Schocken Books, 1990.

Duffett, John, ed., *Against the Crime of Silence: Proceedings of the Russell International War Crimes Tribunal,* New York: O'Hare Books, 1968.

Ember, Lois R., "Worldwide Spread of Chemical Arms Receiving Increased Attention," *Chemical & Engineering News,* 14 April 1986.

Ember, Lois R., "Yellow Rain," *Chemical & Engineering News,* 9 Jan. 1984.

Emerson, Steven A., and Cristina Del Sesto, *Terrorist,* New York: Villard Books, 1991.

Emerson, Steven, and Brian Duffy, *The Fall of Pan Am 103,* New York: G.P. Putnam's Sons, 1990.

Engelberg, Stephen, "Iran and Iraq Got 'Doctored' Data, U.S. Officials Say," *NYT,* 12 Jan. 1987.

EPICA, *The Caribbean: Survival, Struggle and Sovereignty,* 2nd ed., Boston: South End Press, 1988.

Farhang, Mansour, "The Iran-Israel Connection," in *Consistency of U.S. Foreign Policy: The Gulf War and the Iran-Contra Affair,* ed. Abbas Alnasrawi and Cheryl Rubenberg, Belmont, MA: AAUG, 1989.

Fasteau, Marc Feigen, *The Male Machine,* New York: Delta, 1975.

Feldman, Shai, *Israeli Nuclear Deterrence,* New York: Columbia UP, 1982.

Ferguson, James, *Grenada: Revolution in Reverse,* London: Latin American Bureau, 1991.

Fetter, Steve, "Weapons of Mass Destruction: What Is The Threat? What Should Be Done?" *International Security,* vol. 16, no. 1, Summer 1991.

Foltz, William J., "Libya's Military Power," in Lemarchand, ed., *Green and the Black.*

Ford, Gerald R., *A Time to Heal,* New York: Harper & Row, 1979.

Franck, Thomas M., and Nigel S. Rodley, "After Bangladesh: The Law of Humanitarian Intervention by Military Force," *American Journal of International Law,* vol. 67, 1973.

Frantz, Douglas, and Murray Waas, "Bush Secret Effort Helped Iraq Build its War Machine," *LAT,* 23 Feb. 1992.

Frantz, Douglas, and Murray Waas, "U.S. Loans Indirectly Financed Iraq Military," *LAT,* 25 Feb. 1992.

Freedman, Robert O., "Soviet Policy Toward the Persian Gulf from the Outbreak of the Iran-Iraq War to the Death of Konstantin Chernenko," in *U.S. Strategic Interests in the Gulf Region,* ed. Wm. J. Olson, Boulder: Westview, 1987.

Frelick, Bill, "The False Promise of Operation Provide Comfort," *Middle East Report,* May-June 1992.

Fukuyama, Francis, *Gorbachev and the New Soviet Agenda in the Third World,* R-3634-A, Santa Monica: Rand Corporation, June 1989.

GAO, *Caribbean Basin Initiative: Impact on Selected Countries,* GAO/NSIAD-88-177, July 1988.

GAO, *The Drug War: Observations on Counternarcotics Aid to Colombia,* GAO/NSIAD-91-296, Sept. 1991.

GAO, *The Drug War: U.S. Programs in Peru Face Serious Obstacles,* GAO/NSIAD-92-36, Oct. 1991.

GAO, *Food Safety and Quality: Five Countries' Efforts to Meet U.S. Requirements on Imported Produce,* GAO/RCED-90-55, March 1990.

GAO, *Impact of DOD's Detection and Monitoring on Cocaine Flow,* GAO/NSIAD-91-297, Sept. 1991.

GAO, *Trade and Health Issues: Dichotomy Between U.S. Tobacco Export Policy and Antismoking Initiatives,* GAO/NSIAD-90-190, May 1990.

Garthoff, Raymond L., *Détente and Confrontation,* Washington, DC: Brookings Institution, 1985.

Gelb, Leslie H., "U.S. Said to Aid Iranian Exiles in Combat and Political Units," *NYT,* 7 Mar. 1982.

George, Alexander, ed., *Western State Terrorism,* New York: Routledge, 1991.

Gervasi, Sean, and Sybil Wong, "The Reagan Doctrine and the Destabilization of Southern Africa," in George, ed., *Western State Terrorism.*

Gilbert, Martin, *Auschwitz and the Allies,* New York: Holt, Rinehart and Winston, 1981.

Gilmore, William C., *The Grenada Intervention: Analysis and Documentation,* New York: Facts on File, 1984.

Gordon, Michael R., "U.S. Weighs A Plan For Arms Control In The Middle East," *NYT,* 14 May 1991.

Gwertzman, Bernard, "Steps to the Invasion: No More 'Paper Tiger'," *NYT,* 30 Oct. 1983.

HR, Appropriations Comm. subcomm., *Department of Defense Appropriations for 1976,* Hearings, part 3, 1975.

HR, Foreign Affairs Comm., subcomm. on Africa, *Libya-Sudan-Chad Triangle: Dilemma for United States Policy,* Hearings, Oct.-Nov. 1981.

HR, Foreign Affairs Comm, subcomms. on International Security and Scientific Affairs and Western Hemisphere Affairs, *U.S. Military Actions in Grenada: Implications for U.S. Policy in the Eastern Caribbean,* Hearings, Nov. 1983.

HR, Foreign Affairs Comm., subcomm. on National Security Policy and Scientific Developments, *Chemical and Biological Warfare: U.S. Policies and International Effects,* Hearings, Nov.-Dec. 1969.

HR, Foreign Affairs Comm., subcomm. on National Security Policy and Scientific Developments, *U.S. Chemical Warfare Policy,* Hearings, May 1974.

HR, Foreign Affairs Comm. subcomm.; Sen., Governmental Affairs Comm. subcomm.; and Congressional Research Service of the Library of Congress, *Nuclear Proliferation Factbook,* August 1985.

HR, International Relations Comm. and its subcomm. on International Political and Military Affairs, *Seizure of the Mayaguez,* Hearings, parts 1-3, May-Sept. 1975; part 4, Committee Print, Oct. 1976.

HR, Merchant Marine and Fisheries Comm., subcomm. on Panama Canal/Outer Continental Shelf, *Offshore Oil and Gas Oversight,* Hearings, 1984.

Haberman, Clyde, "The Kurds in Flight Once Again," *NYT Magazine,* 5 May 1991.

Haley, Edward, *Qaddafi and the United States Since 1969,* New York: Praeger, 1984.

Harris, Elisa D., "The Biological and Toxin Weapons Convention," in Carnesale and Haass, eds., *Superpower Arms Control.*

Harris, Elisa D., "Sverdlovsk and Yellow Rain: Two Cases of Soviet Noncompliance?" *International Security,* vol. 11, no. 4, Spring 1987.

Harris, Lillian Craig, *Libya: Qadhafi's Revolution and the Modern State,* Boulder: Westview, 1986.

Harrison, Selig, *The Widening Gulf: Asian Nationalism and American Policy,* New York: Free Press, 1978.

Heine, Jorge, ed., *A Revolution Aborted: The Lessons of Grenada,* Pittsburgh: University of Pittsburgh Press, 1991.

Heise, Lori, "Unhealthy Alliance," *World Watch,* Sept.-Oct. 1988.

Herman, Edward S., *The Real Terror Network,* Boston: South End Press, 1982.

Herman, Edward, and Gerry O'Sullivan, *The "Terrorism" Industry,* New York: Pantheon, 1989.

Hersh, Seymour M., *The Price of Power: Kissinger in the Nixon White House,* New York: Summit Books, 1983.

Hersh, Seymour M., *The Samson Option,* New York: Random House, 1991.

Hersh, Seymour M., "Target Qaddafi," *NYT Magazine,* 22 Feb. 1987.

Hersh, Seymour M., "U.S. Secretly Gave Aid To Iraq Early In Its War Against Iran," *NYT,* 26 Jan. 1992.

Hiro, Dilip, *Iran Under the Ayatollahs,* London: Routledge & Kegan Paul, 1985.

House of Commons, Second Report from the Foreign Affairs Comm., *Grenada,* Session 1983-84, London: HMSO, 1984.

Hunt, Michael H., *Ideology and U.S. Foreign Policy,* New Haven: Yale UP, 1987.

Hunter, Jane, *Israeli Foreign Policy: South Africa and Central America,* Boston: South End Press, 1987.

Jackson, Robert, *South Asian Crisis: India, Pakistan and Bangla Desh,* New York: Praeger, 1975.

Jacobs, Dan, *The Brutality of Nations,* New York: Knopf, 1987.

Jamieson, Alison, "Global Drug Trafficking," *Conflict Studies,* no. 234, Sept. 1990.

Johnston, David, "No Victory for Panama," *NYT,* 11 April 1992.

Karem, Mahmoud, *A Nuclear-Weapon-Free Zone in the Middle East: Problems and Prospects,* New York: Greenwood Press, 1988.

Karsh, Efraim, "Military Power and Foreign Policy Goals: The Iran-Iraq War Revisited," *International Affairs,* vol. 64, no. 1, Winter 1987/88.

Katzenbach, Nicholas deB., "The Tragedy of Nigeria," 3 Dec. 1968, in *Documents of American Foreign Relations, 1968-69,* ed. Richard P. Stebbins and Elaine P. Adam, New York: Simon & Schuster for the Council on Foreign Relations, 1972.

Kawell, Jo Ann, "Under the Flag of Law Enforcement," *NACLA: Report on the Americas,* vol. 22, no. 6, March 1989.

Kerr, Sarah, "Fujimori's Plot: An Interview with Gustavo Gorriti," *New York Review of Books,* 25 June 1992.

King, R.P.H., "The United Nations and the Iran-Iraq War, 1980-1986," in *The United Nations and the Iran-Iraq War,* ed. Brian Urquhart and Gary Sick, New York: Ford Foundation, August 1987.

Kirk, Robin, "Oh! What a Lovely Drug War in Peru," *Nation,* 30 Sept. 1991.

Kirk, Robin, "Shining Path Is Gaining in Peru," *Nation,* 29 April 1991.

Kirk, Robin, "Sowing Violence in Peru," *Progressive,* July 1991.

Kirk-Greene, A.H.M., *Crisis and Conflict in Nigeria: A Documentary Sourcebook 1966-1970,* vol. 2, London: Oxford UP, 1971.

Kissinger, Henry, *White House Years,* Boston: Little, Brown, 1979.

Kissinger, Henry, *Years of Upheaval,* Boston: Little, Brown, 1982.

Klare, Michael T., "Fighting Drugs with the Military," *Nation,* 1 Jan. 1990.

Klare, Michael T., "The RDF: Newest 'Fire Brigade' for U.S. Intervention in the Third World," in Meo, ed., *U.S. Strategy in the Gulf.*

Kolko, Joyce and Gabriel, *The Limits of Power,* New York: Harper & Row, 1972.

Krauss, Clifford, *Inside Central America,* New York: Summit Books, 1991.

Krauss, Clifford, "U.S. Will Assist Peru's Army in Fighting Cocaine and Rebels," *NYT,* 25 Jan. 1992.

Kuper, Leo, *The Prevention of Genocide,* New Haven: Yale UP, 1985.

LaFeber, Walter, *America, Russia, and the Cold War, 1945-1980,* 4th ed., New York: John Wiley, 1980.

Lane, Charles, et al., "Peru: Into the Crossfire," *Newsweek,* 19 Aug. 1991.

Leckow, Ross, "The Iran-Iraq Conflict in the Gulf: The Law of War Zones," *International and Comparative Law Quarterly,* vol. 37, July 1988.

Ledogar, Robert J., *Hungry for Profits: U.S. Food and Drug Multinationals in Latin America,* New York: IDOC/North America, 1975.

Lee, Rensselaer W. III, *The White Labyrinth: Cocaine and Political Power,* New Brunswick: Transaction Publishers, 1989.

Leffler, Melvyn P., "Adherence to Agreements: Yalta and the Experiences of the Early Cold War," *International Security*, vol. 11, no. 1, Summer 1986.

Lemarchand, René, "The Case of Chad," in Lemarchand, ed., *Green and the Black*.

Lemarchand, René, "The Crisis in Chad," in Bender, et al., eds., *African Crisis Areas*.

Lemarchand, René, ed., *The Green and the Black: Qadhafi's Policies in Africa*, Bloomington: Indiana UP, 1988.

Lemarchand, René, and David Martin, *Selective Genocide in Burundi*, London: Minority Rights Group, Report No. 20, 1974.

Levitin, Michael J., "The Law of Force and the Force of Law: Grenada, the Falklands, and Humanitarian Intervention," *Harvard International Law Journal*, vol. 27, no. 2, Spring 1986.

Lewis, Gordon K., *Grenada: The Jewel Despoiled*, Baltimore: Johns Hopkins UP, 1987.

Lifschultz, Lawrence, *Bangladesh: The Unfinished Revolution*, London: Zed Press, 1979.

Lillich, Richard B., ed., *Humanitarian Intervention and the United Nations*, Charlottesville: UP of Virgina, 1973.

Littauer, Ralph, and Norman Uphoff, eds., *The Air War in Indochina*, rev. ed., Boston: Beacon Press, 1972.

Little, Douglas, "Cold War and Colonialism in Africa: The United States, France, and the Madagascar Revolt of 1947," *Pacific Historical Review*, vol. 59, no. 4, Nov. 1990.

Love, Kennett, *Suez: the Twice-Fought War*, New York: McGraw Hill, 1969.

Lowenthal, Abraham F., *The Dominican Intervention*, Cambridge, MA: Harvard UP, 1972.

Lynn-Jones, Sean M., Steven E. Miller, and Stephen Van Evera, eds., *Soviet Military Policy*, Cambridge, MA: MIT Press, 1989.

Mamdani, Mahmood, *Imperialism and Fascism in Uganda*, Trenton, NJ: Africa World Press, 1984.

Marshall, Patrick G., "Tobacco Industry: On the Defensive, But Still Strong," *Editorial Research Reports*, vol. 1, no. 35, Sept. 21, 1990.

Massing, Michael, "Noriega in Miami," *Nation*, 2 Dec. 1991.

McCarthy, Richard D., *The Ultimate Folly*, New York: Knopf, 1970.

McConnell, Jeff, "Libya: Propaganda and Covert Operations," *CounterSpy*, vol. 6, no. 1, Nov. 1981-Jan. 1982.

McCoy, Alfred W., *The Politics of Heroin: CIA Complicity in the Global Drug Trade*, Westport, CT: Lawrence Hill, 1991.

McDermott, Jeanne, *The Killing Winds*, New York: Arbor House, 1987.

McHenry, Donald F., and Kai Bird, "Food Bungle in Bangladesh," *Foreign Policy*, no. 27, Summer 1977.

Meisler, Stanley, "Burundi," in Frank Chalk and Kurt Jonassohn, *The History and Sociology of Genocide.*

Melady, Thomas, and Margaret Melady, *Idi Amin Dada: Hitler in Africa,* Kansas City: Sheed Andrews and McMeel, 1977.

Melady, Thomas Patrick, *Burundi: The Tragic Years,* Maryknoll, NY: Orbis Books, 1974.

Meo, Leila, ed., *U.S. Strategy in the Gulf: Intervention Against Liberation,* Belmont, MA: AAUG, 1981.

Milhollin, Gary, "Building Saddam Hussein's Bomb," *NYT Magazine,* 8 March 1992.

Miliband, Ralph, John Saville, & Marcel Liebman, eds., *Socialist Register, 1984: The Uses of Anti-Communism,* London: Merlin, 1984.

Miller, Judith, and Laurie Mylroie, *Saddam Hussein and the Crisis in the Gulf,* New York: Times Books, 1990.

Mintz, Morton, "Tobacco Roads," *Progressive,* May 1991.

Moore, J. D. L., *South Africa and Nuclear Proliferation,* New York: St. Martin's, 1987.

Moore, John Norton, "Grenada and the International Double Standard," *American Journal of International Law,* vol. 78, 1984.

Morales, Edmundo, *Cocaine: White Gold Rush in Peru,* Tucson: University of Arizona Press, 1989.

Morris, Roger, *Uncertain Greatness: Henry Kissinger and American Foreign Policy,* New York: Harper & Row, 1977.

Myrdal, Alva, *The Game of Disarmament: How the United States and Russia Run the Arms Race,* New York: Pantheon, 1976.

Nash, Nathaniel C., "In the Drug War, U.S. Sows Dollars, Reaps Hate," *NYT,* 13 March 1992.

Nash, Nathaniel C., "10 Die a Day, or Disappear, and Peru Goes Numb," *NYT,* 14 July 1991.

Nessen, Ron, *It Sure Looks Different from the Inside,* New York: Simon & Schuster distributor for Playboy Press, 1978.

Norris, Ruth, ed., *Pills, Pesticides & Profits,* Croton-on-Hudson, NY: North River Press, 1982.

Nye, Joseph S., "The Superpowers and the Non-proliferation Treaty," in Carnesale and Haass, eds., *Superpower Arms Control.*

O'Rourke, Ronald, "Gulf Ops," *Proceedings,* U.S. Naval Institute, May 1989.

O'Rourke, Ronald, "The Tanker War," *Proceedings,* U.S. Naval Institute, May 1988.

O'Shaughnessy, Hugh, *Grenada,* New York: Dodd, Mead & Co., 1984.

Oppenheim, V. H., "Why Oil Prices Go Up; The Past: We Pushed Them," *Foreign Policy,* no. 25, Winter 1976-77.

Pachter, Henry, "The Problem of Imperialism," *Dissent,* Sept.- Oct. 1970.

Parks, W. Hays, "Crossing the Line," *Proceedings,* U.S. Naval Institute, Nov. 1986.

Pastor, Robert, "The United States and the Grenada Revolution: Who Pushed First and Why?" in Heine, ed., *Revolution Aborted.*

Paust, Jordan J., "The Seizure and Recovery of the *Mayaguez,"* *Yale Law Journal,* vol. 85, 1976.

Pearce, Jenny, "The People's War," *NACLA: Report on the Americas,* vol. 23, no. 6, April 1990.

Pelletiere, Stephen C., Douglas V. Johnson II, and Leif R. Rosenberger, *Iraqi Power and U.S. Security in the Middle East,* Carlisle Barracks, PA: Strategic Studies Institute, U.S. Army War College, 1990.

Peterzell, Jay, "The Secret War Against Qaddafi," *Nation,* 21 Jan. 1984.

Pierre, Andrew J., *The Global Politics of Arms Sales,* Princeton: Princeton UP, 1982.

Piller, Charles, and Keith R. Yamamoto, *Gene Wars: Military Control Over the New Genetic Technologies,* New York: William Morrow, 1988.

Ponce De Leon, Clara, "Colombia: Another 'Dirty War'?" *NACLA: Report on the Americas,* July-Aug. 1987.

Powell, John W., "Japan's Germ Warfare: The U.S. Cover-up of a War Crime," *Bulletin of Concerned Asian Scholars,* vol. 12, no. 4, Oct.-Dec. 1980.

Power, Paul F., "Preventing Nuclear Conflict in the Middle East: The Free-Zone Strategy," *Middle East Journal,* vol. 37, Autumn 1983.

Pry, Peter, *Israel's Nuclear Arsenal,* Boulder: Westview, 1984.

Quandt, William B., *Decade of Decisions,* Berkeley: University of California Press, 1977.

Raviv, Dan, and Yossi Melman, *Every Prince A Spy,* Boston: Houghton Mifflin, 1990.

Robinson, Julian, Jeanne Guilleman, and Matthew Meselson, "Yellow Rain: the Story Collapses," *Foreign Policy,* no. 68, Fall 1987.

Rohter, Larry, "After 7 Months and a Final Skirmish, the Noriega Case Goes to the Jury," *NYT,* 5 April 1992.

Rohter, Larry, "More Than an Ex-dictator's Future at Stake As Trial of Noriega Begins," *NYT,* 5 Sept. 1991.

Rohter, Larry, "U.S. Jury Convicts Noriega of Drug-Trafficking Role as the Leader of Panama," *NYT,* 10 April 1992.

Rosenthal, Andrew, "President Calls Panama Slaying A Great Outrage," *NYT,* 19 Dec. 1989.

Rowan, Roy, *The Four Days of Mayaguez,* New York: Norton, 1975.

Rowan, Roy, "Pan Am 103: Why Did They Die?" *Time,* 27 April 1992

Rubner, Michael, "Antiterrorism and the Withering of the 1973 War Powers Resolution," *Political Science Quarterly,* vol. 102, no. 2, Summer 1987.

Russell, Diana E.H., ed., *Exposing Nuclear Phallacies,* New York: Pergamon, 1989.

Ryan, Selwyn, "The Restoration of Electoral Politics in Grenada," in Heine, ed., *Revolution Aborted.*

Sandford, Gregory, and Richard Vigilante, *Grenada: The Untold Story,* Lanham, MD: Madison Books, 1984.

Scarlott, Jennifer, "Nuclear Proliferation After the Cold War," *World Policy Journal,* vol. 8, no. 4, Fall 1991.

Scheer, Robert, *With Enough Shovels,* New York: Vintage, 1983.

Schmeisser, Peter, "Pushing Cigarettes Overseas," *NYT Magazine,* 10 July 1988.

Schoenhals, Kai P., and Richard A. Melanson, *Revolution and Intervention in Grenada: The New Jewel Movement, the United States, and the Caribbean,* Boulder: Westview, 1985.

Schumacher, Edward, "The United States and Libya," *Foreign Affairs,* vol. 65, Winter 1986-87.

Scott, Peter Dale, and Jonathan Marshall, *Cocaine Politics: Drugs, Armies, and the CIA in Central America,* Berkeley: University of California Press, 1991.

Seale, Patrick, *Abu Nidal: A Gun for Hire,* New York: Random House, 1992.

Sen., Foreign Relations Comm., *War in the Persian Gulf: The U.S. Takes Sides,* staff report, Committee Print S. Prt. 100-60, Nov. 1987.

Sen., Foreign Relations Comm., subcomm. on African Affairs and Near Eastern and South Asian Affairs, *Libyan Activities,* Hearings, July 1981.

Sen., Foreign Relations Comm., subcomm. on Terrorism, Narcotics, and International Operations, *Drugs, Law Enforcement and Foreign Policy,* Report, Committee Print S. Prt. 100-165, Dec. 1988.

Sen., Judiciary Comm., subcomm. on Security and Terrorism, *Libyan Sponsored Terrorism: A Dilemma for Policymakers,* Hearings, Feb. 1986.

Sen., Judiciary Comm., subcomm. to Investigate Problems with Refugees and Escapees, *Relief Problems in Nigeria-Biafra,* Hearings, July 1969, Jan. 1970.

Sen., Judiciary Comm., subcomm. to Investigate Problems with Refugees and Escapees, *Relief Problems in East Pakistan and India,* Hearings, June, Sept. 1971.

Sen., Labor and Human Resources Comm., *Smoking and World Health,* Hearings, May 1990.

Shalom, Stephen R., "Trading Off Foreign Military Bases in the Philippines and Vietnam: The Strategic Implications," *Pilipinas,* no. 10, Spring 1988.

Shalom, Stephen R., "The United States and the Philippines: 'Sentimental' Imperialism or Standard Imperialism?" in *Art and Politics in Southeast Asia: Six Perspectives,* ed. Robert Van Niel, Southeast Asia Papers Number 32, Center for Southeast Asian Studies, University of Hawaii at Manoa, 1989.

Shannon, Elaine, *Desperados: Latin Drug Lords, U.S. Lawmen, and the War America Can't Win,* New York: Viking Penguin, 1988.

Shawcross, William, *The Quality of Mercy: Cambodia, Holocaust and Modern Conscience,* New York: Touchstone, 1985.

Shawcross, William, *Sideshow: Kissinger, Nixon and the Destruction of Cambodia,* New York: Pocket Books, 1979.

Sick, Gary, "Failure and Danger in the Gulf," *NYT,* 6 July 1988.

Sick, Gary, *October Surprise: America's Hostages in Iran and the Election of Ronald Reagan,* New York: Times Books, 1991.

Sick, Gary, "Trial By Error: Reflections on the Iran-Iraq War," *Middle East Journal,* vol. 43, no. 2, Spring 1989.

Sicker, Martin, *The Making of a Pariah State: the Adventurist Politics of Muammar Qaddafi,* New York: Praeger, 1987.

Sifry, Micah L., and Christopher Cerf, eds., *The Gulf War Reader,* New York: Times Books, 1991.

Silverman, Milton, *The Drugging of the Americas: How Multinational Drug Companies Say One Thing about Their Products to Physicians in the United States, and Another Thing to Physicians in Latin America,* Berkeley: University of California Press, 1976.

Silverman, Milton, Philip R. Lee, and Mia Lydecker, *Prescriptions for Death: The Drugging of the Third World,* Berkeley: University of California Press, 1982.

Sisson, Richard, and Leo E. Rose, *War and Secession: Pakistan, India, and the Creation of Bangladesh,* Berkeley: University of California Press, 1990.

Sklar, Holly, *Washington's War on Nicaragua,* Boston: South End Press, 1988.

Slater, Jerome, *Intervention and Negotiation: The United States and the Dominican Republic,* New York: Harper & Row, 1970.

Slater, Jerome, "Is United States Foreign Policy 'Imperialist' or 'Imperial'?" *Political Science Quarterly,* vol. 91, no. 1, Spring 1976.

Smith, Hedrick, "Ex-U.S. Official Cites Ease in Leaving Grenada Day Before Invasion," *NYT,* 29 Oct. 1983.

Smith, Phillip, "Grappling with Shining Path," *New Politics,* vol. 3, no. 4 (new series), whole number 12, Winter 1992.

Solomon, Stephen, "The Controversy Over Infant Formula," *NYT Magazine,* 6 Dec. 1981.

Spector, Leonard S., *Nuclear Proliferation Today,* New York: Vintage, 1984.

Spiers, Edward M., *Chemical Warfare,* Urbana: University of Illinois Press, 1986.

St. John, Ronald B., *Qadhafi's World Design: Libyan Foreign Policy, 1969-1987,* London: Saqi Books, 1987.

St. Jorre, John de, *The Brothers' War: Biafra and Nigeria,* Boston: Houghton Mifflin, 1972.

Steinem, Gloria, "The Myth of Masculine Mystique," in *Men and Masculinity,* ed. Joseph H. Pleck and Jack Sawyer, Englewood Cliffs, NJ: Prentice Hall, 1974.

Sterling, Claire, *The Terror Network*, New York: Berkley, 1982.

Stobaugh, Robert B., "The Oil Companies in the Crisis," in Vernon, ed., *Oil Crisis*.

Stork, Joe, *Middle East Oil and the Energy Crisis*, New York: Monthly Review Press, 1975.

Stremlau, John J., *The International Politics of the Nigerian Civil War, 1967-1970*, Princeton: Princeton UP, 1977.

Stumpf, Robert E., "Air War with Libya," *Proceedings*, U.S. Naval Institute, Aug. 1986.

Taylor, Peter, *The Smoke Ring: Tobacco, Money, and Multinational Politics*, New York: Pantheon, 1984.

Taylor, Stuart Jr., "In Wake of Invasion, Much Official Misinformation By U.S. Comes to Light," NYT, 6 Nov. 1983.

Thant, U, *View from the U.N.*, Garden City, NY: Doubleday, 1978.

Thomson, James C. Jr., Peter W. Stanley, and John Curtis Perry, *Sentimental Imperialists: The American Experience in East Asia*, New York: Harper & Row, 1981.

Toolis, Kevin, "The Man Behind Iraq's Supergun," *NYT Magazine*, 26 Aug. 1990.

(*The Tower Commission Report*), *President's Special Review Board*, New York: Bantam Books/Times Books, 1987 (cited as Tower Commission).

Treaster, Joseph B., "Cocaine Is Again Surging Out of Panama," *NYT*, 13 Aug. 1991.

Valenta, Jiri, and Herbert J. Ellison, eds., *Grenada and Soviet/Cuban Policy: Internal Crisis and U.S./OECS Intervention*, Boulder: Westview, 1986.

van Ginneken, Jaap, "Bacteriological Warfare," *Journal of Contemporary Asia*, vol. 7, no. 2, 1977.

Van Hollen, Christopher, "The Tilt Policy Revisited: Nixon-Kissinger Geopolitics and South Asia," *Asian Survey*, vol. 20, no. 4, April 1980.

Vargas Llosa, Mario, "The Road to Barbarism," *NYT*, 12 April 1992.

Vernon, Raymond, ed., *The Oil Crisis*, New York: Norton, 1976.

Vincent, C. Paul, *The Politics of Hunger: The Allied Blockade of Germany, 1915-1919*, Athens: Ohio UP, 1985.

Waas, Murray, "Made for Each Other: The Secret History of George Bush and Manuel Noriega," *Village Voice*, 6 Feb. 1990.

Washington Office on Latin America (WOLA), *Clear and Present Danger: The U.S. Military and the War on Drugs in the Andes*, Washington, DC, Oct. 1991.

Waters, Maurice, "The Invasion of Grenada, 1983, and the Collapse of Legal Norms," *Journal of Peace Research*, vol. 23, no. 3, 1986.

Weeks, John, and Phil Gunson, *Panama: Made in the USA*, London: Latin America Bureau, 1991.

Wenger, Martha, "The Central Command: Getting to the War on Time," *MERIP Reports*, no. 128, Nov.-Dec. 1984.

Weston, Rubin Francis, *Racism in U.S. Imperialism: The Influence of Racial Assumptions on American Foreign Policy, 1893-1946,* Columbia: University of South Carolina Press, 1972.

Whelan, Elizabeth M., *A Smoking Gun: How the Tobacco Industry Gets Away With Murder,* Philadelphia: George F. Stickley Co., 1984.

White, Larry C., *Merchants of Death: The American Tobacco Industry,* New York: William Morrow, 1988.

Williams, Walter L., "United States Indian Policy and the Debate over Philippine Annexation: Implications for the Origins of American Imperialism," *Journal of American History,* vol. 66, March 1980.

Wines, Michael, "U.S. Will Try Diplomatic Action Before A Military Strike On Libya," *NYT,* 16 Nov. 1991.

Woodward, Bob, *Veil: The Secret Wars of the CIA, 1981-1987,* New York: Simon & Schuster, 1987.

Wright, Claudia, "Libya and the West: Headlong into Confrontation," *International Affairs,* Winter 1981-82.

Wright, John, *Libya: A Modern History,* Baltimore: Johns Hopkins UP, 1982.

Wright, John, *Libya, Chad and the Central Sahara,* Totowa, NJ: Barnes and Noble Books, 1989.

Wyman, David S., *The Abandonment of the Jews,* New York: Pantheon, 1984.

Wyman, David S., *Paper Walls: America and the Refugee Crisis, 1938-1941,* New York: Pantheon, 1968.

Yost, David S., "French Policy in Chad: The Libyan Challenge," *Orbis,* vol. 21, no. 1, Winter 1983.

Youngers, Coletta, "Body Count," *Nation,* 2 July 1990.

Zimbalist, Andrew, and John Weeks, *Panama at the Crossroads: Economic Development and Political Change in the Twentieth Century,* Berkeley: University of California Press, 1991.

Index

A

The Abandonment of the Jews, 115
Abrams, Elliott, 167
Abu Nidal organization, 142-43, 146, 158, 239n13, 239n14, 241n36, 241n41
Abyssinia, 45. *See also* Ethiopia
Acheson, Dean, 25-26
Adelman, Kenneth L., 50-51
advertising, 51, 167-71
Afghanistan: airliner shot down in, 147; chemical warfare in, 49-50; drugs and, 174-75; Soviet invasion of, 24, 36, 56, 71, 72, 134, 211n58
Africa: arms supplies to, 42; Burundi and, 131; France and, 163; living standards in, 184, 197; Nigerian civil war and, 122; Portugal and, 47; prescription drugs in, 167; Qaddafi and, 150, 161; U.S. intervention in, 7, 131; U.S. racism and, 13, 16, 120. *See also* Africans; *and specific countries*
African Americans, 13, 16, 46, 120. *See also* racism
African swine fever, 49
Africans, 12-13, 194
Agent Orange, 48
Agnew, Spiro, 19
agreement on the Prevention of Nuclear War, 54
Agriculture Department (U.S.), 170, 188, 189
Aguinaldo, Emilio, 14
AIDS, 157
Air America, 173
Air Defense Identification Zones, 154
Air Force (U.S.), 95, 97-98, 148, 154. *See also specific countries*
Air Force Academy, 62
Air Malta flight 180, 161
aircraft carriers, 30, 78, 95, 129
airliners, 80-81, 143, 147, 153, 158, 160, 241n48, 241n49. *See also* Air Malta flight 180; Pan Am flight 103; UTA flight 772; *and specific countries*
Al-Ahram, 152

Al Ittihad, 79
Alabama, 147
Alaska, 65
Alexander, Yonah, 141,
Algeria, 83, 155
Allen, Richard V., 59, 171
Allende, Salvador, 11, 201n14, 202n29. *See also* Chile
Amal, 147
Ambassador at Large for Counterterrorism (U.S.), 157
"Amber and the Amberines," 100
America's Watch, 145
American Association for the Advancement of Science, 48
American Bar Association's committee on international law, 94
American Civil Liberties Union, 23
American Embassy Club, 155
"The American Experience in Asia," 5
American Indians. *See* Native Americans
American Institute of Marine Underwriters, 93
American Society of International Law, 89
Amin, Idi, 135, 162
Amini, Ali, 73
Anaconda, 202n29
Andean strategy, 259n215. *See also* drug war
Anderson, Jack, 241n51
Anglo-Saxons, 13-14, 16
Angola, 61
Ankara, 157. *See also* Turkey
anthrax, 211n58
Anti-Ballistic Missile treaty, 6
anti-imperialists, 14
anti-Semitism, 114-15, 231n9. *See also* Jews
Aouzou strip, 162-64
Apaches, 14
apartheid, 16. *See also* South Africa
Aquino, Corazon, 34. *See also* Philippines
Arab League, 159
Arab states: Egypt and, 69; embargo by, 65-66; Gulf closing and, 78; Iran-Contra scandal, reaction to, 76, 81, 85; mass destruction weapons and, 52, 59, 62, 217n172; oil producers and, 66; term

About South End Press

South End Press is a nonprofit, collectively-run book publisher with over 170 titles in print. Since our founding in 1977, we have tried to meet the needs of readers who are exploring, or are already committed to, the politics of radical social change.

Our goal is to publish books that encourage critical thinking and constructive action on the key political, cultural, social, economic, and ecological issues shaping life in the United States and in the world. In this way, we hope to give expression to a wide diversity of democratic social movements and to provide an alternative to the products of corporate publishing.

Through the Institute for Social and Cultural Change, South End Press works with other political media projects—Z Magazine; Speak Out!, speakers bureau; the Publishers Support Project, and the New Liberation News Service—to expand access to information and critical analysis. If you would like a free catalog of South End Press books, please write to us at South End Press, 116 Saint Botolph Street, Boston, MA 02115. Also consider becoming a South End Press member: your $40 annual donation entitles you to two free books and a 40% discount on our entire list.

Other titles of interest from South End Press